Nov 8   p 3-47
Nov 12   p 48-99
Nov 19   p 99-143

Dec 3   p 144-188

Dec 10   p 189-203

Metapolitics

THE ROOTS OF THE NAZI MIND

(being a revised and enlarged edition of METAPOLITICS: FROM THE ROMANTICS TO HITLER, with a new prefatory essay on the Bonn Republic, based on the author's travels in Germany, up-to-date supplements on Alfred Rosenberg and on bibliography, a new Appendix of unpublished Thomas Mann material, and new revised 1965 material.)

by PETER VIERECK

"The decisive question is for Germany to emerge from the romanticism of the 19th century" — THEODOR HEUSS (1959) *first President of the Bonn Republic, in his nationwide warning of 1959 against Nazi revivals.*

CAPRICORN BOOKS

NEW YORK, N.Y.

*Dedicated to the free
heritage of*
CARL SCHURZ

THE SECOND COMING

Turning and turning in the widening gyre
The falcon cannot hear the falconer;
Things fall apart; the centre cannot hold;
Mere anarchy is loosed upon the world,
The blood-dimmed tide is loosed and everywhere
The ceremony of innocence is drowned;
The best lack all conviction, while the worst
Are full of passionate intensity.

Surely some revelation is at hand;
Surely the Second Coming is at hand.
The Second Coming! Hardly are the words out
When a vast image out of *Spiritus Mundi*
Troubles my sight: somewhere in sands of the desert
A shape with lion body and the head of a man,
A gaze blank and pitiless as the sun,
Is moving its slow thighs, while all about it
Reel shadows of the indignant desert birds.
The darkness drops again; but now I know
That twenty centuries of stony sleep
Were vexed to nightmare by a rocking cradle,
And what rough beast, its hour come round at last,
Slouches towards Bethlehem to be born?

— William Butler Yeats*

* Yeats claims in a private letter of April 1936 to Ethel Mannin:
". . . My horror at the cruelty of governments grows greater . . . If you
have my poems by you, look up a poem called 'The Second Coming.' It
was written 16 or 17 years ago & foretold what is happening." Poem
reprinted by permission of the Macmillan Co.

BOOKS BY PETER VIERECK

I. POETRY:

Terror and Decorum. Charles Scribner's Sons, New York, 1948.
[Won the Pulitzer Prize in 1949.]

Strike Through the Mask! Scribner's, 1950.

The First Morning. Scribner's, 1952.

The Persimmon Tree. Scribner's, 1956.

II. PROSE:

Metapolitics: From the Romantics to Hitler. Alfred A. Knopf, New York. Out of print. (Swedish edition, 1942; Italian edition, 1948.)

Conservatism Revisited and the New Conservatism: What Went Wrong? Free Press Paperbacks, Macmillan, N. Y., 1965.

Shame and Glory of the Intellectuals: Babbitt Jr. vs the Rediscovery of Values. Capricorn Books, G. P. Putnam's Sons, New York, 1965.

Dream and Responsibility: Four Test Cases of the Tension Between Poetry and Society. The University Press of Washington, D.C., 1953.

The Unadjusted Man, A New Hero For Americans. Capricorn Books, G. P. Putnam's Sons, N. Y., 1962.

Conservatism: From John Adams to Churchill. Anvil paperback, Van Nostrand Co., Princeton, New Jersey, 1956. (Japanese edition, 1957 by Japan Institute of Foreign Affairs; Spanish edition in Buenos Aires, 1959; Korean edition, 1960.)

Metapolitics: Roots of the Nazi Mind. A Capricorn Book, G. P. Putnam's Sons, New York, 1961.

III. VERSE DRAMA:

The Tree Witch. Scribner's, New York, 1961. Out of print. Available from author.

CONTENTS

~~~~~~

NEW SURVEY FOR THE 1960's   i

I · *The " German Problem "*   3
    KULTUR VERSUS CIVILIZATION   3
    THE FIVE REVOLTS   10

II · *" Romanticism " and the Cult of " Life ": an Attempt at Definition*   16
    ROMANTICISM VERSUS ROMANTICISMS   17
    LIFE-WORSHIP   21
    " THE WEIGHT OF TOO MUCH LIBERTY "   26
    THE THREE ASSUMPTIONS   28
    THE MATHEMATICAL FALLACY   29
    REPETITION   34
    THE FALSE ANALOGY: DYNAMISM   42

III · *From 1648 to 1848: the Two Souls in Action*   48
    IMPORTANCE OF THE THIRTY YEARS' WAR TODAY   49
    FROM HERDER TO THE CORRUPTION OF NATIONALISM   50
    IMPORTANCE OF THE " WAR OF LIBERATION " TODAY   54
    A NEW VIEW OF THE WAR OF LIBERATION AND OF THE REVOLUTION OF 1848   58

IV · *Father Jahn, the First Storm Trooper*   63

    THE GERMAN JACOBIN   65

    VOLK AS A NEW BASIS OF GERMAN LIFE   66

    FROM PROVINCIALISM TO NATIONALISM   70

    MASS PARTICIPATION, FÜHRER, AND ABOLI-
       TION OF CLASS LINES   72

    NATIONALISM VERSUS CHRISTIANITY   75

    STATE EDUCATION TO INDOCTRINATE FOLK-
       DOM   77

    NATIONALISM IN ACTION   80

    THE IMPORTANCE OF JAHN'S HERITAGE IN
       1941   88

V · *Siegfried: the Metapolitics of Richard Wagner*   90

    " FRENCH IDEAS," 1830–43   93

    REVOLUTION, 1848–49   99

    TRANSITION, 1847–51   103

    THE LIFE-FORCE OF DYNAMISM   106

    FÜHRER CONCEPT   110

    PURIFICATION OF THE RACE SOUL   114

    COMMUNISM   120

    FINAL SYNTHESIS   122

VI · *Hitler and Wagner*   126

    WAGNER AND THE SECOND REICH   126

    WAGNER AND NON-GERMAN FASCISTS   128

    WAGNER VERSUS HITLER: WHAT WOULD WAG-
       NER BE TODAY?   129

    WAGNER PLUS HITLER   132

VII · *Greenwich Village Warriors*   144

    THE SECOND ROMANTIC REVOLUTION   145

    HOUSTON CHAMBERLAIN AS HITLER'S JOHN
       THE BAPTIST   147

DÆMONS, FÜHRERS, AND BOORS   150
"WHAT AN ARTIST DIES IN ME!"   152
THE "GERMAN SOUL"   164
LAGARDE AND LANGBEHN   168
FROM "VOLK WITHOUT ROOM" INTO "LEB-
     ENSRAUM"   173
"GREENWICH VILLAGE" VOTES FOR BARAB-
     BAS   176

VIII · *"O Sacred Mediterranean":* Solution to the
German Problem   178

IX · *Realpolitik: Fichte, Hegel, Treitschke, Hitler*   189
FROM FICHTE TO HITLER   189
HEGEL AND DESTINY   199
TREITSCHKE, NIETZSCHE, AND BISMARCK   203

X · *A Different View of the German Republic*   209

XI · *Prophet Laureate of Metapolitics: Part I*   214
WHO IS ROSENBERG?   214
FOREIGN POLICY   219
INFLUENCE OF WAGNER, CHAMBERLAIN, LA-
     GARDE, JAHN   224
ROSENBERG'S BASIC LINGO AND BASIC ASSUMP-
     TIONS   228
RACIAL INTERPRETATION OF HISTORY   232
ART   235
ROSENBERG'S LASTING INFLUENCES   238

XII · *Prophet Laureate of Metapolitics: Part II*   240
THE COMING REICH   240
ROSENBERG AS JOURNALIST   245
ROSENBERG AS EDUCATOR   252

MALE-LEAGUES IN GERMANY 263

RUSSIAN AND EASTERN INFLUENCES ON GERMANY 266

METAPOLITICS VERSUS ITS INTELLECTUAL CRITICS 272

XIII · *Nazi Religion versus Christian Religion* 281

CHRIST ARYANIZED 282

MESSIAH HITLER AND THE NEW "CHOSEN PEOPLE" 287

WAR IS HEAVEN! 294

TWO CURRENT EVENTS 298

THE DARK GODS AWAKEN 299

ON THE OTHER HAND 301

XIV · *Metapolitics in Action: the Theology of Terror* 303

"WORLD-POLITICAL THOUGHT GROOVES" 303

CAPTAIN HITLER OF KÖPENICK 310

NEANDERTHALERS IN AIRPLANES 312

XV · *The Rooted German* (restored 1940 ending) 317

BIBLIOGRAPHY 321

SYNOPSIS OF ROSENBERG'S POSTS AND INFLUENCE 340

ROSENBERG VS. HITLER IN RUSSIA 342

Appendix A: PRO AND CON:
Two Reviews of Original Edition:
Joseph C. Harsch and Jacques Barzun 344

Appendix B: THOMAS MANN ON *Metapolitics* 355

Appendix C: ACKNOWLEDGMENTS, WAGNER'S TRANSVESTISM, & "HARSHNESS" (for the 1965 edition) 365

INDEX 373

METAPOLITICS

NEW SURVEY FOR THE 1960's

Because this book indicted Hitler in terms of the Christian-Judaic ethical traditions and not in terms of the "scientific" sociologies and because it used the forbidden concepts ("semantic blurs") of moral choice and evil instead of "realistic" economic motivations, the climate of the 1940's was in part inauspicious for getting this Hitler-interpretation debated seriously. Only now is the book coming into its own, judging by the increase of appeals for a new up-to-date edition. These appeals also ask the author for a chapter of new introductory comments: on how the book originated; on the post-Hitler Bonn democracy today; on the future of romanticism and Prussianism; on Nietzsche's role in the book; and on the role of ideas in history. In reply this new survey of re-assessments for the 1960's tries to fulfil, in the above order, each one of these main requests.

1. "METAPOLITICS" REVISITED AND BONN RE-ASSESSED

Yesterday, unconditional surrender. Today, very conditional cooperation. Tomorrow ("mark," as the saying goes, "my words") they will be pounding on the table.

"A German with power in his hands," says Nietzsche, "arouses profound and icy distrust." In Europe, yes. But not in America. Not when the Nordic war-god Thor roars as gently as any sucking dove so as not to fright the ladies.

Yet this is only half the story, the half symbolized in Heine's prediction of 1834: "Thor, leaping to life with his giant hammer, will crush the Gothic cathedrals." There is another half in Bonn's still ambiguous and unresolved experiment in freedom. There, amid handicaps from past and present, the men of the future, the free half of the German heritage, are rebuilding against Thor those same cathedrals of western liberties and of the Christian-Judaic ethics. Whether the rebuilding succeeds, depends in part on American policy. That is, on whether we Americans understand the darker roots of German culture and not only those roots we prefer to see because they resemble our own. *Metapolitics* was and is such an attempt to understand.

Metapolitics was written at Harvard and Oxford universities during 1936–40, re-edited 1941 and accepted for a Harvard Ph.D. degree in history, published September 1941 by Alfred A. Knopf, and now reprinted by Capricorn 1961 in a revised and amplified edition. To avoid duplication the book treated only briefly America's all too standard demonology of German nationalists (Fichte, Hegel, Houston Chamberlain, Treitschke, Spengler). Instead, the 1941 edition was the first serious analysis in English of the influence on the Third Reich of the romantic school, Jahn, Wagner, Stefan George, Alfred Rosenberg and, more briefly, Langbehn and Lagarde.

The 1961 edition, in part a reprint and in part an entirely new book, adds the following: (1) the present long introductory chapter of re-appraisals for the 1960's (on book's origins, Bonn, romanticism, Nietzsche, and intellectual history); (2) rear bibliography brought up to date; (3) Alfred Rosenberg's Nazi career brought up to date; (4) some sections particularly relevant today for which no space had been found in the 1940–41 editings; (5) review by Joseph C. Harsch and debate with Jacques Barzun about romanticism; (6) long Thomas Mann letter, never before published in book form, about the book's Wagner-Hitler interpretation.[1]

---

[1] The Mann letter may become an important literary document, because here Mann grants insights into himself and Germany that are found nowhere else in his great *œuvre*.

The opening assessments of current German democracy, romanticism, and Prussianism, also much new research and bibliographical material, are based on the author's current travel and research in Germany (thanks to a herewith gratefully acknowledged assistance from the Rockefeller Foundation, which, however, is in no way responsible for the views expressed.) Where the 1961 additions are major, we have inserted the phrase "1961 postscript" to avoid claiming the 20-20 hindsight of being wise after the event. Our 1940–41 predictions remain, to stand or fall on their own merits.

The revisions and amplifications are mostly documentary and factual rather than interpretative or stylistic. The book is so inextricably part of its 1936–40 era that it was found impossible to revise its constant use of present tense and present participation. There is little to be said for the youthful-emotional immaturity of some of the book's style except that a rewrite of its crisis mood, in terms of middle-aged detachment, would have become a gesture of concession to something even ghastlier: the present American mood of smugness in general and of forgetfulness about the Nazi evil in particular. The book's mood and style reflect the white heat of a crisis-hour when Hitler was conquering the world while America still drowsed in suicidal isolationism. Better an unrevised tone of urgent commitment, at the price of sounding ridiculous to the urbane, than the slightest concession to sleekness and tact in an America forgetful of that crisis-hour and its anti-fascist lessons.

When *Metapolitics* first appeared, three months before Pearl Harbor, its linkage of nazism with German romanticism was considered anti-German war-mongering by many German intellectuals and by some fellow-Americans also.

Nazi resentment went so far as to bring diplomatic pressure upon Switzerland to prevent publication there. Similarly the book was not allowed in Italy till after the fall of Mussolini.[2] By 1951 the lost war had forced German intellectuals to re-examine nazism's ancestry; it no longer caused a scandal among them when our linkage of Nazi and romantic revolts against the west was confirmed by one of their own leading historians, Karl Buchheim:

[In the early 1800's] the force which soon began to control politics was romanticism. Anti-westernism in Germany also has roots in the abysmal Francophobia which developed under foreign rule. It was soon magnified into rejection of what the west calls 'civilization.' A writer like Fichte . . . championed the thesis . . . that German culture was more primal and fundamental than western civilization. Out of this notion, disregard for the values of civilian life could develop only too easily. . . . Thereafter, it became difficult to introduce western political practices and institutions into Germany.[3]

While the Nazi objections to *Metapolitics* were only to be expected, less expected and more worthy of our respect were the objections by decent, freedom-loving, anti-Nazi Americans like Jacques Barzun (see in Appendix A his persuasive side of our debate). Their objections were sometimes on the ground that our denunciation of Nazi crimes, which they likewise detested, was hysterically exaggerated and did insufficient justice to the strength of German democracy. Such objections by American anti-Nazis occurred before the Nazi mass-gassings and crematories had become common knowledge. These abominations not

---

[2] Italian edition of *Metapolitics* is *Dai Romantici a Hitler* (Milan, Einaudi, 1948). Swedish edition: *Nazismens Rötter* (Stockholm, Bokförlaget Natur och Kultur, 1942). Still no German edition.

---

[3] Karl Buchheim, professor at University of Munich, *Leidengeschichte des Zivilen Geistes oder die Demokratie in Deutschland* (Munich, Kösel-Verlag, 1951).

merely vindicate the so-called "hysterical anti-Nazi exaggeration" of the book; they are an evil so deep, so historically unique in an educated nation, that not merely such superficialities as Versailles and economic depression but the very roots of German culture must have contained some moral or psychological responsibility.

Against the able Barzun defense of German romanticism as liberal, we cite none other than Theodor Heuss, first President of the Bonn Republic, in his public warning against neo-Nazi outrages: "The decisive question is for Germany to emerge from the romanticism of the 19th century." Against those who regard Hitler as an unrooted accident in German culture, we cite the late Sir Lewis Namier:

There are people who treat all evil as extraneous and adventitious: to them a sick person is a healthy person plus a disease, not a body in a condition which, whether temporary or permanent, is its own. A similar 'demonology' treats the present Germany as a country of normal, decent people bewitched by Hitler; whereas in reality Hitler's unparalleled rise is due to the fact that he has given expression to some of the deepest instincts of the Germans . . . He is probably one of the most representative Germans that ever lived . . .[4]

Hitler a "representative German?" Of course. So, equally, is the anti-Nazi hero Claus von Stauffenberg, who threw the bomb against Hitler on July 20, 1944 and thereby saved Germany's honor before history by giving her, too, a belated Resistance. In a different but equally valid way, Carl Schurz was a representative German. He was also a representative American; this freedom-loving German-American fought tyranny on two continents. To emphasize that the book's concentration on nazism was not meant

---

[4] Namier, *Conflicts: Studies in Contemporary History* (New York, 1943), p. 81.

to minimize the freedom-loving part of Germany but to emphasize the positive political contribution the free German can make abroad, the title page of *Metapolitics* was dedicated to the tradition of Schurz,[5] a tradition equally American and German.

Janus has two faces. *Metapolitics* differed from one-sided pro-German and one-sided anti-German books by recognizing simultaneously and equally Germany's western and Nazi aspects and by predicting, already then, that the German pendulum would next, after Hitler, swing back to the west and to a Charlemagne-style synthesis with France. Have there not been hints of such a development in the relationship between Adenauer and De Gaulle? National characteristics, being cultural acquisitions and not inherent or "racial," are ever subject to change in that concrete combination of luck, outer material pressure, and inner ethical responsibility which, more than any abstract system or cycle, makes history. And that includes current German history.

Unlike the influential semi-Marxist analyses of nazism (demonstrating it to be an economic tool of western capitalism) published during the Popular Front years, this revised edition requires no embarrassed recantations about Soviet Russia. Already the 1941 edition insisted that communism is likewise a totalitarian menace and contained one of the first explorations in English, now less rare, of the *extrêmes-se-touchent* concept of "national bolshevism" (amplified 1949 by our Appendix on Soviet-Nazi cooperation in *Conservatism Revisited*). The 1941 edition also contained a warning (published before Pearl Harbor) of Nazi

---

[6] Schurz had a personal significance to the author because Schurz fled from Germany at the same time (during the revolution of 1848-1849) as did the author's great-grandfather, William Viereck, a revolutionist against German militarism and the first Viereck to settle in America (a California Forty-Niner).

encouragement of forthcoming Japanese aggression against America in the Pacific.

The phrase "national bolshevism" was meant as shorthand for the post-Rapallo Radek-Reichswehr *amo et odi* relationship by which the basically incompatible but fellow-Hegelian heritages of Russian left and German right might merge temporarily, against the free west. The phrase also had a second meaning *circa* 1930–34, not linked to Russia or foreign policy but referring to the more anti-capitalist domestic policy of the Strasser wing of the Nazi party, the wing Hitler personally distrusted and purged in 1934 but in which even such pro-Hitler stalwarts as Goebbels and Himmler (both of them originally not Hitler's but Gregor Strasser's private secretaries) had their psychological roots. On page 260, *Metapolitics* envisaged the possibility of a second, more radical Nazi revolution, stressing the socialist half of National Socialism. The military defeat of Germany cut short this second revolution which Goebbels, according to his captured diaries, and Himmler, with his hunt against aristocrats, were inaugurating. Yet the expropriation of capitalists like Thyssen, the increasingly Soviet-style subjection of the individual to the party, and Hitler's hanging of army generals and conservatives after July 20, 1944 – all this shows that the second revolution of national bolshevism was at least partly inherent in Hitler's National Socialism.

Today the Nazi "second revolution" – i.e., into national bolshevism – is partly resumed in the Russian-sponsored Socialist Unity party in East Germany. This party combines communist and anti-western Nazi slogans and emotions under Soviet control. It welcomes former SS officers to create, in partnership with the Kremlin, a second totalitarian Germany. For example, Leo Lange, an official of Himmler's Gestapo, was put in charge of radio and press for East Germany; SS Obersturmführer Adelbert Baumler was appointed chief of Russia's political counter-intelli-

gence for West Germany. On July 21, 1950 Otto Grote-
wohl (in 1960 still Moscow's puppet premier of East
Germany) made a public appeal for Nazi support of communism against the west. Ten years later the situation has
become even worse, judging by the 1960 report of the objective International Committee of Free Jurists. They list
75 Nazi criminals holding high East German posts and
supply specific documentation of photos, Nazi party-card
numbers, and other Nazi records, the transition being particularly smooth in two categories: secret police and propagandists. Kurt Lange, a 1960 official of the Ministry of
State Security (Communist secret police), was not only a
Lieutenant-Colonel of Himmler's SS but personally inter-
rogated for Hitler the tortured heroes who had attempted
the anti-Hitler revolt of July 20, 1944. And among propagandists the 1960 department chief of the Communist
National-Zeitung was founder of the equally anti-western
Nazi newspaper, *Freiheitskampf*, as well as a senior officer
of the Storm Troops.

Meanwhile in West Germany the Socialist Reich party,
the leading underground neo-Nazi party, is partly financed by the Kremlin in its neutralist campaign against
Bonn's alliance with American democracy. Renewed alert-
ness against high-placed ex-Nazis in Bonn is indispensable; even a single Theodor Oberländer in the cabinet was
one too many. But meanwhile let us be equally alert for
communism's ex-Nazis in Russia's East German puppet
state. Hitler's famous remark about Communists becoming Nazis, a remark basic to national bolshevism, also works
in reverse today, from nazism back to communism:

There is more that binds us to Bolshevism than separates
us from it. There is, above all, genuine revolutionary feeling. . . . I have always made allowance for this circum-
stance and given orders that former Communists are to be

admitted to the Party at once. The petit-bourgeois Social Democrat and the trade-union boss will never make a National Socialist, but the Communist always will.[6]

To return from enslaved East Germany to free West Germany: Bonn's danger-from-within is not communist, nor national bolshevik, nor neo-Nazi, but non-Nazi rightist-authoritarian. That is why Armin Mohler's widely-circulated book on the "Conservative Revolution"[7] against Weimar does a disservice to genuine Burkean or Rankean conservatism by using that term as part of a nationwide campaign to rehabilitate morally the immoral rightist fellow-travelers of Hitler. Any criticism, not only of Hitler's 1932 collaborators against Weimar but of 19th-century anti-semitic nationalist predecessors like Jahn, gets brushed off as mere anti-German propaganda (when actually it defends a higher Germany). Mohler thus brushes off our Jahn chapter; he clearly implies that its title, "The First Storm Trooper," was coined by us, with mere hindsight, when in truth the phrase is rigorously pertinent precisely because coined in Jahn's own day, not as *post factum* but as prophecy, a fact Mohler saw in our documentation of that phrase but concealed from his readers; he may have

---

[6] Hitler to Hermann Rauschning, *The Voice of Destruction* (New York, 1940), p. 131.

[7] *Die Konservative Revolution In Deutschland 1918–1932* (Stuttgart, 1950).

been counting on the fact that his German readers can find no copy of *Metapolitics* to check back to.

These slippery tactics require exposure, not because of the uninteresting petty rivalry between any two particular historians but because these same tactics of *anti*-anti-nazism recur on more important fronts. Mohler's praise, for example, of Carl Schmitt as a non-Nazi "conservative," helps such successful wreckers of Weimar — Schmitt is still read — to regain their anti-parliamentarian and anti-semitic influence. What Mohler withholds from innocent readers, who may have no other source for getting the real facts, is that Professor Schmitt, with considerable personal gain, was Hitler's leading respectable apologist among jurists, a violent advocate of the need to liquidate any anti-Hitler opposition, an articulate anti-semite, and the man who drew up the legal justification for Hitler's bloody murders of June 1934.[8] Schmitt — who was to call himself the Rousseau of the Nazi revolution and then repudiate it in 1945 — successfully incited his students into nazism and war-worship by such influential dicta as: "War is the essence of everything. The nature of the total war determines the natural form of the total state."

Mohler's acknowledgement section calls "especially

---

[8] On Schmitt, see, for example, the first-hand evidence of his eager service to Hitler in Ernst Niekisch's memoirs, *Gewagtes Leben* (Cologne and Berlin, Kiepenheuer and Witsch, 1958). For Schmitt's perversion into nazism of the untotalitarian conservatism of Donoso Cortés, see P. Viereck, *Conservatism: From John Adams to Churchill* (Anvil paperback, Van Nostrand, Princeton, N.J., 1956), pp. 67–8, 83–4. It must not be thought that Schmitt is only an isolated example in books like Mohler's. Countless equally harmful grave-diggers of Weimar, such as the Jew-baiting economist Werner Sombart, are being rehabilitated as "non-Nazi" pseudo-conservatives or else as "mainly non-ideological" specialists by Mohler and his all too common type, a type including the current apologists for Bonn's erstwhile cabinet minister, Theodor Oberländer (who had supported the Nazis at the University of Königsberg and in Nazi-occupied Russia and had fallen out with them so "decently" only after they were definitely losing the war).

fruitful" his personal pre-publication conversations with "Prof. Dr. Carl Schmitt" as well as with other leading non-Nazi anti-Weimar authoritarians and militarists. Fruitful, yes; but some fruit contains wasps. Amusingly revealing of this whole widespread wasp-activity in Germany today is Mohler's indignation against the insult to the Nazis implied by our book calling them "Neanderthalers in airplanes," a phrase meant to stress the disproportion between their technical and their moral achievements. In view of the documented record of Nazi atrocities, we regret the comparison as an insult not to the Nazis but to the Neanderthalers.

It is unfair to the honorable word "liberal" to let it be misused as window-dressing by the leftist non-party fellow-travelers of communism. It is equally unfair to let the honorable word "conservative" cover up for these rightist non-party fellow-travelers who, while self-righteously denouncing Hitler in defeat, cooperated directly with him under Weimar in deriding individual freedom and overthrowing parliamentary government. It becomes a point of honor to name both kinds of fellow-traveler forthrightly, by their true names, especially when found in intimidatingly high places. This need is realized neither by Germany's new millionaires nor by its masses (nor by America's left or right, depending on whose ox is gored). But fortunately the need is realized and acted upon by an increasing number of the new university youth, Bonn's most promising element.

Freedom is being threatened in the Bonn Republic. The threat does not come from economic or narrowly political factors; Bonn — with its full employment, two-party parliamentary evolution, lack of Free Corps and leftist-rightist extremist movements, lack of scapegoats and stab-in-the-back myths for losing the war, and lack of assassinations and agitations — has brilliantly avoided these chief Weimar weaknesses. Nor does the threat come from the neo-Nazis; to exaggerate the role of these demagogues-without-a-demos only plays into the hands of the real threat — the psychological threat — to individual liberties. An authoritarian psychology still prevails in high places and demos alike: an authoritarian mentality, a respectable authoritarianism that is non-Nazi and even (as with the Adenauer group) very sincerely anti-Nazi but still not rooted in that kind of free society to which liberals, Tory democrats, and social democrats alike are dedicated in western parliaments. According to one of Germany's leading contemporary philosophers, Karl Jaspers:

There does not seem to be any considerable number of Nazis. The majority of Germans wants to be governed authoritatively but decently. Hitler was a terrible disappointment. But the fact that a restoration of the Nazi regime seems unlikely at present is not by itself ground to be reassured. . . . In principle, Hitler is denounced but not the idea of the great leader as such. . . . There is something in our people which believes in the great leader. . . . It can be traced in our classic literature. . . . The average German, then, trusts authority. . . . Not everybody followed [Hitler before 1945], but the majority did. . . . We [Germans] owe our freedom [from Hitler] not to ourselves but to the Western powers.[9]

Here is an imaginary "trialogue" between three viewpoints on the Germany of the 1960's. (Number 1 has his facts wrong: too pessimistic about Germany; number 2 has his facts right but his interpretations wrong: too optimistic.)

[9] Jaspers, "The Political Vacuum in Germany." *Foreign Affairs*, New York, July 1954, pp. 599, 601, 603.

1. Ritualistic Anti-German: "Most or many Germans of the 1960's back an anti-semitic resurgence."

2. Ritualistic Pro-German: "Most Germans sincerely condemn an anti-semitic resurgence, such as the recent swastika outrages on synagogues. This fact proves that contemporary Germans are a free and ethical society, purged of their Nazi heritage."

3. Thoughtful Sceptic: "Most Germans sincerely condemn an anti-semitic resurgence. They do so not because they now realize that anti-semitism prevents a free and ethical society but because they realize that anti-semitism prevents good public relations abroad."

1. Ritualistic Anti-German: "Most or many Germans back the neo-Nazi periodicals and agitators."

2. Ritualistic Pro-German: "Very few Germans back neo-nazism. This fact proves they are no longer authoritarians but freedom-minded."

3. Thoughtful Sceptic: "Very few Germans back the neo-Nazi brand of authoritarianism. This is not because most Germans are now freedom-minded but because they prefer non-Nazi brands of authoritarianism."

1. Ritualistic Anti-German: "Well, that means the Nazi brand of authoritarianism is not yet really discredited in Germany."

2. Ritualistic Pro-German: "Polls and statistics do show that Nazi authoritarianism is indeed discredited in Germany. This fact proves Germany's moral revulsion from nazism and genocide."

3. Thoughtful Sceptic: "Nazi authoritarianism is obviously discredited in Germany. This fact proves Germany's moral revulsion from — failure. Nazism is discredited not because its genocidal infamies are profoundly

understood but because it failed on its own favorite Social-Darwinist criterion: success."

While we believe that number 3 has the best of the above fictional "trialogue," we most sincerely hope that the future evolution of Bonn will prove him wrong and that thereby the free choice of a new, untainted, post-Nazi generation of Germans will justify the replacement of those three voices by a vindicated number 4: "Thoughtful Pro-German."

2. ROMANTICISM AND PRUSSIANISM: FROM SYNTHESIS BACK TO ANTITHESIS

When the hammer of Thor, as predicted by Heine, finally arrived in 1933, the metal composing it was an alloy: steeled (or Prussianized) romanticism. "Steel romanticism" (a favorite Rosenberg and Goebbels credo, discussed on pages 255–56, 311–12) is an instable blend of opposites; through these pages we shall watch its parade of rationally mechanized anti-rationalists, goose-stepping *artistes manqués,* lower-middleclass Siegfrieds,[1] and obsessively orderly bohemians. To vary the metaphor from hammer to blast: the Prussian uranium and romantic plutonium can be joined only exceptionally, only by the special emotional compulsion of what Rosenberg calls "the medicine man as daemonic figure" (Jahn, Wagner, Paster Stöcker, Hitler). Today for at least a generation these two explosive elements will remain further apart than at any time since

---

[1] Cf. the Georg Grosz caricature of a cigar-smoking petit-bourgeois Siegfried in bearskins. In a single pictorial gesture passing beyond the limits of language, that cartoon sums up our whole book. So in a very different sense does William Golding's novel of evil, *Lord of the Flies.*

"Dedicated to Richard Wagner"
(*George Grosz*)

XV

their reconciliation of 1810–13.[2] Their present Apartheid, instead of a freedom-blasting junction, is Bonn's great psychological advantage over Weimar, in addition to Bonn's more familiar and obvious material advantages.

Under Weimar, Prussian nationalists and romantic nationalists coalesced to indict democrats as scapegoats for a lost war. General von Hindenburg in his famous Nibelungen metaphor blamed the loss of World War I on "Hagen's treacherous stab in the back of the German Siegfried"; thereby Prussian militarism — anti-democratic but not romantic nor racist — had meant not Jews but Weimar democrats in general. But by 1930 that same stab meant to nationalist mobs a "Jewish conspiracy" against the nordic master race; two or three generations of the Jew-baiting Jahn and Wagner kind of romanticism had prepared the German people to visualize the foes of nationalism as Jewish intellectuals. During 1933–45 the old romantic-school crusade of folk culture against French and Jewish internationalism, reinforced by Prussian police-hunts against alien "conspiracy," entered a new dimension that can only be called mob paranoia. Xenophobe persecution complex plus delusions of nordic grandeur catapulted a whole nation through the almost clinical paranoid sequence that begins with hysterical distrust and sinister accusations, then lashes out in frenzied aggressions, and concludes with the usual ritual of suicide. In this case the suicide was enacted not only in that lonely bunker in Berlin but in the hybris of a whole mob-nation.

———

[2] When they united in founding the University of Berlin and in a cultural and military war against France. The elegant view (akin to chic views about Ezra Pound) that these early romantics were pure aesthetes, whom it is vulgar to judge in any political or ethical context, is refuted by such frequent vulgar realities as the following: around 1810 some key leaders of the romantic school (Arnim, Brentano, Kleist, etc.) founded a club and explicitly excluded Jews and Frenchmen from membership, a significant linking.

Under Bonn some Prussianism has survived the death of geographic Prussia, and some romantic folk-cult has survived the death of Nazi *Kitsch,* but neither can achieve an anti-democratic comeback without first finding a scapegoat for losing World War II. After the genocide no Jewish goat is left to scape. Nor had Hitler's Gestapo allowed any wartime opposition from ordinary parliamentarians. Hence, the two brands of nationalism in the 1950's and 1960's are forced to blame each other. What is the current neo-Nazi, anti-army stab-legend but romanticism? — namely, the mystic faith in the daemonic bohemian, the somnambulist Führer from the folk, whose inspired intuitions know more than the prosaic book-logic of the military aristocracy. And what is the anti-Hitler, pro-army stab-legend of the endless memoir-writing generals but Prussianism? — namely, the "realistic" faith in the sober, disciplined, unbohemian experts from the Potsdam drill-field. The latter "would have won the war" except for Corporal Hitler, whose dilettante romantic dreams sabotaged their supposedly foolproof strategy. Conversely the neo-Nazis, especially several civilian graduates from the Goebbels ministry, blame the "treason" of the generals and aristocrats, many of whom Hitler hanged after the officers' plot of July 1944.

The fact that these two stab-legends are mutually contradictory has this time prevented either one from catching on among German youth or German masses. Split into its two components, Thor's hammer has lost its magic alloy; reversing Heine's prophecy, may it this time be Germany's cathedrals that crush the heathen message from the north. The final word on the Aryan Anti-Christ turns out to be also the first: "ex oriente" (and not from the north) "lux."

Now, as in the days when Goethe called order more important than justice, German culture has been more concerned with stability and with fear of disorder than has the rest of western civilization. The need of so many Germans for excessive outer order, whether barracks or filing-systems, is caused by their dark half-awareness of their excessive inner disorder.[3] The average West German of the 1960's, neither a neo-Nazi nor a more than apathetic supporter of his own new liberties, will only support the latter if they bring him order as well as freedom. Therefore, any big new instability, whether in emotions, economics, or world diplomacy, would drive this average burgher into a new authoritarian nationalism under a pseudo-respectable non-Nazi label.

To catch on lastingly, the Bonn experiment in freedom needs something more than the present philistine prosperity; needs a deeper appeal than Weimar ever had to the unconscious emotional levels of German culture yet without surrendering to those levels; needs thereby not to reject or ignore the inherent romantic heritage but to "sublimate"[4] its valuable creative potential within the undaemonic limits of the Christian-Judaic ethics, in the same way that England's romantic impulse was ethically canalized by the Burke-Coleridge-Disraeli-Churchill kind of parliamentary, freedom-revering conservatism. Such "Tory democracy,"[5] combining the conservative sense of historic

[3] Cf. our section "Weight of Too Much Liberty," pp. 26–28.

[4] Nietzsche's word and concept (perhaps from Novalis) long before Freud. On sublimating ethically the indispensable creative organic contribution of the romantic "id," cf. p. 46: "Civilization's task is not a question of destroying but of harnessing the eternal romantic element."

[5] The Disraeli-Churchill section of our *Conservatism: From John Adams To Churchill* (Anvil book, Princeton, 1956) and the Roosevelt New Deal section of our *Unadjusted Man* (Boston, 1956) develop at greater length the concept of Tory democracy, a concept often distrusted (owing to the popular confusion of conserver with conformist) by liberals and social democrats when actually it is their needed ally in conserving traditional constitutional liberties against authoritarianism of either right or left.

continuity and concreteness, the liberal sense of minority rights and civilian courage, and the social sense of humane material reforms, stands in noble contrast with the mean-spirited *Realpolitik* and Social Darwinism of Bismarckian conservatives. It stands in still sharper contrast with the democracy-deriding cultivated irresponsibility of Germany's rightist aesthetes and intellectuals (non-Nazi yet rarely anti-Nazi) during 1919-32.

In order at last to remove the explosive "meta" from metapolitics, Bonn's task is this: for the first time in German history to achieve authority without authoritarianism.

3. DEBT TO NIETZSCHE ACKNOWLEDGED

A brief autobiographical intrusion may perhaps be condoned as the only way of acknowledging this book's chief intellectual and ethical debt. The following jingle was scribbled by the author when, as a 19-year-old college student in 1936, he began the essay that grew into *Metapolitics*:

TO THE GERMAN PEOPLE
The paranoiac Cinderella winces;
Feels Versailles persecutes; feels freedom cheats.
"I'm the dark pawnbroker's imprisoned princess,
Gypped Nordic waiting for the shoe that fits."
More beer. More Wagner. More romantic love.
Soon comes the swan-drawn prince for you to mash.
Don't mind his bed-manners; you'll like cave-man stuff.
His name? "Prince Terror." And he swings a lash.

The light they throw on the genesis of *Metapolitics* is the only real interest of these teen-age rhymes; they are so obviously nothing but a footnote to the Nietzsche-Wagner debate, a gauche paraphrase of what Nietzsche said about nazism long before nazism was born: "The Germans think that strength must reveal itself in hardness and cruelty; then they submit with fervor and admiration: they are suddenly rid of their pitiful weakness and their sensitivity over trifles, and they devoutly enjoy their *terror*. That there is strength in mildness and stillness, they do not believe easily." It is Nietzsche, then, who was the sole begetter of the present volume; it is he whose quotations[1] and overlooked chapter-epigraphs were its subterranean leitmotif.

At that time the author was studying Nietzsche's two most wrenching personal breaks: with his best friend Wagner and with his own sister Elisabeth. The latter had married the national socialist (writ small) Bernhard Förster, whose anti-semitic Aryan cult Nietzsche rejected prophetically as the germ of a future German barbarism. Elisabeth hid or altered Nietzsche's warnings against such obscenities (and lived long enough to embrace Adolf Hitler in person, photographed together before a Nietzsche bust). The moral necessity to break, for freedom's sake, with those closest to one — with Wagner's romanticism and with the nationalist barbarism of Elisabeth and Förster — made Nietzsche's situation particularly poignant to the undergraduate of those days.

How did Nietzsche feel about a family relationship causing much of his public, ever since, to associate him with bigotries he happened to detest? The answer lies in a letter of 1887 to his proto-Nazi sister, which she typically suppressed. Though available earlier, his letter that fol-

---

[1] Note esp. our pp. 48, 90, 130, 144, 181–3, 205–6, 303. There is also a Nietzsche chapter in our later book, *The Unadjusted Man* (Boston, Beacon Press, 1956), pp. 53–63, where Nietzsche appears, with Orwell, Thoreau, Irving Babbitt, and others, as models for our theme of unadjustedness. Furthermore, *The Unadjusted Man* re-interprets McCarthyism, pp. 170 ff., in terms of the Nietzschean criteria of anti-élitist *ressentiment*.

lows is wisely being publicized in 1960 by *Deutsche Rundschau* among Germans too long propagandized by Nazi editing of the Nietzsche archives. Translation ours:

> Your link with an anti-Semitic chief [marriage with Förster] expresses something alien to my whole nature. . . . It is a matter of my personal honor to be absolutely clean and unambiguous about anti-Semitism, namely against it. . . . My revulsion against this [anti-Semitic] party (all too eager to exploit my name!) is as emphatic as possible; but being related to Förster . . . keeps making the adherents of this unsavory party imagine I'm one of them. . . . It makes my character mistrusted, as if I reject in public what I favor in secret — and my inability to stop that . . . has almost made me sick.

Since World War II it has become a more common, less esoteric knowledge — *inter alia*, through the de-Nazified Schlechta edition of Nietzsche in Germany, through the creative scholarship of Walter Kaufmann in America, and through the publication of Nietzsche's letters of warning to his sister — how uncannily Nietzsche had predicted the Nazi future.[2] He had done so, half a century in advance, not by guesswork but by insight into cultural roots. See, for example, our quoting (pages 182–3) of his 1889 prophecy that only a unity of "good Europeans," to "abolish Wagner, Bismarck, and all anti-semites," could stop this combination of romanticism, racism and Prussianism from becoming the "destroyers of both German and European culture." In our 1941 edition such Nietzsche

---

[2] K. Schlechta, *Nietzsche-Werke* (Munich, 3 vols., 1954–56), etc. W. Kaufmann, *Nietzsche* (Princeton, 1950). Anton Gros, "Nietzsche und die 'Antisemitische Correspondenz'", in *Deutsche Rundschau*, Baden-Baden, April 1960. For debate and anti-Schlechta viewpoint, see R. Pannwitz's attack on Schlechta in *Merkur*, Stuttgart, November 1957; Schlechta's rebuttal in *Frankfurter Heften*, Frankfurt, February 1958 and his pamphlet *Der Fall Nietzsche* (Munich, Carl Hanser, 1958); and the articles by W. von den Steinen and K. Löwith in *Merkur*, August 1958.

citations, there translated or discussed in English for the first time, collided head-on with the prevailing American view, which blamed the Hitler credo on Nietzsche and saw Wagner as the young 1848 liberal.

However, Nietzsche has many contradictory aspects; to make a savior of this "human, all too human" artist and psychologist is as unrigorous intellectually as to make a devil out of him. Nietzsche quotations, sometimes even correct ones, have long been fascism's adroitest weapon when addressing not street mobs but literati. For example, in "Answer to the Literary Emigrants," widely publicized by Propaganda Minister Goebbels, the poet Gottfried Benn countered Klaus Mann's sensible denunciation of Nazis as violent barbarians by quoting back Nietzsche: "A master race grows only from terrible and violent beginnings. Problem: where are the barbarians of the 20th century?" We should like to be able to prove that such Nietzsche quotes are invariably twisted out of context; mostly they are, but not invariably. At times our "immoralist" seems indeed responsible for his later misuse, owing to his desire to shock the stodgy at all cost. That desire, once justified in short-run skirmishes with a moralizing Victorian philistia, has overshot its mark in a post-stodgy, shockproof world of surrealist gangsters.

Nevertheless, it is in no way Nietzsche's fault that *The Will to Power* — favorite book-title of the Third Reich Will to Crime — fell into German nationalist hands, without his prefatory warning, suppressed by his sister (italics his, translation ours):

The Will to Power. A book for *thinking*, nothing else: it belongs to those to whom thinking is a *delight*, nothing else. That it is written in German is, at the least, untimely; I wish I had written it in French, lest it seem to confirm the aspirations of Reich-Germanism.

To put it almost ludicrously, the most original mind of the century seems, when read literally, to have squandered his genius by alternately handing middleclass liberals and daemonic authoritarians a time-bomb — a ticking quotation — to use against each other. Seems so, when read literally, but then the reader thinks of the magic world evoked by the name Hölderlin (the sublime poet with whom Nietzsche identified in his own verse), and it becomes clear that Nietzsche is listening to neither of the rivals he alternately and ironically incites but to some inner "golden laughter."

4. USE AND ABUSE OF IDEAS IN HISTORY

As for our thesis about the decisive Wagner influence on Hitler: what still seemed to many a wild-eyed hypothesis in 1941, has today not merely been vindicated but become a boring cliché. The new documentation after World War II, ranging from several first-hand reminiscences about Hitler's boyhood to the Wagner citations in Hitler's last conversations, confirms Hitler's lifelong obsession with both the theory and practising of Wagnerian romanticism. Hitler: "At every stage of my life, I come back to Richard Wagner."[1]

According to the friend of Hitler's pre-1914 teen-age days:

Richard Wagner's music dreams were still the object of our undivided love and enthusiasm. For Adolf, nothing could compete with the great mystical world that the Master conjured up for us . . . He no longer felt lonely and outlawed, and mis-

[1] L. Snyder, *Basic History of Modern Germany* (Princeton, 1957), p. 169.

judged by society. He was intoxicated and bewitched. Willingly he let himself be carried away into that mystical universe which was more real to him than the actual workaday world.[2]

Reviewing *Hitler's Table Talk* (conversations with his generals during World War II), *TLS* concludes: "There is nothing here to sustain the view that Hitler was a close student of Nietzsche; it would be nearer the truth to say that he translated Wagner into political terms."[3] Several other post-war, post-*Metapolitics* scholars reach the same conclusion; for example, Robert Rie in *Journal of the History of Ideas*, June 1952:

One can hardly overestimate Wagner's influence, since his entire creative work and activity not only expressed a positive political program, but also determined the frame of mind in which the national life was conducted. . . . Hitler most certainly succeeded in shaping his reign after the pattern of a Wagnerian music-drama, and in performing it accordingly. That is to say, a music-drama of the Wagner who created the *Nibelungen*. . . . Nietzsche is completely innocent of the fact that three decades after his death he was to be considered the prophet of the Third, the Hitler Reich. The Superman whom Zarathustra presents is actually Nietzsche's conception of the ideal Man, who "knows how to conduct the history of man as his *own* history" . . . . , is therefore tolerant and human in a humanitarian sense, which means that he is, in general, much more in accordance with the ideals of the Western democratic world than with those of the German world, to which he is really in opposition.

---

[2] A. Kubizek, *The Young Hitler I Knew* (introduction by H. Trevor-Roper, Boston, 1955), pp. 187, 192. While Franz Jetzinger's indispensable book, *Hitlers Jugend* (Vienna, 1956) finds many errors in Kubizek's reminiscences, his stress on Hitler's Wagnerism has never been put in doubt.

[3] *Times Literary Supplement* (London, January 4, 1952), p. 2, reviewing *Hitlers Tischgespräche*, edited by Gerhard Ritter, Bonn, 1951. Significantly the only foreigner whom Hitler admires in these confidential conversations is Joseph Stalin, whom Hitler calls "a man of real genius."

Opinion will differ about the influence of ideas on history. But however great or small their influence politically, it was ideas that severed Germany psychologically from the entire world. The Third Reich was not only a dictatorship but a unique dictatorship. Its roots in romanticism and Wagnerism set it off not only from the free world but from its fellow dictators. The only other fully totalitarian state, Soviet Russia, has a very different idea-heritage. Clearer and closer to the west than Alfred Rosenberg's cloudy flights are Russia's machinery cult and industrialism-in-a-hurry, Marxism's theoretical lip-service to western democratic ideals, and Marxist Russia's actual practice of the party-terrorist phase of the west's French Revolution, all merging with the old familiar Oriental despotism into a composite: Ford Pasha and Robespierre Khan.

Despite her d'Annunzios and grand-opera balconies, even fascist Italy's police-state differed fundamentally from Germany's. Mussolini's fascist imperialism, never fully totalitarian, lacked the Aryan blood-cult basic to Hitler-Wagner and was far less "socialist," collectivized, or organic. Mass-murder on racial grounds is the typically Nazi kind of murder; mass-murder on economic class grounds is the typically Soviet kind of murder; individual murder on statist political grounds (Matteotti) is the typically fascist kind of murder. All three are evil but very differently evil, and only the first two are totalitarian. Whereas Italian fascists thought of themselves as returning to the Roman tradition, German Nazis thought of themselves as the renewed revolt of nordic Kultur against Roman as well as French civilization. Germany's deliberately anti-rational religion of organic folk and blood is not the same as statism, although including statism; in contrast Soviet statism and Italian-fascist statism seem mechanical, bureaucratic, and at least relatively rational.

Since it is, therefore, not economics nor politics but an idea-heritage that makes Nazi Germany unique, this book belongs to the genre of "history of ideas." That genre is nonsense when written on the abstract assumption that ideas develop in a vacuum without a concrete context or that ideas can single-handed cause political events. Events are an intermeshing of causes from which neither spiritual nor material environment can be extricated. Germany's idea-heritage of Wagnerian romanticism could never have caused the Nazi dictatorship without such worldwide material factors as the crisis in western capitalism and the depression and unemployment of 1929–33. Conversely these material factors — for the reason that they accompanied such different, such democratic non-racist results in America, England, and France in the 1930's — could never have caused the Nazi dictatorship in Germany without the Wagnerian idea-heritage. Because only Germany reacted to the common economic and political problems of the west with the uncommon "solution" of nazism, therefore the economic and political explanations explain nothing at all until intermeshed with Germany's uncommon psychological and spiritual roots.

Nazism's material causes (e.g., effect of inflation on middle class), though of at least equal importance, have already been sufficiently analyzed in other books; it is nazism's psychological and spiritual roots that still require more clarification; hence, the deliberately one-sided emphasis of this book represents no highflown soulful belittling of the familiar down-to-earth material causes.

We are not trying to make bookworms out of the activist Nazi party leaders; unlike Herr Doktor Goebbels most of them were the least intellectual gang of street-brawlers ever to start a revolution, except insofar as garbled philosophy was a mere pretext (as the wrongs of Versailles were a mere pretext) for making the basically decent German nation condone gangster methods. Nevertheless, without a century of romanticist ideas, seeping downward to all levels and then outward from books into bullets, the well-educated and decent German nation would never have become so uniquely susceptible (gullible) toward a meta-thug. Overestimated by ivory-tower subjective idealists and underestimated by capitalist and socialist materialists, ideas do not "cause" history; but they do shape the particular form which history, however caused, will take; this form, this "mere idea," may then become a matter of life or death for millions, especially for those who don't think ideas are a matter of life or death.

Richard Wagner, product of the German romantic school and of the Jahn-influenced student movement, was to the Nazi Revolution — even though less completely and less explicitly — what Rousseau was to the French Revolution and Marx to the Russian Revolution. Rousseau would have been horrified by Robespierre; Marx by Stalin; Wagner by Hitler. But "ideas have consequences" even when, as in all three cases, the consequences were partly due to a vulgar misinterpretation of these ideas by *terribles simplificateurs* and a cynical misuse by demagogues needing window-dressing.

Scholarly causality-hunts, yes; retroactive witch-hunts, no. The fair-minded historian must guard not against all kinds of moralizing but against the facile kind of moralizing of self-righteous hindsight. He must not oversimplify his explanations by combining *cherchez la femme* and *trahison des clercs* into *cherchez le clerc*. To a great extent he must exonerate Rousseau, Marx, Wagner and the German romantic school from consequences they never foresaw. To a great extent, but yet not entirely; sometimes far from entirely. Because unintended political consequences were unforeseen, does not mean they were unforeseeable. By a process of logical deduction and, more important, of psychological deduction and ethical sensitivity about means and ends, the unintended consequence known as the Nazi mind was partly foreseeable in the ideas at its root. Otherwise Heine and Nietzsche would not have so clearly foreseen it in those ideas in their own day. "The power of vested interests is usually exaggerated," says J. M. Keynes, "when compared with the gradual encroachment of ideas. . . . Madmen in authority, who hear voices in the air, are distilling their frenzy from some academic scribbler of a few years back."

— PETER VIERECK
Mount Holyoke College
January, 1961

METAPOLITICS

CHAPTER I

THE "GERMAN PROBLEM"

Zwei Seelen wohnen, ach!, in meiner Brust;
Die eine will sich von der andern trennen.

[Two souls, alas, dwell in my breast together;
The one wants separation from the other. — GOETHE][1]

Nazism is the last phase of the intermittent, ever-
renewed attempt of partially Romanized Germany to
shake itself free of Mediterranean influence.

— BERNARD BERENSON

KULTUR VERSUS CIVILIZATION

The type of politics discussed in this book is not really
"politics" in the unpretentious American sense of the
word but is best described as — well, there is no ordinary
English word for it — as *Metapolitik:* metapolitics. No
English word expresses so well the Weltanschauung
which Hitler has instilled into German youth and which,
backed by German military and economic efficiency, is
the menace of the hour to all free peoples. The composer

---

[1] Johann Wolfgang Goethe: *Faust*, Part I, lines 1112–13. Throughout the book, all references in the notes to lines of *Faust* refer to the line-
numbering used in Goethe's *Werke* (Erste Abtheilung), Vols. XIV, XV
(Weimar: H. Böhlau; 1887, 1888). Some other editions of *Faust* assign
different numbers to the lines.

Richard Wagner's " Circle " of nationalists was the first to use this word *Metapolitik* as Germany's political ideal. Among Wagner's letters from ardent admirers one from a prominent nationalist offered a singularly startling suggestion: " To be genuinely German, politics must soar to metapolitics. The latter is to commonplace pedestrian politics as metaphysics is to physics." [2]

As if abashed by the audacity of his own imagination, this correspondent surged patriotically on without stopping to define the word he had coined. The word is here borrowed advisedly; it expresses, more adequately than any existing dictionary term, the highfalutin mysticism welding the political, economic, and national philosophy of Wagner and Hitler into a unity very much its own — and very German.

I shall use " metapolitics " to mean the semi-political ideology resulting from the intertwining of four distinct strands. These four are romanticism (as interpreted in the chapter following this); the " science " of racism; a vague economic socialism, protesting sometimes demagogically and sometimes sincerely against capitalist materialism; and the alleged supernatural and unconscious forces of Volk collectivity.

In setting up metapolitics against politics, Germany deliberately turns her back on western civilization. Both Germany and the west are agreed on that — and both pugnaciously so. Is the common phrase " western civilization " mere rhetoric? Or can we not find for it a brief definition which both Germany and the west will accept? A rough attempt in a single sentence: loyalty to western civilization means loyalty not to one particular portion of geography — that would be nationalism — but to a uni-

---

[2] Constantin Frantz: " Offener Brief an Richard Wagner," *Bayreuther Blätter,* Jahrgang I, no. 6 (June 1878), p. 169.

versal civilization compounded of three separate heritages: rationalism, classicism, Christianity.

Nazism stands for the opposite of each of these three heritages: for force against reason, for romanticism, for tribal paganism. This states the contrast a bit too naïvely, because, of course, the matter is hardly so simple as this. This contrast is only the framework, requiring qualification and elucidation and, above all, explanation.

Just as Mason and Dixon's line today still runs through the heart of many Americans, so through the centre of German hearts runs the great Roman wall. Speaking metaphorically, on one side of the wall are the classical, rational, legalist, and Christian traditions (often mutually conflicting) of the Romanized German; on the other side (often mutually conflicting) are the paganism of the old Saxons, the barbaric tribal cults of war and blood, and the anti-rationalism and anti-legalism of the romantics. This almost schizophrenic split is manifested in a number of different contrasts. One contrast often is inconsistent with another, yet each has a spark of truth. For example:

Law vs. life, form vs. content, static vs. dynamic, classicism vs. romanticism, politics vs. metapolitics, internationalism vs. racism, liberal capitalism vs. national socialism, pacifism vs. militarism, freedom vs. tribal Führer, individualism vs. totalitarianism, atomism vs. organic Volk, reason vs. force, gold vs. blood, Christ vs. Wotan, the westerner vs. the nordic, civilization vs. Kultur.

By itself each of these formulas, except for the last named, which sums them all up, is an oversimplification and can be misleading. Such formulas are often unfairly worded, unfair according to which side coins them and according to what is omitted. Yet even the crassest oversimplifications are important as crude symptoms of the basic contrast.

Almost every major German figure bears within himself both sides of this contrast. That is why German thinkers and bards talk more of " two souls in one breast " than do the thinkers of any other national culture. From Goethe on, German poets seem to exult secretly in their conflicting souls, even while bemoaning the fact openly. They treat their souls as a fond mother treats an *enfant terrible:* scolding yet egging on. That may make them " geniuses " and " dæmonic," but this inner conflict over the Roman wall is not always so harmless. Sometimes it is psychologically accompanied by projection, fanaticism, hysteria, instability, delusions of persecution plus persecution of others, and convulsive outbursts of physical violence.

These qualities make good romantic poetry perhaps, but bad politics. They have caused those dæmonic, pseudo-mystic elements in nineteenth-century German thought which seem just plain crackpot to the uninitiated westerner. This is the background for the ideas we shall consider in Richard Wagner, Alfred Rosenberg, and the rest.

The contrast of Kultur versus civilization is the root, not always consciously, of the " two souls." It has been pointed out how Fichte, in the early 1800's, was perhaps the first to articulate this contrast consciously:

> If western Europe, international in mind and tendency, looks upon civilization as a system of ways of behavior and spiritual ideas that are humane and susceptible of universal application, the Germans understand by Kultur an intimate union between themselves and the natural forces of the Universe, whose action they alone are capable of apprehending, and as a tribal discipline designed to turn those forces to account. Fichte insisted only the Germans know the method of realizing this intimate union. . . . They, Fichte reminded them, are the " primeval people " (*Ur-Volk*) who speak the primeval, aboriginal

tongue (*Ur-Sprache*) which gives them contact with the
forces of Nature. Therefore, German minds return more
easily than those of other nations to the instincts and concepts of the primitive world from which "*the west,*" *under
the joint influences of Classical thought and of Christianity,* has sought to escape. From Fichte to Hitler . . .
the line runs straight.[3]

A German historian who died the year of the first Nazi
putsch has best summed up this contrast between civilization (the west) and Kultur:

Whoever believes in the existence of a natural, eternal,
and divine Law, I mean in a common and universal basis
of humanity, and sees the very essence of humanity in this
universal basis, will see [in the anti-western part of] German thought a *queer mixture of mysticism and brutality.*
But whoever considers that history is an unceasing creation of living individual forms, which are ordered according to a continually variable law, will see in western ideas
the product of an *arid rationalism,* a levelling *atomism*
— in short, a mixture of platitude and pharisaism.[4]

After the Franco-Prussian War of 1870, *Grenzboten,*
the influential weekly magazine of German "national liberals," stated: "It is easier to accept the smooth superfici-
ality of French civilization in spite of its inner corruption
than to appreciate properly the depth of the German spirit
[Kultur]. This war has shown that in essentials Germany
can never hope to be understood by other peoples than
those of German blood." These words typify volumes of
proto-Nazi thought in their contrast of civilization's "su-

3 Fichte's *Speeches to the German Nation,* delivered in Berlin, 1808;
any edition. H. W. Steed: "Preface," in A. Kolnai: *War against the West*
(New York, 1938), p. 7.

4 Ernst Troeltsch: *Deutscher Geist und Westeuropa* (Tübingen,
1925).

perficiality " and " corruption " with Kultur's subconscious
" depth " and " blood." [5]

The assertion that " Germany can never be understood "
by other races means that the magic word " Kultur " can
never be pinned down. It is understood only by blood, by
the subconscious. It is inexpressible in words. It is expres-
sible only in feeling, the heroic feeling of German blood.

As motto for the title-page of his chief work, the official
Nazi philosopher, Rosenberg, quotes a passage from the
fourteenth-century German mystic, Master Eckehart.
" This message is addressed to no one who does not already possess it as his own life or at least as a yearning of
his heart." This fourteenth-century passage in at least one
respect is identical with the *Grenzboten* passage. Both
rule out rational argument from the start. No wonder that
Eckehart is the Nazis' favourite mediæval mystic. They
see an uncanny foreshadowing of modern German ideology in his mystique of the instinctive wisdom of " subconscious blood." [6]

Let us grant the claim that German thought has, at its
best, sometimes gone deeper than most French thought.
But as propaganda for the semi-educated, long before Versailles, Kultur's partly justified claim of " depth " was perverted. It became a rationalization of barbarism, an overcompensation for the inferiority complex of feeling less
" Romanized " than the Mediterranean world. It became
an easy way to side-step the challenge of sanity, reason,
and logic; in fact, a deliberate revolt not only against
reason but against all moral and political restraints, a revolt against humanity, against universals, against internationalism on behalf of Volk and mother nature.

[5] Hans Kohn: *Revolutions and Dictatorships* (Cambridge: Harvard
University Press; 1939), p. 339.

[6] Alfred Rosenberg: *Mythus des 20. Jahrhunderts,* 142nd ed. (Munich, 1938), pp. iii and 252–9.

Houston Stewart Chamberlain is extremely important as Wagner's chief political apostle and as Hitler's first discoverer and teacher. In 1905 Chamberlain summed up Kultur versus civilization as peasant versus factory worker. " The former is intertwined with living nature, from which he daily learns truth. . . . The factory worker is torn out of all organic union with nature, which teaches subconsciously. . . . Today in Germany millions of such workers obey a handful of immigrant Jews."

The Nazi view of the war of 1940–1 was already applied before Versailles by Houston Chamberlain to the World War. In 1917 he defined the World War as " basically " a war against " Judaism and its closely related Americanism." He accused both Jews and Americans — exactly as Hitler does today — of trying to enslave the world into " boundless plutocracy." In short, concluded Chamberlain, " it is the war of modern mechanical ' civilization ' against the elemental old holy, eternally reborn ' Kultur ' of superior races." [7]

Product of all these predecessors is Chamberlain's pupil Hitler, who announces: " By Kultur I do not mean what is called today by the word ' civilization.' The latter seems to be, on the contrary, rather an enemy of true spiritual and living levels." Footnote to this in *Mein Kampf:* " Civilization means the application of reason to life. Goethe, Schiller, Kant are reflections of the western mind. The patriot prefers to seek the ' life forces,' the irrational impulses, which seem to him more characteristic of the German mind." [8]

[7] H. S. Chamberlain: *Der Seher des dritten Reiches,* 3d ed., selections ed. by G. Schott (Munich, 1939), pp. 116–17, 93.

[8] Adolf Hitler: *Mein Kampf* (New York: Reynal & Hitchcock; 1940), p. 352.

THE FIVE REVOLTS

Can Germany's two souls of Kultur vs. civilization be traced
back through her whole history? This particular section (pp.
10–15) is presented as tentative speculation, an unprovable
hypothesis for background-in-depth, and not as an attempt
to simplify history into deterministic national traits. All national traits are subject to change; history, including German
history, is not a Procrustes of abstract mass blueprints but a
Proteus of interacting free choices and personal responsibil-
ities. You can scientifically "extrapolate a curve" of mathematical dots (mechanically determined) but not of human
beings (creatively unpredictable).

About fifteen centuries ago the Roman Empire, ancestor
of what we call "the west," collapsed before the battleaxes
of the blond barbarians of the north. In 1927 the French
philosopher Henri Massis expressed, in *Defence of the West*,
the prophetic fear that an analogous fate would meet the
the west in our own century. Nazis themselves glory in this
analogy with the Roman and eary Teuton times, so that the
analogy, which is only partly correct, is widely accepted on
both side of the Roman *limes* today. Spengler, too, prophesied a *Decline of the West*, whether with sorrow or malicious glee, and his is one of the few "heavy" books we know
Hitler has read.[9]

Chamberlain and Rosenberg pictured the Teuton invaders
as great heroes who "saved" the Roman Empire from its
decadent, peaceful, legalistic over-civilization. No doubt that
is just how the Nazi invaders of Paris picture themselves
today.

[9] Henri Massis: *Défense de l'Occident* (Paris, 1927). Oswald Spengler: *Der Untergang des Abendlandes* (2 vols., Munich, 1918–22); English translation, *The Decline of the West* (New York: Alfred A. Knopf;
1926–8). Konrad Heiden: *Hitler* (New York: Alfred A. Knopf; 1936), pp.
310–11.

Throughout German history we can trace the resentment, coupled with aggressive inferiority complex, against the two disciplines imposed on Germany by the universal legalism of the Roman Empire and the universal absolutes of Christianity. For almost two thousand years this resentment has flared up periodically in cultural, political, religious, and so-called racial revolts in favour of un-Romanized barbarism, irrational, elemental, powerful, and genuinely brave. That feeling lies behind Wagner's tirade against Christianizing the "health-exuding warriors of the north." These are the warriors, one feels, with whom Hermann the Cheruscan (Arminius), at the battle of Teutoburg Forest, A.D. 9, pushed the Roman world-empire back to the Rhine.

The 1806–13 War of Liberation against France popularized the Hermann symbol in Germany. The great poet-playwright Kleist, strongly influenced by the romantic school, wrote *Hermann's Battle* in 1808 to preach that again Germans must resist French civilization just as they resisted Romanizing in A.D. 9. Most of this influential play sounds as if written by a Nazi today. Hermann's warriors appeal to the pagan god Wotan for victory. "Falseness" is deemed the eternal opposite of "blond hair and blue eyes." The most ruthless militarism and *Realpolitik* are preached, just as Fichte was then preaching them in his Berlin *Speeches*. Hermann is pictured as tricking the Roman Emperor Augustus by a sort of Munich Pact and then suddenly overwhelmingly the effete over-civilized westerners in a glorious massacre.

The important political influence of Kleist's play today is illustrated in the recent summary of it by an enthusiastic admirer. This summary calls the play's chief motive "revenge for suffered wrongs," on a close analogy with Hitler's revenge against Versailles. "For this requirement every human restraint and convention must be withdrawn, even the laws of humanity. The poet considers *all means* justified for Hermann, even lies and deception — the offer of alliance to Augustus — in order to reach the holy goal, the liberation of Germania from the Roman yoke." Again on an analogy with Hitler, the enthusiastic summary concludes that Germans should regard the Hermann of A.D. 9 as a "noble hero, although to reach his goal he is treacherous and cruel." [10]

The spiritual descendants of Hermann's "health-exuding warriors" were the mediæval Saxons. The latter staged the second great German resistance to the west. They fought for their god Wotan against Charlemagne, who tried to Christianize the Saxons and to weld the Romanizing and Teutonic heritages into one civilized world-empire.

Traditionally Germans hailed Charlemagne (*Karl der Grosse*) as one of their greatest heroes. In this they are right! Today, however, Nazi schools follow Rosenberg in sympathizing with the alleged Kultur of the pagan, un-civilized Saxons. Charlemagne is now called "Charles the Saxon-Slaughterer." Certainly Charlemagne's attempt to convert the Saxons to Christ by bloody coercion was scarcely the most tactful (or Christian) way to win Germans to the west!

Indeed, throughout history Germany can argue an excellent case against the west. Tact and peaceful reasoning were not conspicuous in the invasions of Germany by Louis XIV, by the French Revolutionaries, and by Napoleon, or in Versailles and the French 1923 invasion of the Ruhr. But this admission does not invalidate our thesis

---

[10] Heinrich von Kleist: *Werke* (Berlin: Paul Franke Verlag, n.d.); "Die Hermannschlacht," pp. 110, 114, 138; comment by Dr. Willi Koch, p. xi.

that Germany's aggressive inferiority complex against western civilization is the greatest cultural and political tragedy of Europe. Quite another matter is the question of who is more to *blame* for this tragedy, Germany or her neighbours. Let us leave such unsolvable questions to French, English, and German chauvinists to wrangle over. To recognize a historical fact is unpleasant and necessary; to blame whole peoples for a historical fact is enjoyable and pernicious. As Burke said long ago, you can't indict a whole people.

The spirit of Hermann and the Saxons staged its third great revolt against Rome in the time of Luther's Reformation. Chamberlain, Rosenberg, and Hitler read too much of this spirit into Luther himself. Yet they do us the service of pointing out an aspect of the original Protestant revolt of which most American Protestants are unaware. Return to the sources to read such powerful champions of Luther as his friend Ulrich von Hutten, and you find far more tribal German patriotism against the Mediterranean civilization than interest in Christianity. Personally Luther was more aroused by Christian than by nationalist motives. Yet as a popular German movement the Reformation was a nationalist Kultur ousting as alien the Renaissance and humanism, those two superb flowers of Mediterranean and western civilization.

When the glory of Renaissance Italy crumbled into decadence, not Italy but France was the nation most deeply steeped in Roman and classical civilization's high heritage of reason, clarity, universalism, law. During the last three centuries France, more than the decrepit city of Rome itself, has been Germany's chief cultural benefactor (or menace), especially after native German culture was enfeebled by the Thirty Years' War. That is why Germany's fourth and fifth revolts against the Roman Empire's western heritage were directed against France and not against Italy.

Germany's fourth major revolt against the west began in the late eighteenth century with the anti-rational literature of the pre-romantics known as "Storm and Stress" (*Sturm und Drang*) and ran through the great romantic school of 1800 and through the neo-romantics (the "decadents") of the 1890's. In politics the same great wave of this fourth revolt surged through the War of Liberation and the Revolution of 1848, as indicated in the chapters on Father Jahn and Wagner.

Nazism, the fifth revolt, the most radical break ever made with western civilization, would annihilate our liberties, our very bodies and our most basic ethics.

But through the two thousand years covered by these five revolts the "two souls" were equally active. The mediæval Saxon tribes were a colourful minority. The mass of German tribes — above all, in the Rhineland and the south — were steeped like France's Gauls in the Christian tradition of Charlemagne and of the mediæval Holy Roman Empire. They have remained so ever since. Their tradition, not the tradition of the barbaric Saxons, produced most of the great minds Germany has contributed to our common civilization.

Germany's finest political and intellectual heritage from her Holy Roman Empire is the Christian-Roman tradition, universal and anti-nationalist. This heritage is the mission of world brotherhood and is fully as " German " as Hitler's "mission " of world conquest.

Before the romantic revolt Germany participated under Lessing in the west's Age of Enlightenment. During many decades before the Nazis, a large majority of votes under both the Kaiser and the Republic were held by the Social Democrats, the Catholic Centrists, and the liberals, all thoroughly " western." Every German revolt against the west has been followed by an even longer and equally typical period of mutual synthesis. Inadmissible, therefore, are the claims of a Hermann or a Hitler to typify Germans as a whole. Germany's ceaseless cultural pendulum will swing back to its western pole.

CHAPTER II

"ROMANTICISM"
AND THE CULT OF "LIFE":
AN ATTEMPT AT DEFINITION

~~~~~~

The romantic rebellion against discipline, measure, and sanity, that is to say against civilization, [is] the chief problem in European culture — philosophy and art no less than politics — for the last 200 years; a problem too deep for any " economic interpretation." The disastrous surge of the elemental has been made possible only because the educated have betrayed civilization and exalted the abyss. " Better a tragic and magnificent Götterdämmerung than a thousand years of peace!" It is the apologists of dynamic chaos who have pushed the world back into chaos.

— ALBERT GUÉRARD [1]

At first glance, there may seem scant connection between the earlier German romanticism and nazism. But the former evolved step by step into the latter over the complex period of a hundred years. We can enter the ideological house that Hitler built only by entering through the underground passage — apparently far off, apparently un-Nazi — of romanticism.

[1] *New York Herald Tribune Books,* Sunday, October 8, 1939, p. 20.

ROMANTICISM VERSUS ROMANTICISMS

Why has the word "romanticism" always been so hard to pin down? Surely not because it lacks connotations. On the contrary, romanticism has too many. On hearing it, the mind is certainly conditioned to an immediate reaction. Yet what one pictures is as vague, blurred, misty in outline as those moonlit landscapes which romantic poets cherished. Such intuitive "feeling for" the meaning of romanticism is completely adequate for the romantic himself. For his critics, a concept must be found which is more precise, consistent, clear.

A precise response to the word "romantic" is impossible if only because there have been too many authoritative definitions. Romanticism has been defined at great length — and differently in each case — by Goethe, the Schlegel brothers, Novalis, Heinrich Heine, Eichendorff, Victor Hugo, Stendhal, Coleridge, Carlyle, Georg Brandes, Irving Babbitt, and many others equally authoritative. They all conflict.[2] Consequently I cannot hope to avoid conflicting

---

[2] Among early nineteenth-century Germans, the two most fruitful examples of conflicting viewpoints toward romanticism are, on the one hand, the articles by A. W. Schlegel, Friedrich Schlegel, Novalis, and Schleiermacher in the periodical *Athenäum* (3 vols., Berlin, 1798–1800) — and, on the other hand, Heinrich Heine: *Die romantische Schule* (Hamburg, 1836).

Among more recent discussions of romanticism, the following books and magazine articles are suggested to the reader as the minimum of a preliminary introduction to a study of the subject. Georg Brandes: *Main Currents in Nineteenth-Century Literature* (6 vols., London, 1901–24), Vol. II, on Germany. G. A. Borgese: *Storia della Critica Romantica*, (2nd ed., Milan, 1920). Hans Böhm, ed.: *Gedankendichtung der Frühromantik*, Vol. XXVII of *Kunstwart-Bücherei* (Munich, 1935); an anthology of the romantic school's new ideas. Paul Kluckhohn: *Die deutsche Romantik* (Leipzig, 1924). Richard Benz: *Die deutsche Romantik* (Leipzig, 1937). Friedrich Gundolf: *Romantiker* (2 vols., Berlin, 1930–1). L. A. Willoughby: *The Romantic Movement in Germany* (London, 1930). Ricarda Huch: *Die Romantik* (2nd ed., Leipzig, 1924). H. N. Fairchild: *The Romantic Quest* (New York, 1931). Hans Kohn: *Force or Reason*

with much of them. But one may seek some common denominator by inquiring whether the authorities do not so
much disagree as contemplate romanticism on different
planes of reference.

The American philosopher Arthur Lovejoy, perhaps
the most penetrating modern authority on romanticism,
stresses that the word " romanticism " has become almost
meaningless and speaks, instead, of many quite different
"romanticisms." [3] It seems to me that these differences
have two chief causes: First, the opposite creeds within the
fold of German romanticism itself. (One example of such
opposites is the bohemian individualism of the romantic
school's earliest phase versus the totalitarian collectivism
of a Fichte, Hegel, and Hitler.) Second, the differences
between German romanticism and the romanticisms of
France, England, and America.

Often two different romanticisms are really the same
great romantic movement applied to different planes. In
the case of bohemian individualism versus totalitarianism,
one is on the plane of the ego and the other on that of the
state. But both — and this is the point to be stressed —

(Cambridge, Mass., 1937). Mario Praz: *The Romantic Agony* (London,
1933). Fritz Strich: *Deutsche Klassik und Romantik* (Munich, 1922).
Irving Babbitt: *The New Laokoön* (Boston and New York, 1910), and
Rousseau and Romanticism (Boston and New York, 1919). Arthur O.
Lovejoy: " On the Discrimination of Romanticisms," in *Publications of the
Modern Language Association*, New York and Menasha, Wisconsin, Vol.
XXXIX (1924). "Romanticism: A Symposium," by J. C. Blankenagel,
G. R. Havens, H. N. Fairchild, K. McKenzie, F. C. Tarr, and Elizabeth
Nitchie, in *P.M.L.A.*, Vol. LV (March 1940). Jacques Barzun: "To the
Rescue of Romanticism," in *American Scholar*, New York, Spring 1940
(which I recommend as a brilliant defence of romanticism and for a view-
point directly opposite to my own).

[3] Lovejoy, loc cit. (pp. 229–53). For further aspects of romanticism,
see also the following works of Lovejoy: *Bergson and Romantic Evolution-
ism* (Berkeley: University of California; 1913): *The Great Chain of Being*
(Cambridge, Mass., Harvard University Press; 1936), lectures 10 and 11;
Optimism and Romanticism (Baltimore: Mod. Lang. Assoc.; 1927); reprinted from *P.M.L.A.*, Vol. XLII, no. 4, December 1927, pp. 921–45.

apply to their respective planes the identical romantic philosophy of ceaseless lawless expansion and of self-justified self-worship.

The second cause for confusion we can take in our stride, for we are concerned chiefly with German romanticism. So-called romantic movements did also exist in France and England. Sometimes these did indeed stand for the same things as the original romanticism, that of Germany, but never as a widespread national movement. To a large extent I accept the following statement:

> Romanticism is Germanic and reached its purest expression in those territories which are freest from Roman colonization. Everything that is regarded as an essential aspect of the romantic spirit, irrationalism, the mystic welding together of subject and object, the tendency to intermingle the arts, the longing for the far-away and the strange, the feeling for the infinite and the continuity of historic development — all these are characteristic of German romanticism and so much so that their union remains unintelligible to the Latins. What is known as romanticism in France has *only its name in common* with German romanticism.[4]

Romanticism is typically "Germanic" in its broadest versions, but never exclusively so and with many exceptions. Even further, one may treat romanticism not only as the "purest expression in those territories freest from Roman colonization" but also, and more important, as a cultural and political reaction against the Roman-French-Mediterranean spirit of clarity, rationalism, form, and universal standards. Thereby romanticism is really the nineteenth century's version of the perennial German revolt against the western heritage.

---

[4] Gustav Pauli, quoted in Vol. IV of Georg Dehio: *Geschichte der deutschen Kunst* (4 vols., Berlin, 1919–34).

In other words, romanticism, no matter how far afield
it may seem from current Nazi politics, is the most influential modern phase of Germany's old "two souls in one
breast," the German cultural schizophrenia which made
nazism possible.

As a further clarification, one may distinguish between
an all-inclusive and a single-plane romanticism. The
former applies the romantic assumptions to all possible
planes of reference. This generally occurs only in Germany. But on many of the single planes romanticism is not
only a German but a European movement.

The chief of these European planes is the nineteenth-
century revolt against reason, against that eighteenth-
century faith in rationalism which could not survive the
French Revolution, which it had helped cause. The kernel
of this revolt is an innate element of human nature — the
element of periodic protest, sometimes destructive and
sometimes revitalizing, of the instinctive "natural man"
against external form and against limitation by reason. He
protests against the classicist and civilized (that is, conditioned and unnatural) discipline of law. The stock defences of form, æsthetic and moral respectively, are:
Baudelaire's "*Je hais le mouvement qui déplace les lignes*"
("I hate motion that displaces lines") and Goethe's "*in
der Beschränkung zeigt sich erst der Meister*" ("the master is revealed only by [ability to work within] limitation").[5]

A most frequent source of confusion is the habit of past
critics of classifying men according to what particular
golden age they worshipped, Hellas in the case of classicists, and the Middle Ages in the case of romantics. Many
classicists are unjustifiably listed as romantics simply be-

---

[5] From Baudelaire's sonnet *La Beauté* and Goethe's sonnet *Natur und
Kunst*.

cause they are social conservatives and hence like the Middle Ages. Many romantics are unjustifiably listed as classicists because they fancied themselves noble Hellenes born too late.

Critics will reach no practical nor precise definition until they agree that the decisive criterion is not what historical era you like but why you like it and how you define it and what particular values of your own you read into it. The greatest German romantic poet, Hölderlin, and the greatest German classicist, Winckelmann, both worshipped ancient Greece, but they were worshipping two quite different shrines. We must never automatically accept a person's definition of himself or of his ideas, no matter how sincerely the definition is intended.

LIFE-WORSHIP

The distinction must be drawn between romanticism and emotional sentimentalism. The latter dubs romantic any sort of stereotyped wallowing in the picturesque or emotional, from adventurous Wild West to holding hands under a full moon. German romanticism, in contrast, is an earnest and extremely intelligent attempt at an all-embracing code of life ("Weltanschauung"). Its theories are the product of intensive cerebration, no matter how much they exalt the emotions.

The two Schlegel brothers will always remain a chief primary source for a definition. They were the recognized founders and the two chief theorists of Europe's original "romantic school," the German school of around 1800. They were "romantics," with all the anti-intellectual connotations of that word; yet it is hard to imagine two more completely intellectual personalities. If the critic will only refuse to take them at their own word, their cerebral *tour*

de force becomes apparent. They glorified simple pious
faith, emotional spontaneity, organic traditionalism rooted
in folk-instinct or in church. But in them and in numerous
other romantics these qualities were really the sophisticated products of starved and self-dissatisfied intellectualism, desperate disillusionment, and awareness of the
danger to society of their own undue rootlessness.[6]

At one point intellectual romanticism does indeed try to
overlap with the tinsel romanticism of Hollywood and of
the lurid pulp magazines. Rousseau, that French-speaking
Swiss with the most German of hearts, wailed that he did
not wish to " die without having lived " ("*mourir sans
avoir vécu*"). This wish became the daily prayer of his
admirers, the German romantic school. This wish, in its
most universal and normally human expression, is summed
up in Flaubert's character of Madame Bovary and in
Thomas Mann's "little Herr Friedemann."[7] How desperately they did not want to " die without having lived,"
these characters, both fictional and real! Their " bovarism " — a quite indispensable word — implies a definition
of " Life " (with capital " L ") which is hardly scientific
and can only be described as romantic.

Germany's most immortal and most influential personification of this definition of " Life " is Goethe's Faust. The
early, still " erring " Faust of Part One has had an incal-
culable influence on German minds — indirectly even, as
we shall see later, on German politics. Not prosaic-factual

    [6] For complete works of the Schlegels, see A. W. Schlegel: *Sämmtliche
Werke*, 12 vols., ed. E. Böcking (Leipzig, 1846–7), and Friedrich Schlegel:
Sämmtliche Werke, 2nd ed., 15 vols. (Vienna, 1846). For romanticism,
note especially their articles in *Athenäum*, 1798–1801, and Friedrich
Schlegel's philosophic novel *Lucinde* (Berlin, 1799), and his *Prosäische
Jugendschriften* (ed. Jakob Minor, Vienna, 1906).
    [7] Gustave Flaubert: *Madame Bovary* (Paris, 1857). A translation of
Thomas Mann's *Der kleine Herr Friedemann* is included in his *Stories of
Three Decades* (New York: Alfred A. Knopf; 1936).

but intoxicating-ecstatic is the romantic definition of Life. For the cult of Life means "dynamism," key word of romanticism and of nazism. This ecstatic definition of Life underlies Faust's famous reference to "living Nature" (*"die lebendige Natur"*), surely accompanied, we can almost visualize, by a "dynamic" gesture, by some broad and generous sweep of his arm. The same definition underlies Faust's "Let us hurl ourselves into time's dynamic sweep [*Rauschen*]" and his:

> I have long been disgusted with all knowledge.
> In the depths of natural-sensuality [*Sinnlichkeit*],
> Let us appease burning passions.[8]

No romanticist, whether in real life or in fiction, whether in private emotions or in public statesmanship, is ever reconciled sanely and classically to experiencing or dominating solely a partial aspect of the things of this earth. Old Doctor Faust, too, moans that he has never really lived. Though it would be sacrilege to say so to Goethe-snobs (those philosophical blood-suckers of Goethe's greatness), the Faustian and Hollywood definitions of "really living" mean identically the same thing on their separate planes. They mean: knowing all and, ah, experiencing all. This pother of the German Faustians about really living is a more snobbish and pretentious version of the bored American shopgirl on her day off who vaguely yearns to Go Places and Do Things.

Faust makes his famous wager with the devil: Mephistopheles is to "satisfy" Faust at the price of his soul. To "satisfy" him, Mephisto rejuvenates him into a hot-blooded young cavalier, ready alike for heroic or amorous adventure. Yet the plain and universally ignored fact of

---

[8] Goethe: *Faust*, Part I, lines 414, 1754, 1749–52. For explanation of references to line-numbers in *Faust*, cf. the first note to the previous chapter.

the matter is that Herr Doktor Faust inherently can't get
very far in this business of living fully (of "intoxication"
and "deep sensuality") for the simple reason that he is
prevented by his incurable habit of turning all such raw
life into a metaphysical debauch, an orgy of abstract theorizing. Such a soul even Satan's most luscious wiles are
powerless to seduce long from his "dark urge" ("*dunkler
Drang*").[9]

To be sure, Faust loves and destroys blonde little Gretchen. But ultimately even that stirring tragedy is so much
grist for further philosophizing. Faust constantly forces
Mephisto, the *grand seigneur* who is bored to death by
such things, into subtle philosophic and moral debates
until at last he exclaims in despair: "You're still full of
Ph.D!" ("*Dir steckt der Doktor noch im Leib!*")[10]

And what else would Mephisto's comment be on the
recherché naturalness and folk-spirit of the Schlegel school
or the heroic Spartan blood-baths and self-consciously
"hard-boiled" power-politics of Professor Nietzsche, Professor Treitschke, Professor Lagarde, Herr Doktor Spengler (all these bovaristic souls) — what else but: You're
still full of Ph.D.!

The romantic and Faustian man feels he is "missing
something" — namely, simple spontaneous sensuality —
and his vanity rationalizes this matter-of-course physical
need into the highbrow philosophy of Life-worship. Let
us not ask embarrassing questions about precisely what is
meant by Rousseau, Faust, Madame Bovary, and little
Herr Friedemann when they complain of "missing Life";
Freud, after all, had a word for it. Vulgarity is always
wiser than pretentiousness, and so the cheap pulp magazines serve to pierce the smoke-screen of philosophic ra-

---

[9] *Faust*, Part I, lines 1692–1710, 328.
[10] Ibid., I, line 3277.

tionalization. The following typical quotation from a pulp magazine throws more light on the romantic Life-cult than many a smooth-paper philosophical journal.

The quotation ends a thriller in *Fantastic Mysteries* describing the last hour of the last two survivors at doomsday (when the universe explodes apparently just in time to save the trembling-voiced character named Eastwood · from the somewhat demonstrative Alice):

> "Kiss me!" she whispered suddenly, throwing her arms around his neck. "Hold me in your arms. I want you to love me — now — now. . . . Let us *live* a little at the very last!"
>
> "This is the end, Alice, . . . of human life," said Eastwood, and his voice trembled.
>
> "I don't fear it, not death. But I have never *lived*. I have never *felt* or known anything. I have always been timid; — and I've almost wished for suffering rather than to be . . . *dead*, as I've always been. I've never *lived*, and now we must die together!"
>
> A strange passion intoxicated him as his lips met hers, an intoxication and passion more poignant for the certainty of coming death. . . . She looked at him, her eyes shining with softness. . . .
>
> "Try to face it bravely," stammered Eastwood.[11]

How refreshingly the shopgirl level of this pulp quotation strips naked that fancy mystic meaning which "Life" has for certain timid inhibited intellectuals! However, Life generally includes far more for romantics than the hearty phallism of pulps and D. H. Lawrence. Generally Life has the broader, more grandiose meaning of *all* instinctive life-forces, of mother nature as a whole. To worship nature's allness as God, as so many German romantics

---

[11] *Famous Fantastic Mysteries*, New York, May–June 1940, p. 122.

did and do, is the heathen religion known as pantheism. Their modern pantheism is a more philosophic version of the nature-worship of the pre-Christian Teuton Wotan-religion. The pantheists' god is the direct opposite of the Christian and Jewish God, who, in contrast, stands separate from and above the natural life He created.

"THE WEIGHT OF TOO MUCH LIBERTY"

Some readers may object that the stress on schizoid polarity in German minds, on inner swings of the pendulum, is inconsistent with stress on the German craving for discipline, authority, ruthless order. But is it inconsistent? Is not, rather, the excessive and traditional discipline by the German state the direct product of the excessive lack of inner discipline of the individual German? In Germany as in America the increase in centralization of state power is the process by which the state is sucked into the vacuum created by the default in responsibility of the individual citizen. Anarchy and tyranny are merely opposite faces of a single coin.

The key to modern German psychology is nineteenth-century romanticism. Is this thesis refuted by the dominant — or erstwhile dominant — role in Germany of something so unromantic as Prussia and Prussianism?

Actually, through most of their history Germans considered Prussia the least German of German states. They considered Prussia merely the crude semi-Slavic Prætorian Guard of the German northeast border. Prussia was not accepted as a German model nor as the dominating German state until well on in the nineteenth century — the *romantic* nineteenth century — and that is just the point: Germans accepted authoritarian Prussianism so enthusiastically precisely because it was so un-German. They accepted it as the opposite extreme, the needed overcompensation, of what they unconsciously sensed as their most dangerous and most typical quality: their intoxication with chaos, their anarchic Faustian romanticism.

But even in this reaction Germans could not escape themselves. In fact, nothing is more typical of the chaotic romantic temperament than this very attempt to escape from itself into the prison of limitless authoritarianism.

Germans have a strange habit of fleeing not from prisons but into prisons. Wordsworth, the English Lake-school romantic, found salvation in that same process when he reacted against the excessive freedom of his youthful "French ideas." He expressed that reaction, more perfectly than anyone before or after, in his pæan to the narrow stone "cell" as the sweetest refuge from "the weight of too much liberty." [12]

"Stone walls do not a prison make," or at least not nearly so unbreakable a one as — words. The cell into which generation after generation of German romantics have finally fled from liberty's weight is a word-cell. Their cell is their fanatic faith in some rigid authoritarian dogma, whether of church or state.

This apparent paradox behind German discipline has found its most striking summary in no German writer but in America's widest-read feminine columnist. "The German does not accept discipline because of a neat love of order. He accepts it the way a drunkard delivers himself into a sanitarium. He wants some one to impose it on him *because* he cannot impose it on himself." Because his inner polarity makes him "anguished, divided, at loose in the cosmos," he finally welcomes a nation-wide prison

---

[12] From Wordsworth's sonnet "Nuns Fret Not."

camp, for prison at least gives him "four walls and a rou-
tine."[13]

The masses worship a prison-camp type of state with
fanatic hysteria so long as it saves each of them, as romantic individuals, from his inner mental and emotional anarchy. But let Hitler take warning! Once the German Volk
grow long accustomed to the prison they yearned for, they
will yearn — and act with boundless violence — to get out
again. Invariably, and sooner than expected, their tem-
peramental polarity undergoes its pendulum-swing from
tyranny back again to — freedom or chaos?

THE THREE ASSUMPTIONS

In the official periodical of the German romantic school,
in 1798, Friedrich Schlegel defined romanticism as "an
evolving universal-poesy . . . in a state of becoming."
Keep this definition in mind, especially the term "evolving" and the stress on "becoming" as opposed to "being,"
for I shall try to show that these terms have lethal political
consequences today as well as harmless poetic ones.[14]

After his conversion to classicism the great Goethe
warned Germany against the future menace of romanticism's lack of form and law. Goethe pontificated his own
definition of romanticism with all the bitterness one might
expect from a former semi-romantic: "The classical I call
the healthy, and the romantic the diseased." Yet romanticism, especially in its broader, world-wide aspects of revolt against reason and law, is not a "disease." A disease
by definition is an abnormal condition. The romantic impulse is normal, all too normal. Its very normality, its be-

---

[13] Dorothy Thompson: "The Problem Child of Europe," in *Foreign
Affairs,* New York, Vol. 18, no. 3 (April 1940), pp. 389–414, at p. 399.
[14] Quoted from editorial by Friedrich Schlegel in *Athenäum,* Vol. I.

ing so typically human a failing, makes it a far deeper and more permanent menace to human society, to intellectual, emotional, and political stability, than any disease.[15]

Romanticism has a far more consistent internal logic than might be expected of an anti-formal movement. At its base are three sweeping assumptions of dubious logic. They may be conveniently though arbitrarily called *mathematical fallacy, repetition,* and *false analogy.* References to them will recur as leitmotivs throughout this book. Unromantic philosophies often accept one or even two of the tenets. The unique essence of romanticism is that it combines all three inextricably.

THE MATHEMATICAL FALLACY

In mankind's ordinary, Euclidean mathematics, the whole must always equal the sum of its parts. In romantic mathematics, the whole is greater than the sum of its parts. This first romantic postulate may be restated as the ideal of organic synthesis on all planes, what some philosophers call the hypothesis of "emergence" or "creative synthesis."

Let us keep in mind, throughout, the historical background of the original romantic school. The romantics were partly right in attributing the vicious side of the great French Revolution — namely, its chaos and its consequent ghastly bloodshed — to the disruptive effects of destructive rationalist analysis.

The original romantic school and modern nazism triumphed in part for the same reason. Both were welcomed by many as a synthesizing counter-poison to the alleged disintegrating effects of an aggressive rationalism. The French and Russian world-revolutions were the respective

[15] Goethe: *Gespräche mit Eckermann,* standard Insel edition (Leipzig), p. 467.

bêtes noires. The French and the Jews were the respective bogy men.

Romanticism was the most influential literary movement in German history, penetrating and transforming every single aspect of human society. It had the courage to call its aim " a universal synthesis." This synthesis was applied philosophically and religiously, scientifically, poetically, politically.

Philosophically and Religiously. — The philosophy or religion most typical of the romantic school is vitalistic pantheism. This is illustrated by the very title of the book by the influential romantic philosopher Schelling: *World-Soul* (1798). The universe is greater than the sum of all its parts and contains a vital omnipresent spirit which analysis can never find. Schelling defines the entire universe as a single indivisible " organism." [16] Romantic philosophy, especially Schelling's, was moulded by Goethe, himself only temporarily a romantic. Goethe loved to hyphenate " God-Nature " (" *Gott-Natur* ") as one unified organism. A. W. Schlegel's university lectures on vitalism helped to romanticize the youth of Germany and Austria. Today Henri Bergson's philosophy of the *élan vital* is the famous French application of Germany's old romantic tradition of vitalism.

Scientifically. — Science was told to treat nature organically rather than mechanically. Analysis has been invariably coupled with the adjective " destructive " by romantics. By dissolving the whole into its component parts, scientific analysis is accused of losing that invisible force which makes the whole greater than the total parts. Synthesis was set up for science as the counter-ideal to mechanistic analysis. This was the message of Fichte's

---

[16] Friedrich W. Schelling: *Von der Weltseele* (2nd revised ed., Hamburg, 1806; 1st ed., 1798).

theory of science. Its importance is shown by the fact that the German romantic school's official magazine in 1800 hailed Fichte's organic theory of science as one of the three "greatest tendencies of the age." The other two were the French Revolution (the counter-credo to romanticism) and the romantic Part One of *Wilhelm Meister* (Goethe's prose counterpart to the Part One of *Faust*).[17]

Poetically. — The repercussions of the organic view upon literary content are obvious. A simple example is the amount of space which all romantic literature devotes to deeply felt scenic beauty. Vitalistic pantheism is what makes romantic poets of all nations feel so "at one" with so-called nature. Less obvious but no less significant are the repercussions of the organic view upon technical form.

The difference between neo-classic and romantic techniques is the difference between the static and the flowing. The typical neo-classic poem is atomistic; it consists of distinctly divided lines or couplets. The romantic's typical poem is quite as organic a unit as his universe or his political society.

In our own English literature the two most familiar examples of this contrast are Dryden and Pope versus Shelley and Keats. Pope's famous *Essay on Man* consists of self-sufficient rhymed couplets ("heroic couplets") making perfectly good sense each by itself. The opening ten couplets can be read in reverse or mixed-up order and still remain satisfactory. In contrast, the couplets of Keats and Shelley flow into one another so that their order cannot possibly be changed: they are organically welded.

Politically. — When this organic approach was applied to state or nation or race instead of to universe or science or poem, the result was political romanticism. Without it Hitler's Third Reich is inconceivable. But the political

---

[17] *Athenäum*, Vol. II, last issue.

application only followed after the æsthetic application,
under the stress of the wars against France; and so our
earlier attention to æsthetic and philosophic romanticism,
far from being irrelevant to nazism, is its historical introduction.

Rousseau, the Swiss semi-romantic, coined the two contrasting phrases: " general will " and " will of all." These
his German admirers used all too successfully to bolster up
their organic view of the nation. The will of all is the mere
sum of citizens' individual (atomistic) wills, what modern
democracy deems synonymous with the will of the people.
The general will is the indivisible state-organism's vaster
will, what nazism deems synonymous with the will of the
people.[18]

Living at the height of French rationalism, against
which he only partly revolted, Rousseau never intended
the general will as the sheer mysticism it became in Germany. The catch is that no objective criterion exists for
deciding correctly what man or party is the true interpreter
of the state's voice. Counting noses in elections is ruled out
as mere will of all. Consequently, the general will, though
never so intended by the more liberal Rousseau, became in
Robespierre's French Revolution the mask for the republican Reign of Terror and became in Hitler's German Revolution the mask for limitless anti-republican despotism.

Innumerable writers of all lands have used terms treating the nation as an indivisible organism, but these were
generally only useful and picturesque metaphors for the
need of national unity. To German political romantics,
however, the organic state was not metaphor but concrete
reality. The recognized political oracle of the German romantic school was Adam Müller, just as the Schlegel brothers were the joint literary oracle. Adam Müller called the

---

[18] Jean Jacques Rousseau: *Le Contrat Social.*

state " a vast individual enveloping all the little individuals " and called human society " solely a single noble and complete person." He wanted the state to cease being an " instrument in the hands of a person " and to become, instead, " a person itself, a freely evolving whole," to which all citizens must piously sacrifice their mere individual freedoms.[19]

Novalis is usually remembered as the greatest of romantic ivory-tower poets; but he, too, illustrates the all-embracing quality of Germany's romanticism, which applied the principles of its " universal-poesy " to all planes, including politics. Impatient foreign critics have again and again dubbed nazism " political insanity." That is praise rather than insult to many a German romantic. Novalis rhapsodized that " collective insanity," in contrast with individual insanity, " ceases to be insanity and becomes magic." Its magic is holy; he elsewhere compares it with that of God: " From each true state-citizen glows forth the soul of the state, just as in a religious community a single personal God manifests Himself as if in thousands of shapes." Novalis defines each citizen as a mere " limb " of the state organism, which is " alive and personal." [20]

More familiar examples are Hegel's evolving state organism, incarnating God's idea, and Fichte's totalitarian national-socialism. Hitler's speeches and *Mein Kampf* are a lowbrow version of political romanticism. Here the race instead of the state is the mystic whole greater than the total of its parts, welded by purity of blood. The democratic parliamentary system would atomistically divide

---

[19] Friedrich Meinecke: *Weltbürgertum und Nationalstaat* (7th ed., Munich and Berlin, 1928), pp. 148–9. Reinhold Aris: *Die Staatslehre Adam Müllers in ihrem Verhältnis zur deutschen Romantik* (Tübingen, 1929) shows Müller's crucial and neglected importance in political romanticism.

[20] Novalis quoted in the Böhm anthology: *Gedankendichtung*, p. 71, and in Meinecke, op. cit., pp. 65, 67–8.

this welded unit into separate parties. The Volk unit's general will speaks only through its oracle of the Führer.

This romantic metaphysics of race organically unites possessors of the same blood even when they live in separate states. Thus were sown in nineteenth-century thought the seeds of ceaseless future wars. In order to justify war against sovereign states with German minorities, the Nazi periodical *Rheinfront* said in 1937:

> Primarily we are not citizens of states but racial comrades. The certificate of state citizenship is an easily exchanged possession, but membership within one's Volk is something immutable, granted by God. . . . The law of blood-brotherhood . . . produces a great community of German kind which has its members in all states of the world and which finds its proud refuge and kernel in the Reich of Adolf Hitler.[21]

REPETITION

The second assumption, repetition, attempts to justify the organic assumption ethically. By itself, the organic view is a mere statement of fact, not a judgment of value. It merely says that, for better or worse, the particular plane where it is applied (life, the universe, the ego, the poem, or the state) is an organic unity. To say so (as do certain modern philosophers of organic synthesis and the *Gestalt* psychologists) does not by itself make you a romantic. The romantic is the fellow who goes on to say: it is always *good* that the unit is organic. He goes still further to say — this is the crucial romantic credo — that it is always bad to let any outside law or standard, ethical or political, limit the particular unit he worships.

---

[21] Josef Huenerfauth in *N.S.Z. Rheinfront*, quoted in *New York Times*, Sunday Magazine Section, November 21, 1937, p. 16.

Romantics who contradict one another are generally holding to the same philosophy but merely applying it on conflicting planes. The plane of the organic state as an end in itself clashes with the organic unity of the individual ego or of the pantheistic universe. Conversely, the unlimited romantic ego splits up the state into anarchy. The ego, in turn, disintegrates when emotions are unlimited by reason. Within the nation-plane itself, the unlimited nationalisms contradict and destroy one another. So do the unlimited free personalities within the ego-scale.

The ethical justification and guide for conduct of any unity must come from within and not from without, because otherwise they would not be an organic part of that unity. But that makes romantic ethics a begging of the question. The organic nation, for example, is an end in itself which nothing must limit. Why? Well, *because* it is the nation.

Similarly, on the " life " scale, all experiences are part of an organic unity named " life." They must all be swallowed whole and with smacking of lips. For they all are good. Atomistic analysis must not split their unity into good and bad.

Why life for life's sake? Always the same answer: because it is life. Nothing is being said except that life is life, nation is nation, ego is ego, x equals x. These modest truths have restated, not answered, the question of value judgment. The simplest dictionary definition of tautology is " a useless repeating of an idea in different words; needless repetition which adds nothing to the sense." [22]

This romantic justification keeps trying the trick of lifting itself by its own boot-straps. This boot-strap logic revolutionized every field in the nineteenth century. The im-

---

[22] *The Winston Simplified Dictionary* (advanced ed., Philadelphia, etc., 1930), p. 1018.

mediate effect was beneficial or harmful depending on
whether the external laws that were swept away are
deemed bad or good. Literature especially benefited when
freed from neo-classicism's restrictions. But the long-range
effect was the destruction of objective standards everywhere. The romantic value-judgment was applied on different planes. Following are concrete examples of how the
romantic value-judgment was applied on the diverse planes
of so-called " life," art, the state, Volk, the ego, and emotions.

So-called " life." — Faust we found was the most influential German ideal of the full life. The full life includes,
if need be, your own unhappiness and the violent destruction of your neighbours. Faust prays: " All mankind's portion I want to feel within myself, seize with my soul the
highest *and lowest,* its joy *and woe* " (italics mine).[23]

Not only here, but on all scales the romantic, by rejecting all limits, is forced into the position of desiring the infinite as his only satisfaction. But no mortal can attain the
infinite. Consequently the romantic is doomed to ceaseless
dissatisfaction and ceaseless striving, like Faust, who finds
his very salvation in such dissatisfied " eternal striving."
Schleiermacher, the greatest romantic theologian, significantly defined religion not as a system of ethical laws and
limits but as " sense and taste for the infinite." [24]

Art. — Totality of self-expression in both life and art
includes expression of elements hitherto repressed, the
morbid as well as the normal, the unmoral and even the
diabolistic as well as the moral. Classicism fastidiously dis-
criminates and excludes. It is far more incompatible with
naturalism and realism than is romanticism. Romanticism,

---

[23] Goethe: *Faust,* I, lines 1770–3.
[24] Ibid., II, lines 11451–2, 11936–7. Friedrich Schleiermacher: *Über
die Religion* (1st ed., Berlin, 1799), the second of its five speeches.

the "universal-poesy," for the first time made respectable every possible subject-matter, even the most commonplace and "proletarian." Modern realism, unromantic as it may often be, is possible only because romanticism cleared its path.[25]

The State. — The organic view was valuable in unifying so loose a federation as the Germany of the eighteenth century and of the pre-Bismarck nineteenth century. Such an all too "atomistic" Germany was, we must remember, the historical context of the romantic revolt against atomism. By itself, the organic assumption, as propagated by the proto-romantics like Herder, was not aggressively nationalist nor morally and physically destructive. None of this (no revolt against external law) was in the typical quotations previously cited from Novalis and Adam Müller.

The quotations from them made the bare statement that the state is a single superhuman individual. If we read on in these two, we watch this needed unifying force become a force of chaos at the subtle point where the mathematical fallacy passes into the repetition. Novalis goes on to say: "*All* culture springs from a man's relations with the state." [26] Adam Müller goes on to say that nothing inorganic should fetter these superhuman individuals, the states— no human law, no league of nations.

Novalis wanted a special uniform for the citizens of the state, especially for those who most fully incarnated the "state soul." The wearers of this uniform have turned out

---

[25] The works of the romantic school's best story-teller, Ludwig Tieck, illustrate perfectly the natural transition between romanticism and modern realism. The late Irving Babbitt in his Harvard lectures defined realism as romanticism grown "decadent" and the naturalist school as "romanticism on all fours."

[26] Novalis (pseudonym of Friedrich von Hardenberg): *Works,* ed. Miner, II, 272.

to be Hitler's Storm Troopers, a not illogical development which would have horrified Novalis and every single one of the other early romantics.

The self-justified state, like the Faustian man, must not let ethical discrimination hamper its experience of life's totality. So we are not surprised to find Adam Müller end with bloody hymns to war. The result of Hegel's state-worship, too, was that the state became the ethical end in itself in much influential German political thought. All individuals, all the external restrictions of international morality, and all the concretely existing internal parts of the state must be sacrificed to its mathematically non-existent whole, which is mystically greater than its total parts.

Volk. — Gradually this exalted organic unity of political romanticism was applied to the plane of race instead of the state. Modern nordic racism is to a surprising extent a product of nineteenth-century German romanticism. It took the Germans to revive the old Jewish concept of a Chosen People who have been defeated, dispersed, and cruelly partitioned but are messianically destined.

No romantic unity must have its organic oneness divided by external lines. The poem's unity must not be divided by classical lines nor the Volk's by class lines. No part of the Volk's totality must be despised. In the Nazi labour camps all youths, rich and poor without exception, are forced to dwell together six months in the same Spartan circumstances. The aim is to give them, in Hitler's words, " a true national community feeling . . . and above all a proper respect for manual labour." (No mention, of course, of respect for mental labour.)

Though most early romantics, unlike Fichte, still retained functional class lines, they strove successfully to wear down cultural class lines. They it is who discovered and enthroned the previously despised folk-literature.

They convinced Germany that the basic and best German Kultur lay in the folksongs, epics, and symbolic myths which they collected amid the aristocratic sneers of the classicists. These writings were claimed to be not the works of individual authors but of the impersonal force of Volk, a sort of collective author. This was Herder's folksong theory. The Grimm brothers, collecting the famous *Grimm Fairy Tales,* did most to convert Germany to this theory.

All individuals, but especially educated individuals, were ruled out as the authors of folk art. Education allegedly made individuals too artificial, too unprimitive. Only the indivisible primeval "Volk-soul" had the required creative powers.

The mysterious dormant powers of the "common people," the mute inglorious Miltons that bloom to blush unseen, have perhaps been exaggerated. In any case, the romantic Grimm theory has been completely discredited by the most thorough later examinations. These have exposed folksongs and the quaint, apparently "native" folk-costumes as slow seepages downward from court and educated circles, as simplified borrowings from above and almost never as creations.[27]

The first romantic generation, the Jena school of the Schlegels, Tieck, Novalis, was less important in propagating Herder's ideas of folk art than was the second generation, the Heidelberg romantic school of the Grimm brothers and Arnim and Brentano. The latter two writers published the most famous German folksong collection (*The Boy's Magic Horn*) during Napoleon's rule over Germany. Later the great Prussian Minister Stein commended

---

[27] John Meier: *Kunstlieder im Volksmunde* (Halle an der Saale, 1906); and *Kunstlied und Volkslied in Deutschland* (Halle a. d. S., 1906). Hans Naumann: *Grundzüge der deutschen Volkskunde* (Leipzig, 1922).

this single book of poems for its important part in arousing
Volk patriotism to overthrow the French! So we see how
close is the connection between poetry and politics in romantic Germany.[28]

Arnim and Brentano declared they had taken these folksongs down orally from the lips of the common people.
Germans believed this, basing their worship of Volk to an
incredible extent on this single epoch-making book and its
surrounding folk-wisdom cults. Since then the book's so-
called folksongs have been traced. Almost all were found
copied from books of individual poets of the upper and
middle classes. Some of the best and most "natural" and
"primitive" of these songs, supposedly collected from the
ancient lore of the race, were secretly written by the talented Brentano himself.[29]

In England the same gullible age went into ecstasies
over those primitive products of the Celtic soul, Macpherson's forged *Poems of Ossian*. The worshipful attitude toward Volk gave tremendous impetus to both democracy
and nationalism, the two greatest political forces of the
nineteenth century, but also — via nationalism — to nazism.

Ego and Emotions. — The introspective literary works
of the romantics broke down the partition separating reason and emotion inside the individual ego. By that act
romanticism brilliantly anticipated modern psychology.
But, unlike the Freudians, the romantics exulted rather
than grieved over their important discovery of the role
primitive emotions play in supposedly objective thinking.

---

[28] L. A. von Arnim and Clemens Brentano, eds.: *Des Knaben Wunderhorn* (3 vols., Heidelberg, 1808, 1819). Stein's comment cited in Johannes
Janssen: *Johann Friedrich Böhmers Leben* (3 vols., Freiburg im Breisgau,
1868), I, 439.

[29] Karl Bode: *Die Bearbeitungen der Vorlagen in "Des Knaben
Wunderhorn"* (Berlin, 1909; Vol. LXXVI of Palaestra series).

The terrors and hates of the French Revolution and its wars blasted down the already leaking dikes of eighteenth-century rationalism. Europe was inundated by the long pent-up flow of violent emotions. The new emotionalism ranged from the most sensual to the most religious, generally combining both, as in Novalis's mystic-sexual *Hymns to Night* of 1800. In contrast to the dry didactic verse of the eighteenth-century neo-classicists, the romantics expressed that deeper human tendency which Novalis called "the internally related association of voluptuousness, religion, and cruelty." [30]

The new emotionalism was one plane of romanticism completely European rather than German. "O for a life of sensations rather than of thought!" exclaimed Keats in a letter of about 1820. That strain persisted throughout the century, growing ever more trite. Oscar Wilde in the 1890's wrote: "For, sweet, to feel is better than to know," rhyming with "youth's first fiery glow." [31]

Such lines anyone, by any definition, would label "romantic." But that may lead to the serious mistake of treating romanticism as chiefly an emotional spree. Romanticism need not exalt the emotions above all else. It merely applies its organic and repetition assumptions to all planes, including God, universe, state, poetic technique, ego. On the last of these planes the *whole* ego must be exalted, its mind as well as its emotions.

To be sure, the exaltation of emotions became tremendous in practice. With extreme intellectuals like the scholarly Schlegel brothers, the emotionalism was feigned and compensatory, a remedy for their own lack. More often

---

[30] Novalis (Hardenberg): *Hymnen an die Nacht* (1800), included in *Novalis Schriften,* ed. L. Tieck and F. Schlegel (3d ed., 2 vols, Berlin, 1915). Quotation from the Böhm anthology, p. 65.

[31] The Keats quotation is from John Keats: *Letters* (2 vols., 2nd ed., New York, 1931); the Wilde quotation from Wilde's poem "Panthea."

it was genuine, resulting from the special historical context of the first romantics. Reason did not need to be exalted, because at that historical period the eighteenth-century rationalists had long been exalting it already. The emotions were a brave new world to explore, and the romantics were its most daring and deepest explorers. The ideal of their novels was the complete man, who experiences everything, simply everything.[32]

The romantic ego is summed up in two words: arbitrary caprice. Completeness of expression includes every whim, whether saintly or diabolic. The ego must run the gamut of unrestricted emotional and intellectual self-expression. In practice romantic caprice had twin results: it made possible the rankest bohemianism; it also made possible a richer expression of latent abilities and new approaches in everything from art and philosophy to politics and war.

The word " conventions " is the bugbear of the ego-plane romantic. He demands that conventions and morals stop hampering the inspired expansion of the ego, especially the superman's ego — that is to say, his own. He rightly complains that conventions too often enthrone mediocrity. But the classicist rightly responds that the absence of conventions always ends in a general decline of standards to even less than mediocrity.

THE FALSE ANALOGY: DYNAMISM

The third romantic assumption seems the most plausible of the three. It might be called the spirit of the modern

---

[32] The following are the most important novels of the German romantic school illustrating this new emotionalism and egoism; Novalis: *Heinrich von Ofterdingen* (1800, included in *Novalis Schriften*); Friedrich Schlegel: *Lucinde* (Berlin, 1799); Jean Paul Richter: *Titan* (1800); J. von Eichendorff: *Ahnung und Gegenwart* (1815); L. Tieck: *Sternbald* (1798); C. Brentano: *Godwi*. Though it is no novel, mention must be

world. This is the spirit of dynamic evolution, producing relativism of truth, of morals, of law, of — absolutely everything.

The concept of dynamism is an old one in Germany; we shall find it fully developed already in Wagner. But Nazi education has dusted it off and preaches it in order to justify the Nazi immoralism and aggressive expansion. Hitler's ex-aide Rauschning even calls dynamism the single basis of everything whatsoever in current Nazi deeds and words.[33] Dynamism and life-worship combine in the slavish worship of so-called men of action, of change for change's sake, of unceasing aggressive nihilism against all stable lines whether in thought or in international politics. The dynamism of old romantic theory became the dynamite of Nazi deeds.

Fundamental are the associations of static with classic and of dynamic with romantic. Applied on all possible planes, the former is external law, the latter is life, using life in the romantic sense of ceaseless vital movement. The former favours form, the latter favours content, and like land and sea their adherents can never cease battling. At best, the former is peace and order, and the latter is liberating change and progress. At worst, the former is tyranny, and the latter anarchy. According to temperament, most men incline more toward one side than the other.

Our age's tragedy is its failure to harmonize these two battling forces, as if form and content sought but never found each other. Too few have acted on the truth that the two opposed ideals need each other, that life and law must always battle, yet cannot exist apart. Law without life is death by decay, a dry shell crumbling into dust at

---

made of W. H. Wackenroder's all-important *Herzensergiessungen eines kunstliebenden Klosterbruders* (1797).

[33] Hermann Rauschning: *The Revolution of Nihilism* (New York, 1939), *passim*, especially pp. xi–xvii, 3–97.

reality's touch. Life without law is death by suicide, a tidal wave of chaos without direction or meaning.

The German romantics, and the semi-romantic Herder and Goethe, were evolutionists long before Darwin. They were committed to the evolutionary creed long before Darwinism supplied its scientific bolsters.

Why label this assumption "false analogy"? The romantics applied to every single human, moral, and civilized unit this evolutionary spirit, which they rightly discovered in many of the physical units around them in the sphere of unhumanized nature. Doing so, they were carrying a sound analogy unsoundly far; hence, "the false analogy."

Neo-classicism in literature and *ancien régime* in politics failed to discover a sufficient place for change. As an attitude applicable to all planes, this negative attitude toward change will here be called pseudo-classicism. The romantic discovered nothing but change. His discovery proved as history-making as his step from the organic mathematical fallacy to the ethical repetition.

The pseudo-classicist denies the existence of flux. The classicist proper, as here defined, never denies flux (certainly not in unhumanized nature) but, unlike the relativists, is guided by knowledge of something permanent beneath the flux. The classicist stands firmly on an island of what he deems eternal verities and absolute standards, crying to the tides of flux: "So far and no farther!" But in today's chaos he seems no more successful than King Canute.

> World-soul, come penetrate us! . . .
> The eternal moves onward through all:
> For all must decay into nothing
> If it seeks the static stage of being.[34]

---

[34] From 2nd and 4th stanzas of Goethe's poem *Eins und Alles*.

The poem of Goethe quoted above sums up the third romantic assumption. It makes clear the previously considered self-definition of the German romantic school: romanticism as an " evolving universal-poesy . . . in a state of becoming." The key words are " evolving " and " becoming." Where each classicist treats his particular plane as being, each romantic treats his particular plane as becoming. Never, in this romantic false analogy, must a unit cease becoming, for the instant that it is static, it dies. By this paradox (despite Hamlet) " to be " *is* " not to be."

As usual, we turn to *Faust* as our best model for romanticism. (It is also the model for classicism and anything and everything else, the great treasure-house of Goethe's all-inclusive genius.) Restated in the terms of our definition, the wager between the devil and Faust is the contrast between being and becoming. Faust says: " When I cease moving, I am a slave." Faust forfeits his soul if he " says to the passing moment: tarry, you are so fair." The angels rescue his soul because " we can save him who strives eternally." Such salvation is notoriously not dependent on any ethical discrimination to discipline this striving.[35]

Faust's highest goal is to " find torment and joy in ever moving onward, every moment dissatisfied." Such a creed necessarily despises happiness. " Torment and joy," evil and good, are all really good, because all are part of " life's " organic totality.[36]

Time and again romanticism has been correctly refuted, but it always survives its refuters. How many thinkers have won their spurs slaying this dragon in its myriad different names and disguises! Yet it always turns up again on some new plane more vigorous than ever. Its pressure

---

[35] Goethe: *Faust*, I, lines 1688–1711; II, lines 11936–7.
[36] Ibid., II, lines 11451–2.

of life against external law will always be with us. The
practical question is how to allocate each to its propor-
tionate place. In other words:

*Civilization's task is not a question of destroying but of
harnessing the eternal romantic element.*

Romantic striving has Schleiermacher's "taste for the
infinite." Form limits a unit from infinite expansion.
Never must the living whole, whether ego or nation, freeze
into form. Classicism's static law is as deadly to the living
organism as the dissecting analysis of French rationalism:
"We murder to dissect." For the romantic, "the law kill-
eth"; it is freedom's strait-jacket. For the classicist, "law
alone can give us freedom" [37] (as Goethe put it in his final
classic phase).

Romantic converts thronged the Catholic church because of its apparent organic unity and its æsthetic stained-
glass windows. But the pantheistic god whom the romantics worshipped in these apparent conversions to
Catholicism was rarely the Catholic or Protestant God. He
was more like Goethe's earth-spirit (*"Erdgeist"*), the
ceaselessly changing force of nature, "an eternal sea, a
glowing life." [38]

The so-called "mediæval Christianity" of the romantic
school really meant idolizing a Bergsonian *élan vital*, un-
detached from nature, instead of the truly mediæval and
Christian God, who, being moral, is detached from nature.
Christianity is as irreconcilable with pantheism as with
atheism. Part of this pantheist religion is the romantic philosophy of self-justified "striving" and "life": "Heathenism is the religion of will, the faith which life has in itself
because it is life and in its aims because it is pursuing them.
. . . The Germans have been groping for four hundred

[37] Last line of Goethe's poem *Natur und Kunst*.
[38] *Faust*, I, lines 501–9.

years toward a restoration of their primitive heathenism." [39]

All three romantic assumptions coalesce neatly whether in German paganism, poetry, or politics. The unity must not only be organic (first assumption) and indiscriminately accepted for its own sake (second assumption), but evolving in ceaseless dynamism (third assumption). The most important political application of the dynamism assumption is Germany's combination of *Realpolitik* with Hegel's philosophy. This combination will be treated in the chapter on " *Realpolitik*."

Romantics are proud that romanticism, like life itself, is self-contradictory and eludes definition, a ceaseless becoming. Novalis was systematically romantic when he chose as his slogan " systemlessness as a system." We sense exultant pride behind the remark of one Schlegel to the other that any " definition " of the mere word " romantic " would take him 125 quarto pages.[40]

The whole romantic movement stands self-condemned in a single stray sentence of Hugo von Hofmannsthal, who was the pre-1914 Vienna incarnate. Intended solely as æsthetic criticism, his comment on dynamism is even more valid in politics, philosophy, and ethics:

" The chief trouble with all the bad writers of our day is that they do not try to view Life from any proper perspective but are dictated by an absurd and positively corybantic prostration before it." [41]

---

[39] George Santayana: *Egotism in German Philosophy* (revised ed., New York, 1940), pp. 131–2.

[40] From Novalis's letters: " *Systemlosigkeit in ein System gebracht.*" Friedrich Schegel to A. W. Schlegel, in a letter of 1797.

[41] Quoted from Stefan George's periodical: *Blätter für die Kunst,* in A. Eloesser: *Modern German Literature* (New York: Alfred A. Knopf; 1933), p. 189.

CHAPTER III

FROM 1648 TO 1848:
THE TWO SOULS IN ACTION

~~~~~~

We see the old German nationalism after its grand flaming up in the Wars of Liberation (1813), after its deepest foundation by Fichte, after its explosive rise through Stein and Arndt . . . the unqualified greatness of those men who in 1813 again led Germany from the abyss to the heights.

— ALFRED ROSENBERG, *official Nazi Director of Weltanschauung* [1]

The Germans . . . with their Wars of Liberation (1813) . . . are to blame for nationalism, this disease and madness most inimical to culture. . . . Abolish Wagner, Bismarck, and all anti-Semites . . . Fichte's lying but patriotic flatteries and exaggerations. . . . Sluggish, hesitating races would require half a century ere they could surmount such atavistic attacks of patriotism and soil-attachment and return once more to reason; that is to say, to " good Europeanism."

— NIETZSCHE [2]

---

[1] Alfred Rosenberg: *Mythus* (142d ed., Munich, 1938), pp. 539–41.
[2] E. Podach: *Nietzsche's Zusammenbruch* (Heidelberg, 1930), pp. 75, 85. F. Nietzsche: *Beyond Good and Evil* (Modern Library ed., New York), pp. 176, 171–2.

IMPORTANCE OF THE THIRTY YEARS' WAR TODAY

According to persistent Associated Press reports, Hitler will call his next victorious world peace conference at Münster. There he would avenge the Thirty Years' War, just as he avenged the World War at Versailles in the early summer of 1940. At Münster in 1648 the German states signed the humiliating, disunifying peace terms of Westphalia, which ended that bloodiest of all European wars. The world has had dinned into its ears the German resentment against the Versailles humiliations of 1919. Americans have been made far less aware of the significance of Münster. Yet historically Hitler would be acting very profoundly in choosing Münster, because the Thirty Years' War did far more than over-publicized Versailles to ruin Germany physically and to warp German mentality.

From 1618 to 1648 Germany's neighbours exploited her religious and political conflicts in order to wage on her soil and resources the most devastating world war in European history. By sword and by starvation this "Thirty Years' War" slaughtered literally the majority of Germany's population. The majority of her flourishing towns were burnt down and turned into wildernesses. The war wiped out in Germany those free institutions which the burghers of all lands were then building up against their political lords. Ever after, Germans have been backward politically in resisting all forms of statism and authoritarianism.

Germany's physical weakness and loss of cultural self-assurance after that exhausting war made her fall slavishly under French and alien influence for a century. Cultured society spoke only French and mocked everything German, snobbishly blind to the immortal greatness of German culture and the German tongue. This situation,

which could not but lead eventually to an equally unjust
anti-alien reaction, accounts for the all-important German
inferiority complex. The inferiority complex expressed itself in bumptious sabre-rattling and in a hysterical reaction
against "French ideas" and against western civilization
as a whole.

History yokes the future to the remote past. We must
go back to the terrible Thirty Years' War of the seventeenth
century to understand the politics and ideas of 1940 Germany. In view of the consequences of that remote war, as
well as the analogous and more obvious consequences of
Versailles, Germany's neighbours bear as heavy a guilt as
Germany for much of what they rightly loathe in Germany
today. They can say of the Germans what a great German
poet has said of the Jews:

"We lame them and then hate them for limping."[3]

FROM HERDER TO THE CORRUPTION OF NATIONALISM

Herder was the first to make German romanticists enthusiastic for the "organic, plantlike unfolding of Volk-souls."[4]
This was toward the close of the eighteenth century, and
his words referred not merely to Germany but to all Volk-
souls. Here romantic politics was still in the eighteenth-
century tradition of cosmopolitan humanitarianism. This
was sloughed off during the transition from books to bullets. The right to "unfold organically" became restricted
to the German "Volk-soul" alone. Father Jahn, the youth

---

[3] From Franz Grillparzer's drama *Die Jüdin von Toledo:*
    Ich selber lieb es nicht, dies Volk, doch weiss ich,
    Was sie verunziert, es ist unser Werk;
    Wir lähmen sie und grollen, wenn sie hinken.
[4] H. O. Ziegler: *Die moderne Nation* (Tübingen, 1931).

leader of the Napoleonic era, best personified this transition.

The early romantics, from Herder up to the wars with the French Revolutionaries and Napoleon, saw the Volk-soul chiefly as a medium for beautiful literature, as the Rousseauist lispings of the "noble savage." But Jahn and Fichte were more interested in beating France and French thought than in art for art's sake. They, and German leaders ever after, used this folk-literature as a political medium to inculcate nationalism in the young.

Herder was the highminded founder of the Volk cults of both Germans and Slavs. He anthologized and encouraged the national literatures of every Volk impartially. His goal was the peaceful co-operation of all nationalisms. Ironically, his national anthologies later became the fountainheads of both aggressive Pan-Germanism and aggressive Pan-Slavism.

The crowning irony is Herder's theory that an age of really passionate nationalism would make war impossible forever. Past wars he explained as the products of unnational atomistic states. But an organic national state would so enjoy the fruits of its unfolding Volk-soul that it would want all other Volk-souls to have the same enjoyments and would encourage them, too, to unfold without restriction. Herder envisaged a utopia of perpetual peace in which passionate nationalisms unfolded sweetly side by side like different-coloured roses in one common garden.

This goal has all our sympathies, but we question Herder's faith in nationalism as the means. From Rousseau's untenable faith in the natural goodness of man, Herder derived his untenable faith in the goodness of nations who act "naturally." His are the romantic postulates: acting "naturally" meant unfolding organically the instincts of the national ego and being "freed" from the artificial restraints of external law. But to classicists and conservatives the essence of freedom is these traffic lights of universal external law. Without these the natural and instinctive unfolding — whether on the plane of individual or nation — means unchecked egoism and the war of all against all.

The goal of Herder's nationalism was negated when Jahn angrily denounced the "love of the German for his foreign brethren" and glorified aggressive war.[5] Yet Jahn and all later Volk nationalists through Hitler are inconceivable without Herder. That is why Nazi schoolbooks make Herder a chief hero. The Nazi and Wagnerian cult of the organic instinctive Volk could not have existed without him. Yet he would be jailed as a pacifist and internationalist if he lived in Germany today.

The trouble is the old and very human one that we cannot reach our goals without using means tough enough to be effective. And then — the means have the disconcerting habit of getting the bit in their teeth.

From a Herder to a Hitler! Was this corruption of nationalism inevitable or merely a tragic accident? Probably inevitable, but we can never really know. What we do know is that this corruption is a basic motif of the last hundred years. Not only in Germany but in all lands nationalism passed from the humane, the peaceful, and the tolerant to the war of all against all. From Herder to Hitler in Germany, from Mazzini to Mussolini in Italy, from Wordsworth to Kipling in England.

The gradual stages of this downward transition should not be slurred over as negligible nuances. The descent inside Germany appears in three distinct stages: from the literary romantics down to the active leader Jahn; from

---

[5] Quoted in H. von Treitschke: *History of Germany in the 19th Century* (New York, 1919), V, 249, 244.

Jahn down to the racial determinism and Aryan cult of Wagner and Houston Chamberlain; from the talkers Wagner and Chamberlain down to the rock bottom of the active leader Hitler.

Each stage is accompanied by an ever broader class and mass appeal, requiring an ever lower and less educated and more demagogic common denominator. The first Volk-worshippers of the romantic school are like Marie Antoinette playing in the artificial " naturalness " of her Arcadian little shepherdess costume. Their nationalism was the sophisticated affectation of literary snobs and life-starved professors. Through them, nationalism saturated German literature and universities and history books. Through the universities, the books, the student leagues, Jahn's storm-trooper gymnasts, and the battlefields of Leipzig and Waterloo, German nationalism saturated the middle classes. Then Wagner, anticipating a more industrialized age, transferred nationalism from middle class to proletariat, from capitalism to economic socialism. With Hitler and Goebbels nationalism has reached the broadest and lowest possible common denominator.

The greatest demagogues of our age have won their proletariat — at least for the time being — to a national socialism. Until Hitler, nationalism seemed almost a class monopoly of the bourgeoisie. Hitler called " this bourgeois world . . . a class doomed by fate to decline." He shrewdly observed that the earlier " Pan-German movement was nationalistic but unfortunately *not social enough* to win the masses." [6] Therefore . . .

---

[6] Hitler: *Mein Kampf* (ed. cit.), pp. 984, 158.

IMPORTANCE OF THE "WAR OF LIBERA- TION" TODAY

Between revolutionary ideas and revolutionary action there is generally a lag of at least a generation. In the late eighteenth century, in the " Storm and Stress " school and the kindred romantic school, the psychological revolt against French culture was for the first time generally expressed in books. In bullets it was first generally expressed by what Germans call the " War of Liberation " against Napoleon. The proto-Nazi ideas which partly accompanied this war did not arise in a vacuum. They arose from the earth-shaking collision between the new social order of the French Revolution and Germany's old social order of the eighteenth century. Smashed forever was the old order, but a sketch of it is here indispensable as social background for what followed.

What was Germany really like before the physical and intellectual invasion by the French Revolution and Napoleon changed forever her map and her ideas? Before then even the word " Germany " is misleading. " The Germanys " is a more fitting label for the 360 pygmy states composing the Holy Roman Empire. The latter amiable anachronism may have been, as Voltaire said, neither holy, Roman, nor an empire, but it was certainly largely German: German in language though not yet German in united national feeling.

Under these 360 semi-independent princelings life was easy-going, static, unadventurous. A cultured aristocracy flourished with gentlemanly inefficiency. The economic standards of living were low from our viewpoint, but really high compared with those of the earlier seventeenth century. From this mellow atmosphere, so rich with accumulated tradition, ripened the very finest fruits of German culture. Even the pettiest courts vied at attracting creative intellects. The court of the tiny Duchy of Weimar was simultaneously graced by Goethe, Schiller, Wieland, Jean Paul, and Herder. This is more cultural greatness in a feeble state of a few square miles than the whole modern German state and most modern power-states can boast.

This fruitful but overripe culture was the product of the creative idleness of upper-middle-class humanists dependent on aristocratic patronage from above. The patronage was forthcoming because some of the courts — enough of them to keep any Goethe or Humboldt from being slave to economic needs — were models of taste and urbane discrimination. All this was swept away by the awakening of nationalism and capitalism in the new bourgeoisie. The Germanys, the land of musicians and poets, was step by step replaced by a unified centralized Germany, a land of far greater political power and far greater economic prosperity and yet in one sense far less great.

The process of unification from atomistic Germanys to organic Germany, from 1800 to 1940, was not gradual but a number of abrupt jolting jumps. Under Napoleon the French took the first and largest step toward reducing the number of independent German states. Thereby the French unified their future conqueror for the first time and sealed their own doom. In 1806 the Holy Roman Empire was officially dissolved. Napoleon gave more than three hundred of the tiny states to the middle-sized states loyal to him. These enlarged states refused to disgorge their prey after Napoleon's fall, so that the number was reduced from 360 to 39 by 1815.

The next great jump was caused by Bismarck, who reduced the states to 25 by 1871. The Weimar Republic reduced them to 17, ousting the princes but still retaining much local autonomy. Hitler, though retaining some local

state names, has co-ordinated all into one completely centralized totalitarian unit. Thus was the romantic dream of
an intensive organic unity achieved over a hundred and
fifty years.[7]

In the mellow pre-1806 order there were very little active popular politics and almost no national politics. The
old order preferred to leave what was — or seemed — well
enough alone. When France's soldiers and ideas killed the
old order, they in some respects did a service to Germany,
unifying and modernizing it and giving it more rational
laws. All sides agree that the French Revolution and Napoleon vastly modernized Germany, and we can use the word
"modernize" either as reverently or as sarcastically as we
please, since it was a blessing but a far from unmixed one.
Its spirit is logic, an anti-traditional and rootless logic, yet
very useful and universally valid. The best symbol of its
spirit is the metric system of weights and measures, which
the French armies spread in their wake over most of Europe.

At Waterloo Germany threw off French political and
military rule forever. But she never threw off the influence
of the French Revolution. She retained, along with its
metric system, the revolutionary anti-traditional efficiency
which that symbolized. The perennial German rebel
against "French ideas" unconsciously retains many of their
essentials. When he fancies he is fighting them most
fiercely, he often only readjusts them to German needs.
The most unbeatable German reply to a western revolution has always been not conservatism but an even more
radical German revolution. This key thesis will be illustrated in Jahn, Wagner, and Hitler.

Granted that conquest by the French Revolution and

[7] The process is best summarized in Pierre Benaerts: *L'Unité alle-
mande* (Paris, 1939).

Napoleon did Germany the service of modernizing and liberalizing her life and laws and sowing the seeds of freer popular politics and more liberal ideas. But with what psychological result? Unfortunately, such unasked service, coming from external military conquerors, is rarely appreciated by any people, especially a proud people and one with an inferiority complex toward France already. As a result, the Germans felt the second of their three most crucial psychological humiliations, the first being the peace of misery after the Thirty Years' War and the third being Versailles.

Napoleon's armies forced most German states to become dependencies of France. Much evidence indicates that this may have been to their vast political, intellectual, and economic benefit. But it was the opposite of psychological benefit, because it was done only partly with their consent. Crushed by the battle of Jena of 1806, Prussia, the proudest-minded German state of all, was yoked to France. Its territory was dismembered. Berlin was occupied by French troops. German patriots swore vengeance.

The nationalism of this great and tormented land has ever after been excessively intolerant, the desperate counter-irritant to excessive injustice from its neighbours. Humiliations under France engendered in the peaceful, unnationalistic Germanys emotions analogous to those engendered after 1919 by Versailles. The former injustice produced Jahn as the latter helped produce Hitler. The former led to the War of Liberation; the latter ended in the 1939 war against the unsatisfactory Polish settlement.

It is significant that the schoolbooks of monarchic, republican, and Nazi Germany alike exalt the War of Liberation as Germany's most glorious war. The reason is that this revolt against French rule in 1813 united almost all the Germanys in a common cause for the first time in modern history. To be sure, nationalism was already a political objective in the Germanys before the War of Liberation. German nativism played an important part in Martin Luther's revolution against the Latin Renaissance culture and against the internationalism of the Catholic church. Despite all that, the Volk state as the be-all and end-all of social life did not become the fanatic goal of many important German leaders till after defeat and humiliation from Napoleon.

Thus considered, Jena becomes one of the most decisive battles of modern history. By winning it the French won perhaps the most costly Pyrrhic victory of modern times. Their physical victory, accompanied by their aggressive intellectual influence, became a social catalyst. This French catalyst changed German nationalism for the first time from æsthetic dilettantism to political dynamite. Hard to conceive fully without Jena and without the subsequent War of Liberation are many of the political and intellectual developments which made a Hitler even remotely possible.

A NEW VIEW OF THE WAR OF LIBERATION AND OF THE REVOLUTION OF 1848

During 1806–15 the idea of thoroughly reorganizing the Germanys on nationalist lines for the first time captured the imagination of an influential group of Germans. This was led by the students, professors, gymnastic societies, and literati. This early nationalism is generally and mistakenly deemed the necessary concomitant of nineteenth-century liberalism, simply because both revolted against the conservative internationalism of the Hapsburg Chancellor Metternich. Actually, certain of these early German nationalists are more in harmony with Hitler's radical totalitarianism than with the bourgeois liberalism of the intervening years.

Nazi historians like Alfred Rosenberg and all Nazi schoolbooks violently denounce Metternich and the " Metternich system "; that hardly makes them liberals. We must distinguish between two types of nineteenth-century revolutionists, often overlapping. The first group are those who revolted against the old Metternich order because it was, in their opinion, too oppressive. The second group are those who revolted mainly because it was international and who preferred a nationalism that would turn out to be many times more oppressive.

Only the former group should technically be labelled "liberals." The second group of rebels tended toward an organic and totalitarian Volk state and were romantics. The first group were rationalists, individualists, constitutionalists. That is, they wanted what Wagnerites not quite fairly call an "atomistic society." A fairer definition would be: a society where the individual does not exist for the state (not even for a classless Volk state), but where the state exists for the individual and hence has its power limited by a constitution, by inalienable civil liberties (Bill of Rights), and by rule of law instead of arbitrary men.

Against the common enemy both groups of rebels joined. The irreconcilable difference inside their own camps they tragically ignored or minimized. This confusion, which began in the anti-Napoleonic wars, even continued into the 1860's and 1870's. For example, Treitschke (and to some extent Houston Chamberlain!) considered himself a liberal, what he called a "national liberal," because he loathed the old order of international conservatism. Yet today we see that his aggressive war-exalting nationalism and anti-Semitic Aryan cult are more like nazism than like what the west knows as liberalism.

The German Revolution of 1848 is generally and falsely called a liberal revolution, as if it were part of the same world-wide movement that caused France's liberal revolution of 1848. The immediate cause of both revolutions was the same: the middle class's increasing resentment against the Metternich system and the latter's decreasing ability to defend itself. But the long-range cause of 1848 Germany was not French liberalism but the very opposite: the revolt of the War of Liberation against the ideas of the French Revolution.

Napoleon was taken by hostile Germans less as the symbol of dictatorship than as the symbol of the French Revolution's rationalism, liberalism, and legalism, as introduced into Germany by the Code Napoléon. These are the very isms which Hitler stamps out. Napoleon's rule, despite its evils, never left the fold of western civilization. Hitler is the culmination of anti-western Kultur, of romanticism's revolt against Napoleon, the " good European." Hitler and Napoleon are direct opposites as cultural symbols. But it seems futile to hope that journalists will desist from their superficially plausible but absurdly misleading comparisons of the little Corsican and the little Austrian, who is even labelled " the second Napoleon."

Outwardly the German rebels of 1848 (even Wagner at first) still used the phrases of atomistic liberalism and constitutional democracy because these were the correct and fashionable phrases of the time for all anti-Metternichians. But inwardly many, possibly most, had already passed from that phase into the phase of organic nationalism. The time has come to revise those history books which call 1848 the " international liberal revolution." That is only true of France. So far as Germany is concerned, both 1848 and the War of Liberation are better called nationalistic revolutions with a thin liberal veneer.

Ever since Bismarck's ruthless war of 1870, the German Revolution of 1848 has, in contrast, become to Germans the stock symbol of the pacific Herder brand of nationalism. In reality, the German '48 was already then, in part, of the aggressive brand of nationalism. Its first deeds were intolerance of all other nationalisms. It waged war against the Danes over the Danish King's partly German, partly Danish state of Schleswig-Holstein and threatened with Germanization the independence of Czechs and Poles.

Germany's Revolution of 1848 is best summed up as a pathetic muddle. It was led by what were literally "absent-minded professors." Like so many frustrated pedants, many of them were disciples of the famous romantic school of 1800, which they hoped to translate from poetry into political reality by passing resolutions. The revolution's schizophrenic muddle is what rendered it impotent against the swift counter-revolutions of the Hapsburgs and of the conservative aristocrats. In its crises its leaders could never make up their minds whether they were revolting for the sake of cosmopolitan liberalism ("French ideas") or for aggressive nationalism.

Until 1933 many western liberal historians assumed that all German revolutions must be liberal simply because all other western revolutions of the nineteenth century happened to be liberal. Such historians (for example, Hazen [8]) assumed that a German revolution must have the same liberal goal as they themselves. This mistake is a typical nineteenth-century provincialism. Too many modern liberals have never emerged intellectually from the nineteenth century. For example, Woodrow Wilson. Instead of preserving in modernized form the international Danubian community of the Hapsburg Empire, he Balkanized Europe into rabid little nationalist states because he still

---

[8] Charles Hazen throughout his *Europe since 1815* (New York, 1910).

shared Mazzini's dreams of keeping nationalism liberal.

Even today books subsume Jahn, Wagner, and 1848 under the cliché heading: "liberal revolt" (against scapegoat Metternich). In contrast this book presents evidence linking them to the Nazi revolt against western freedom. But in fairness to the free half of the German heritage, never forget how many other Germans did stay true to the west (i.e., freedom-minded and parliamentary, whether as liberals, conservatives, or democratic socialists). Freedom predominated on verbal or conscious levels in 1848 over authoritarianism; the former was top current, the latter undercurrent; in 1933 top current becomes undercurrent, but not even the Hitler terror can stop their periodic *alternation* from being the essence of German culture. . . . Our next chapter deals with Jahn and is the first study of him to appear in English.

1961 postscript: The great German Catholic historian, Franz Schnabel, now writes, "Because [Germans] lacked a genuine tradition, romanticism contrived a tradition for them. Jahn and the applause he gained were warning signs of the unhistorical and destructive results this new tradition would have."[9] And five years after the publication of *Metapolitics*, the great Wagner biographer, Ernest Newman, now similarly confirms our Jahn-Wagner link. Newman calls Jahn's definition of Volk "essentially the same definition as Wagner's" and adds: "These views were not original or even peculiar to Wagner . . . the seed of all of them is to be found in Father Jahn . . . Jahn anticipated the Nazi mentality . . . was an anti-semite . . . approved the public burning of books . . . yearned for a Führer . . . believed in 'blood and soil' as fervently as Wagner and Alfred Rosenberg."[10]

---

[9] Schnabel essay in *Hochland*, Munich, October 1949.
[10] Newman, *Life of Richard Wagner* (N.Y., 1946), VI, 96–7.

CHAPTER IV

FATHER JAHN, THE FIRST STORM TROOPER

～～～～～～～～～～～～～～～～～～～～～～～～

*In Jahn arose another world, a new human type. . . .
"Only the overthrow of the nineteenth century by National Socialism has enabled us to see freely and purely
the figure of Jahn."*

— BUNGARDT, *a Nazi historian, 1938* [1]

*As inventor of the word "folkdom," Jahn is the natural
starting-point for every analysis of the concept of Volk.*

— THEUNE, *another Nazi historian, 1937* [2]

Friedrich Ludwig Jahn, whose ideas and deeds best
typify the combination of romantic ideas and social changes
in the early 1800's, was born in 1778, son of a Protestant
preacher. The birthplace was a small town in the province
of Priegnitz, part of the ancient Brandenburg nucleus of
the Kingdom of Prussia. He evolved from local Prussian

---

[1] K. M. Bungardt: *Friedrich Ludwig Jahn* (Würzburg, 1938), p. 2.
The quotation within this quotation is from Alfred Bäumler: *Politik und
Erziehung* (Berlin, 1937).
[2] B. Theune: *Volk und Nation bei Jahn, Rotteck, Welcker und Dahlmann* (Berlin, 1937), p. 13

provincialism, for which he wrote a pamphlet in 1800, into the broader German nationalism for which he volunteered in the anti-French crusades of 1806 and 1813. During 1796–1802, he had been studying at the famous old universities of Halle, Jena, and Greifswald. His doctor's degree he received in philology at Leipzig in 1806 for a book on the German language, which he later strove to " purify " of all un-Germanic words. His university years, above all, steeped him in the basic assumptions of the romantic school, in its new credo of Volk and of " organic versus atomistic society."

Jahn earned his living as a private tutor, public lecturer, and school teacher; he also received Prussian subsidies for agitating the masses against Napoleon. In 1811 he organized among young students his first gymnastic society and simultaneously his first secret nationalist society. As his huge beard grew in dignity and length, his youthful gangs, who worshipped him fanatically as a Führer, gave him his famous nickname " Father Jahn."

Father Jahn's life is one of ceaseless wandering through Germany, orating and writing on behalf of German unity. In 1819 the Prussian government, joining the conservative anti-nationalist reaction of the " Metternich system," suddenly arrested Jahn as a dangerous rebel. For a few years he was dragged from prison to prison; and even after his release his movements were restricted to limited localities under police supervision, until the advent of a more friendly Prussian king in 1840. At the age of seventy Father Jahn was chosen as a delegate to the revolutionary national parliament of 1848. There the former extremist now was called too conservative by the new generation of nationalists, and there he saw his lifelong dream of German unity chattered away. He survived by only four years (till 1852) his slain hopes.

THE GERMAN JACOBIN

The French invaders destroyed the old order of Frederick
the Great's time in Germany. What would replace it? Under Stein, the Prussian Minister, the most efficient reforms
of the French Revolution were introduced peacefully from
above by that revolution's worst enemies. Fanatic nationalism plus sane social reform was the dual creed of
Germany's bright young men. So long as Napoleon threatened externally, the enfeebled old order had to let these
men of ideas take over internally. After Napoleon fell, the
old order under Metternich began to oust and crush them;
they had served their purpose.

But getting rid of them was easier said than done. The
consequences of their work from 1806 to 1819 have
moulded Germany to this very day. During those years
Father Jahn was nationalism's storm-centre. By 1819,
when he was jailed, his agitation had permanently shocked
the middle class and the intellectuals out of their former
aloofness from politics. Ever after, much of Germany's future was shaped by those college and high-school lads who
had learned Jahn's gospel from his lips and his organizations.

Jahn's conservative critics damned him as a " German
Jacobin." [3] " Jacobin " was a fighting word in those days.
It meant a radical who attacked the very basis of the old
system Metternich was rebuilding. Jahn was ferocious in
his denunciation of the new revolutionary doctrines which
France was spreading over the world, just as Hitler de-
nounced the revolutionary doctrines spread by Russia.
But Jahn denounced "Liberty, Equality, Fraternity"

---

[3] H. von Srbik: *Metternich, der Staatsmann und der Mensch* (2 vols.,
Berlin, 1931), I, 167. F. G. Schultheiss: *Friedrich Ludwig Jahn* (Berlin,
1894), pp. 113–14.

probably not so much for its revolutionary implications but
because it was written in French. In just that fashion the
Nazis denounced the Soviet's "bolshevism," "godless-
ness," and "terror" not because the Nazis are any less
state-socialist, anti-Christian, or violent, but because Russia is a rival and Marx a Jew.

With the "true German costume" of his books and
speeches, Jahn was actually clothing many of the "dangerous French ideas." [4] Jahn's program was German Jacobinism in the same way that Hitler's program is Brown
Bolshevism. Jahn was at first beamed upon by conservative Prussian authorities just as Hitler, before his gradual
expropriation of German capital, was beamed upon by the
capitalist Thyssens. Only after years of financial and
propagandist support [5] did the German authorities suppress Jahn and his young Storm Troopers as "revolutionary national-Jacobins." Too late — the snowball had begun to roll.

VOLK AS A NEW BASIS OF GERMAN LIFE

Even a passionate nationalist like Treitschke called Jahn a
"crude peasant" and a "noisy barbarian." Coarse and
boisterous Jahn was, but not for lack of education and intelligence. He was frank and unsophisticated in speech, offensive and unpolished in manner — as a matter of policy.
To him virtue meant the tough, straightforward nordic in
contrast with the sly French dandy. Goethe satirized this
attitude in *Faust* through the character of a young romantic
enthusiast who exclaims: "In German you're a liar if

---

[4] M. Antonowytsch: *Friedrich Ludwig Jahn, Ein Beitrag der Anfänge
des deutschen Nationalismus*, No. 230 of "Historische Studien" (Berlin,
1933), pp. 17–20.

[5] Carl Euler: *Friedrich Ludwig Jahn* (Berlin, 1881), pp. 221, 425–6.
Schultheiss, op. cit., p. 79.

you're polite!" Ever since, German nationalists have quoted this line as if Goethe meant it seriously. When a low varlet plays the boor, that is unpleasant enough. An intelligent and educated man like Jahn could think up a thousand brand-new vulgarisms. His boorishness was a refined art! [6]

By 1815 Jahn permanently wore the " true German costume " of his own invention. This invention was a hermit-like gown of unbleached cloth into which he wanted to force all German citizens.[7] The Nazi brownshirt achieves his dream of a distinctively national dress for civilians; but Jahn's invention was a far more sloppy affair:

> Jahn's long hair, which had turned gray in a single day after the battle of Jena, hung down uncombed upon his shoulders; his neck was exposed, for the servile stock and the effeminate waistcoat were equally unsuitable for the free German. The low-cut neckband of his dirty coat was covered by a wide shirt-collar. With great self-satisfaction, he extolled this questionable get-up as "the genuine Old German costume." [8]

Thus clad, Jahn swaggered through the streets of conquered Paris, whither he came in the entourage of Prussian officials. Staff in hand, with hair and beard flowing in the wind, he harangued crowds on the virtues of unspoilt primitive Teutonism. His proudest exploit in the French capital was to climb its Arc de Triomphe and knock the tuba from the mouth of the goddess of victory. And why not — were not Vandals a primitive Teutonic tribe? Gleefully Jahn quoted French journals which dubbed him

---

[6] H. von Treitschke: *History of Germany* (6 vols., New York, 1915–19), I, 358. Goethe: *Faust*, II, line 6771: " *Im deutschen lügt man, wenn man höflich ist.*"

[7] Schultheiss, op. cit., p. 92. Euler, op. cit., p. 376.

[8] Treitschke, op. cit., III, 5.

"Chief of the Corps of Vengeance." At the Congress of
Vienna he contrasted dramatically with the suave diplomats.[9] Jahn's self-dramatization had this advantage: it
hypnotized fellow enthusiasts even though its absurdity
repelled detached observers.

Jahn's cult of primitivism and of Teuton boorishness was
accompanied by the most grotesque phenomena. Logical
young extremists began dressing in bear-skins, as did
Jahn's acquaintance Sand, who killed an anti-nationalist
writer with a primitive dagger. Jahn himself, while a student, lived for a while in a cave, scorning such decadent
artificialities as houses. From his cave, like a besieged
caveman of the Stone Age, Jahn would roll huge boulders
down on jeering throngs of anti-nationalists. After Jahn
became a nationally famous leader, his young fanatics
would roam the streets like bands of Storm Troopers. Each
band would surround and hoot at any outnumbered pass-
ers-by who looked un-German or too well dressed or gave
signs of French politeness. Thus Teutonic heroism thrived
again and the Volk-soul was "regenerated."[10]

The gymnast Jahn and the poet Arndt were called "the
popularizers of the teachings of the Volk-soul."[11] A parliamentary committee of the German Diet classified Jahn's
German Folkdom of 1810 with Fichte's *Speeches to the
German Nation* of 1808 as "the spiritual godfathers of the
newer Germany."[12] Both works were written while French
troops still occupied Germany; this background accounts
for the fanatic bitterness of Jahn's and Fichte's nationalism.

Fichte's work was limited in its appeal by its abstruse

[9] Euler, op. cit., pp. 433–4, 439, 422–3. Jahn: *Friedrich Ludwig
Jahns Werke*, ed. by Carl Euler (2 vols., Hof, 1884–7), I, 491–7.

[10] Treitschke, op. cit., III, 7.

[11] F. Schnabel: *Deutsche Geschichte im Neunzehnten Jahrhundert*,
(4 vols., Freiburg, 1929–37), I, 306.

[12] J. Friedrich: *Jahn als Erzieher* (Munich, 1895), p. 48.

metaphysics. Jahn's book offered a more practical program, in colorful demagogic style. General Blücher, the German co-victor at Waterloo, called Jahn's book "the Germanest verbal gun [*sic*]." [13] *German Folkdom* is halfway between scientific scholarship and demagogics — that half-way point which sounds so thrilling and convincing to the half-educated.

Jahn's credo was that the unconscious force of Volk shapes all history. To describe this force Jahn coined the word "folkdom" (*Volkstum*), today one of the most important Nazi words. Folkdom he called "that which the Volk has in common, its inner existence, its movement, its ability to propagate. Because of it, there courses through all the veins of a Volk a folkic thinking and feeling, loving and hating, intuition and faith." [14]

Cosmopolitanism Jahn spurned because "humanity appears nowhere by itself pure and simple but only as incarnated by folkdoms." [15] The Greeks and Germans are "humanity's holy people." [16] Later Hegel devoted many volumes to describing how Greeks and Germans, in turn, incarnated God's idea. "How odd of God to choose the Jews," German nationalists seem to wail, when the Germans would make a Chosen People so much superior.

Jahn attempted no new philosophic foundation. Almost all his ideas derive from the German romantics, in whom he was steeped. The romantic school's organic assumption, when applied to the plane of nation and in the context of the war with France, produced Jahn's book *Folkdom*.

Folkdom is devoted to methods for nationalizing Germany's way of life or, rather, "awakening" its allegedly innate nationalism. Without Hitler's cynicism, the book

13 Jahn, op. cit. (Euler's introduction), I, xlvi–xlvii.
14 Euler, op. cit., p. 111. Jahn, op. cit., I, 154, 156.
15 Jahn, op. cit., I, 158.
16 Ibid., I, 162.

foreshadows *Mein Kampf* by its shrewd outline of propaganda techniques and educational indoctrination. So does Jahn's appeal for biological Volk purity.[17] "Animal hybrids have no genuine power of propagation, and hybrid peoples have just as little posterity." "The purer a people, the better; the more mixed, the worse." Every Volk should lead an isolated existence. The founding of a world government " is the last moment of humanity."[18]

Volk is the only true basis of a state. "A state without Volk is nothing, a soulless artifice," wrote Jahn. "A Volk without a state is nothing, a lifeless frivolous phantom like the vagabond gypsies and Jews. Only state and Volk in one make a Reich. Its power of survival is its folkdom."[19] Today that sounds more trite than startling, although attempts to change the map of Europe on that basis will always mean chaos and war. Metternich, the Hapsburg Chancellor and urbane "good European," first viewed more with amusement than horror "that newfangled notion of nationality."[20] But even in his own day it became the most frightening reality of modern progress.

FROM PROVINCIALISM TO NATIONALISM

Jahn's original creed was not nationalism but provincial Prussian patriotism.[21] Not till Prussia's isolation caused her annihilation at Jena did Jahn see German unity as the sole salvation against Napoleon. He witnessed that battle; he said its horror turned his beard grey![22] He now damned

---

17 Theune, op. cit., p. 124.

18 Jahn, op cit., I, 164–8.

19 Ibid., I, 160.

20 W. Monypenny and G. Buckle: *Life of Benjamin Disraeli* (new ed., 2 vols., New York, 1929), I, 997–1003.

21 Antonowytsch, op. cit., p. 14. See "Beförderung des Patriotismus in Preussen" in Jahn, op. cit., I, 3–32.

22 Euler, op. cit., p. 78.

the boundaries separating the Germanys. Traditional local patriotism must be exterminated to make way for Jahn's national patriotism. His reaction to Jena was typical of that of thousands of German leaders. Jena was the vision of Damascus converting many thousands of provincialist Sauls into nationalist Pauls.

But the " particularism " of Bavarians, Prussians, Saxons, Swabians, Austrians had roots so much deeper than the new nationalism that Jahn's dream had to wait a whole century. Hitler is the first German strong enough to abolish the old provincial names and lines. After union with the Reich in 1938, the thousand-year-old name " Austria " was changed to " East Province." Today separate Bavarian or Prussian or Austrian loyalties are treason. Hitler's speeches constantly rage against alleged English plans of again splitting Germany into Germanys.

To overcome patriotism for the old *provincial* capitals like Munich and Berlin, Jahn planned to build a new *national* capital. He located it with mathematical exactness at Germany's geographical centre and named it " Teutonia." For efficiency, he drew new local subdivisions along natural lines to replace both arbitrary and traditional lines. Jahn knew where national tradition must end and efficiency begin.[23]

All these recommendations smack of the *departements* of the French Revolution. These, too, broke up France's old provincial lines. Extremely radical for his time was Jahn's demand for unification (preferably under Prussian leadership). It meant the overthrow or subjection of most of Germany's old established ruling houses.

The prophetic Metternich warned that the anti-French wars enabled " the revolutionary spirit " to hide " under the veil of patriotism." Among the eager Germans, " ha-

---

[23] Jahn, op. cit., I, 169–75, 206.

tred of the military despotism of Bonaparte " too often became linked with hatred of " the legitimate power of their masters." " Prussia," concluded Metternich, " committed a grave fault in calling to her aid such dangerous weapons " as nationalism.[24]

In his *German Folkdom* of 1810 Jahn seemed content with uniting Germany proper. In 1814 his war experience inflated his demands. He now added the Swiss, the Netherlanders, and the Danes to the Germanic peoples to be incorporated. Germany's central position, he pointed out, makes her the battlefield of Europe unless she is armed to the teeth and fanatically united.[25] In a war-torn world, there was logic in this demand. Since Jahn's day, the idea has been expanded into Hitler's concept of *Lebensraum*.

MASS PARTICIPATION, FÜHRER, AND ABOLITION OF CLASS LINES

Jahn proposed a new nobility of merit. The traditional nobles must do more than " count their ancestors." They must earn new titles of merit. The new nobility must be open to even the humblest-born citizen because " Volkhonour makes every member of the Volk a man of honour." [26] Like Hitler and unlike Junker nationalists, Jahn knew that fanatic nationalism can be long sustained only by a mass movement enabling the lower classes and the uneducated to reach the top. Good citizens, Jahn decided, are only made through mass participation in government.[27]

Does this make Jahn a sincere partisan of representative

---

[24] From " Confession of Faith " to Czar Alexander, Prince Clemens Metternich: *Memoirs of Prince Metternich* (5 vols., London, 1880), III, 463.

[25] Jahn, op. cit., I, 417–18.

[26] Ibid., I, 290–2; II, 701, 952–3.

[27] Ibid., I, 177–8.

government? Most liberal historians think so, and beam upon his youth movement. They overlook his dictatorial tendencies and his enthusiasm for some coming German Führer. Invariably Jahn was suspiciously vague about the powers and functions he would actually grant the Reichstag.

He was less interested in one form of government or another than in a strong, united, nationalist government, no matter whether parliamentary or dictatorial in form. Therefore his views on form of government varied with the changing needs of the moment. He was never a liberal nationalist or a republican. Generally he favoured a centralized national monarchy with advisory parliament and constitution. But when exasperated, he favoured a dictator.

In 1814 Jahn called for a "unity-creator," an unparliamentary dictator, a Führer. By 1814, experiences had proved to him the strength of provincialism. He wanted a Führer to burn it out by Hippocrates' cure for cancer: "What medicine does not heal is healed by iron; what iron does not heal is healed by fire." Half a century later Bismarck orated that problems are settled by "blood and iron " and not by parliamentary chatter. Jahn said of his " iron and fire" Führer: "The Volk will honour him as saviour and forgive him all his sins." [28]

The logic of organic nationalism leads to collectivism, to mass levelling and socializing. Jahn's slogan: "Participation of the individual in the happiness and suffering of the whole," had a social goal similar to that of the favourite Nazi slogan: "Collective good before individual good " (" *Gemeinnutz vor Eigennutz* ").[29] Only the unity of the

[28] Ibid., I, 419.
[29] Antonowytsch, op. cit., p. 81. P. Piechowski: *Friedrich Ludwig Jahn — Vom Turnvater zum Volkserzieher* (Gotha, 1928), p. 14. Jahn, op. cit., I, 194–6.

masses with the state, preached Jahn, can clothe " the skeleton of state " with " the warm flesh and blood of folkdom." " The longing for unity is the first self-consciousness of an awakening Volk. . . . *One* God, *one* Fatherland, *one* House, *one* Love! " [30] Thus Jahn. The official posters of Nazi plebiscites: " *One* Volk, *one* State, *one* Führer."

Jahn demanded universal national citizenship not for the sake of liberty but for the sake of spreading nationalism. Nationalism is best spread by the " participation of individuals in the happiness and suffering of the whole." [31] To " remove separating factors," Jahn would abolish class privileges and Germany's feudal traditions; " there is but one Master: the state." Jahn called for such reforms as free ownership of land for all. [32] These reforms were soon introduced into Prussia by Stein. Both Stein and Jahn wanted to unite the army with the broad mass of citizens and wanted a common public-school education for children of all classes. Jahn was equally against class lines and provincial lines. Class consciousness splits the organic unity of Volk into class atoms.

Prophetic of Hitler are the grounds Jahn lists for depriving a German of citizenship in this coming nationalist utopia. Three of Jahn's " criminal " grounds are: besmirching the honour of the Volk in foreign lands, marriage with an unnaturalized foreigner, and remaining a bachelor while healthy, potent, and capable of supporting a family. [33] The citizen must serve the state with pen, loins, and spade. Jahn would be pleased that Hitler not only bans interracial marriages but subsidizes intraracial breeding.

---

[30] Jahn, op. cit., I, 194–211. Piechowski, op. cit., p. 12.
[31] Jahn, op. cit., I, 194.
[32] Ibid., I, 197.
[33] Ibid., I, 287.

NATIONALISM VERSUS CHRISTIANITY

Nationalism is our century's new pagan religion. This development was prophesied by Heinrich Steffens, a more moderate romantic than Jahn. Watching Jahn's gymnasts march by like Storm Troopers, Steffens feared that "this vague German patriotism was taking on a *religious* character and becoming ever more threatening." [34]

Political nationalism clashes with Christianity in Germany more than elsewhere. The historical reason is that religion has overlapped politics in Germany more than elsewhere. The very term "Holy Roman Empire" indicated inextricable overlapping. The historical fact that Germany did not become either all Protestant or all Catholic has had tragic consequences. The Catholic-Protestant split was a major cause of the terrible Thirty Years' War. Ever after, this split was encouraged and exploited by Germany's neighbours — especially exploited, Jahn correctly charged, by French intervention. [35]

Therefore Jahn demanded a single united German church, purged of international ties. "The church should not be placed above the state, nor under it, nor next to it; it should be integrated with it." By integration, Jahn meant fusing church and state into organic unity. [36] His state is a Volk state nationalizing private and public activities in all-inclusive (totalitarian) fashion. How can religion escape such state co-ordination? In practice, Jahn's term "integration" would work out not so differently from Hitler's integration of Pastor Niemöller into "free positive Christianity."

---

[34] Heinrich Steffens: *Was Ich Erlebte* (8 vols., Breslau, 1843), VIII, 314.

[35] Jahn, op. cit., I, 220.

[36] Ibid., I, 212.

True Christianity Jahn identified with what he called "northern Christianity." Son of a Lutheran preacher, he charged that Luther's "northern" Christianity was being plotted against by scheming un-nordic Jesuits and Hapsburgs. Jahn used Christianity rather conveniently to justify the traditional German expansion eastward (*Drang nach Osten*). Germany's mission was to Christianize — by conquest — the "inferior" Slavs and Balts of the east.[37]

Neither Jahn nor Hitler have much interest in questions of Christian dogma except on political grounds. Their basic dogma is strictly secular: folkdom.[38] Ever since Henry VIII, England, too, has had a national church — but not subjected to a totalitarian framework. As sweeping totalitarians, Jahn and Hitler would actually go much, much further than Henry VIII, whom they profess to imitate.

Jahn and Hitler are far-seeing and wise in trying to end Germany's bloody feud between Catholic and Protestant sects. At last Hitler has achieved this great feat of unifying them: not by the "German Christianity" he set up under Müller, who proved a failure, but by persecution!

Jahn's term "integration" provokes two questions: Would Christianity still be Christian without its dogma of universal brotherhood? Are the modern nationalist values compatible with either Protestant or Catholic Christianity? In the act of throwing the first stone at Hitler, let nationalists of all countries pause to answer these questions.

[37] Ibid., I, 223–8; II, 540 ff. Piechowski, op. cit., p. 21.
[38] Theune, op. cit., pp. 27, 117.

STATE EDUCATION TO INDOCTRINATE FOLKDOM

Jahn insisted on the same elementary state education for children of all classes. His political motive for this was twofold: to break down class prejudices and to nationalize the masses. Universities, too, were to become vehicles of folkdom. His was a broad concept of education, including both culture for its own sake and propaganda. In the development of nationalism in every land, state-controlled universal education has proved the most reliable agency for nationalizing the masses.[39]

Nietzsche once defined nationality as people who read the same newspapers. The language a man reads is the medium for his indoctrination. That is why all nationalists stress language. Jahn helped found Germany's first " Language Purification Society." An example of the results is that because " university" is a word of un-nordic, Latin origin, one of Jahn's disciples replaced it with the name " Institute of Mental Gymnastics." [40] The Nazis are consciously Jahn's disciples in purging German of foreign words.

Today German is the basic language of all Germans, as a matter of course. Not so in Jahn's day. French was the language of culture and diplomacy. Frederick the Great's court dismissed German as " that coachman's language (*Kutschersprache*)." Right through Jahn's lifetime, nobility and middle class trained their children in French. Herder and the romantic school's interest in folksongs paved Jahn's way by reviving German as a language for polite society.

---

[39] Jahn, op. cit., I, 185–7, 193. C. J. H. Hayes: *Essays on Nationalism*, (New York, 1937), p. 86.

[40] Euler, op. cit., p. 445. Treitschke, op. cit., III, 9.

The differences in grammar and language-structure between German and French may help determine the characteristic national differences in thought-structure and
philosophy of life between the Germans and the French.
That is why Jahn was so worried about Germans who also
spoke French. A typical example of Jahn logic: " Man has
but *one* mother; *one* mother tongue is enough for him."
French for Jahn was the language of gay seducers. " Unhappy Germany," he wailed, " neglect of your mother
tongue has been fearfully revenged upon you. . . . This
language [French] has rendered impotent your men, led
your children astray, dishonoured your wives." [41]

In 1817 Jahn thundered to a lecture hall crowded with
Berlin's most polished society: " The father who lets his
daughter learn French is just as good as the man who ap-
prentices his daughter to whoredom." A Prussian officer
in the audience took offence at thus being called a pimp
for letting his daughter brazenly conjugate French irregu-
lar verbs in public! The result was a *cause célèbre,* with
further pressure by the Prussian government to hush Jahn.
Such incidents typify the coarseness of speech which Jahn
urged as Teutonic.[42] Herder and many of the romantic
school cultivated the folksongs and traditions of *all* nationalities. Jahn turned this broad cultural interest into
narrow, anti-alien politics.

To instil proper national sentiment into pupils, Jahn
proposed a whole new series of books and anthologies.
These were to include German songs, the sagas of German
heroes, and a national bible of folkic Weltanschauung.
The purpose of this, later fulfilled by Nazi educators, was
far more political than literary.[43]

---

41 Jahn, op. cit., I, 244–5.
42 Euler, op. cit., pp. 483–4.
43 Jahn, op. cit., I, 343–59.

Jahn wanted to popularize as well as nationalize art.[44] He would probably stroke his long beard in approval over Hitler's Munich "House of German Art." The bronzed and sturdy nordic lads and lasses would be to his taste. To Jahn, folkdom is not only a subject for art but the object of art.

As the best means for schools to inculcate folkdom, Jahn urged the study of history. "The Fatherland's history inspires to deeds by its living example."[45] Hitler in *Mein Kampf* lists the two decisive influences of his schooling: "First, I became a nationalist. Second, I learned to grasp and to understand the meaning of *history*." Hitler lauds his favourite teacher for not "rattling forth historical facts" but finding "the forces" which shape history. "When Hitler speaks of . . . history as the science which demonstrates that one's own people is always right, he is echoing Jahn."[46]

History that "inspires to deeds" by "its living example" can be read in the elementary texts of every land. Are not our own professional patriots ever alert for allegedly un-American texts? Goethe said: "Patriotism corrupts history." Madariaga's attractive cure for nationalist war is to make every Hans and Gretchen read only French history texts and to bring every French child up on German histories.

Jahn viewed his program for national public education with nineteenth-century optimism: "The effects of such a German popular education will be infinite. . . . Popular education is the true spiritual creator of the Volk." A people thus organically united can never be destroyed by foreign conquests.[47] Hitler's educational ideas as expressed in

---

[44] Ibid., I, 264.
[45] Ibid., I, 256.
[46] *Mein Kampf*, ed. cit., p. 19; also editor's footnote, p. 19.
[47] Jahn, op. cit., I, 282.

Mein Kampf " are in part the common property of all who
have gone to school and in part the legacy of Jahn." [48] The
nationalizing effects of a century of state education bear
out Jahn's predictions and plans.

NATIONALISM IN ACTION

Jahn's agitation helped achieve in action the theories of his
book *German Folkdom*. His nationalism in action took
three chief forms: the gymnastic societies, the volunteer
Free Corps, and the fanatic nationalizing of German student leagues. These three institutions first infected German youth with the virulent germ of activist nationalism.

As the " Father " of gymnastics, Father Jahn is a national
saint of the Nazis. In an unpolitical form, decent innocu-
ous *Turnvereins* in Milwaukee and St. Louis continue his
work. Gymnastic societies of Slav patriots still imitate
Jahn's organization. Till Hitler's occupation, the gymnastic *Sokols* indoctrinated Czech nationalism. Jahn's gymnasts personified that anti-intellectual " regeneration "
which ivory-tower intellectuals were demanding. Jahn
combined patriotism with good health to make boys physically and spiritually fit for national war against the French
conqueror. When not training them in mock battles, he
was marching them off to lectures on the old Nibelungen
saga. Under the very noses of French officers and spies,
active nationalism was being bred.

Jahn's gymnasts (*Turner*) were dressed in special uniform. "With the gymnast costume, every distinction of
rank automatically disappeared." His boys were very
noisy and jeered at youths who did not participate.[49] Jahn's

[48] *Mein Kampf*, ed. cit., p. 19, ed. note.
[49] Euler, op. cit., 180, 185–6, 199.

aristocratic enemies complained that he was turning polite middle-class youngsters into ruffians. In other words, he fired their enthusiasm.

When the government called for anti-French volunteers in 1813, most of Jahn's youthful enthusiasts followed him into the Free Corps.[50] The government then subsidized his activities. His gymnast craze spread rapidly. In Jahn's home territory, Berlin, the craze reached its peak in 1817 with 1,074 participants. The same year two important universities gave Jahn honorary degrees.[51]

But reaction was growing. Jahn's gymnasts were allied to other radical nationalist groups. Moderates feared all this as a menace to the new peace and order of 1815. In 1817 and 1818 two vigorous paper battles stirred all Germany: the " Berlin gymnastic feud " and the " Breslau gymnastic fight." Most leading intellectuals were forced to take sides. Breslau's learned society, before which a Jahn disciple read an inflammatory pro-gymnast paper, was thrown into a riot. The society was dissolved in consequence.[52]

Under pressure from Metternich, the King of Prussia closed down the gymnastic fields.[53] They were eventually reopened under careful government supervision (after Jahn was jailed, in 1819). The real fight was not about physical education but about the nationalization (today, read " radicalization ") of youth. In 1818 Metternich warned Prussia: " The gymnastic institution is the real training ground for the university mischief. . . . The inventor [Jahn], the invention, and the execution come from Prussia. . . . The lower institutions are like the branch

---

[50] Schultheiss, op. cit., p. 101.

[51] Friedrich, op. cit., p. 25; Schultheiss, op. cit., pp. 94, 42; Euler, op. cit., pp. 535–6.

[52] Euler, op. cit., pp. 494–510, 562–7.

[53] Ibid., pp. 474–8.

lodges of a mother lodge. One has to grasp the evil by the roots."[54]

Jahn's youths were both civilian gymnasts and volunteer soldiers in the Free Corps against France. From this combination sprang the concept of what are now known as Storm Troops. The concept was foreshadowed by Jahn's peace-time bands of organized youth. Wagner in 1848 and Röhm in 1933 wanted to organize all civilian masses into an amateur political army. From old Teutonic lore and from the military success of the French Revolution's "nation in arms," Jahn and fellow nationalists reach a common conclusion: an awakened mass of patriots is invincible![55] The practical result was universal military training throughout Europe.

Under the old order in Germany, middle-class society had abhorred militarism and the soldier's life.[56] Frederick the Great would not let the bourgeoisie become officers because he felt a tradesman class lacked the requisite aristocratic "sense of honour." For the non-commissioned ranks, only country oafs and ruffians would dream of volunteering and then only as mercenaries. Jahn swore to change all that. In national-Jacobin fashion his book *Folkdom* imported the French Revolution's concept of a "nation in arms." From above, Stein's brain-trusters introduced these class-levelling reforms in Prussia.

Meanwhile from below, Jahn's network of agitators started converting the whole German middle class to the glories of service in the ranks. Reorganized by the reformers, Prussia took up arms to avenge Jena. Prussia proclaimed the famous "Free Corps" of volunteers against France. It was a successful experiment in tapping a

---

54 Ibid., pp. 568–9.
55 Schultheiss, op. cit., p. 83. Antonowytsch, op. cit., pp. 20–5
56 Euler, op. cit., pp. 201–2.

broader level of national enthusiasm. Middle-class volunteers were also evoked from *non*-Prussian states by
Jahn in order to make the Free Corps a unifying national
force.[57]

Jahn was tipped off in advance of the Free Corps procla-
mation. His disciples circulated quietly through German
universities and skilfully prepared the ground. When the
call to arms was trumpeted, student volunteers streamed
from all German provinces. Jahn himself was given command of two incomplete companies. He enlisted,
equipped, and helped train enough men for a full bat-
talion — one third of the entire Free Corps! [58]

Napoleon paid the movement sufficient attention to
curse Jahn because of his volunteers.[59] Their military
value was slight.[60] Their real importance was in filling the
young volunteers with unquenchable fanatic nationalism.
To volunteer was the bath of fire for which life-starved and
Faustian souls yearn. A typical sentimental incident records that a slender maiden was found dead on the battlefield; in story-book style, she had disguised herself as a
boy.[61]

The Free Corps was a unique collection of students and
their professors, scientists and preachers, exotic poets and
drab government bureaucrats; all volunteered. Professional soldiers distrusted this undisciplined horde. Its implication of a politically united nation made the separate
German states tremble. Therefore the *national* Free Corps
was deprived of its independence and eventually split up

[57] Paul Wentzke: *Geschichte der deutschen Burschenschaft* (Heidelberg, 1919), p. 96.

[58] Ibid., p. 96. Schultheiss, op. cit., pp. 83–4, 87–8.

[59] Schultheiss, op. cit., p. 88.

[60] A hotly debated issue. Euler, op. cit., pp. 335–45. Wentzke, op.
cit., pp. 99–103. Schultheiss, op. cit., pp. 86–7.

[61] Euler, op. cit., p. 335.

among the armies of the *independent separate* states.[62]
Jahn's dream was foiled for the time being.

Originally, Jahn intended the Volk army to be purely
defensive. His book on *Folkdom* piously denounced " aggression " — so long as the aggressor was France and not
Germany. But like many German nationalists he found
the peace of 1815 intolerable to Germany's political interests. He now thundered: " Germany needs a war of her
own in order to feel her power; she needs a feud with
Frenchdom to develop her national way of life in all its
fullness. This occasion will not fail to come. . . ." [63] It
came long after Jahn's death. Only by such an anti-French
crusade could Bismarck in 1870 unite Germany at last.

Nationalist sentiment in the universities reached the
pitch of frenzy after the War of Liberation.[64] Returning
from the Free Corps, students organized nationalist fraternities. Thirty years later it was the Herr Professors
(these same boys grown up) who led the 1848 Revolution
for German unity.

A chief spiritual godfather of these nationalist student
leagues was Father Jahn. In his own university days he
had fought the aristocratic fraternities (*Landmannsschaf-
ten*) because they were organized on the basis of separate
provinces. In 1811–12 Jahn and a collaborator had proposed the organization of *national* student leagues (*Burschenschaften*), but Fichte had turned the idea down.
During Free Corps days Jahn again preached the idea to
all, and at last it was put into practice.[65]

From their very start, Jahn was the idol of these noisy
new fraternities. Many units imitated his draft constitu-

---

[62] Schultheiss, op. cit., pp. 87–9.

[63] Euler, op. cit., 440–1.

[64] Treitschke, op. cit., III, 38, *passim*. Theodor Ziegler: *Die geistigen
und sozialen Strömungen des 19. Jahrhunderts* (Berlin, 1899), p. 116.

[65] Wentzke, op. cit., pp. 80–5, 150.

tion. His disciples led in founding them. In turn, these national student leagues were the most active supporters of gymnastics. Throughout Germany the leagues co-operated against their foes. Jahn's student influence was sometimes direct, sometimes indirect through his network of middlemen. He and the poet Arndt were worshipped hysterically; so much so that Metternich vowed to free Germany from what he called the " dictatorship of such men as Jahn and Arndt. . . ." [66]

Jahn had lit a stick of dynamite under the ivory tower of German universities. The effect was permanent.

Student hysteria reached its climax in the fanatic book-burning episode of 1817. Jahn from afar was its guiding spirit. At the Wartburg castle gathered a stormy youth congress of student representatives from all Germany. They fed to huge bonfires the reactionary and anti-national books most hated by Jahn, amid frenzied nationalist resolutions. Nazi book-burnings consciously imitated Jahn's notorious deed.

Both horror and enthusiasm shook central Europe after the Wartburg youth congress. Most moderates now turned against Jahn.[67] He could no longer control the forces he had set in motion. The youth he inspired went far beyond his approval in their radicalism.

An example of such radicalism is the revolutionist Follen. This debonair madcap finally had to flee to America, where he charmed Harvard tea-parties and to this day has a street near Harvard named after him. Prophetically Follen called Jahn's gymnast movement the future " Storm Troopers " of a future nationalist seizure of power.[68]

---

[66] Ibid., pp. 118 ff., 131, 167–8, 181–3, 299–301. Treitschke, op. cit., II, 432.

[67] Wentzke, op. cit., pp. 213–18. Euler, op. cit., pp. 525–39.

[68] Srbik, op. cit., I, 590–1.

As an agitator Jahn did many propagandist jobs for the
government before 1815. He wrote and distributed influential leaflets appealing to the common people. Prussian ministers took him along to the Congress of Vienna
to drum up nationalism whenever it happened to suit their
policy. In this he was their tool — so they thought. But
when nationalism no longer suited their policy, their tool
not only refused to stop but now turned his nationalism
against them. Against the aristocratic Austrian and Prussian governments Jahn's totalitarian nationalists now often
made common cause with those liberal and republican
rebels with whom Jahn is generally and mistakenly identified in English and American history books.

In 1819, on partly false charges of revolutionary conspiracy, the aristocratic Prussian government threw Jahn
into jail.[69] He was victim of that general anti-nationalist
repression whose pretext was the Sand incident. Karl
Sand, an insane student acquaintance of Jahn's, had murdered a reactionary anti-national playwright in horrible
fashion. Waving his bloody dagger, Sand had vainly proclaimed a nationalist revolution against all the existing
German governments. Metternich, conservatism's Cas-
sandra, was frankly ecstatic with delight over this assassination plot. It justified all his gloomy warnings. It gave
him his long awaited pretext for the famous and highly debatable " persecution of demagogues " that followed.[70]

Till 1824 Father Jahn was clamped in semi-confinement.
Thereafter a police supervision to restrict his travel and
conduct generally succeeded in keeping him from touring

---

[69] Heinrich Prohle: *Friedrich Ludwig Jahns Leben* (Berlin, 1855)
contains the full report made by the poet Hoffmann, exonerating Jahn,
pp. 321–425.

[70] Metternich: *Memoirs*, III, 260–1. In a private letter he wrote: " It
will be my care to draw from the affair [the assassination by Sand] the best
possible results."

the universities and from organizing and agitating. Upon regaining comparative freedom under the new Prussian King in 1840, Jahn denounced internationalism as bitterly as ever but had to pose for safety's sake as a far more conservative nationalist than before.[71] Until the Revolution of 1848, Prussia still continued to ban or control public gymnastics in order to wipe out the secret student societies and grand-opera conspiracies for national unity which accompanied Jahn's setting-up exercises.

The nationalism of Jahn's movement was partly — and only partly — linked with anti-Semitism. Occasionally tolerant, at other times Jahn vented the coarsest sort of fury upon all Jewry. German anti-Semitism in the early nineteenth century was partly a social and economic reaction to the liberalized laws of Stein, which opened to Jews professions previously barred.[72] Napoleon won much Jewish support inside Germany by bestowing civic equality upon Jews in the German lands he conquered. From those days dates the modern German concept of Jewry as a Trojan Horse, as a stab in the back, which has been exploited to the hilt by Hitler.[73]

When not busy addressing delegations of gymnasts, Jahn campaigned against the large-scale emigration to America as sapping the Volk's blood. He lived to see the Revolution of 1848. He became an elected delegate to its revolutionary Frankfurt Diet, where he was trotted about with his long white beard by the younger nationalists as the living symbol of their movement's continuity.[74]

---

[71] Euler, op. cit., pp. 578–84.

[72] Theune, op. cit., p. 112; Treitschke, op. cit., III, 44.

[73] Cf. *Mein Kampf*, ed. cit., p. 251, ed. note.

[74] V. Valentin: *Geschiehte der deutschen Revolution von 1848* (2 vols., Berlin, 1931), II, 583–4.

THE IMPORTANCE OF JAHN'S HERITAGE
IN 1941

As early as 1810 Jahn had foreseen and popularized the totalitarian implications of the organic Volk state. Ever after, he demanded that the state subordinate every institution, every thought and deed, to enhancing aggressive nationalism. In this he is the father of the Nazi system of education.

Much of Nazi Germany would horrify Jahn personally, just as he was shocked in his own day — too late — by the extremists inevitably produced by his agitation. But Jahn, boor by policy, was the first to demonstrate the inherent barbarism of modern nationalism-in-action, in contrast with Herder's humanitarian nationalism-in-literature. Hitler's Director of Weltanschauung, Rosenberg, cites as leitmotiv for his book on " The Coming Reich " the words on Volk of Father Jahn.[75]

Jahn's lasting importance was bringing violent nationalism from a few intellectuals to the broad middle and lower middle classes. Not even he reached the lowest classes, the peasants and proletarians, because there were then no politically aware masses to respond. The logical final step, of nationalizing even the proletariat, awaited the national socialism of Wagner and Hitler.

The young men inspired by Jahn — in Free Corps, in gymnastics, in national student leagues — became nationalism's germ-bearers. These same young men later permeated all German life and made solid, lasting institutions of Jahn's dreams. In the schools, taught by these middle-class teachers, the broader masses in turn were nationalized. On that foundation Hitler built his house.

---

[75] Rosenberg: *Mythus,* Book III, " The Coming Reich," p. 451.

Today the organic state utterly subjects all individuals to the whole. This whole is now deemed incalculably "greater than the sum of its parts." These new ideas and attitudes of romanticism were first popularized by men like Jahn. Potential in his Volk state lurked the Germany of 1941. He and his comrades of the War of Liberation form the connecting link between romantic folksong and efficient folk-army.[76]

---

[76] It was Jahn more than Fichte who was the inspirer of the War of Liberation, despite Treitschke, who found Jahn "too boorish" to be a hero. H. Engelbrecht, *Fichte* (N.Y., 1933, pp. 124–35) proves that in reality Fichte's *Speeches* in 1808 reached "very meager audiences . . . attracted hardly any notice." Only later did they attain the influence we analyze on p. 192.

CHAPTER V

SIEGFRIED: THE METAPOLITICS OF RICHARD WAGNER

∽∽∽∽∽∽∽∽∽∽∽∽∽∽∽∽∽∽∽∽∽∽∽∽∽∽∽∽∽∽∽∽∽∽∽

German youth honours in Wagner a dictator . . . in the name of the "Chosen People," the Germans! Wagner belongs to the demagogues of art, knowing how to play upon the instincts of the masses and thereby knowing how to win over the instincts of such youths as crave power. . . . Wagner became now an oracle, a telephone from the other world. . . . I like not the agitators dressed up as heroes [like Siegfried] . . . the anti-Semites who excite the blockhead elements of the populace. The invariable success of intellectual charlatanism in present-day Germany [1887] hangs together with the desolation of the German mind, whose cause I look for in a too exclusive diet of papers, politics, beer, and Wagnerian music, not forgetting the condition precedent of this diet, the national vanity, "Germany, Germany above everything." . . . Richard Wagner [is] leading us to ruin.

— NINETZSCHE (1887) [1]

---

[1] Nietzsche: *Die Unschuld des Werdens: Der Nachlass* (ed. A. Bäumler, Leipzig, 1931), I, 160. Nietzsche: *Genealogy of Morals* (New York: Modern Library; n.d.), pp. 102, 172–3, 185.

At a typically fashionable American concert of Wagnerian music a speaker explained the concert somewhat like this: "Here in free America we honour tonight not the Germany of Hitler, of dictatorship and persecution, but the Germany of Richard Wagner, of free art and racial tolerance and democracy." My mind could not help straying to the Wagner festivals going on at that very same time in "the Germany of Hitler." In 1933, on the day the Nazis seized power, they had ordered Berlin to celebrate by performing Wagner's nationalistic opera *Die Meistersinger* as nazism's official artistic symbol. Which is right in claiming Wagner as its symbol, the fashionable American school or the Nazi German? Let the evidence of Wagner's own works decide.

The evidence presented in these pages, substantiated by documentary sources in the notes, exposes Wagner's warped genius as the most important single fountainhead of current Nazi ideology. His incalculably influential political writings and orations are little known to Americans and to most Germans. Though widely circulated, his proto-Nazi tirades, published in his official Bayreuth magazine, scarcely reached the broader masses directly. How, then, can his ideas be so influential? The explanation is that his ideas saturated the masses indirectly, through his popularizers.

The popularizers of his ideas, and those of his good friend the racist Gobineau, were known as the "Wagner circle." After the maestro's death in 1883, this became known as the Bayreuth circle. The most familiar names of the Wagner and Bayreuth circles are Wagner's widow, Cosima, his son Siegfried Wagner and son-in-law Houston Stewart Chamberlain, and their friends Alfred Rosenberg, Dietrich Eckart, Goebbels, and Hitler.

Rosenberg later became the official Nazi philosopher, and Eckart was an amusing drunken poet of Munich's bohemia. In his spare time between drinks, Eckart was a leading founder of the original Nazi party and taught his young disciple Hitler the Chamberlain-Wagner theory of Aryan racial purity. In 1923, Eckart brought young Hitler into the fold of Frau Wagner's Bayreuth circle.

The purpose of the two chapters on Wagner here presented is threefold: first, to explain Wagner's change from pedestrian, everyday politics to his more soaring metapolitics; second, to co-ordinate and define as precisely as possible his vague metapolitical ideas; third, to indicate their importance for Nazi Germany and the world.

These pages must strictly exclude all discussion of Wagner's music *qua* music (even though Thomas Mann recently wrote: " I go a little farther than Peter Viereck. I find an element of nazism not only in Wagner's questionable literature; I find it also in his ' music ' " [2]).

The intense emotional subjectivity behind Wagner's philosophy must be stressed vigorously. The " one great need of his life " was his " lust for domination," an aspect in which he closely resembles Hitler.[3] To what does Wagner frankly attribute his petulance against Bismarck's empire of 1871? Partly to governmental thwarting of his whim to greet the returning army personally with a self-composed victory hymn! [4] He was not joking when he remarked to a friend: " Bismarck is certainly a great politician but not a great man, for he has no comprehension

---

[2] Thomas Mann in *Common Sense,* New York, January 1940, p. 13, in reply to my articles on " Hitler and Wagner " in the November and December 1939 issues of *Common Sense.*

[3] Ernest Newman: *Wagner as Man and Artist* (London, 1914), pp. 3–4. Heiden: *Hitler,* p. 310.

[4] Richard Wagner: " Was ist Deutsch? " *Bayreuther Blätter,* Jg. I, No. 2 (February 1878), pp. 41–2.

of Bayreuth." [5] This subjective and egocentric approach
is typical of Wagner from beginning to end.

How shall we classify Wagner's ideas and his psychological development? On this score his biographers and
critics of all schools are for once unanimous. His fiercest
enemy, Nordau, calls him " the last mushroom on the dung-
hill of romanticism." His ablest admirer, Thomas Mann,
finds " the concept of the romantic is still the best label for
him." In between are literally dozens of such titles of
Wagner studies as, for example, *The Romantic Structure
of Wagner's Cogitation.* Quite correctly, Wagner himself
stresses his kinship to the German romantic school by his
terminology, operatic themes, literary allusions, and basic
postulates. He worships the first romantics, be it noted,
for " arousing the Volk spirit in the War of Liberation." [6]

"FRENCH IDEAS," 1830–43

" At one bound I became a revolutionist," said Wagner of
the second French revolution, that of 1830.[7] It was his
first step from music into politics. He became also a democratic internationalist. Like young Mussolini, young Wag-

[5] Berthold Kellermann: *Erinnerungen, ein Künstlerleben* (Zurich,
1932), p. 77. Ernest Newman: *The Life of Richard Wagner* (3 vols.; New
York: Alfred A. Knopf; 1933, 1937, 1941), II, 552–3.

[6] Max Nordau: *Degeneration* (translated from 2nd German ed., New
York, 1895), p. 194. Thomas Mann: *Leiden und Grösse der Meister* (Ber-
lin, 1935), pp. 135–6. (From this book of essays the essay on Wagner
appears in English translation, in somewhat condensed form, in Thomas
Mann: *Freud, Goethe, Wagner* (New York: Alfred A. Knopf; 1937), pp.
101–211.) Kurt Knopf: *Die Romantische Struktur des Denkens Wagners*
(Jena, 1932). Arthur Kiessling: *Der Geist des Romantischen im Denken
und Schaffen Wagners* (Leipzig, 1925). Wagner: *Richard Wagner's Prose
Works* (8 vols., trans. and ed. by W. A. Ellis, London, 1895–9), I, 311;
IV, 59.

[7] Wagner: *Prose,* I, 6. K. W. Zinnius: *Die Schriften Richard Wagners
in ihrem Verhältnis zur zeitgeschichtlichen Lage* (Heidelberg, 1936),
p. 11.

ner once wrote manifestoes against the "vanity" of nationalism.

Wagner was then a student at the University of Leipzig.
There he was inspired with world-revolutionary zeal by
the dashing Polish refugees from czardom. Simultaneously he was inspired with national-revolutionary zeal by
his membership in the national student league (*Burschenschaft*) which Father Jahn had founded.[8] Which of the
two zeals would win out in Wagner?

During this first period Wagner's most ardent zeal was
still the international one which the French Revolution
had stirred in him. In his first published essay, 1834, he
prayed that "the master will come who writes in neither
Italian, French, nor German fashion." Instead, art's mission is to rise above "national vanity" to a "feeling of
universality." In such a mood Wagner moved to Paris
in 1839, hailing it as the capital of world culture, "the
capital of free France, where a press exposes all wrongs,
where only merit wins applause." [9]

Steeped in what Germans call the "French ideas" of
rationalism and atomistic liberalism, Wagner then called
himself proudly an "anti-mystical materialist." Philosophically he belonged to Feuerbach's "Young Hegelians." Feuerbach, connecting link between Hegel and
Marxism, preached a more materialistic and socialistic
version of Hegel. Politically, Wagner sympathized with
the self-styled "Young Germany" group, whose leaders
(Heinrich Heine and Börne) were actually Jewish exiles
in Paris. There they wittily challenged sentimental German patriotism from their more utilitarian and rationalist
criteria. Among his Parisian compatriots, Wagner was in-

---

[8] Wagner: *Mein Leben* (2 vols., Munich, 1911), I, 75. Newman:
Life, I, 89. Wagner: *Prose*, IV, 47.

[9] From Wagner's "German Opera" and "On Meyerbeer's *Huguenots*." Zinnius, op. cit., pp. 14, 15.

fluenced musically by his chief patron, the Jew Meyerbeer; intellectually, by the Jew Heine.[10] An anti-Semite
in theory, Wagner had a reputation for preferring Jews
to other Germans as his intimate friends.

The facts about Wagner's birth, now known at last, must
be frankly uncovered, not as gossip but for the sake of
psychoanalysing the origins of his projection complex
toward Jews and his revolutionary inferiority complex
against the " respectable " aristocratic world. In 1938
Henri Malherbe's authoritative French study[11] proved
beyond reasonable doubt that Richard Wagner's real
father was not his mother's husband, Frederick Wagner,
but the allegedly Jewish actor Ludwig Geyer. Ancient
hotel records, recently uncovered, prove that Wagner's
mother during her husband's lifetime had been living
with Geyer during secret trips out of town.

At almost the same time Herr Frederick Wagner died,
and she married Geyer. In his " respectable " autobiography, full of pious forgeries, Richard Wagner names
Frederick Wagner as his father. But the original unre-
touched draft of Richard's autobiography names Geyer as
his real father, according to Nietzsche (who had seen it),
unpublished letters, and several published sources — an
admission Richard also made to his Isolde, Mathilde
Wesendonk.

Probably no drop of the Wagner family's blood ever
flowed in young Richard's veins. But it is far from proba-
ble that Geyer was of Jewish extraction, despite the fact
that Richard himself was unsure and anguished on that
score. Also despite the following piquant fact: Wagner's

[10] E. Weller: *Richard Wagner und der völkische Gedanke* (Tübingen,
1927), pp. 20–4, 46–8. Zinnius, op. cit., pp. 11–15.

[11] Henri Malherbe: *Richard Wagner, Révolutionnaire* (Paris: Albert
Michel; 1938).

rivals in anti-Semitism in his own day published cartoons
of Wagner with so-called Semitic traits and editorials
damning his operas as "Jewish music," simply because
Wagner, for some curious reason, was the favourite musician of German Jews as he became of Hitler! The question of Wagner's "race" should, of course, in a civilized
or democratic community, be of little importance. Yet
events have lent it vast importance (it decides whether
or not he can be played in Germany today).[12]

Consider also Wagner's emotional inclination for certain
habits of luxury and unmanliness. (Nordau even ludicrously concludes: "Richard Wagner is in himself alone
charged with a greater abundance of degeneracy than all
the degenerates put together.") Consider those mysterious imported perfumes from Paris, those ermine gowns
and brocaded roses, his lace shirts and satin street clothes.

---

[12] The paragraphs on the Geyer question are based on the following
sources, which include important new discoveries on that subject. Richard
Wagner is proved Geyer's illegitimate son by Henri Malherbe, op. cit. For
further important evidence, see the following: Franz Blei: *Erzählung eines
Lebens* (Leipzig: Paul List Verlag), p. 207. Letters in the partly unpublished collection of Mrs. Burrell. Wagner's own admission in Richard
Wagner and Mathilde Wesendonk: *Tagebuchblätter und Briefe, 1853–
1871* (37th ed., Berlin [?], 1910), p. 48. *New York Times*, July 8, 1939,
news section, "Wagner Again Called Jew." Professor A. Lorenz in
Allgemeine Musikzeitung, Nov. 20 (Munich, May 13, 1938), cites Wagner's own private admissions that Geyer was his father and publishes recent research revealing Geyer's family tree, refuting the widespread belief that Geyer was Jewish.

The family tree published by Lorenz is probably authentic; on the
other hand, readers should be made cautious by the fact that the German
press is no longer free and that Hitler would probably not allow publication of any evidence impeaching Wagner's "Aryanism." Valuable evidence on the Wagner-Geyer-Jewish questions is also presented by Walter
Rauchenberger: "Richard Wagners Abstammung und Rassenmerkmale,"
Die Sonne, Vol. XI (1937), and unpublished letters from Rauchenberger
to Dr. Siegfried Placzek, cited to me by the latter; Newman: *Wagner as
Man and Artist*, p. 121; Newman; *Life*, II, 608–13, and III, Appendix;
New York Times, January 23, 1941, "Wagner, Nazi Idol, Held Son of
Jew."

With the projection theory in mind, we are not in the least surprised to find his works consistently exalting nordic Spartanism and damning the luxurious and effeminate decadence of the French. Demanding the annihilation of "luxury-cravers" in life or music, he thunders that "the luxury of the upper classes feeds only on the strangulation of the lower, labouring classes." As usual, he is really condemning and projecting his own self.[13]

By 1842, after three years in Paris, Wagner's inevitable anti-French reaction begins. His *Autobiographical Sketch* of 1843 accuses Frenchmen of "making music only for gold." Note already the Wagnerian leitmotiv of gold, symbol of materialism in his operas, symbol of Judaism and French decadence in his metapolitics. In France he "had not only suffered material miseries; his idealism had been outraged." The 1843 autobiography ends with a sincere explosion: "For the first time I saw the Rhine. With hot tears in my eyes, I, poor artist, swore eternal fidelity to my German fatherland."[14]

What caused the young internationalist of 1839 thus suddenly, in 1843, to recognize his emotional need for a German fatherland? The answer lies in his remark that "what awoke my longing for my German homeland was the feeling of homelessness in Paris."[15] He himself recognized this as a longing to become an organic part of a greater unity that is trusted and beloved. Here is the key to his transition toward metapolitics: rationalistic atomism would not satisfy his emotional needs, his lonely "homelessness."

[13] Nordau: *Degeneration*, p. 171. Mann: *Leiden*, p. 146. Newman: *Wagner as Man, and Artist*, pp. 122–3. Wagner: *Prose*, I, 85, 313.

[14] Wagner: *Prose*, I, "Autobiographical Sketch," pp. 15, 19, etc. Newman: *Life*, I, 324.

[15] Quoted from his 1851 *"Communication to My Friends,"* in Zinnius, op. cit., p. 19.

Ever after, his longing was to fuse organically with his own Volk. "It is the Volk-soul that speaks through Wagner," suggests Thomas Mann (sceptically); "he is only its mouthpiece."[16] To be the mouthpiece of the Volk organism (non-existent, as it happens), that was certainly Wagner's lifelong ambition. As with so many extreme nationalists, Wagner's spirit "found itself" abroad.

Wagner's new mood caused him in 1845 to begin the *Meistersinger,* in contrast with the mood of *Rienzi.* Thereafter, his operas are based on Germanic themes. Identifying himself with the Nuremberg folk-poet Hans Sachs of the *Meistersinger,* Wagner ends this favourite Nazi opera with the famous chorus warning Germans against the "corrupting" influence of the Romanized west (which he calls "*welsch,*" a significant German adjective meaning the Latin and French world). Thereby this opera, which Nietzsche calls "a lance against civilization," has come to symbolize to thousands of Germans that old contrast of Kultur versus civilization.

It is significant not only that the *Meistersinger* is Hitler's favourite opera but that, like Wagner, "Hitler likes to picture himself as Hans Sachs particularly. Hitler knows all [Wagner's] scores and finds emotional relief and inspiration for his actions in their rendition."[17] The influence of the *Meistersinger* is illustrated by Hitler's choice of little old Nuremberg, the town which Wagner personified in Hans Sachs, as the official site of all the annual Nazi party congresses.

By 1843, even before the '48 Revolution, the two chief threads of Wagner's metapolitics are already clear. These

[16] Mann: *Leiden,* p. 140.
[17] Sermon by Dr. W. H. Mellish, *New York Herald Tribune,* September 13, 1940, p. 14.

are his attitudes toward Germany ("Volk") and toward
the French and Jews ("gold"). Where his view of society passes from the atomistic into the organic, that is the
crucial point at which his politics "soars" into metapolitics.

REVOLUTION, 1848–9

In the early nineteenth century a "liberal revolution"
meant a nationalist revolution. It also meant a bourgeois,
anti-aristocratic crusade against class distinctions. But
being bourgeois, its indignation was limited to political,
not economic, class distinctions. What was Wagner's relation to the famous Revolution of 1848–9?

In May 1849 the most revolutionary wing of the Saxon
parliament seized Dresden, the capital of Saxony. Wagner
was an active leader of this Saxon revolution with his
friends Röckel, a journalist, and Bakunin, the melodra-
matic Russian anarchist. These three anti-capitalist leaders were hurrying the bourgeois revolution ahead into a
socialist revolution when the Prussian troops suppressed
it with bloodshed.

To what extent did Wagner participate in this revolution? To no great or active extent, according to historians
Houston Chamberlain, Glasenapp, Ellis, and Wagner's
own later stuffed-shirt memoirs. This school tries to create
a "respectable" Wagner, whose revolutionary activities
were never too radical or illegal. But these historians were
later refuted successfully by historians Newman, Dinger,
Georg Müller, and others. The latter school offers overwhelming evidence for Wagner's full, active, and illegal
participation in the 1849 Revolution. Evidence includes
his secret storage of rebel hand-grenades, his articles and

concealed editorship of Röckel's rebel journal, his distribution of mutinous handbills to the army, his job as tower
watchman over the proletarian barricades.[18]

Wagner nonchalantly took in his stride this abrupt
change from ivory tower to the literal tower of battle.
With deadly bullets hurtling all around him in his watch-
tower over the barricades, he felt, in his own words, a
" spiritual intoxication " of ecstasy: " I experienced a
strange sense of extravagant delight in playing with something so serious." The identical sentiment was then being
experienced in revolutionary Paris by Baudelaire, the poet
and later Wagner-worshipper. This pose of the dandy
æsthete, playfully " living dangerously," remains basic to
Wagner's active metapolitics. For the romantic æsthete,
revolution of any sort whatever is better than boredom.
Baudelaire wrote: " Boredom, this dainty monster, dreams
of scaffolds while smoking his pipe." The revealing psychological affinity between these two great decadent artists, Wagner and Baudelaire, is stressed by both Nietzsche
and Thomas Mann.[19]

Wagner's two strongest motives for seeking to overthrow the whole order of centuries were, as usual, subjective. One was " the disdain with which I found my earnest

[18] Carl Glasenapp: *Das Leben Richard Wagners* (6 vols., Leipzig,
1894–1911); for the Wagnerian legend's official soft-pedalling of his
revolutionary activity, see II, sec. 1, 278–338. Ed. notes of Ellis to Wagner: *Prose;* and Ellis: " *1849: A Vindication* " (London, 1892). Wagner:
Mein Leben, I. Hugo Dinger: *Richard Wagners Geistige Entwicklung*
(Danzig, 1892), pp. 183–6. Newman: *Life,* II, 3–103, especially pp.
62–4, 72–4, 78–86. Georg Müller: *Das Recht bei Richard Wagner* (Berlin, 1914), pp. 3–6. Paul Wiegler: *Geschichte der Deutschen Literatur*
(2 vols., Berlin, 1930), II, 504–6. Wagner: *Richard Wagner's Letters to
August Roeckel,* ed. H. S. Chamberlain (Bristol, London, n.d.).

[19] Wagner: *Prose,* IV, 8. Newman: *Life,* II, 69. Baudelaire: *Fleurs
du mal:* " *C'est l'Ennui! . . . ce monstre délicat . . . il rêve d'échafauds
en fumant son houka.*" Nietzsche: *The Case against Wagner* (2nd ed.,
Edinburgh, 1911), pp. 22, 28, 69. Mann: *Freud, Goethe, Wagner* (New
York, 1937), pp. 205–7.

art-ideal regarded " by the more classical taste of aristocratic societies.[20] As the other motive, an economic interpretation would stress his unpayable debts. These were
twenty times his annual income! The debts were caused
to a large extent by the strange fact that he could not
create his music without his imported Parisian perfumes
and unless attired in his luxurious womanly robes of expensive lace and ermine. A fine proletarian rebel!

What exactly did Wagner want done in the '48 Revolution? He wanted to unify all lands of German blood into
a super-state, bringing about an artistic and economic
utopia and abolishing class distinctions and property.
What were his specific practical measures to achieve this?
A typical measure, whose self-styled practicality speaks
for itself, appears in his dramatic oration of June 14, 1848.
To " emancipate humanity " at one stroke, he demands the
abolition of money, that " demoniac idea." How and with
what results? Don't worry; just " abolish " it, orates Wagner, and " God will give us light." Note the Rousseauist
implication about the natural goodness of things primitive.[21]

As the revolution progressed, Wagner big-heartedly decided also to " abolish " poverty and work. This was just
as easy: by abolishing the leisure class and equalizing work
for all, no man need work more than a few hours daily.
The freed masses would thereupon, according to Wagner's Rousseauist optimism, devote themselves to great
art — meaning his own operas, of course. As usual, he
offers no more specific measures than vague rhetoric:

> The legions from the factories are naked, frozen, hungry;
> for not to them belongs the fruit of all their labour but to
> the rich. . . . Their daughters walk the city streets with

[20] Wagner: *Prose*, IV, 5.
[21] Wagner: *Prose*, IV, 139, speech at Vaterland Verein.

the burden of their shame, an offering to the baser lusts of the rich and the mighty. They all are waiting for the Revolution, creator of a new world blessing all.[22]

During the revolution Wagner was still in the throes of his own internal revolution (against " French ideas " and against Feuerbach). Begun in 1843, his inner revolution was not wholly victorious till 1854. Meanwhile Wagner joined his rationalist revolutionary colleagues in demanding from the German National Assembly the usual planks of contemporary liberalism. The following are Wagner's more specific demands at divers times during 1848–9:

An offensive and defensive alliance between revolutionary Germany and revolutionary France — this demand is the swan-song of his early French phase. For both men and women he demanded " the unconditional right to vote " in national plebiscites. He demanded a German unity based on equal-sized states. Big states like Prussia must be split up to prevent Prussian dominance over his native Saxony. He wrote a letter to Frankfurt urging the National Assembly to seize sole power and then name a new ruler for united Germany. Arguing that children born in the free Germany will be " like unto gods," Wagner proclaimed their mission to " civilize " the rest of the world by settling " little Germanys " all over the globe. From the aristocracy he demanded voluntary surrender, or else " the contest will be a bloody one." [23]

To " abolish " each class distinction, he continued, an amateur political army of the masses must be founded. This must absorb and replace the regular army (Reichswehr), in a dream akin to what Röhm in 1934 envisaged for his Storm Troopers. As a further death-blow to class

---

[22] Ibid., VIII, 234–5, " The Revolution."
[23] Ibid., IV, 138. Newman: *Life*, II, 7–10.

distinction: " The Volk is but one, and there should be but one sole house of the people's deputies." [24]

TRANSITION, 1847–51

Wagner's political program of this period has been treated first in order to get rid of it before coming to his more important metapolitics. He himself got rid of it shortly. In 1849 the conservative, anti-nationalist governments regained power in Germany. Wagner barely escaped to Switzerland as a political refugee. His unhappy exile lasted eleven years, under an imminent death sentence. Such conditions made him receptive to the mystic pessimism of Schopenhauer, whose complete convert he now became for a while.

As *Rienzi* and *Die Meistersinger* had expressed æsthetically his previous two intellectual changes, so *Tristan* did his newest creed. As Wagner typifies for us the new German nationalism of the 1840's, so in the 1850's he typifies Germany's sudden Schopenhauer cult. Published in 1819, not until a generation later was the philosopher's work read by the public. His sudden popularity was a social symptom of the wave of despair following the lost revolution's high hopes.

The impact of the new philosophy had a marked effect upon Wagner's opinions and behaviour.[25] He repudiated what he now contemptuously called his former " optimistic faith in reason and progress." He repudiated Feuer-

---

[24] Wagner: *Prose*, IV, 137–9.
[25] Müller: *Recht*, p. 13. Wiegler: *Geschichte*, II, 506. Weller: *Wagner*, pp. 21–2. Mann: *Leiden*, pp. 127 ff. Wagner: *Prose*, IV, 8, etc. H. S. Chamberlain: *Richard Wagner* (London, 1900), pp. 151–61. Dinger: *Entwicklung*, is the most thorough book on Wagner's transition from Feuerbach to Schopenhauer.

bach's Young Hegelians and their doctrines of materialism, progress, universal happiness. He lost his French remnant of rationalism and of atomistic liberalism. Most important, he became fanatically convinced that no individuals can plot their own destiny, nor can reason and consciousness serve. Events are shaped solely by Schopenhauer's pantheistic Will, which is unconscious, supernatural, eternal. "Nothing really happens but what has issued from this Will," Wagner now wrote, "a headlong blind impulse." [26]

Consequently, not only were all individual politics futile, but also any *conscious* politics of the Volk, such as parliaments and voting. Futile were all the conscious reforms he had been urging as a revolutionary leader. From that time Wagner consistently abstained from urging any narrowly political measures. It was not long before he even repudiated the political side of his 1848 Revolution as "entirely un-German," imported from France by Jews: "Democracy in Germany is a purely translated thing. This translated Franco-Judaico-German democracy exists merely in the press." [27]

Even before he read Schopenhauer, in the 1840's Wagner's future metapolitics had already been germinal in him. Fighting bravely together on the same side of the barricades, he and his liberal colleagues never realized that the gap between him and them was greater than between them and the conservative enemy. While acting liberal politics with them, Wagner was writing metapolitics.

Some time in the 1840's Wagner acquired his apparently original "discovery" that music divides into German and Jewish. The former is a Good Thing, the latter a Bad Thing. This is the tenor of his *Judaism in Music,* published in 1850. This influential anti-Semitic tract is an ungrate-

[26] Zinnius: *Wagner,* p. 36. Wagner: *Prose,* IV, 10.
[27] Wagner: *Prose,* IV, 166.

ful tirade against his friend and former patron, the Jewish musician Meyerbeer.[28]

The following separate aphorisms, selected from Wagner's various works during 1847–51, are the quintessence of metapolitics. He wrote them privately while publicly risking his life for a supposedly liberal and rationalist political revolution! If we be so picayune as to find them sheer dangerous nonsense, Wagner refutes us in advance by explaining we must " be brave enough to deny our intellect."

> Ye err when ye seek the revolutionary force in consciousness and would fain operate through the intellect. Not ye will bring the new to pass but the Volk which deals unconsciously and, for that very reason, from a Nature-instinct. . . . The Volk has ever been the only true inventor; the unit cannot invent. . . . The artisthood of the future [must rest] on the principle of *communism*. . . . The Volk must burst the chain of hindering consciousness.[29]

Crucial are Wagner's definitions of Volk, revolution, freedom: " The Volk are those who deal instinctively. . . . Revolution is the movement of the *mass* toward acquisition and employment of the force hitherto in the hands of the *unit*. The mass attains to the same force as the individual, and only on this standpoint is freedom possible." [30]

By these definitions Wagner remained a revolutionist to the end. Their hidden dynamite is the concept that only collective, never individual, freedom exists. The mass must be made collectively free from, say, Versailles or capitalism, at the cost, if necessary, of enslaving each of its individuals. As a Nazi Storm Troop song puts it, " We spit on

28 Reprinted in ibid., III.
29 Ibid., VIII, 345–7, in 1847–51; I, 80, in 1849.
30 Ibid., VIII, 348, 370–1.

freedom, the Volk must be free." [31] In the midst of the so-called " liberal revolution," Wagner is exactly reversing the attitude of nineteenth-century liberalism toward the state and individual freedom. That is why the ablest Nazi pane-gyric of him is entitled: *Richard Wagner, the Revolutionist against the Nineteenth Century*.[32]

By one of his brilliant false analogies, Wagner transfers bodily the qualities of Schopenhauer's world-Will to Ger-many's Volk-Will; that is, to the supernatural organic unity behind the mortal individual atoms. Granted the existence of this, then no more politics of consciousness, of intellect, or of individuals can save the national organism. But then how can metapolitics save it? Through three supernatural concepts: the mystic life-force of dynamism; the Führer concept; the purification of the race-soul.

The importance of these three concepts for Nazi Ger-many is too obvious to require explicit emphasis. They were demonstrably present in Wagner during his transi-tion period of 1847–51. How were they systematized dur-ing the rest of his long life? This is better answered topi-cally than chronologically.

THE LIFE-FORCE OF DYNAMISM

What Wagner arbitrarily labels " Life " has both the blind and the pantheistic attributes of Schopenhauer's Will. Schopenhauer hated this dark brooding force, wanted it resisted and destroyed by human spirit. So, too, the pessi-mistic Wagner of the temporary *Tristan* phase sought only " the Will's dignified self-annulment." [33] But in his treat-

---

[31] Stephen Roberts: *The House that Hitler Built* (New York, 1938), p. 57.

[32] K. R. Ganzer: *Richard Wagner, der Revolutionär gegen das neun-zehnte Jahrhundert* (Munich, 1934).

[33] Wagner: *Prose*, IV, 8.

ment of legality and of national politics he always retained the romantic school's cult of Life-worship.

Wagner incarnates perfectly the three assumptions defined in the chapter on "Romanticism." On all possible planes Wagner and his many disciples exalt Life (*élan vital*) against law, content against form, instinct against reason, synthesis against analysis, the organic against the atomistic, Volk legend against scientific truth; above all, the dynamic against the static.

By the 1870's this spirit had an incredible and exotic culmination, which is apparently — but only apparently — unpolitical: frogs! Vivisection of frogs Wagner calls "the *curse* of our civilization." Demagogically Wagner urges the Volk, in true lynch-mob fashion, to smash the laboratories, boot out the scientists, rescue the little martyrs. A sort of moral Armageddon must decide between those "who free trussed animals" and those "who truss them to torture them." Because Bismarck's empire fails to untruss these, the suppressed socialists are right in being the "enemies of the state." The fiendish scientist's torture of quadrupeds, says Wagner, is all of one piece with the fiendish capitalist's living torture of the proletariat. In addition, it is "already too late to avert the curse brought down on us by animal food." [34]

In Wagnerian metapolitics such supernatural curses, not mere politics, are what destroy a great nation. Why supernatural? Because animals are dynamic with sacred capitalized Life. But Wagner's vegetarianism? — don't vegetables also possess Life? No, he had no intention of starving to death. After all, vegetables, though technically

---

[34] Ibid., VI, 197, 208, 241–3, and "Against Vivisection, A Letter to E. von Weber," VIII, 391–4. Wagner: *Bayreuther Blätter*, editorials of October–December 1880 and February–March 1881. Nordau: *Degeneration*, pp. 209–10.

" alive," must have seemed tiresomely static to Wagner's unscientific eye. In contrast with the dynamic animal kingdom, vegetables may have the *vital* but lacked that sacred *élan*!

It will not do to dismiss patronizingly Wagner's anti-vivisectionism and vegetarianism as the mere crank failings of a great man. That would be to miss their whole significance. By no means crackpot or arbitrary, they form the logical culmination of his metapolitics. Life's organic unity must not be destroyed politically by the atomistic state, mentally by analysis, physically by vivisection. Behind the second of these sacrileges, that of destructive intellectualism, lurk the Jews. In his little Bayreuth magazine Wagner " exposes " their plot to destroy Germany " by might of pen." [35]

Wagner's aim in life is " artistically conveying my purpose to the true emotional, *not* critical, understanding of spectators." [36] The same Wagnerian outlook is applied to the most diverse fields, weaving them into a single philosophy. The same Wagnerian spirit favouring in music the revolt of emotional inspiration against classical rules favours in politics the revolt of instinctive Volk against law. This spirit can only be labelled romantic.

Wagner's article on *Revolution* best shows this spirit in politics. [37] It also shows that in his younger days he was capable of beautiful prose, although his later writings, with their bombast and endless sentences, are undoubtedly the stylistic model for *Mein Kampf*. *Revolution* was published just before the Dresden revolution of May 1849. Already then Wagner's revolutionary motives were both more æsthetic and more mystic than political. All existing so-

---

[35] Wagner: " Modern," *Bayreuther Blätter*, Jg. I, n. 3 (March 1879), pp. 59–63.

[36] Wagner: *Prose*, I, 391.

[37] Ibid., VIII " The Revolution," pp. 232–8.

ciety and its governments must fall. As reasons he cites his personal hate of their bureaucracy's uninspired "dusty office-desks." In "these modern torture-rooms" — note the significant anti-vivisection phraseology — "between files of documents and contracts, the hearts of live humanity are pressed like gathered leaves."

The "lofty goddess REVOLUTION" (capitals his) Wagner defines as a "supernatural force." And he means it, for is she not dynamic Life? "I am the ever rejuvenating, ever fashioning Life. I pour young life through all your veins." Whatever is a state of being instead of becoming "must fall." "I will break the power of the mighty, of law, of property. *Life is law unto itself.*"

In other words, down with law! But Wagner's liberal colleagues in this same revolution were shedding their blood for ideals of legalism: social contract and written constitution.

In 1865 Wagner at last openly repudiated Germany's '48 Revolution as a Jewish importation of French rationalism.[38] He has been accused of thereby selling out his ideals in order to please his patron, the mad King Ludwig of Bavaria. His writings during the '48 Revolution refute this accusation. They reveal already the unbridgeable gulf separating him from rationalist liberals. Once he and they were no longer fighting the common enemy of the Metternich system, his eventual realization of the gulf was inevitable. This does not exclude the additional phenomenon of sudden success reconciling the starving bohemian with bourgeois respectability. But as his disciple Houston Chamberlain said,

> You cannot sever his artistic from his social convictions.
> . . . To revolt against corrupt art is to revolt against the

[38] Ibid., IV, 166.

corrupt society from which this art springs. In this sense
Wagner was a revolutionist since 1840 down to the day of
his death.[39]

During 1848 Wagner also wrote two plays, on Siegfried
and Jesus.[40] Both heroes are made to incarnate the very
same dynamism as his " sublime goddess REVOLUTION, destroying and blessing." Siegfried and Jesus are revolutionists for subconscious, supernatural inspiration against
the static legalism and conscious reason of the gods and
the Pharisees respectively.

Wagner's sweeping anti-legalism does not mean he
wanted chaos or anarchism, despite Bakunin's "uncanny
fascination" over him.[41] The invisible supernatural unity
of Life and the living Volk would keep better order than
the visible, material unity of law or parliaments. But since
all political and conscious measures are futile, how is this
unifying Will to manifest itself to Germany? Here we
come to Wagner's Führer concept. Being more than mortal, the inspired Führer of the future, like the Siegfried
of the past, is to practise the metapolitics which Wagner
himself can only preach.

FÜHRER CONCEPT

Wagner treats the great leader as neither man nor god but
as demigod. As an individual, the leader is a mere atomistic mortal; as personification of the German Volk, he shares
its divinity. Wagner must be conceded amazing powers of
prophecy for his part in contributing the Führer concept
to modern German history. Later, Houston Chamberlain
and that weird drunken poet Dietrich Eckart, to whom the

---

[39] Chamberlain: *Wagner,* pp. 15, 33–4.
[40] Reprinted in Wagner: *Prose,* VIII.
[41] Newman: *Life,* II, 49–51.

close of *Mein Kampf* is dedicated, instilled this Wagnerian concept into their young disciple Hitler.[42]

Instead of the word " Führer," Wagner often expresses this concept by a number of other terms, especially " hero," " folk-king," and " Barbarossa." Wagner calls the mediæval Kaiser Frederick Barbarossa a mystic spiritual reincarnation of Siegfried, the legendary Nibelung warrior and first nordic superman. Barbarossa-Siegfried will some day return to save his German people in time of deepest need.[43] This prophecy of a third incarnation of Barbarossa and Siegfried, became the hope of patriotic Wagnerians. Incidentally, according to the old legend, the site where the sleeping Barbarossa is to reawaken and resume his rule over Germany is — Berchtesgaden.[44]

Wagner's Führer concept went through three distinct stages. The first stage is on the surface still moderate and reasonable. An example is Wagner's public speech of June 1848.[45] This distinguishes sharply between king and monarch and between republicanism and democracy. Monarchy and democracy Wagner flays; kinghood and republicanism he wishes combined. Abolish monarchy, he urges his hearers, but " emancipate the kinghood."

By the existing system, he complains, a German ruler is a monarch, defined as merely first of the aristocracy. The revolution must transform him into a king, defined as " the first of the Volk." The king is the " man of Providence."

---

42 See Eckart in index of Roberts: *Hitler*, and of Heiden: *Hitler*.

43 Wagner: *Prose*, VII, " The Wibelungen," pp. 257–99; VIII, the Barbarossa fragment; etc.

44 James Bryce: *The Holy Roman Empire* (8th ed., New York, 1887), pp. 180–1: " [In] Berchtesgaden . . . among its limestone crags, in a spot scarcely accessible to human foot, the peasants of the valley point out to the traveller the black mouth of a cavern and tell him that, within, Barbarossa lies in an enchanted sleep . . . waiting to descend with his crusaders and bring back to Germany the golden age."

45 Wagner: *Prose*, IV, 141, 144, for speech that follows.

As such, he must no longer " cast in his lot with one exclusive, smaller section of his Volk " but with all. To become the Volk's mouthpiece, he must abolish Wagner's pet hate of " class distinction." Wagner appeals sentimentally to his King of Saxony " to be the first and most sterling republican of us all."

By " republican," Wagner does not mean democrat nor the constitutional parliamentary monarch of Louis Philippe or England. These rest on the system Wagner so detests, a system of several parties and of warfare of separate interests. Wagner uses " republican " in the sense of *res publica,* the interest of the public as a unit. None of us can be " so pure a republican as the prince," because his " eye is single to the whole." In contrast, we ordinary individuals, not being " men of Providence," are blind to the whole. We can only follow selfish personal or class interests. Similarly parliamentary constitutional states, whether monarchies or democracies, can only follow party interests.

That — by the analogy suggested earlier — means vivisecting the living national organism into parts, as if it were one of Wagner's hapless " trussed " frogs. It is also vivisection to split the Volk from its mouthpiece by a lifeless, legalistic constitution. " Each advance of constitutionalism is a humiliation to the ruler " because tantamount to " a vote of want of confidence."

Constitutions, want of confidence, opposition parties are needed for governments representing the Volk indirectly. Such are parliaments, which merely stand for a majority of interests, and monarchy, which merely stands for aristocratic class interests. But the king does not represent the Volk; he *is* the Volk, its direct and collective mouthpiece. So why should the Volk restrict or divide the power of its own self, its personification?

These monstrous sophistries are the philosophic basis

of the Hitler dictatorship. It, too, claims to be based on the whole Volk instead of on separate classes. Hence its logical suppression of rival parties, parliament, constitution, and all atomistic individualism. Through Wagnerian disciples like Chamberlain, Nazis are steeped in Wagner's pet paradox that democracy is not the rule of the people. Democracy Wagner calls a foreign dictatorship over Germany by Jewish finance and un-folkic " French ideas." Only through the dictatorship of a demigod Führer comes " true " rule by the people — not as individuals, to be sure, but as an (unfortunately non-existent) collective will. Again we are reminded of Wagner's replacing individual by collective freedom and of the Storm Troop song: " We spit on freedom, the Volk must be free! "

Why can't a democratic system simply add up and satisfy its component individual interests till it achieves this vaunted collective interest? Because the whole of the Volk is infinitely greater than the sum of its parts. The sum of the democratic atom-interests produces a collectivity, but an inorganic one, a corpse. The invisible supernatural element that makes a nation, its dynamism, is lacking. This vanishes when the sacred synthesis is analysed (vivisected) into its components.

Wagner bolsters these concepts by reading them into ancient Germanic history. " Monarchy " he calls a " foreign and un-German notion " imported from the aristocratic French. In contrast, we must " search back among Germanic nations for the kinghood's meaning." [46] Wagner does not explain this Delphic utterance, but probably he is harking back to the custom of " raising on shields." Instead of accepting hereditary dynastic monarchs, many primeval Saxon tribes elected one of their number popu-

---

[46] Ibid., IV, 144.

larly by raising him on their shields and endowing him with dictatorial power. The analogy speaks for itself.

The second stage of Wagner's Führer concept comes in an essay of 1864. This time Wagner is addressing not the unimaginative Saxon King but Wagner's intimate friend King Ludwig of Bavaria. Wagner urges Ludwig to head a united German republic. The king is now explicitly, instead of implicitly as in the first stage, called the "live embodiment" of the "patriotic Wahn." By *Wahn*, a key-word of Wagner, too ambiguous for safe translation, he means something between pragmatic myth and glorious madness. This *Wahn* is produced by the supernatural "spirit of the race." The king's function is now more frankly defined as overriding "the interests of the parties" for "the safety of the whole." Thereby the king "occupies a position wellnigh *superhuman*." [47]

The third stage of his Führer concept Wagner evolves only in his unripe old age. It is illustrated by his essay "Herodom" (1881). [48] Conveniently for Hitler, the "man of Providence" is now no longer called a king, nor is he contemporary, like Ludwig, nor of the past, like Barbarossa. He is the divine hero of the future. As important as these changes is the change in the Führer's mission. To the functions urged upon the Saxon and Bavarian kings Wagner adds redemption of Germany's lost Aryan purity. At this point Wagner's second metapolitical concept fuses with his third, that of purification.

PURIFICATION OF THE RACE SOUL

The two founders of Nazi Germany's doctrines of nordic superiority were a Frenchman and an Englishman. Count

[47] Ibid., IV, 12, 16.
[48] In *Bayreuther Blätter,* September 1881.

Gobineau was Wagner's friend; Houston Stewart Chamberlain was Wagner's disciple and son-in-law. The Wagner circle introduced Gobineau's ideas from France into Germany and popularized Chamberlain's. In vulgarized form the ideas of these two men were drilled into the German masses from ever more lowbrow concentric circles, but the centre of emanation was the highbrow Wagner cult in the opera town of Bayreuth.

According to Thomas Mann and others, Wagner's aim in Bayreuth was to found there a classless society upon his metapolitical ideas and from this pure nucleus to convert all Germany. In Chamberlain's prophetic words of 1900, " The festival house at Bayreuth is an emblem of battle " — (against " corrupt society," democracy, and the Jews) — " a standard for armed warriors to rally around. . . . For only in battle do forces nerve themselves for action." A generation later Hitler did indeed bring, as his Storm Troops, these " armed warriors to rally around " the battle emblem of Bayreuth.[49]

In the works of Chamberlain, " the *Meister* [Wagner] lives on." [50] Chamberlain, in turn, lives on in Eckart, Rosenberg, Hitler. In 1923 Chamberlain declared himself " enraptured with Hitler " after their meeting in Bayreuth. " Through Chamberlain Hitler learnt to expound Wagner." Thus the concentric circles ever widen in Germany until few people realize that in their centre stands the musician Richard Wagner.[51]

" Is Wagner a man at all? " asked his former best friend,

---

[49] Mann: *Leiden,* 161. Erich Valentin: " Wagners politischer Glaube," *Bayreuther Blätter,* Jg. 60, winter issue (1937), pp. 8–16. Chamberlain: *Wagner,* 379.

[50] Weller: *Wagner,* p. 60. Note especially Chamberlain's *Foundations of the 19th Century* (New York, 1914) and *Arische Weltanschauung* (Munich, 1916).

[51] Heiden: *Hitler,* p. 95. *Mein Kampf,* ed. cit., p. 359, note.

Nietzsche. " Is he not rather a disease? " [52] Wagner's
youthful Nazi-worshippers make Wagner posthumously
into a tiresomely undiseased and heroic figure, a thorough
philistine. Imagine their shudders could they guess his ab-
normalities or glimpse the psychological subtleties behind
his effusions for his square-shouldered, clean-shaven German Spartanism. At heart, after all, he remained Baudelaire's *alter ego*. Wagner's nordic effusions were as much
the æsthetic pose of a bored Parisian café decadent as the
naïve seriousness of a German chauvinist. Wagner's life
proves there is such a thing as becoming too blasé even for
vice. At that point, health and simplicity (and solid old-
fashioned patriotism) are the last, recherché stimulus for
the jaded.

Before 1881 Wagner's anti-Semitism was more cultural
than racial. In 1881 he steeped himself in Gobineau's *Essay on the Inequality of the Human Races*. The results
show in Wagner's two articles from which the following
aphorisms are gleaned.[53]

Not politics, not concrete laws and conscious reforms,
but the unconscious race-force will end Germany's woes
— provided the race-force is purified again. " These
[Aryan] stocks are distinguished from the others throughout our whole world-history " because " like Siegfried and
Hercules they are conscious of divine descent." In contrast
with others, who spring in prosaic Darwinian fashion
" from monkeys," they " trace back their origin to gods."
No wonder that they are " marked out for rulership."

Among Aryans, in turn, the " pure-bred Germanic
branches " form a sort of cream of the cream because

---

[52] Nietzsche: *The Case against Wagner*, p. 11.
[53] Arthur Gobineau: *Essai sur l'inégalité des races humaines* (2 vols.,
2nd ed., Paris, 1884). Wagner: *Prose*, VI, 269–9, 276–9, for quotations
that follow.

theirs are the "root qualities." The qualities Wagner cites as particularly Germanic are fearlessness, pride, honour, and — hate of luxury. Moreover, "a lie to them was inconceivable." But Wagner dangles this golden picture before his flattered readers only to snatch it away by thundering that today a "depravity of the blood" has robbed Germany of these virtues. "The accident of the Germans becoming masters of the great Latino-Semitic realm was fatal to them," because "great characters come almost solely from pure-bred races." Wagner opposes mixed marriages as uncompromisingly as does the Old Testament's Book of Ezra, whose patriotic phraseology so resembles that of the German chosen people.

But suddenly Wagner turns to his Jewish readers with a generous offer: they too, even they, can contribute their humble widow's mite to the world's redemption. As follows: "Bear your share in this work of redemption by self-immolation. There can be only one release from the curse which rests on you: . . . destruction! " The reason is that they are "the dæmon of man's downfall." For innate in their blood is "an instinct shut against all idealism." In contrast, the soaring German soul is simply chock-full of it.[54]

This idea of innate racial philosophy was in Wagner long before Gobineau. Already in the 1840's, as we have seen, he accused the French and Jews of following the profit motive ("gold"). Like the later Hitler in *Mein Kampf*, Wagner solemnly shakes his head over the "total Semitizing" of the "so-called Latin world."[55]

In 1867 Wagner more dogmatically defines "the unbridgeable gulf which separates the German spirit from

[54] Chamberlain: *Wagner*, p. 176. Wagner: *Prose*, VI, 277.

[55] Wagner: "Know Thyself," *Bayreuther Blätter*, February–March 1881.

the French." He defines " what is German " as " that which one does for its own sake." He defines what is French or Jewish as what one does solely for " utilitarian " profit. The greatest disaster in German history is that its luxurious aristocracy, whom he threatens with revolution, were insidiously corrupted by French fashions and thoughts.[56]

Freedom of the press is another Wagnerian phobia. "French materialism," he charges, is "instilled into the German Volk by journalistic propaganda." So long as Germany allows freedom to the Jews, the free press is not really free: "There is scarcely a newspaper or magazine that is not directly or indirectly conducted by Jews." Hence his persecution complex about journalists: " I was my whole life long the victim of unheard-of persecutions from the press." Behind the scenes (whether through Marxist or capitalist materialism) international Jewry is the secret "administrator of European civilization." [57]

The Volk organism will be healthy again, with all its infallible subconscious "instincts," once it is purged of things alien. Though the Jews and French are the main alien influence, Wagner occasionally points to a third: Christianity. Punning on two common German names, in 1850 he accuses it of turning the "Siegfrieds" into "Gottliebs," healthy instinct into sissy decadence.[58]

Like Hitler, with his "positive Christianity," Wagner claims that he is a " true " Christian, and that all the other Christians are out of step. When he was not too busy being a true Buddhist, true Hellene, or true nordic, he doubtless sincerely deemed himself a true Christian. There are others besides himself who deem him one, on the basis of the hocus-pocus religiosity of his *Parsifal*. But Wagner re-

---

[56] Wagner: *Prose,* IV, 100, 107.
[57] Wagner: *Prose,* IV, 54, 60; VI, 43. Wagner: *Mein Leben,* I, 282.
[58] Weller: *Wagner,* p. 45. Wagner: *Prose,* I, 249–66.

veals frankly his other role as fountainhead of Nazi paganism when he wails: "Our clergy-ridden, *pandect* [legalistic] civilization had reduced the health-exuding warriors of the north to weak-nerved cripples [by] its entire variance with our nature." [59] Wagner's Nibelungen operas have made him the most influential modern popularizer of nordic paganism.

In his old age Wagner made one great pot-pourri of all his purification crotchets. The result is a truly original program for the "regeneration of the human race." "Present-day socialism," he urges in his monthly magazine, "must combine in true and hearty fellowship with the vegetarians, the protectors of animals, and the friends of temperance." Only such a united front of purifiers, such a Wagnerian collective security, he urges, can save mankind from Jewish aggression. For let no one think Wagner, old codger though he be, is caught napping by the latest of world-Jewry's sinister plots: against vegetarianism! The proof? Wagner tears the veil from "the striking fact that the Jewish God found Abel's fatted lamb more savoury than Cain's offer" of a vegetable.

But how can even the truest and heartiest fellowship escape this "curse of animal food"? Well, if "animal food is indispensable in northern climates, what prevents a sensibly conducted migration to South America?" Wagner's metapolitics is nothing if not "sensibly conducted," and he conjures up a charming vista in which "our unions" would "devote their greatest energy to emigration . . . and these northern lands [all Europe!] would soon be abandoned again" to their pristine jungles and wild beasts. [60]

The great man was getting along in years. . . .

[59] Wagner: *Prose*, I, 259.
[60] Ibid., VI, 241-3.

COMMUNISM

Wagner always clung to one important remnant of his former materialism. This was his communism. He proudly called himself a " communist " in the sense of Bakunin and Proudhon, who both influenced him in the 1840's, but not in the sense of Karl Marx, a Jew. Wagner's communism in economics seems inconsistent with his metapolitics, which spurns mere political reform and all such materialistic fields as economics.

In both Wagnerian and Nazi economics, the labourer is the source of all material wealth, just as the Volk is the source of all spiritual wealth. A little-known fact is that Hitler originally wanted to name the Nazi party the " Social Revolutionary party," in honour of the Russian anticzarist *but* anti-bolshevik party of that name, in order to indicate that he stood for socialism but not for the rival brand of Marx and Lenin.[61]

Wagner's three pet hates are money, property, and the capitalist class; they should be " abolished." In an essay of 1849 Wagner attacks artists who stay aloof in the ivory tower and justifies his own leading role in the national and socialist Saxon revolution of that year. The artist and the proletariat are really in the same boat; they must stick together because both are exploited. The capitalist theatre-owner does not produce " art for its own pure sake " (Germanism), but for profit (Judaism). Similarly, the " slave of industry " in " our modern factories " undergoes " the deepest degradation of man." [62]

However hard-boiled it may sound, Wagner's communism is essentially an æsthetic reaction: a tormented soul's flight from the reality of industrialism. This is shown by

---

[61] Heiden: *Hitler*, p. 105.
[62] Wagner: *Prose*, I, " Art and Revolution," pp. 27, 31–2, 48–9.

another essay of 1849, where he speaks with terror of " the cold and heartless machine" and "seeks the opposite path" of "absorption into nature." With the prophetic sensitivity of the artist, Wagner foresees and suffers the industrial mechanization of life more than twenty years before the real beginning of the German industrial revolution! As the grand egotist and genius, he cannot bear the thought of mass production crushing his personality and standardizing his art into the "busy strokes of a machine." [63]

In conveying this feeling, Wagner is at his best, his most honest and moving. For once he is human and unaffected, in welcome contrast to his poses of mystical Germanism. Many years before, he anticipates the latent menace, then unguessed, in industrial " efficiency" and expresses the simple human reaction to it. This is a feat of amazing psychological insight.

On behalf of his communism, a vague and utopian brand, Wagner sincerely propagandized throughout his long life. In 1851 he wrote that from property, "which wondrously enough is looked on as the foundation of good order, originate all the crimes in history." [64] The accursed gold of the *Ring of the Nibelung*, according to Bernard Shaw and others, represents the curse of capitalism. [65] After the Empire of 1871 Wagner attacked its parliament as a tool of the rich. Just before his death he wrote: " The state's adoption of the concept of property has driven a stake through humanity's body." [66]

---

[63] Ibid., I, 85, 48–9. Discussion in K. A. von Müller: "Wagner und das 19. Jahrhundert," *Corona*, Munich, April 1933, p. 420.

[64] Wagner: *Prose*, II, 192.

[65] Bernard Shaw: *The Perfect Wagnerite* (Chicago and New York, 1899), chapter on " Wagner as a Revolutionist," pp. 32–41. Wiegler: *Geschichte*, II, 506.

[66] Wagner: *Prose*, VI, " Know Thyself."

FINAL SYNTHESIS

In 1879 Wagner calls the legally elected Reichstag "un-German barbarians" who "know everything except the seat of German power" — namely, "German labour." This passage begins like Karl Marx, but it soon continues like Adolf Hitler. The anti-Semitic attack on parliament which follows it resembles word for word the typical Nazi attack on the German Republic, but it was written by Wagner in 1879:

> What is our "universal-suffrage" parliament doing with these German workmen? It compels the ablest hands to emigrate and leaves the rest to rot in squalor. . . . But what care they [the Jews] for the deluge coming after? . . . Those [Jews] mock our want, since [it is] alien to them. . . . With the aid of all related branches of the German stock, we might steep the whole world in art creations peculiar to ourselves. Holland, Denmark, Sweden, Switzerland — not one of them shows dread of our predominance.[67]

In its morbid sort of way, this synthesis of communism and racial chauvinism is a stroke of genius. Like Wagner's Führer concept, it springs from a great and all too prophetic mind. Its greatness is the simple fact that it hit upon the *one way to sell nationalism* to the proletariat of an industrial age. And the one way to sell state communism to the middle classes! When Wagner was writing, nationalism seemed doomed among the German urban masses. This was partly because of Marxist teachings by labour unions, partly because most German nationalists stood too obviously for the upper-class interests of either the Junkers or the capitalists.

---

[67] Ibid., VI, 124–6.

The nationalism of the romantic movement had till now appealed chiefly to middle-class youths, who imbibed it in their universities or in Father Jahn's gymnast societies. Such appeals worked brilliantly back in the days of Germany's War of Liberation, half a century before her industrial revolution. Whether consciously or intuitively, Wagner sensed that such appeals were now outdated as propaganda. They could no longer rouse sufficient mass movement, just as Hitler's rivals of the conservative Nationalist party could score few votes. Numerically, in an age of quantitative mass politics, aristocratic and educated voters are, as Wagner sensed, futile against the irresistible mob force of the Volk.

Wagnerian metapolitics is Janus-faced. Simultaneously it looks back to romanticism and ahead to a machine age of wage slaves and unemployed. The result is a streamlined romanticism. As such, it is marvellously suited, economically and psychologically, for the prosaic monotony of industrialism and for bored shopkeepers with too many usurious debts and too little excitement.

Wagner's non-political, purely musical appeal has similar roots. His are the only operas in America today drawing vast popular audiences. In so far as their popularity is emotional as well as musical, they are the sociological index of a nation's *Bovarisme*. One of their most poignant appeals is to starved individual emotion (the love-duets of *Tristan*) and, in Germany's case, to frustrated national egotism (the Siegfried cycle).

As Wagner himself explained, his art and weird genius aim " not at the critical understanding " but at the pent-up emotions of the subconscious. These he wants to arouse against law, static morality, and intellect, as if reviving a dying nation by a sudden burst of Wagnerian frenzy. " I pour young Life through all your veins; Life is law unto itself." "We must be brave enough to deny our intellect." "The Volk must burst the chain of hindering consciousness."

Those are his words, the words of the politically most influential artist of modern times. Similarly, to quote the words of his disciple, Propaganda Minister Goebbels, the Nazi mission is "to cause outbreaks of fury, to set masses of men on the march, to organize hate and suspicion with ice-cold calculation, to *unchain volcanic passions.*" [68] Our century is witnessing merely the first spark of the dynamite latent in political mass-exploitation of the subconscious. All over the world, in mutually hostile forms, an untapped new force stirs beneath the conscious and at least semi-rational realm of politics. This new mass force is metapolitics.

An electrifying and terrifying example of this new mass force at work was the Nazi Party Congress of 1936 in Nuremberg. My own impressions of this mass-meeting are best confirmed by the following authoritative eyewitness account of that same meeting:

> At intervals, a curious tremor swept the crowd, and all around me individuals uttered a strange cry, a kind of emotional sigh, that invariably *changed* into a shout of "Heil Hitler." It was a definite struggle to remain rational in a horde so surcharged with tense emotionalism. . . . Hitler's triumph was that of emotion and instinct over reason, a great upsurge of the subconscious in the German people. . . . He gave visions of ultimate expression to the repressed . . . some romance that would take away the drabness of their recent suffering.[69]

[68] Goebbels in "Background for War," p. 2, reprint from *Time,* New York, May 1, 1939.
[69] Roberts: *Hitler,* pp. 139, 37, 38.

At bottom, Wagner's goals had never really changed from those of the original romantic school of 1800: anti-French, anti-rational, worshipping subconscious, lawless "Life." Even his combination of these goals with collectivist socialism lurks in Fichte, though not in terms of industrial society. Wagner's originality, in addition to his elaborate Führer concept, lay in adapting the romantic values to another age. Not to the past, not even to his own age, but to the age his nerves foresaw of complete material and spiritual mechanization. Thereby he found the synthesis for which he had groped all his life: Schopenhauer plus Feuerbach: Volk plus communism: circus plus bread: National Socialism. With this synthesis Wagner's system of metapolitics is complete.

* * *

1961 postscript: The chapter that follows examines Wagner's influence on Hitler, both in general inspiration and in specific programs and ideas. Hitler himself recognized "no predecessors except Wagner."[70] Kubizek, Hitler's youthful friend of 1904–08, describes their visit to Wagner's *Rienzi* in Linz and how the opera inspired the teenage Hitler to ecstatic outbursts about becoming the future Rienzi-tribune of his *Volk*; much later, in describing the very same Wagner evening to Wagner's pro-Nazi widow Cosima, Hitler told her: "In that hour, it [the Nazi dream] began."[71]

[70] In conversation with H. Rauschning: *Gespräche mit Hitler* (Zurich, 1940), p. 215.

[71] W. Daim: *Der Mann der Hitler die Ideen Gab* (Munich, 1958), pp. 45–46, 251; A. Kubizek: *Adolf Hitler, Mein Jugendfreund* (Graz and Göttingen, 1954), pp. 140–2 ff. (Eng. tr.: *The Young Hitler I Knew,* Boston, 1955, p. 290, etc.) Professor H. Trevor-Roper writes, "By all external checks Kubizek's account is reliable, and to anyone who has studied the mind and character of Hitler it is also inherently plausible." F. Jetzinger (*Hitlers Jugend,* Vienna, 1956) does find errors in Kubizek but none changing Kubizek's picture of Wagner's influence as decisive in molding young Hitler, an influence Daim also accepts. Actually both the rival accounts of Hitler (Jetzinger and Kubizek) are valuable, as assessed in Daim, pp. 28–32, 249, and also in W. Jenks, *Vienna and the Young Hitler* (New York, 1960), pp. vii–viii, another post-war book documenting the key influence of Wagner's anti-semitism.

CHAPTER VI

HITLER AND WAGNER

~~~~~~

Whoever wants to understand National Socialist Germany must know Wagner.

— CHANCELLOR ADOLF HITLER

WAGNER AND THE SECOND REICH

Before looking at Wagner's links with the Third Reich of Hitler, it is necessary briefly to look at Wagner's links with the Second Reich of Bismarck.

In 1871 Bismarck united the Germans for the first time since the Holy Roman Empire of the Middle Ages. The latter was incarnated for German patriots in the Emperor Frederick Barbarossa and the First Reich. Bismarck's Prussian-led empire was called the Second Reich because a new empire must be bolstered in prestige by improvising some continuity with the grand old past. For the same reason Hitler's empire is called the Third Reich.

In Bismarck's Reich the spiritual, non-economic needs were left unsatisfied both by the ruling classes of Junkers and industrialists and by the rebel Marxists. This spiritual starvation amid economic and political prosperity helps account for the tremendous power of Bayreuth from the 1870's on. From 1876 through 1941 Bayreuth has been a sort of religious shrine in Germany. In 1876 the German princes gathered in Bayreuth to worship what Wagner's *Meistersinger* chorus calls " the holy German art." From then on, the prestige of Bayreuth and the prestige of the Second Reich were allied, to mutual advantage.

To win the German Volk, the new German state of 1871 had to acquire the prestige-giving emotional connotations of romanticism. That meant an alliance with music, an alliance between Potsdam and Bayreuth. Bayreuth stood for romanticism's brand of nationalism, for the cults of Siegfried, Barbarossa, and Hans Sachs. Without these romantic appeals, the dry, sober, basically un-German Prussianism could have no appeal, no ideological glamour, for the German masses.

Bismarck and Wagner sulkily dismissed each other as an unmusical philistine and a mad bohemian. None the less they allowed their respective disciples (the above-mentioned princes of 1876 and the Wagner circle of Cosima and Siegfried Wagner) to found the Potsdam-Bayreuth alliance. "Without Bayreuth — this one can say without exaggeration — the German spirit could hardly have endured Bismarck's [unromantic] state." [1]

Bayreuth became the smart shrine of all who were culturally *nouveaux riches* in the same way that Potsdam became the shrine of the political *novus homo*. Wagner was a shrewd enough propagandist to exploit a good thing when he saw it, no matter what his private feelings against Prussia. That is why, to quote Thomas Mann, "Wagner attached his cause to the Bismarckian Reich " as soon as

---

[1] Eugen Rosenstock-Hüssy: *Die europäischen Revolutionen* (Jena, 1931), p. 429.

he saw it was an " unparalleled success," in order to make
" the European hegemony of his art the cultural hanger-on
of Bismarck's political hegemony." To amuse posterity,
says Nietzsche, the Second Reich should have had " a genuine Bayreuthian stuffed or, better still, preserved in *spirit*
— for that is exactly what is lacking — with this inscription
below: ' A specimen of the spirit on which the German empire was founded.' " [2]

WAGNER AND NON-GERMAN FASCISTS

On an analogy with the Marxist " Comintern," we may
speak of a world-wide " fascintern." Wagner's metapolitics is the fountainhead of more than nazism; it is the intellectual fountainhead of the fascintern, of fascism outside
Germany as well as inside. A passionate Wagnerite was
the greatest French philosopher of fascism, Maurice Barrès,
a patron saint of the French regime of 1941. The Frenchman Count Gobineau, the founder of modern racism, was
a personal friend and admirer of Wagner himself. As for
the English semi-fascist D. H. Lawrence, " no one, not
even the Führer, was ever more devoted " to Wagner as
oracle; " those to whom Wagner seems profound, have discovered in Lawrence their perfect expression." [3]

The Italian poet d'Annunzio is to Mussolini and fascism
the same inspiration that Wagner is to Hitler and nazism.
But whence d'Annunzio's rather unoriginal ideas and heroic posturings? He was the admirer and eager imitator
of none other than Richard Wagner — and also, signifi-

[2] Thomas Mann: *Leiden*, p. 155. Nietzsche: *Ecce Homo*, Modern Library ed., New York, pp. 81–2.

[3] Thomas Mann: *Freud, Goethe, Wagner*, pp. 207–8. D. H. Lawrence's novel: *The Trespasser*. W. Tindale: *D. H. Lawrence* (New York,
1939), pp. 170, 211–12, and cf. the chapter " Lawrence among the Fascists," pp. 162–80. Mann in *Common Sense*, January 1940, p. 11.

cantly, the good friend of his fellow Wagnerian fascist Maurice Barrès, and of the German poet Stefan George.

When Wagner died, in Venice in 1883, d'Annunzio personally carried his sacred coffin. After the World War d'Annunzio became Italian fascism's literary saint. He settled permanently in Wagner's former villa on Lake Garda, given to d'Annunzio by Wagner's fascist-minded family. There the Italian metapolitician swore to die heroically like "his beloved Siegfried" of Wagner, but he died of mere old age. Similarly, Mussolini himself greatly admires Wagner — and considers him quite un-German.[4]

Hitler's official philosopher, Rosenberg, says Wagner "fought alone against the whole bourgeois-capitalist world" of the Jews and "foresaw the dawn" of nazism. "In all countries," adds Rosenberg, "Bayreuth found sympathetic souls."[5] A separate book would have to be written on these sympathetic souls of all countries; there is no further space for them here.

WAGNER VERSUS HITLER:
WHAT WOULD WAGNER BE TODAY?

Back in the mid-nineteenth century Wagner's operas preached nationalism because he wanted to convert the beer-drinking German philistines to this exhilarating new religion of the Nation. But in the twentieth century the Kultur-Babbitts, the philistines, are precisely those most converted to the Nation, making it no longer suitable æsthetically for opera, poetry, and philosophy but thoroughly banal and beer-drenched — in fact, making na-

---

[4] Bernard Wall: "Gabriele D'Annunzio," *The Colosseum*, quarterly, Vol. IV, no. 18 (London, July 1938), pp. 93–4. G. A. Borgese: *Goliath* (revised ed., New York, 1938), pp. 290, 185.

[5] Rosenberg: *Mythus*, pp. 443–4.

tionalism and philistinism synonymous. In such circumstances (as Thomas Mann once put it) what could
Wagner have been today but one of Hitler's subversive
Kulturbolsheviks? Wagnerian music would have been
added to the banned list of " degenerate art."

Needless to say, Wagner should not be blamed too much
for what the Wagnerites did with him at Bayreuth. At
heart he always quietly retained much of the civilized
cosmopolitanism of his early French period. The Wagnerites were often more Nazi-minded than he. Wagner's
tragedy is that finally he himself became a Wagnerite. In
so far as he did so, he became the fountainhead of the Nazi
religion and deserves to be blamed for his share of its most
intolerant and lawless and racist doctrines. Nietzsche, who
had loved Wagner the cosmopolitan and who hated Wagner the nordic nationalist, sadly summed up the transition:

> I hardly recognized Wagner. What had happened?
> Wagner had been translated into German! The Wagner-
> ite had triumphed over Wagner. Those of us who knew
> to what refined artists, to what *cosmopolitanism* of taste
> Wagner's art can alone appeal, were beside ourselves at
> the sight of Wagner bedecked with German virtues. . . .
> Not a single abortion was missing — not even the anti-
> Semite. Poor Wagner! To what pass had he come? . . .
> The idealists of the Bayreuth press . . . that crowd was
> enough to make your hair stand on end! [6]

Not only Wagner the great musician but even Wagner
the national socialist must be ranked miles above the Nazi
level. Like most dreamers of new movements, he would
unquestionably have rejected the coercive means needed to
carry out his ends. Like Bakunin, he was an anarchist
toward the visible state. His racist and national-socialist
goals were to come not through force nor through any ma-

---

[6] Nietzsche: *Ecce Homo,* pp. 80–1.

terial institutions but through art and music and the invisible Volk-soul. For Wagner, as for Marx and Lenin, the state was the bad means which would " wither away " as soon as the goal of killing capitalist democracy was achieved. But neither Hitler's nor Stalin's state seems breathlessly eager to " wither."

The German Volk-soul, Wagner assumed, would be angelic again when racially purified of its Jewish and French " poisons." To be sure, it must have its mystical Führer as dictatorial mouthpiece, but he was often described by Wagner as a saintlike, almost priggish creature, with no more than a Chocolate Soldier reign of terror. This namby-pamby side of Wagner, though as basic as his Siegfried side, naturally has no more practical political results today than Lenin's dogma of the state withering.

Wagner cites the Thirty Years' War to prove that Germany can be destroyed materially — that scarcely worries him — without destroying the German soul, which is indifferent to military success. Likewise, even the *Meistersinger* ends with the theme that Germany's " Holy Roman Empire " can " disintegrate " but is less important than her immortal " Holy German Art." Wagner was an æsthete through and through, not a politician. Germany should dominate the world, of course — that was the destiny of her Aryan blood — but by her superb music and philosophy, not by Blitzkriegs. Germans are " marked not for rulers but for ennoblers of the world." [7]

This more pleasing side of Wagner is basic, but it is not this side of him that concerns us here. For it is not this side of him that moulded Hitler, Goebbels, Rosenberg, and the rest of his disciples who now seek to rule but not ennoble the world.

---

[7] Wagner: *Prose*, VI, 124. Weller: *Wagner*, pp. 41–4. Mann: *Leiden*, p. 152. Last chorus of *Die Meistersinger*.

More important in balancing Wagner against Hitler is
the almost complete agreement between Wagner's and
Hitler's metapolitics, their common national-socialist credo
and goals. Only indirectly does Wagner bear guilt for the
criminal means used to achieve his goals. Yet his guilt, no
matter how " indirect," is still enormous: what else but
some form of Nazi barbarism could be the inevitable " indirect " result of romanticism's hundred years of billings-
gate against classic form and law? " Life is law unto itself."

WAGNER PLUS HITLER

Wagner plus Hitler is historically more important today
than Wagner versus Hitler. Hitler entered his present
World War amid Wagnerian strains. Through much of the
war crisis of July and August 1939 he was attending the
Bayreuth Wagner festival with his good friends Frau Winifred Wagner and Verena Wagner. Winifred is called
" keeper of the Wagnerian tradition " and " dictator of the
Bayreuth festival." Hitler was once expected to marry her
and used to visit her constantly at Bayreuth.[8] She is the
widow of the composer's son, Siegfried Wagner, who was
also a good friend of Hitler's. The Führer is " particularly
fond " (more than of adult company) " of Wagner's blond
grandchildren, who treat him like an old uncle." [9]

Hitler has said: " Whoever wants to understand National Socialist Germany must know Wagner." According
to Goebbels, Hitler has seen *Die Meistersinger* more than

---

[8] *Münchner Neueste Nachrichten*, Munich, July 26, 1939, p. 1. *New
York Times*, Sunday, July 30, 1939, p. 2–E. Heiden: *Hitler*, pp. 324–5.

[9] G. W.: " Hitler at Fifty," *The Living Age*, New York, July 1939,
pp. 452–4; tr. from *Nationalzeitung*, Basel, Switzerland. *Time*, New York,
December 16, 1940, pp. 40–2.

one hundred times! In the 1920's Hitler used to effuse to Bayreuth meetings about the mystic " destiny " linking his struggle eternally to Wagner's.[10]

Since youthful influences are often the deepest, what effect had Wagner on the Führer's childhood? A youthful friend described young Hitler's almost hysterical excitement during Wagnerian music: " Wagner was a fighter," so Hitler loved him and proclaimed that " opera is really the best divine service." [11] Had Hitler entered a plodding bureaucratic career, as his petty-bourgeois father demanded, Hitler would not now be ruling Germany. What decided him against becoming a local official and what filled him with restlessness for a vaguely artistic and bohemian life, was Wagner's music. To quote the Führer's own words:

At the age of twelve, I saw the first opera of my life, Wagner's *Lohengrin*. I was captivated at once. My youthful enthusiasm for the master of Bayreuth knew no bounds. Again and again I was drawn to his works . . . seeing increasingly better productions. All this served to confirm my deep-rooted aversion for the career my father had chosen for me. I wanted to become a painter, and no power on earth could ever make an official of me.[12]

The reader will recall Wagner's description of his convulsive spiritual transformation from the so-called French and Jewish ideas of a citizen of the world into an anti-Semitic nationalist. This same transformation, the typical youthful crisis of romantic psychology, was experienced by Hitler and described in similar language. In *Mein Kampf* he writes that, in his first youthful years in Vienna, he was

[10] Joseph Goebbels: *Vom Kaiserhof zur Reichskanzlei* (22d ed., Munich, 1937). *Münchner Neueste Nachrichten,* July 22, 1939, p. 4.

[11] Reinhold Hanisch: " I Was Hitler's Buddy," Part II, *New Republic,* New York, April 12, 1939, pp. 270–2.

[12] Hitler: *Mein Kampf,* ed. cit., p. 23.

an internationalist and was sincerely horrified by anti-
Semitism as "mediæval" bigotry. But, adds the future
Führer, "there came for me the time of the *greatest in-
ternal transformation* which I ever underwent. From a
feeble *citizen of the world* I became a fanatic anti-
Semite." [13] In other words, even the holy incarnation of
Siegfried-Barbarossa (just as in the case of the anti-
Semitism and anti-luxurious Spartanism of his teacher,
Wagner) is to some extent waging his war against — him-
self.

Thus Hitler's youth. And as he grew older, his "favourite reading" is listed as none other than the "political
compositions of Richard Wagner." [14]

No wonder the diabolically clever combination of appeals with which Hitler won the masses consists of the
very same appeals which compose Wagner's metapolitics.
These are: Pan-German nationalism; vague promises of
economic socialism (that "true," anti-Marxist brand); fanatic anti-Semitism, both economic and racist; revolt
against legalism; revolt against reason, especially against
"alien" intellectualism; the Führer principle; yearning for
the organic Volk state without class distinctions; hatred of
free speech and parliamentary democracy and of the international bankers supposed to control democracy; misty
nordic primitivism of the Siegfried and Nibelungen sagas.

Neither Wagner nor his pupil Hitler invented any one of
these appeals. Wagner's historical importance is this: he
is the focal point where all these contradictory doctrines
coalesce into one single program of irresistible demagogic
appeal to the mass man. Hitler's historical importance is
as the genius who actually did the job, the Horatio Alger
of metapolitics who, though born without a brown shirt

---

[13] Hitler: *Mein Kampf*, 13th German ed., Munich, 1932, p. 69.
[14] Heiden: *Hitler*, p. 310.

on his back, orated his way from office boy to president of the world's most efficient death factory.

Hitler's love for Wagner's prose also had stylistic consequences. It is not only the model for the political ideas of *Mein Kampf* but also for its turgid, orgasmic, and grammatically involved prose. Wagner's style, says Mann, "doubtless has a strong National Socialist element" even when "regarded purely as prose and apart from all content." [15]

Hitler's book and speeches inherit Wagner's stylistic faults: painful repetition, crank tangents, offensive grandiloquence, emotion to the point of hysteria. But Hitler's book and speeches equally inherit Wagner's stylistic assets: a vigour and energy ("dynamism") sweeping along impressionable listeners, especially when *en masse;* vague mystic soaring and striving, making readers and listeners feel heroic and uplifted, especially youth reared in the tradition of German romanticism — and both Wagnerism and Hitlerism are most magnetic as youth movements.

The techniques of showmanship in Wagner's opera settings are also imitated effectively by Hitler. These techniques, whose aim is to flabbergast the audience with awe, are the model for Hitler's stage-managing of the Nazi party congresses. The torchlight parades, the mob choruses, the grand gestures of the nordic heroes, the reiteration of leitmotivs and ever rising climaxes — all these have been reproduced from Bayreuth in Nuremberg.

Also in private life Hitler adopts the much rarer Wagnerian crochets, such as vegetarianism, and has issued decrees limiting what Wagner called "the curse of vivisection."

In 1923 Hitler's Munich beer-hall putsch failed. In 1924 he was sentenced, for treason, to his comfortable Bavarian

[15] Thomas Mann in *Common Sense,* January 1940, p. 12.

prison. Naturally he made a point of taking along a porta-
ble phonograph and a set of recordings from Wagner's
operas.[16] During the thirteen months in his cell, he dictated to Rudolf Hess the tome of philosophy and autobiography known as *Mein Kampf*. It is no coincidence that
this work was composed amid the heroic bray of Wagnerian phonograph records. Ever after, Hitler had the
habit of humming Wagnerian music to himself during political conversations.[17]

One of the world's leading orchestra conductors, Sir
Ernest MacMillan, insists: " From the time that I first saw
Hitler in Bayreuth in 1933, I have felt a perverted Wagnerism in *all* his actions and speeches. His very speeches
suggest a parody of Wagner. . . . Hitler identifies himself in his own mind with many a Wagnerian hero." One
such hero, as we have already seen, is Hans Sachs. Another is Lohengrin, the " knight in shining armour." Hitler compares his last-minute rescue of Germany by glorious
bloodshed to Lohengrin's similar rescue of Elsa. In Hitler's
own " House of German Art " at Munich hangs a painting
of Sir Adolf on horseback dressed in — shining white
armour! When Hitler entered the present World War, the
sword motif of Wagner's *Ring der Nibelungen* rang con-
tinuously in his ears, and he felt himself " Siegfried setting
forth to slay the dragon." In fact, his premonitions of his
" approaching death," revealed by members of his entourage and by his own speech of September 1, 1939, suggest
that for him this war is a grand Wagnerian *Götterdämmerung* (Twilight of the Gods) " with the whole of Europe afire as a funeral pyre for Adolf Hitler. Anyone who
thinks such a picture too outrageously disproportionate for

---

[16] B. Lansing: " Adolf Hitler," *Life,* New York, September 25, 1939,
p. 48.

[17] *Time,* February 26, 1940, p. 90. H. Rauschning: *The Voice of Destruction* (New York, 1940).

even Hitler's imagination cannot have followed his career carefully." [18]

In 1920 the young Nazi party issued its "Twenty-five Points," which ever since have remained its official program. The Twenty-five Points are a weird medley of (would-be) aristocratic racism and plebeian socialism. This double-barrelled appeal, to both top-dog and under-dog psychology, is what brought in the votes. The debt-ridden under dog of the inflation era is promised "ruthless war" against "usurers and profiteers," "unearned income," and "*Zinsknechtschaft*" ("the tyranny of taking interest"). How many of these twenty-five promises were later kept is quite another matter. But, considered solely as demagogic technique, they helped make the National Socialists the largest single party under Germany's last two free elections, of July and November 1932. The Twenty-five Points without exception coincide with Wagner's Bayreuth program.[19]

The Nazi program received an "emphatic endorsement" from Houston Chamberlain at Bayreuth. "In the apotheosis of Germanism which Wagner represents, Chamberlain found a living justification of his theories." Whole long passages of *Mein Kampf* on the need for Führer, war, and racism are borrowed from Chamberlain, Wagner's English son-in-law. In 1924 Hitler pouted that "the official authorities of the government passed by the

---

[18] Quotations in this paragraph are from the speech delivered at Vancouver, Canada, October 7, 1939, by Sir Ernest MacMillan, Principal of the Toronto Conservatory of Music and conductor of the Toronto Symphony Orchestra. My source is the unpublished full text of this speech, lent me through the courtesy of Sir Ernest. A brief summary can be found in the *New York Times*, Edition P, Sunday, October 8, 1939, p. 33.

[19] The official version of the original "Twenty-five Points" is in Rosenberg: *Wesen, Grundsätze, und Ziele der Nationalsozialistischen Deutschen Arbeiterpartei* (Munich, 1933), and in many earlier and later editions.

observations of a Houston Stewart Chamberlain indiffer-
ently. . . ." Today the opposite is true. Hitler has had a
street in Berlin named for Chamberlain. The only catch is
that, after Britain took up arms to defend Poland, the
official Nazi news agency had to announce to the German
people that Chamberlainstrasse referred to Houston and
not to Neville.[20]

Goebbels's published diary throw much light on himself
and Hitler. After an evening at *Die Meistersinger* in 1932,
Goebbels's eulogy of "the giant Wagner" ends: "As the
great 'Awake' chorus begins, you feel the stimulation in
your *blood*. Germany, too, will soon feel the same and be
called to an awakening. We *must* attain to power!" And
on attaining to "power," the first Nazi victory decree is
the playing of that same chorus. "Now [Wagner's] radi-
ant 'Awake' chorus has regained its true significance,"
gloats Goebbels in his 1933 diary — after Hitler became
dictator under the slogan: "*Deutschland erwache!*"
("Germany awake!").

Elsewhere Goebbels notes: "Hear the Valkyrie at the
State Opera. Wagner's sublime music is *mingled* with the
sound of marching of the Steel Helmet troops, who have
celebrated their great day in Berlin and are now passing
the opera house." This is the quintessence of the Nazi
mind, this "mingling" of Wagnerian romanticism with the
efficient brutal marching of militarism.[21]

The revival of the Nibelungen-Siegfried legends began
with the early romantic school, despite Goethe's prophetic
warning of their barbaric ancestors. Not till Wagner's

[20] *Mein Kampf* (Reynal & Hitchcock ed.), p. 269; passages on need
of Führer, war, and racism, pp. 116–7, 387–420; ed. notes, pp. 116, 395,
413. On Chamberlain Street, cf. Associated Press dispatch, Berlin, December 14, 1939.
[21] Goebbels: *My Part in Germany's Fight*, translated by K. Fiedler
(London, 1935), pp. 131, 268, 257.

operas did these legends become familiar to the mass of ordinary Germans. Wagner it was who almost single-handed steeped all Germany in the tales of Siegfried, his wonderful sword, the horrible capitalistic dragon, the not quite Aryan little dwarfs with their hoard of corrupting gold. The following concrete examples of how these opera versions of Siegfried have moulded everyday German life will illustrate the stranglehold Wagner has on the modern German imagination.

The Nazi excuse for Germany's 1918 defeat was that her unbeatable armies were stabbed in the back by the Jews and democrats at home. Why did Germans swallow this propaganda with such gullible gusto? Because, explains Elmer Davis, " three generations of Germans have been conditioned by [Wagner's] *Ring* operas to the conviction that the German Hero can never be struck down except by a stab in the back," such as dark Hagen administered to blond Siegfried. Because of the " parliamentary footpads," to quote Hitler's own words, " the warring German Siegfried received a stealthy stab in the back." [22]

Hitler says of the first meeting of the Nazi party: " Out of its flames was bound to come the sword which was to regain the freedom of the German Siegfried." With this Siegfried motif he concludes the first volume of his autobiography.[23] During the years of the German Republic, when Versailles still kept Germany partially disarmed, opera audiences went wild with enthusiasm over the symbolic scene where Siegfried forges the German sword. When Nazi Germany finished its huge western line of forts, the German people and foreign journalists unanimously referred to it as " the Siegfried Line." This shows how

---

[22] Elmer Davis: *Not to Mention the War* (New York, 1939), pp. 205–6, footnote. Hitler: *Mein Kampf,* ed. cit., p. 912.

[23] *Mein Kampf,* pp. 513–14.

widely Wagner has popularized Siegfried with the masses, for the official government title of the forts was not " Siegfried Line." The official title, however, is equally symbolic, being named after the *limes* line, which in ancient Roman days was the barrier between western civilization and the warlike barbarian invaders from the Teutonic north.

Early in 1940 Robert Ley, Führer of the Labour Front, made an important speech to the German working class with the purpose of converting them to Hitler's war. Significantly, Ley was able to assume that his listeners, though humble ill-read proletarians, knew the legend of Siegfried and the dragon. He summed up the war as a crusade against the decadent English dragon, who deprives the German Siegfried of the Nibelungen hoard, which in this case is *Lebensraum,* raw materials, colonies. Ley said: "Workers of all lands, unite — to smash the rule of English capitalism! You young upward-striving nations of the earth, combine to annihilate the old English dragon who blocks the treasures of the earth and withholds from you the riches of the world." These words show not only how deeply Wagner has penetrated the masses but how cleverly the Nazis have been stealing the Marxist thunder, even appropriating the slogan: " Workers of all lands, unite! " [24]

Wagner is far closer in spirit to the Nazi Third Reich of steeled romanticism than to the Prussian Second Reich of orderly bureaucracy. The latter exalted the state, whereas Wagner and Hitler exalt the Volk. The state to romantics represents lifeless form; it is static legality. The Volk represents living content; it dynamically overlaps and smashes state lines. That is why young Hitler, a most unpatriotic state citizen, prayed for the destruction of his Hapsburg state — for the sake of the German Volk.

[24] *Time,* February 26, 1940, p. 24. *New Republic,* February 26, 1940, p. 260.

After 1871 the Hohenzollern and Bismarckian state was territorially saturated and thoroughly conservative; for almost half a century, it was a peaceful and law-abiding upholder of the European *status quo*. Americans tend toward the serious error of identifying the Second with the Third Reich. This overlooks the whole revolutionary, expansive, romantic side of nazism. The plebeian Hitler throws out not only the Junker spirit of class distinctions but also the admirable non-political civil service and non-political Reichswehr autonomy so typical of the Kaiser's bureaucratic state.

In fact, Hitler mocks as a " mad concept " the Prussian ideal, which he sneeringly describes as " doglike adoration for so-called ' state authority. ' " Such a " dead mechanism," he explains, must be replaced by a " living organism," based on " the herd instinct, which appears when all are of one blood." In the 1920's " the Jewish-democratic *state* (Reich) has become a real curse to the German *Volk* (nation)." That is because " we as Aryans can only picture the state as the living organism of a nationality." [25] Here the Führer is repeating Wagner almost word for word.

When Hitler annexed the Czechs and began his chain of conquest, many Americans thought that his annexation of non-Germans was inconsistent with the Nazi racial ideology and that hence Nazi ideology was no longer a determining force. Actually there was no inconsistency whatever, because Hitler never includes Czechs, Poles, and other nations organically in his Volk; he merely adds them to his state. Here the distinction between Volk and state makes all the difference in the world. It means that

[25] Hitler: *My Battle,* the abridged Dugdale edition (Boston and New York, 1933), pp. 157, 159–61, 247. *Mein Kampf* (German ed.), p. 426; (Reynal & Hitchcock ed.), p. 601.

the Poles, though appendages of the German state, are
as " racial inferiors " the slaves of the German Volk. They
can never rise from slavery to equal citizenship. Similarly,
Germans of the Jewish group are, for both Wagner and
Hitler, in the German state but not in its Volk.

To sum up, Wagner's moulding of Hitler's mind was
twofold: direct, through Hitler's " favourite reading " of
" Wagner's political compositions "; indirect, as we have
seen, through Houston Chamberlain, the Wagner family,
Eckart, Rosenberg. A man of action, without even a full
high-school education, Hitler could not be particularly well
read. If, none the less, he knew his Wagner so thoroughly,
these same Wagnerian influences must have been similarly
moulding millions of other ordinary Germans, no matter
how indirectly. In a yet more indirect sense, one hundred
years of romantic literature and philosophy made Germany more susceptible to Nazi concepts than any other
country in the world, already long before Versailles.

After Versailles the question for romantic nationalists
was how to destroy the old Versailles order of international
capitalism or Marxism, how to destroy the Jews blamed
for that order, and hence how to save and purify the Volk.
Who would do this ruthless job? Would it be by democracy or Prussian monarchy or army or — something
new? Wagner both anticipated and answered these
questions.

He answered them in advance by nurturing his Führer
concept from its modest pale bud of " kinghood " (1849)
to its gaudiest bloom of 1881. Wagner said in 1881: " We
must now seek the Hero " of the future, who " turns against
the ruin of his race." Doing this, " the Hero wondrously
becomes divine." [26] Siegfried and Barbarossa were to have
their third incarnation!

[26] Wagner: *Prose*, VI, 279.

Hero? Wondrously divine? In 1924 Hitler was on trial of his life for treason. He informed his judges that they were dragging him to court just as two thousand years ago a divine hero in Jerusalem had been dragged by the same race to His apparent death. " I wanted to be the destroyer of Marxism. I mean to solve this task," shouted Hitler from his prisoner's box, adding: " When I stood for the first time before Richard Wagner's grave, my heart swelled with pride. . . ." In Hitler's list of the three greatest Germans " nearest to the heart of the Volk," the sole modern he names is Wagner.[27]

" We must now seek the Hero." For half a century learned pedants dismissed Wagner's metapolitics as unimportant because unscientific. Their fate in contemporary Germany speaks for itself, both the dismal fate of aloof learning and the triumphant fate of Wagner's metapolitics. In an age of emotional mass politics, it is not important that Wagner's fanatic hates and enthusiasms were perhaps pathological and certainly unsound. Important are such mawkish scenes as young Hitler standing at Wagner's grave, heroically dedicating himself, the Siegfried of the lower middle class, with grim, non-Wagnerian efficiency acting out Germany's last Wagnerian melodrama.

[27] *Der Hitler-Prozess*, edited by the newspaper *Münchner Neueste Nachrichten* (Munich, 1924). Heiden: *Hitler*, pp. 317–18. Hitler: *Mein Kampf* (Reynal & Hitchcock ed.), p. 287.

CHAPTER VII

GREENWICH VILLAGE WARRIORS

~~~~~~

The Germans are always so badly deceived because they try to find a deceiver. If only they have a heady wine for the senses, they will put up with bad bread. Intoxication means more to them than nourishment; that is the hook they will always bite on. A popular leader [Führer] must hold up before them the prospect of conquests and splendour; then he will be believed. They always obey, and will do more than obey provided they can get intoxicated in the process.

— NIETZSCHE [1]

This [Nazi] government is composed of members half of whom are men who originally intended to devote themselves to some creative work. . . . This government, rooted in opposition to rationalism, is well aware of the nameless longing of the Volk . . . which can be explained and expressed only by the artist.

— HANS BLUNCK, *President of the Reich Chamber of Literature, 1938*

---

[1] *The Political Quarterly*, London, Vol. XI, no. 1 (January–March 1940), p. 27.

THE SECOND ROMANTIC REVOLUTION

So far I have spoken only of the original romantic movement (except for such independent later romantics as Wagner). But Germany produced another such large-scale and interconnected romantic movement, almost as important as the first. This second romantic revolt triumphed in German literature in the 1890's, and in German politics (books into bullets) with Hitler.

Europe's 1890's were the height of a brilliant æsthetic and intellectual revival, international in scope though varying according to national characteristics. It was known in Germany as neo-romanticism and in France and England as the "decadent" movement. The first romantics, about 1800, had revolted against French rationalism. The second revolted against the realistic, scientific school of writing associated with Emile Zola. They revolted against the faith in smug materialism and in an unduly utilitarian brand of democracy. This materialist-democrat faith was then widespread not only in France, England, and America but in Germany herself.

The second romantic revolt, like the first, was partly justified and wholly inevitable. European culture was indeed choking in the narrow smug Victorian cult of "progress" produced by the rather shallow but "stupendous" material success of the new industrialism. In so far as a revolt against this was justified, the revolt also triumphed by the 1890's in western culture under the influence of the so-called decadent school. The familiar names are Baudelaire, Gautier, Verlaine, Rimbaud, Mallarmé, and their flamboyant English imitators Swinburne, Oscar Wilde, Ernest Dowson. Regarded first as clowns, then as Satans, then as saints by the shocked and titillated bourgeois, they have been unduly laughed at, unduly persecuted, and unduly adored.

Though they rarely could cope with their liquor or their sex lives, the decadents showed more real common sense in diagnosing the fatal weaknesses of their age and of liberal bourgeois prosperity than did all the vaunted common sense of the canny businessmen. The "solid," "sound" way of life of the latter seems certainly precarious today, and its doom was predicted in the 1890's, and for the right reasons, by those whom the respectable citizen dismissed as clowns. When every other word of the decadent poets was "ennui," that seemed mere æsthetic affectation and sickly languor. Yet they rightly sensed that mankind sometimes prefers the bloodiest revolt against reason to an industrialism which is just plain dull and a material progress which starves the emotions and the imagination.

The liberal bourgeois democracy enjoyed the height of its material and psychological prosperity in that Victorian lull before the storm. It did so with the smug self-confidence of a cuckold. For (at least in Germany) it could no more satisfy the romantic aspirations of the masses than Monsieur Bovary could "satisfy" Madame Bovary. It simply lacked the sex appeal (metaphorically speaking) of a Wagnerian opera or a fiery demagogic oration.

In addition to these psychological weaknesses, and equally underestimated and equally important, were the familiar economic weaknesses of capitalist society. These every decadent considered too prosaic to notice, and the job of prophesying their doom was left to the Marxist Cassandras. The latter were often justified if taken as purely destructive critics. They should have been listened to more then and should be listened to more today. But being anti-Christian, the materialism of the Marxists was and is and will be as helpless as the capitalist brand of materialism to forestall fascism. Fascism can only be forestalled by satisfying the emotional and religious needs of the masses in addition to all the indispensable economic needs. By default, therefore, Wagner it was who by the 1870's and 1880's became priest, pander, and physician to Europe's emotionally and religiously starved.

Where the second romantic revolution differs from the first is in political method. Here the romantic "will to power" no longer *rejects* the "uninspired" world of materialism-efficiency-industrialism but *swallows* it, swallows and thereby assimilates it. Thus, in the person of Wagner, the romantic "spirit of music" combines with a tough, practical, and politically shrewd nazism. Thus, in the whole movement of nazism itself, the fantastic goals of romanticism are sought in 1941 not with the inefficient "blue flower" of the earlier, ivory-tower romantics but with the most rational and scientific means of modern technics, modern propaganda, modern war. This swallowing and assimilation of its direct opposite, of rational technics, which alone explains the victories of Hitler's Germany, is what makes the second romantic revolution the most important "event" of the last hundred years.

HOUSTON CHAMBERLAIN AS HITLER'S JOHN THE BAPTIST

The mystagogue of Bayreuth was the Master's English son-in-law, Houston Stewart Chamberlain. The æsthetic wave of the second romantic revolution combined with the nationalist wave of Bismarck's Second Reich to make Bayreuth the national shrine of art. There the Master's brew of fascist metapolitics intoxicated more and more of German youth.

Ever stirring and reflavouring and sampling the brew, Chamberlain devoted his life to fermenting the Master's concoction for *Der Tag*, which both *knew* would come. And sure enough, this became the official intoxicant of the Third Reich after a frustrated artist and a frustrated poet and a frustrated philosopher and a frustrated playwright, named Hitler and Eckart and Rosenberg and Goebbels, respectively, became ecstatic initiates of Chamberlain at Bayreuth.

For the German Chosen People, Wagner was the Moses who would never see the Promised Land, and Chamberlain was the John the Baptist who discovered Hitler and baptized him in the holy fire-water of metapolitics. Wagner's plucky wife Cosima had her doubts about Hitler, at least until 1933. But Chamberlain and Winifred Wagner and supposedly Siegfried Wagner, the Master's son, saw in Hitler the fulfillment of all the Old Testament prophecies of Richard Wagner. To them Hitler was not demagogue but demigod. He was that Siegfried-Barbarossa reincarnation for whom Wagner had yearned to save Germany from Wagner's three abominations: democracy, finance-capitalism, and the Jews.

In 1923 Chamberlain wrote Hitler an amazing letter. It was written even before Hitler temporarily won the local headlines with his disastrous beer-hall putsch of that year. In this letter Chamberlain compared himself to John the Baptist, who could die in peace now that he had found the Saviour he had always sought. "At one stroke you have transformed the state of my soul. Germany in her hour of direst need gives birth to a Hitler. . . . Now I may justly go to sleep and need never again awaken. God protect you!" In 1923 he called Hitler a "cosmos-creating" force and an "awakener of souls." In 1924 he called Hitler

" heaven-sent " and " the most creative mind in statecraft since Bismarck." [2]

Before that, almost identical predictions were made by Dietrich Eckart, Hitler's original discoverer and impresario, and by none other than Rudolf Hess, the man who shared Hitler's prison cell after their joint 1923 putsch, the man to whom Hitler dictated his *Mein Kampf*, the man who was official head of the whole Nazi party-organization and the next in succession after Hitler and Göring — and the man who suddenly parachuted into a Scottish field in May 1941. Prior to 1923 both Eckart and Hess had ecstatically hailed the unemployed, unknown Austrian postcard-painter as the future dictator and saviour.

Consider three facts. First, all these intoxicated prophecies. Second, the fact that in the years 1920–4 Hitler was either completely unknown or a laughing-stock; his party had not a single Reichstag seat and comparatively only a handful of members, almost all in Munich, consisting mostly of tough Free Corps soldiers like Röhm, sousing æsthetes like Eckart, and unemployed lower-middle-class youngsters. Considering these two facts from the viewpoint of 1923 and not of today, we as rationalists would consider these prophecies about Hitler by Chamberlain and Eckart as mad, even though both men were nationally famous literary figures.

Then as the third fact consider Hitler's successive victory marches through Vienna, Prague, Warsaw, Paris. Now it is we rationalists who seem the mad ones, for having scoffed at these fulfilled prophecies. Suppose Hitler had always remained an unemployed, uneducated, and

[2] H. S. Chamberlain: *Der Seher des Dritten Reiches* (selected works, ed. by G. Schott, 3d ed., Munich, 1939), pp. 11–15. R. Olden: *Hitler* (New York, 1936), p. 151.

frustrated artist. Even then he must have had some extraordinary magnetic power, yet to be explained by psychologists, in order to elicit such prophecies from nationally famous writers at a time when he was so unknown to the nation and such an apparent failure in everything. This power Chamberlain described, in a letter to Hitler, by a strange metaphor which numerous German witnesses of Hitler's oratory were to confirm:

" Your eye acts as if gifted with many hands; it seizes a man and holds him tight! "[3]

These are the qualities German romantics often mean by the twin concepts " dæmonic " and " superman."

DÆMONS, FÜHRERS, AND BOORS

A book on German metapolitics owes to American readers a clear definition of that perennial proto-Nazi word " dæmonic." But the more German romantics I read, the more I must confess my incompetency to define the word. Either you feel that sacred misty dæmonic glow or you don't, and we shall have to leave it at that. But not quite at that. A few hints can escape through the veil even to unbelievers. Though admittedly unclear, a tentative definition might be: a " dæmonic " man is a mortal demigod driven along beyond good and evil by the invisible elemental forces he incarnates.

In order to explain Byron and Napoleon, the word " dæmonic " in its modern sense was first used by Goethe. It was misused ever after by the romantics of all countries — especially in Germany. There it is an earmark of profundity among modern Nazi thinkers and nineteenth-century proto-Nazis; the more often you use it in a paragraph, the " deeper " your philosophy is. Anyone who is

[3] Chamberlain, loc. cit.

ill-mannered, boorish, irrational, and egotistic, provided he is intolerably so, is likely to be called dæmonic in nineteenth- and twentieth-century Germany — or at least be called a genius. (In Greenwich Village days, it was called artistic temperament.)

The mystic or dæmonic view of Hitler has been widely accepted, especially among Germans. Anti-Hitler arguments, to be effective, must be able to refute this view on its own rarefied level, as well as on a rational level. The chapter on "Nazi Religion" will quote influential German leaders calling Hitler literally the nordic "Christ." On such levels of argument, suffice it to point out the following old apocalyptic prophecy. To human eyes the Antichrist will appear identical with the Christ in magnetic attraction, in performance of material miracles, and in supernatural power to command adoration. The one difference is the all-important hair's-breadth distinction between good and evil.

Actually, of course, those who call Hitler the Antichrist or Satan incarnate are as hysterical as the Nazis who call him the Christ. We have plenty of more tangible reasons for opposing him. But those who do judge politics metapolitically will find it hard to justify Hitler even on their own questionable level. They may find a tiny, all-important mistake in spelling is being palmed off on them. Suppose you are romantic enough and German enough to believe in the "dæmonic." Then you are also liable to believe in the existence of the "demonic." Since only a hair's breadth separates the two, can you ever be quite sure which way to spell your Nazi supermen?

"WHAT AN ARTIST DIES IN ME!"

Wagner as philosopher-musician was the great connecting link between the first and second romantic revolutions. Like the first, the second was avowedly based on the "spirit of music." As proclaimed by earlier romantics, by Wackenroder, Tieck, and E. T. A. Hoffmann, music is both the highest and most romantic art, the divinest human activity, because the "spirit of music" (to them) is the incarnation of all that is most vague, formless, expansive, most emotional and subjective, escaping from uninspired reason into the infinite yearning and infinite striving of the dæmonic subconscious. Note how this violently unclassical definition of the musical art combines with the chief jargon-terms of so many anti-western *political* prophets, the meta-politicians. That is why art, especially Wagner's music, was expected somehow to "regenerate" all of life, even politics and foreign policy. To the politician-æsthetes of the second romantic revolution, music symbolized the revolt of the Volk's instinctive mass dynamism against legality, reason, and static morality.

During his Wagnerite and anti-western period, Nietzsche significantly gave the title *The Birth of Tragedy from the Spirit of Music* to that early book of his which ends predicting the birth of a triumphant new Germany from these four "Dionysian" blessings: an æsthetic national "tragic myth"; "the ecstatic luring call" of Wagner "the bird"; the consequent "elimination of foreign elements" from Germany; the "bloody glory of the late war" against France (the war of 1870) and against France's Romanizing, westernizing influence on Germany.[4]

---

[4] Friedrich Nietzsche: *The Birth of Tragedy from the Spirit of Music*, translated by Clifton Fadiman, in *Ecce Homo and the Birth of Tragedy* (Modern Library ed., New York), pp. 331–8. The original German edition appeared in 1872.

A famous modern German art-critic expressed an attitude more typical of large masses of Germans than of almost any other country when he said: "Among us Germans, art was not a class distinction, an enervating form of dilettantism, or a luxury, but the one and *only* reality, the ultimate altar, the final bond holding humanity together . . . heroism."[5]

The benefits of this German attitude are as obvious as Germany's immortal artistic contributions to humanity. Less obvious are the dangers of this attitude. It has the unexpected consequence of art voluntarily synthesizing with vast untrained popular tastes. Often these are not merely vulgar (*kitsch*) but demand a fanatic and intolerant nationalism whose propaganda-handmaiden art must become.

Germany would gain in both art and sane politics if she had either a lot more or a lot less of solid, stodgy, undiluted Babbitts. She needs a more unambiguous dividing line between her spiritual Rotary Clubs and her spiritual Greenwich Villages. When both get mixed up, the result is dæmonic bank clerks, lower-middle-class Siegfrieds, and what Nietzsche called Kultur-philistines. The mixture is dangerous because thereby every metapolitical lunacy, instead of being harmless, is welded to irresistible business-like efficiency.

In relative proportion to other countries, almost every Tom, Dick, and Harry of the German semi-educated seems an amateur æsthete, a Greenwich Village Babbitt, unfortunately retaining the knack of handling a machine-gun competently. Actually, of course, even in Germany these are a small minority. But in proportion to other countries

---

[5] Julius Meier-Graefe, quoted in A. Eloesser: *Modern German Literature* (New York, 1933), p. 236.

they played an enormous role, especially among the proto-Nazis and the Nazi party itself.

Fantastically, stunningly high is the proportion of frustrated æsthetes among the founders of the Nazi party in the 1920's. They would gather in Munich's Greenwich Village for their beer-parties. There flawlessly efficient plans for a war of extermination against France would alternate with tearful wails against Jewish critics for damning their paintings or poems. That is why a leading Munich journalist labelled the Nazi party of the early 1920's "an armed bohemia." This was no idle *bon mot* nor intended as a scornful epithet. Nor did it minimize their menace, but rather was intended to maximize it.

In pursuit of both their political and their æsthetic ambitions, the Nazis have organized German æsthetes into a "Kultur Senate" and a "Reich Chamber of Literature." Member of the former and 1938 President of the latter is the poet Hans Blunck. In 1938 many chief Nazi officials in all fields wrote an important joint anthology, *Germany Speaks,* to present the Nazi Weltanschauung in up-to-date form. Blunck was chosen to write the official article on Nazi "Kultur policy." His highly interesting arguments are additional evidence for the "Greenwich Village warrior" approach to the psychology of Nazi leaders.

Blunck begins by stressing how "strange" yet "symbolic" is the state's selection of himself, "a poet and writer of fairy-tales," for this article on state policy when the state could easily have selected one of its strictly political leaders. He makes the selection symbolize the following three facts about the link between nazism and artistic temperament:

First, the Republic was overthrown in Germany partly by the opposition of many influential artist-intellectuals. From 1918 on, these "idealists" acted as they did for nazism against democracy because they consciously carried on the militant nationalism which earlier romantics had set, in the War of Liberation, as a sacred tradition for German artist-intellectuals ever after.

Second, artists rank as chief gainers (this is Blunck speaking!) from Hitler's dictatorship. As evidence, Blunck boasts that the amount of grand opera (!) has increased (especially Wagner's) and that Hitler has abolished unemployment among the poor starving artists, the musicians among whom had been fifty per cent unemployed. These citations may well be statistically correct; but Blunck naturally ignores the question of how far art and intellect " gain " from this economic rescue of the unemployed among their members when art and intellect must now be prostituted into propaganda for tyranny and nonsense.

Third and most important, " this [Nazi] government is composed of members half of whom are men who originally intended to devote themselves to some creative work." That fact gives the Nazi leaders " religious convictions " about the " importance of artists " as the Volk's " mediators." That fact also explains the Hitlerites' strong psychological hold on Germany, their hold on the romantic " German soul." For, as Blunck concludes with extreme shrewdness, " This government, rooted in opposition to *rationalism*, is well aware of the nameless longing of the Volk it governs, of their dreams that sway between heaven and earth, which can be explained and expressed only by the *artist*." [6]

Unique in history is a dictatorship by leaders " half of whom originally intended " a career of creative art. That could happen in almost no other country than Germany. It would be the highest compliment to Germany for attach-

---

[6] *Germany Speaks* (London, 1938), Blunck's article, pp. 229, 234, 243, 238–9.

ing such importance to culture — except for one fact: they are almost all very bad artists. Almost all were failures, not only by the usual vulgar criterion of success but by their own artistic criteria. Almost all blamed Jewry for their failures. They blamed the alleged Jewish control of press, of publishing, of æsthetic criticism.

Blunck makes a bad slip on their behalf when he writes elsewhere: " Every one of them has produced a life's work which at this late stage [*after* the Hitler dictatorship] is appearing before the public for recognition and appreciation for the first time." That sentence unintentionally admits their failure except under prejudiced Nazi subsidy. But sometimes Blunck achieves a really wise analysis of them. He rightly traces their spiritual ancestry back to those members of the romantic school whose work passed from books into bullets in the War of Liberation. He rightly credits nazism's " secret poets " with much of the successful appeal of the Nazi revolution. What he calls their anti-democratic " *Fronde* " of " romantic nationalism " did indeed " transmute politics by applying ' the eternal German romanticism.' Scepticism and negation were swept aside, and in their place was a new creative will." [7]

To " transmute politics " is another way of saying that when a frustrated romantic artist vents his spleen in politics he transmutes politics into metapolitics. In no country but Germany (and Japan) is it taken as a matter of course that a ferocious battle-scarred soldier and Storm Troop leader like Röhm dashed off his thoughts in hexameters. Some of his verse, which at least scans well, he addressed to Hitler, as did Eckart and Schirach. An armed bohemia!

Following are examples of key founders of nazism whose most burning ambition, before they entered politics, was

[7] Roberts: *House*, pp. 243–5.

in spheres of art and inspirational philosophy. Hitler: painting of romantic landscapes, architecture. Goebbels: drama, novel, poetry. Rosenberg: architecture, philosophy. Eckart: poetry, drama. Baldur von Schirach (leader of the Hitler Youth and Governor of Austria): poetry. Funk (Nazi Minister of Economics): music. C. Schmitt: philosophy. H. Grimm: novel. Houston Chamberlain: literature, philosophy. The Nazi half of Stefan George's circle, such as Ludwig Klages, Blüher, Friedrich Wolters: poetry, philosophy. The Nazi half of the Bayreuth circle: music. Widely broadcast by Goebbels in 1933, the slyest Nazi rebuttal to anti-Nazi refugees was typically not by a politician but a leading poet: Gottfried Benn. Benn's reward for calling Hitler "the Führer we all worship": becoming Hitler's "Acting Leader of the Poetry Section, Prussian Academy of Arts," whence true arts were hounded — and soon Benn himself, his "worship" sincerely over.

W. Funk exemplifies the arty frustrated musician who becomes a high Nazi. Earlier, he had worked with Jewish bankers, those same Jewish bankers called by the Nazis the "secret dictatorship of gold" known as plutodemocracy.

(This anti-Semitic myth stems partly from Wagner's similar one about Jewish capitalists. In Hitler's speeches it now includes Aryan as well as Jewish capitalists, even after his 1941 break with his Soviet ally, because of the increasingly radical dynamics of his mass revolution. According to this popular Nazi and Wagnerian myth, all democracy is a secret dictatorship of Jewish capitalists who mask themselves by financing puppet Marxist parties. They allegedly " fool the workers " by pretending to be socialists and by stealing the anti-capitalist phrases of the self-styled " true " (national) socialism of Fichte, Wagner, the nationally-socialist Jew Lassalle, and Hitler. This cruel Nazi lie about Jewish gold has been often and easily disproved. Yet it was sincerely believed by a large part of the German lower classes, above all among the unemployed and the lower middle class.)

Despite all Funk's former Jewish connections, Hitler has chosen him both as Minister of Economics and president of the Reichsbank. America would tend to fill both such jobs with men leaning temperamentally more toward the prosaic than toward Greenwich Village. Funk puts dash and glamour into economics for the masses by hymns from Wagner against " gold " (symbol of capitalism, Jewish usury, and the Versailles reparations). Funk's burning ambition was and is to be a great musician. He himself declares his artistic destiny " thwarted " by his " economic calling." It is a fact that this *rara avis* among orthodox economists " is more frequently seen in the company of artists than with tried economists at directors' meetings." [8]

For all these Nazi leaders, art was a chief ambition. Even for many of the rest, art was at least a more important side-issue than it would be in most non-German countries. A specific example: the Nazi Foreign Minister Ribbentrop personally penned a play in the 1920's, called *In the Path of the Führer*. Another example: Hess, Germany's erstwhile deputy-Führer, takes very seriously his romantic poetry. It could find no publisher until after 1933; the same is true of the literary efforts of most of the other Nazi would-be geniuses. Even the grotesque Julius Streicher, Führer of the Franconian province and editor of the unspeakable *Stürmer,* is no exception. According to the Nazi *Who's Who,* he nurses ambitions as a water-colour artist.

The highest placed exception is Göring. Appropriately he is Governor of Germany's most unbohemian province, Prussia. In personal life Göring's role, partly pose and

[8] Oswald Dutch: *Hitler's Twelve Apostles* (New York, 1940), p. 201.

partly reality, is as the bluff, hearty, no-nonsense-now sort of fellow who prefers hunting with an English Ambassador to sitting with Hitler and Goebbels at a five-hour Wagner concert. No wonder British Tories, before the war, fell for Göring hook, line, and sinker, as the admiring reports of their Ambassador Henderson indicate.

Not having gone to Eton, all Nazis are cads to British diplomats. But the latter pinned their hopes on Göring as being the nearest approach to a gentleman of which a Nazi is capable. In sharp contrast with both Germans and French, many British gentlemen find artistic temperament simultaneously too sinister and too enthusiastic to be respectable. The result of this English faith in Göring is that today he is no longer confined, as during Henderson's sojourn, to hunting boars in East Prussia; he now hunts human game with his air force in England.

The amateur artists among Nazi leaders are often closely allied with some of the leading professional artists. The latter include Blunck, the " poet and writer of fairy-tales "; Hanns Johst, the poet and official Nazi dramatist; and such widely read novelists as Hans Grimm and Kolbenheyer. All did their bit in undermining loyalty to the Weimar Republic.

Not all these literary nationalist grave-diggers of democracy were Nazis. Many formed the ultra-nationalist *" Fronde "* of the "Wartburg circle." Many wrote before 1933 for the influential magazine *Die Tat* and for similar political-romantic-æsthetic magazines. Such romantic ultra-nationalists were rarely Nazi party members, but often they acted in alliance with the Nazis against the common enemy, democracy, and paved the Nazi way.

Like the Nazi leaders themselves, and much earlier, the pre-Nazi founders of nationalism as a religion were almost all men of intense æsthetic ambitions. That includes the

Herder school, the "Storm and Stress," the romantic school
of 1800, the neo-romantics of the 1890's, the musician
Wagner and his Bayreuth circle.

The would-be tough-minded, feet-on-the-ground materialist will doubt the importance of æsthetic motive in Nazi
psychology. He will treat these artistic ambitions of Nazi
leaders as mere hobbies. On the contrary, these ambitions
were originally far deeper than political ambitions in most
of the cases we have named and were integral parts of
their personalities. The two deepest emotional experiences
of Hitler's youth were æsthetic. The one was an ecstatic
experience, the other his deepest anguish. The former was
his hysterical and almost religious worship of Wagnerian
music. The latter was when the Vienna Art Academy
ended his artistic career by rejecting his paintings as officially "below standard."

Even since his triumph as dictator, the worship of cheering millions cannot heal that psychological wound. It is
still his anguish today. Hitler was for once not the cunning
demagogue nor the ruthless *Realpolitiker,* but he was
wearing his heart on his sleeve when he declared just before the World War of 1939:

"All my life I have wanted to be a great painter in oils.
I am tired of politics. As soon as I have carried out my program for Germany, I shall take up my painting. I feel that
I have it in my soul to become one of the *great artists of
the age* and that future historians will remember me *not*
for what I have done for Germany, but for my art." [9]

If Hitler could conquer all he wants to conquer, I'd
imagine his dramatic retirement from the Führership into
the Olympian heights of Berchtesgaden to paint and to

---

[9] According to British Ambassador Henderson. Nevile Henderson:
Failure of a Mission (New York, 1940). *Time,* New York, September 11,
1939, p. 29.

write sentimental memoirs. Like Nero, his dying words might be: "What an artist dies in me!" And somehow a Hitler would never think of dying unless in front of a mirror and surrounded by reporters and photographers. As perhaps with Nero, so with the Nazis, the æsthetic frustration helps explain the bitter cruelty. A basic observation of psychiatrists is that frustration finds its outlet in aggression. Look over the speeches and writings of Hitler, Goebbels, Rosenberg, and the rest. In these men hate, revenge, and persecution complex predominate emotionally over love, peace, and construction.

Conceivably some readers, laudably eager to treat enemies with fair play, may feel that these frustrated æsthetes were really men of æsthetic ability. The only answer is to read their works and look at their paintings, and then decide for yourself. Even in Nazi Germany the decision is nearly unanimous on that score.

Conceivably a few readers might even go further and half-believe the fanatic and probably sincere convictions of Hitler and the rest that their failures under the Republic were due not to lack of merit but to unfair Jewish critics. In a few cases such unfair treatment probably existed to a small degree, but basically and generally this slanderous excuse for almost all the Nazi failures is due to frustration and persecution complex. That is not merely a personal guess but a fact easily proved. The most obvious proof is an ironic one: even in Nazi Germany, with Nazi critics, these failures generally are just as great as in the days of Jewish critics. For example, one of the first Nazi acts was to produce the lyrical romantic dramas of Goebbels and of the deceased Eckart. But the plays of both had to be dropped as complete failures. Earlier, alleged Jewish press influence could be blamed for their rejection. Who is to blame this time?

Eckart had even resorted to signing his plays with Jewish pseudonyms. He inserted sympathetic Jewish characters in them, though naturally with his fingers crossed. He honestly expected that a Jewish name would automatically win him the success so long denied him as an anti-Semitic Wagnerite. He was honestly baffled when his plays were rejected as emphatically as ever. Who was to blame this time? [10]

Schirach's lyrics now have state backing. He inserts them in the official anthologies he controls. But even Nazi readers consider his verse a sentimental imitation of Stefan George without the original's fine frenzy and poetic fire. Rosenberg's philosophy, to be sure, has triumphed at last inside Germany; its pretensions to merit will be scrutinized in detail in a separate chapter. As for Hitler's vague romantic paintings, the reader can judge for himself.

Consider the notorious public "burning of the books." In this the disappointed playwright Goebbels was imitating a similar episode in which Father Jahn was the leader, not long after the War of Liberation. Most of the books the Nazi youth tossed into the bonfires were not political but literary. Among their authors were so-called Kultur-bolshevists, Jews, many conservative and liberal western-minded writers, internationalists, and writers against whom Nazis bore special grudges, like Thomas and Heinrich Mann.

The burning was interpreted abroad as proving the Nazis hostile or indifferent to art. The direct opposite is true. It proves how much more seriously Germany takes art than most countries, how much more excited she gets over it — excited enough to burn it. Even today Germans buy and read proportionately far more literary books, far more poetry above all, than do Americans, just as they still

---

[10] A. Reich: *Dietrich Eckart* (Munich, 1933), pp. 49–53.

under Hitler far exceed us in widespread appreciation of serious music.

What the book-burning does show is the bad artistic taste of the Nazis; but bad taste in art does not mean indifference or hostility nor absence of artistic temperament. Often it is the symptom of too much arty temperament, to the point of bohemianism. In the Nazi leaders bad taste is a symptom of a love for the arts which is unduly romantic and subjective and fanatic, and hence undiscriminating. In short, the book-burning, often cited to refute the following point, only confirms it: that in Germany the political leaders take æsthetics far more seriously than in America or most other countries.

The Nazis and the Nationalists were the Republic's two chief opposition parties of expansive nationalism. The former was socialistic; the latter was conservative and Junker, and was dissolved by Hitler after 1933. But before 1933 they often worked closely together against their common enemies. Hugenberg was the leader of the Nationalist party. He first made Hitler respectable and helped finance him on his way to power. If the leader of the Nazi party is an ex-painter, the leader of the former Nationalist party is a former lyric poet whose verse had been published before the World War.

Partly as a direct consequence, both Hitler and Hugenberg were men of unusual and daring imagination in politics, not to mention the all too imaginative Goebbels and the rest. This consequence was not only a symptom of their artistic temperament but a victory-achieving sublimation of it. In contrast, consider the unimaginative, dry-as-dust politics of the Social Democrat trade-union bureaucracy, uninspiring and hence ineffectual.

Almost no political public is more susceptible to romantic appeals than the German. The Republic and its Social

Democrat leaders never really caught the public's imagination. What did they ever know of the Volk's " dreams that sway between heaven and earth "? (Blunck should have added: " and hell," and his mob psychology would be complete.) More than all the Weimar bureaucrats, a moody, romantic ex-artist like Hitler can play, as on a musical instrument, on " the nameless longing of the Volk, which can be explained only by the artist."

THE ''GERMAN SOUL''

The example of Italy, Germany, and even Spain may suggest to some that fascism triumphs most easily in the countries steeped in grand opera. Such a provocative generalization borders, of course, on absurdity. Still, it is a suitable take-off for a flight into what romantics call the " German soul."

Grand opera! The operatic and æsthetic-bohemian side of Nazi leaders will seem to many Americans more compatible with feminine softness than with animal ferocity, concentration camps, and war. That holds true in our American *mores*. But the opposite is true of Germany, as my many examples of Nazi leaders have indicated. In fact, the un-arty slums of Chicago have produced few such tough guys as a sensitive æsthete named Hitler and his lethal comrades.

Emotional artiness and a sentimental attitude toward history are in modern Germany (as in Japan — and in the Marquis de Sade!) compatible not with softness and inefficiency but with cruelty, military courage, and a burning ruthless will to power. Indeed, that same juxtaposition of qualities characterizes to even greater extremes the non-Aryan member of the Axis. The Japanese are the most sensitive, courteous, and beauty-loving of peoples, the most delicate painters of vases, the most refined composers of *hokku* verse, and — the sackers of Nanking in what was the most brutal and sadistic atrocity of this century.

To catch the spirit of nazism's most nauseating strain, picture something like this: Picture two blond young Storm Troopers, battle-scarred but starry-eyed, burning a defenceless synagogue or kicking in the stomach a concentration-camp prisoner while murmuring dreamily: "We Germans are incurable romantics!" Strange indeed are the ways of romantic idealism and Teutonic heroism. If our Storm Troopers were more literate (as fans, say, of Krieck or Schirach or Goebbels), they might have added: "Always following the gleam of the blue flower of idealistic yearning — like Faust or Horst Wessel or that true nordic, Jesus. Becoming instead of being. Striving instead of bourgeois contentment. Blood instead of gold."

Goebbels's novel, Ernst Krieck's magazine *Volk in Becoming,* and the writings and speeches of Hitler and Rosenberg teem with such purple passages. Novalis was a chief founder of romanticism in 1798. His one novel created the famous search for the unattainable "blue flower" ("*die blaue Blume der Romantik*"). Later generations have made this ceaseless futile search for the mystic flower into the best-known symbol of the "German soul," symbol of its ceaseless longing (*Sehnsucht,* a key-word) and its ceaseless striving (*Streben,* another key-word). A hundred years of such vague ecstasy about the German soul have ended by equating its "ceaseless longing" with that particular "nameless longing of the Volk" (Blunck) of which Hitler's military dictatorship is the sole official oracle.[11]

The German soul! It is a favourite sport of Germans, not

[11] Joseph Goebbels: *Michael* (2nd ed., Munich, 1931). E. Krieck, editor: *Volk im Werden,* monthly (Leipzig, from 1933 on). Novalis (pseudonym of Friedrich von Hardenberg): the novel *Heinrich von Ofterdingen,* included in *Novalis Schriften* (2 vols., 3d ed., Berlin, 1815).

only intellectuals, to introspect with awe-struck adoration
the misty labyrinths of their own " German soul." In almost all intellectual or literary books devoted to explaining
Germany, whether by Nazi or anti-Nazi romantics, the
phrase " the German soul " crops up at the core of every
problem. In fact, several different books on Germany have
that very phrase as title.

The writings about the German soul must follow certain
tacit conventions. That means treating it simultaneously
in two ways: as tenderly as a sensitive, exotic butterfly
wing, yet as brutally as befits a " dæmonic," " cosmic "
" Life-force " (all key-words) capable of putting the whole
globe to the sword by sheer military efficiency.

No doubting Thomas has ever succeeded in touching
this German soul, and none of us doubters has ever seen
it. No, no, you must take it on faith and on the " healthy
Volk-instinct " and " Will to Destiny " of your subconscious
Faustian " Life-force," or else you are nothing but an un-
nordic rationalist and Kultur-bolshevist. As with " dæmon," any definition in mere words is out of the question;
one must be noble enough to feel the inner glow.

All these phrases from the philosophers of subjective
idealism make the whole subject of the German soul sound
loftily impractical and ethereally unselfish. Yet its cash
value (" We artists must live ") is not to be sneezed at.
Though we still don't know what it means, we have learned
to appreciate with something like awe the German soul's
vast material usefulness, its protean *convenience.* It is the
most convenient excuse ever devised by ambition for escaping the obligations of decent external law, whether
moral, political, international, or artistic. In this function
of freeing the egotist from normal human obligations, it
resembles what psychiatrists define as a neurosis.

The lesser breeds, who lack this marvellous convenient

neurosis, have in the past committed just as many crimes as the Germans; to deny this would be to slander Germany. But with these undæmonic lesser breeds, a crime is a crime (except for a certain type of moralizing Anglo-Saxon hypocrite); it is something one feels a bit squeamish and uncomfortable about. The beautiful convenience of the German soul is that it enables one (like Goethe's caddish Faust) to commit a crime and yet feel ecstatic and romantic about it.

Picture, if possible, a handsome, clean-shaven, and good-naturedly sadistic gangster, who kills for love of killing and yet always looks like a boy scout following the gleam. Picture him sobbing tearfully over Wagner's *Liebestod* motif and banning Jewish kosher cooking as inhumane to poor defenceless animals. You are picturing the Horst Wessel strain of Nazi psychology. You are picturing the ideal of many of the more educated section of Storm Troop leaders.

When the German soul deigns to speak through its oracles, whether in politics or literature, it speaks in cloudy rhetoric. Rhetoric is its trademark, the best proof of its *bona fide* genuineness. This brings us back to Germany's second romantic revolution of the 1890's. French writers of all schools were finally taking rhetoric behind the barn and wringing its neck. Verlaine pled: "*Prends l'éloquence et tords-lui le cou!*" At that same time, always contrary to the French, many German neo-romantics were wringing the neck of clarity and banishing understatement, restraint, and law as uninspired. Above all, they were resubmerging all "deep" philosophy and poetry and politics in vague, highfalutin rhetoric.

This second romantic revolution often resumed from the first romantics the contrast between Kultur and civilization, the revolt of the Teutonic tribes (Volk) against western values. Since 1933 this revolt has sometimes become very barbarous. But just as often, originally, it was very sophisticated and merely *would-be* primitive. It was in the romantic tradition of the anti-intellectual intellectuals, the mystical atheists, the rootless traditionalists, the scarlet-sinning pedants, the dark-haired preachers of blond superiority, and the university Volk-proletarians.

This revolt for Kultur was becoming ever more popular and fanatic already by 1914. So the Treaty of Versailles was more acceleratory than causal in function. I cannot agree with those to whom Versailles explains everything, nor with those who deny historic causality to movements of ideas and confine politics to economic causes.

The neo-romantic æsthetes were followed by the same books-into-bullets evolution as has already been noted from Herder on. When words are sword-words, they are deeds as much as anything achieved by the self-styled man of action. The sneering distinction between men of books and men of deeds is made false by the fact that in the long run books *are* bullets. What neo-romantic æsthetes writing in the last quarter of the nineteenth century most moulded today's Nazi metapolitics? Any answer must surely include Wagner, Houston Chamberlain, Langbehn, Lagarde, Spengler *malgré lui*, the less worthy half of Nietzsche's and Stefan George's politically-split disciples.

LAGARDE AND LANGBEHN

Already in the 1880's Professor Paul de Lagarde was rejecting much of Christianity as Jewish. He replaced it by a compromise between Christianity and a new racist religion of the German Volk. From these ideas of Lagarde and Houston Chamberlain sprang Hitler's "positive Christianity," which is instilled into German youth today. For the

German Volk, Lagarde coined the label " the Master Volk,"
a favourite phrase of Hitler and all Nazis.[12]

Paul Anton de Lagarde was born in Berlin in 1827 and
died in 1891. Lagarde is his adopted name; his real name
was the very commonplace one of Bötticher. After studying theology and Oriental languages at Berlin, Halle, London, and Paris, he received the high post of Professor of
Oriental Languages at Göttingen in 1869. Like Gobineau
and so many other racists, Lagarde was a learned Orien-
talist. The brief article which the *Encyclopædia Britannica* devotes to Lagarde deals almost exclusively with his
pedantic research into Asiatic philology, now mostly forgotten by the world, and devotes only a line or two —
" Lagarde also took some part in politics " — to what is
historically his most important side today. For his Oriental
scholarship led him to a new interpretation of the Bible by
which the Jews are the arch-fiends of history and by which
the Christian churches, save where purged of their Jewish
origins by a German " awakening," are the curse of the
nordic super-race.

Lagarde's new interpretation made such an influential
sensation in the 1880's that Richard Wagner enviously accused him of trying to make anti-Semitism and the new
German nationalism his private monopoly. It will be seen
how Lagarde's anti-Semitic Biblical criticisms were to be
applied in modern German church politics by his loyal disciple, the Nazi educator Alfred Rosenberg.

Lagarde is a leading founder of the extremely important
concept of *Mitteleuropa*. This means an economic and
semi-political union of central and Balkan Europe administered by efficient German technicians in a vast German-
dominated empire. The idiotic Versailles system, by de-

---

[12] The summary of Lagarde (real name: Bötticher) is from his
Deutsche Schriften (2 vols., Göttingen, 1878–81).

stroying the ancient Hapsburg Empire, turned central and southeastern Europe into a lot of autonomous little snarling nationalisms committing economic suicide by their mutually destructive tariff walls. In contrast with this Versailles system the *Mitteleuropa* concept has a great deal to recommend it to all concerned — provided the non-Germans retain certain basic liberties and suffer no racist discrimination. But this proviso will hardly be possible under a Hitlerian mentality.

In 1915 Friedrich Naumann's book *Mitteleuropa* converted German liberals during the World War to a tolerant and liberal version of this sensible concept.[13] Haushofer (the "geopolitician") and Rosenberg converted young Hitler to this concept, reverting to the original intolerant and illiberal version of Lagarde. Today Hitler and his technicians have made *Mitteleuropa* an economic and political and military fact. Like all his ambitions, this dream (aside from its obvious economic causes) originated not from resentment of the cruelties of Versailles but with all these romantic nationalists and neo-romantics of the nineteenth century.

In 1890 appeared one of the most important proto-Nazi books, *Rembrandt as Educator,* by Julius Langbehn.[14] It ran through many editions in the neo-romantic 1890's and has again been popularly revived by the Nazis. Langbehn signed himself anonymously as "the Rembrandt-German," a label which quickly caught the popular fancy. By strained arguments Langbehn forced the helpless dead Rembrandt to be his chief symbol, but that is not the main point. The point is what the symbol stood for. Langbehn made it stand for the primitive and unspoilt Saxon, the

---

[13] Friedrich Naumann: *Central Europe,* translated by C. Meredith (London, 1916).

[14] J. Langbehn: *Rembrandt als Erzieher* (4th ed., Leipzig, 1890).

" true " German of the north, as opposed to the decadent Romanized German of the southwest.

Two of Langbehn's chief chapters are on " German Art " and " German Politics," two topics which are almost synonymous in romantic metapolitics. His ideas are mostly derived from Lagarde, but are made far more readable and reached a far wider public. These ideas of Langbehn's book prepared his large German public for Hitler, so a brief summary of them is needed today. To be German is a matter of blood, Kultur, and heroic temperament. Therefore Rembrandt and Shakespeare are typical German artists, Holland and England being mere geographical expressions. To a great extent blood subconsciously determines all art and all political ideology and action.

The future would be a contest of speed between the races. The goal is world dominion, with the Aryan naturally Langbehn's favourite horse and the Semite as a sinister dark horse plotting to steal victory by some dirty trick. Aryan blood has two supreme expressions: art and war, the former for itself and the latter for its neighbours.

Logically, no particular link unites art and war. Yet these two are coupled as a single Janus-faced idol by most of these Greenwich Village warriors, from the speeches of Fichte through the speeches of Hitler and the books of Langbehn, Lagarde, Chamberlain, George, Rosenberg, Goebbels. Their philosophy is that of æsthetes with brass knuckles. Specifically, art and war mean only romantic art and efficient totalitarian war. Both are practised successfully to the full in the Third Reich. But in everyday German life, in the hands of the Nazi Kultur-Babbitts, the twin heroisms of art and war degenerate into the twin sordidnesses of sentimentality and brutality.

Langbehn's book is another example of how almost every Nazi tenet was being widely circulated three decades before Versailles. He tries to prove that the German race is the natural ruling race all over the globe, whether in Europe or America. The sturdy Saxon stock of Germany is to dominate the globe by means of the instinctive subconscious forces conjured up by cultivating its own organic folkdom. All this was taken over by Alfred Rosenberg, including Langbehn's evidence that most great geniuses, including Shakespeare, were really Germans.

Fantastic are Langbehn's visits to the anti-nationalist Nietzsche in his lunatic asylum. Langbehn boastfully and foolishly announced beforehand that his magic folkic powers would exorcize the demons haunting Nietzsche's soul and would thereby restore him to sanity. The demons must have been shamelessly unfolkic, for poor Nietzsche still had enough sane moments left to beg that Langbehn be thrown out as a fraud. Langbehn explained away his failure by charging that devils of hell irrevocably possessed Nietzsche's soul.[15]

Langbehn has been summed up as a man who " wanted to be a sort of secret potentate and laid claim to a magical power, which he did, as a matter of fact, exert for a time." [16] But do these words not also describe a large number of the other Germans we have been considering? " Secret potentate " and " magical power ": were not these also in part the ambition of Nietzsche, Wagner, Stefan George, many of the earlier romantics, Father Jahn, and Hitler himself? This ambition is linked to the German concept of the dæmonic superman.

These dæmonic ambitions are found in German literature and life far more prominently than in most other countries. These elements make the average western reader and observer distinctly uneasy. They seem, to his more ra-

---

[15] Cf. Podach: *Nietzsches Zusammenbruch.*
[16] Eloesser, op. cit., p. 347.

tional and material outlook, morbid and potentially dangerous to the world, sinister and yet a bit fascinating. They help account for the frequent, often exaggerated accusations of "megalomania" and "paranoia" hurled against Germany. During the 1914 World War, Santayana cast such accusations upon Germany's chief thinkers in his *Egotism in German Philosophy*.[17] Ever since the romantic school, Germany has exceeded most countries in gullible love for "secret potentates" with "magic power," of whom the brilliant word-magician Stefan George is the extreme example.

FROM "VOLK WITHOUT ROOM" INTO "LEBENSRAUM"

In Hitler's Germany, Langbehn and Lagarde naturally have far more disciples than in their own lifetime. Among their disciples, Hans Grimm is clearly one of the most intelligent and influential. He is one of the ablest writers active in Nazi Germany.

Grimm's epoch-making book is *Volk without Room* (*Volk ohne Raum*), a Pan-German classic since 1926. This is the book that popularized the concept of *Lebensraum* (national living-space), with which Germans today salve their conscience for all territorial expansion. Grimm's writings don't stop at proving the economic need of cramped Germany to expand. Besides the prosaic need, they prove the romantic duty; for the "nordic nations" have a "mission" to "lead the peoples of this earth."[18]

Grimm had spent his life in Africa before the World War. He loved Germany with all the fervour of the intel-

---

[17] G. Santayana: *Egotism in German Philosophy* (New York, reprinted, 1940).

[18] H. Grimm: *Volk ohne Raum* (2 vols., Munich, 1929; 1st ed., 1926); and *Amerikanische Rede* (Munich, 1936).

lectual whose fear of becoming rootless makes him lean over backwards toward peasant earthiness. Important is a certain ideal figure exalted by Grimm's book, also exalted by Lagarde and Langbehn, and given a rosy poetic glow in non-political German literature by excellent writers like Immermann. This ideal figure is the sturdy north-Saxon peasant. The ideal, at least as retouched by German painting and literature, is an attractive one. Taken by itself, it is just as compatible with the American farmer-democracy of Jefferson and Jackson as with nazism. But Nazi writers make this ideal peasant justify any number of their aims, not always implausibly, from the revolt against urban " French ideas " to aggressive expansion to win him more *Lebensraum*.

We are starting off on the wrong foot if we seek to explain Nazi Germany's persistent demands for *Lebensraum* solely by her economic needs. Other countries are more overpopulated and economically cramped than the Germany of the Republic or of Hitler; yet they have not developed this " Volk without room " psychology. The boundaries of pre-1914 Germany were sufficient to give Germany the greatest economic prosperity she has ever had before or since. They were emphatically good enough for Bismarck. He called Germany a " saturated nation." He considered that further expansion would be one of those useless blunders which are worse than crimes. He did all he could to discourage the expansive program of the Pan-Germans, who were then demanding exactly the same empire of *Lebensraum* (the Balkans, Austria, Czechoslovakia, Holland) which Hitler was later to seize.

To sum up, this *Lebensraum* expansion not only has economic and strictly political causes but would be unthinkable unless these factors were reinforced by the books-into-bullets of a century of romantic nationalists, whose motives were more æsthetic and philosophic than economic.

It is hard to explain the frenzied emotional pressure behind the German urge for expansion. Yet this pressure is real and is something more subtle and more tragic than the mere brutal lust for aggression which it seems to anti-Germans today. All the writers we have been considering, with their pressure for ceaseless expansive "becoming" in all fields (intellectual as much as territorial), have an air of being ever on the verge of suffocation in a cramped hall-bedroom. A blend between a cunning unscrupulous "con" man and a very daring, very restless Faust, Hitler temperamentally is like the claustrophobe who feels smothered in any closed room, no matter how large, and must smash all its windows, gasping: "Give me air!" [19] This pathologically *cramped* feeling of needing to smash out wildly in all directions is typical of many aspects of modern German life as a whole. Consider this feeling in conjunction with the tense emotional atmosphere of the following lines of Yeats, in which the fanatic German "Volk without room" need only be substituted for Ireland. Explaining why "nothing said or done can reach my fanatic heart," the poet cries:

> Out of Ireland have we come.
> *Great hatred, little room,*
> Maimed us at the start.
> I carry from my mother's womb
> A fanatic heart.[20]

[19] Virginia Woolf called the great Irish novelist James Joyce "a desperate man who feels that in order to breathe he must break the windows." Max Lerner has brilliantly applied this remark to the Führer in "Hitler as a Thinker," *New Republic*, New York, November 22, 1939, pp. 132–3.

[20] W. B. Yeats: *Collected Poems* (New York, 1938), p. 293. Quoted by permission of The Macmillan Company, publishers. Italics mine.

"GREENWICH VILLAGE" VOTES FOR
BARABBAS

Many leading intellectuals of the world as a whole took a conspicuous stand against Hitler from the start. This fact has led many outside Germany into the illusion that nazism was a movement of illiterates and boorish cavemen and had somehow less "ideology" and fewer intellectuals among its leaders than other new political philosophies, such as communism. Nazi ideology was dismissed abroad as something hastily improvised, something not taken seriously by even the Nazis, a mere rationalization for murder and sadistic terror; in short, something without such old and serious philosophical roots as Marxism. This illusion is still widespread today outside Germany.

Actually, the more avowedly anti-intellectual and folkic or proletarian a movement is, the more will certain intellectuals crowd around it like bees around honey. This was true of the original romantic school and of the neo-romantics and in the 1920's and 1930's of Hitler's political romantics. Surely even among the quibbling pedants-in-overalls of Marxism you will find few more intellectual anti-intellectuals than some of the men here examined.

Most of these leading Nazi ideologists (except for the brilliant George circle) may justly be denied the status of first-class thinkers. But neither do they deserve to be dismissed with the haughty contempt usually accorded them in America. Rather, these German word-warriors (like Langbehn, Lagarde, Eckart, Gottfried Feder, Darré, Ernst Krieck, Count Reventlow, Funk, Goebbels, Rosenberg) generally have a status midway in-between the first and the third rate. They strike an unhappy medium between "Cosmic Circles" and Babbitt, between Parnassus and propaganda.

Professors, philosophers, and creative artists, these men were often of the highest education and mental gifts, and truth was their calling. But when the cock crowed in Germany's hour of need, they denied truth, and truth was dragged to execution and to concentration camps. After 1933 many of them repented. Many courageously strode to torture and prison (like F. G. Jünger) for openly calling Hitler a false saviour, scoundrel, and destroyer of German culture. But too late.

Many of the most talented German intellectuals (including Blunck, Grimm, Ludwig Klages, Krieck, Reventlow, and the rest) still support Hitler right through the worst. They have won nice book-reviews for themselves, comfortable professorships and editorships, and a halo of national glory; they have become saints. All this the repentant proto-Nazi intellectuals like Jünger and Rauschning and Otto Strasser and Edgar Jung might have had too. But they scorned it in favour of jail (Jünger), exile (Rauschning and Strasser), or death (Jung).

More important, thousands of spirits who had always been " western," and anti-Nazi even from the start, sensed that in the Third Reich the honourable, self-respecting place, the Christian place for the loyal servant of truth, is in jail and not in the bemedalled presidency of some official Kultur society.

It is bad enough when the masses shout: " Not Christ but Barabbas," though that seems to be the perennial cry of the mass man, but the Nazi philosophers sin more deeply than that. For they become not the frank hired thugs but the sainted apostles of Barabbas' streamlined Kingdom of Heaven.

CHAPTER VIII

"O SACRED MEDITERRANEAN": SOLUTION TO THE GERMAN PROBLEM

~~~~~~

Of thee the Northman by his beachèd galley
Dreamt . . . O sacred Mediterranean.

Among the chief figures cited among the " Greenwich Village warriors " were Langbehn, Spengler, Nietzsche, Wagner, and Stefan George. These thinkers exerted a tremendous anti-western influence upon Germany. Yet these very same Greenwich Village militarists were troubled by a pro-western phase. The return of these prodigal sons back from Kultur to civilization is an amazing phenomenon by itself, but it is more than that; it is a happy omen of the future of Germany as a whole.

The symbol of the return of these Germans to the west can shed light on the solution of the " German problem." The symbol is the Mediterranean. When these figures, like most great Germans, made their compromise with the west, the Mediterranean was almost always the symbol of their compromise, the harmonizer of their " two souls in one breast." Before coming to the bizarre conversions of these men, we must briefly survey what the Mediterranean actually symbolizes culturally and politically.

Metaphorically, the two different geographical terms " the Mediterranean " and " the west " are often used synonymously. That is because so many basic values of western civilization, though universal, were first consciously proclaimed in certain ancient lands of the Mediterranean shore, notably the Syrian and Greek coasts. From Palestine, Hellas, and the Roman Empire these values spread west and north and then over the whole globe. Aiming at objective validity for all, they cut across subjective national boundaries and cults. They civilized and Romanized and finally Christianized the wild Germanic and Celtic forest tribes from whom the modern English, French, Germans, and Scandinavians are descended. Today these heritages from the little " middle " sea are cherished as a matter of course in such far-off continents as America and Australia.

Our chief Mediterranean heritages are three in number: liberty, legalism, and Christianity, which we inherited respectively from the Greeks, the Romans, and the Jews. Their values, unlike Hitler's, can be universally adopted by mankind because they are not matters of racial blood and soil but of tradition and environment.

Athens was the first to develop deeply the ideal of individual liberty, the ideal of free self-expression whether in philosophy, art, or politics. That is why we can talk today about civil liberties, the Bill of Rights, the " Rights of Man."

Rome passed on to us the ideal of a law common to all. In the words of Luigi Sturzo, " The protection of a law common to all, without distinction of race or opinion, is the first, the lowest rung of freedom. If this no longer exists, a country has no right to call itself civilized or Christian."[1] Legalism is the necessary supplement to rule of reason and to Christian equity. Legalism means the west's striving, however imperfect, toward objective and universal justice. The Roman Empire, whose citizenship was open to all nationalities on equal terms, spread this ideal of law wherever Romanization pushed back the frontiers of barbarism.

Christianity added peace, neighbourly love, mercy, and charity to the more warlike classic heritage of Hellas and Rome. Christianity bore the good tidings that all men are equal before God. Christian equality, combined with Christian love toward all, outlawed morally that blemish of classical culture, slavery.[2]

These three heritages of liberty, law, and Christian love are all Mediterranean in origin. They are the ideals toward which our western civilization is ever striving, despite all our admitted economic inefficiencies and social injustices. Against these three heritages nazism consciously revolts, with all its admitted economic efficiency, in an atavistic return to the pre-Roman Teutons.

In the preceding chapter, Langbehn was cited as the Nazi hero of 1890 who crusaded against these civilizing influences and for an atavistic return to the barbarian Saxon tribes. But the story of Langbehn's end was recently suppressed in a Nazi biography of him. For he ended by repudiating his best-selling Rembrandt-Saxon book; he ended by calling for a synthesis of German Kultur with all these western values as the only salvation. He even switched from the Saxon tribes to their Christian tamer, Charlemagne, by becoming — while Hermann the Che-

---

[1] *Political Quarterly*, London, Vol. XI, no. 1 (January-March 1940), p. 5.

[2] R. A. Scott-James in the "Weekly Magazine Section," *Christian Science Monitor*, Boston, July 27, 1940, p. 11.

ruscan, Witukind, and Jahn writhed in their graves — a Roman Catholic.

Langbehn turned to the Roman church not so much for reasons of religious dogma as to symbolize his rise from nordic tribal exclusiveness to universalism; the most traditional symbol of universalism happens to be Rome. But this heritage of the political and cultural Roman world-empire is no monopoly of the Roman church as opposed to the Protestant. Protestant Christianity is every whit as western (except for the German-nationalist part of the Lutheran movement). The significance of his conversion is not a matter of the dogma of any one brand of Christianity.

Its significance is the awareness that tribal nationalism must be subordinated to the Christianity of a common humanity. The same significance, rather than a matter of specifically Catholic or Protestant dogma, applies to the dramatic and little-known last appeals to the Pope by Spengler and Nietzsche. Before his death in 1936, Spengler said that " for the world's sake the Pope should excommunicate Hitler." [3]

This was an unexpected though commendable deathbed repentance. Most of his life Spengler took " Kultur versus civilization " as his motto and glorified bloody war for its " Faustian dynamism " and "nordic vital sense." He mocked and sapped in Germany the Christian concepts of peace and humanity. He rhapsodized over "man as a heroic beast of prey." Shortly before Hitler, he gloated to thousands of impressionable readers that "ancient Barbary is reawakening . . . a sound warlike relish of one's own power." [4] Yet after three years of Hitler and after being outraged and nauseated by the bloodthirsty 1934

---

[3] *Mein Kampf* (Reynal & Hitchcock ed.), p. 761, footnote.

[4] Kolnai, op. cit., p. 216.

purge, Spengler's doting on beasts of prey turns into stark horror. Now he learns to think in terms of international humanity: "for the world's sake." Now he appeals — rightly and logically — to Christianity as humanity's best bulwark against this new barbarism.

Analogously, Nietzsche, Langbehn, and George had also indulged in a cult of war similar to Spengler's. Often they were just as fascinated as he by the atavism of what Nietzsche called "the blond beast," the healthy predatory barbarian. A few years under Hitler would have been the best cure and return to sanity for all the nineteenth-century proto-Nazis we have been discussing, including Wagner and Jahn, just as it was for Rauschning and would be for nazism's æsthete-intellectual sympathizers abroad. A proto-fascist intellectual smiles delightedly at beasts of prey so long as he is on the right side of the zoo's railing. But in the end (as in the famous limerick about the devoured lady of Niger) the smile is on the face of the tiger.

In January 1889 Nietzsche begged the Pope for a sort of League of Nations to save Germany from her coming internal barbarism and to save international civilization from Germany. Since Nietzsche signed this document "Nietzsche Cæsar," he was declared insane, no doubt rightly. As a result, the document was casually dismissed as lunatic ravings and has been ignored by historians. Yet the piquant and little-known fact is: already in that year he named the ingredients of his predicted future barbarism *specifically* as the Wagner cult (Nietzsche called the *Meistersinger* "a lance against civilization"), anti-Semitism, "atavistic attacks" of racial nationalism, and Bismarckian *Realpolitik*.

Again and again Nietzsche warned that "the Germans . . . with their Wars of Liberation . . . are to blame for

nationalism, this disease and madness most inimical to culture." Today the Nazis make a national hero of him.
Rosenberg calls him one of nazism's four intellectual grand-
parents, along with Wagner, Lagarde, Chamberlain.
Goebbels became a Nietzsche-worshipper via his Jewish
Professor Gundolf, and the hero of Goebbels's autobiographical novel carries and quotes a copy of Nietzsche's
Zarathustra with him wherever he goes. Hitler has hon-
oured the present Nietzsche shrine at Weimar with a personal pilgrimage. Some tactful friend should call to their
attention the last letters Nietzsche ever wrote.

In these letters Nietzsche urged Europe's rulers to become " good Europeans " and form " an anti-German league
to encircle the Reich " in order to " abolish Wagner, Bismarck, and all anti-Semites " and all the militaristic Pan-
German nationalists. He warned that unless this were
done now, these Wagnerites, goose-stepping nationalists,
and anti-Semites would so increase in power in Germany
that, in a future romantic " revolt against reason," they
would become the " destroyers of both German and European culture " by conquering their more rational neighbours. Are these the ravings of a madman or some of the
sanest warnings ever uttered? How would Nietzsche's
contemporary Nazi admirers answer this question? [5]

These views of Nietzsche were carried on by his ad-
mirer, the exotic poet-prophet Stefan George. When
Goebbels and the press were hailing George as a sort of
Nazi poet laureate, George expressed his horror and dis-

[5] Podach, op. cit., pp. 77, 85–6. Nietzsche: *Beyond Good and Evil*
(Modern Library), pp. 171–2; *Ecce Homo* (Modern Library), p. 127;
Unschuld des Werdens, Der Nachlass, ed. A. Bäumler (Leipzig, 1931), I,
119. Thomas Mann: " In Defense of Wagner," *Common Sense*, January
1940, p. 11. Joseph Goebbels: *Michael* (2nd ed., Munich, 1931). Alfred
Rosenberg: *Gestaltung der Idee* (7th ed., Munich, 1938), p. 17.

gust at nazism by willing that his body under no circumstances be buried in German soil. He lies buried in posthumous self-exile in Switzerland.

Like Nietzsche, the highly influential George flirted with
proto-Nazi ideas. The consequences of this, as we have
seen, were disastrous to Germany and beneficial to the
Nazis. But, like Nietzsche, George adhered in the last
analysis to his Romanized and Mediterraneanized creed.
This creed of Nietzsche and George was that Germans will
relapse into their pre-Roman barbarism unless steeped in
the civilizing influences of *la belle France.* Tenderly
George poeticized " the Frank returning to the sweet land
of France," which is a " mother to the stranger, to the
unrecognized, and to the persecuted." [6] This creed sounds
poignantly pathetic in the year 1941, when all France
("mother to the stranger and the persecuted"!) is surrendering her free way of life and being steeped in German
Kultur in turn. In fact, this creed sounds unintentionally
ironic and almost macabre today, for the carpet-bagging
descendants of the ancient Germanic tribe of " the Frank "
are only too eagerly " returning to the sweet land of
France."

The western conversion of Langbehn, Nietzsche,
George, Spengler, and the rest, if it is to be a really workable solution of the German problem, does not mean the
repudiation of all Germanism. It means the union, mutually fruitful, of the best in Germanism and in universal
Christianity, the co-operative union of the two conflicting
souls in one breast. The key to this solution is that these
tension-torn Northmen found peace and truth and harmony at last only when their minds wandered southward
to the Mediterranean-Latin-French civilization, which
lured and charmed them as if they were " belated strag-

---

[6] George: *Der siebente Ring,* the poem " Franken."

glers of the great migrations of the Germanic peoples, the *Völkerwanderung,*" still wide-eyed with wonder at the brave new world whose southern sun assuaged them of their frosty northern strife.[7]

Too frequent in German psychology to be mere coincidences are the examples of this "Mediterraneanizing" process in Langbehn, Nietzsche, Stefan George, Spengler. These four examples help justify the following generalizations about the very core of German thought. First consider what all four thinkers have in common. All four during part of their lives represented the most dangerous and brutal qualities of nazism and of aggressive egotistic militarism. All four had a tremendous influence in paving the way for Hitler's triumph. The first three, at least, are among the very chief Nazi heroes today. The final return of all four to the fold of the west is carefully suppressed from the public.

Add to this Wagner's "collapse before the Cross" in *Parsifal.* Nazis soft-pedal this phase of Wagner as much as they soft-pedal Nietzsche's and Spengler's final appeals to the Pope against German nationalism. Most of these men were not interested in Catholic-Protestant feuds about dogma as such. By turning to Rome, these five German thinkers were performing a profound symbolic act. Their act was a repetition of Charlemagne and Otto the Great and all the other German kings marching to Rome and becoming transformed from tribal German kings into universal non-national emperors of a "Holy Roman Empire."

In effect, all these proto-Nazis (Langbehn, Nietzsche, George, Spengler, and even Wagner) were saying in their highest moment: "We are Germans, but we are Romanized Germans. We want synthesis with the west. We want

---

[7] Eloesser, op. cit., p. 351.

to undo the battle of Teutoburg Forest, when Hermann
cut half the barbaric Germanic tribes off from the civilizing influences of the great world-empire. We want to save
Germany and Europe from the revolt of Kultur versus civilization, which would destroy the standards and heritages
and acquired decencies of two thousand years. In short,
we want to save Germany and Europe from all that is
meant by the terrible name Hitler, for whom we ourselves
are so much to blame." No, they could not all have named
Hitler's name in this imaginary appeal; technically that
would be quite unchronological. But Hitler and nazism
had not a single characteristic which these men did not
know and name — which they did not first worship and
then warn against long before Hitler. And long before
Versailles.

That is how these men ended, and Goethe had already
anticipated it all. Goethe strongly opposed the War of
Liberation, warned Germany against German nationalism,
and accepted both cultural and political synthesis with
France. Goethe particularly warned Germany against romanticism's revival of the Nibelungen saga as a dangerous
symptom of atavistic return to that pre-Roman barbarism
which Germans must do everything possible to restrain
and civilize. Yet — this is the paradox of all these German
leaders — Goethe, too, in his romantic and early-Faustian
half, paved the way for many Nazi traits, such as unmoral
dynamism. But Goethe's final verdict was that a German is
really great and really German only when he passes beyond Germanism.

Among the greatest Germans that Goethean tradition
has continued unbroken. It continues in exile in Thomas
Mann today. He is not only Germany's greatest living
writer but also one of her most courageous and subtlest
thinkers. Like Nietzsche, to whose inspiration Mann has

attributed his best side, and like most great Germans, Mann at different stages expressed each of the "two souls." The first World War inspired Mann to certain defences of German militarism and to setting anti-western Kultur against civilization. He was then somewhat of a German nationalist; he denounced that "civilization-intellectual" (*Zivilisationsliterat*) who can only ape the French democracy.[8] But during the present war Mann is a universalist; and thereby, by being more than German, he is being a greater German than Hitler and perhaps even more German than Hitler. For despite Hitler, the one soul is as typical of the German breast as the other, and the soul which most of the greatest Germans ended by choosing, from Goethe through Nietzsche to Mann, is not the one Hitler claims to incarnate.

Once north meets south and west in Europe, then at last comes the dawn of the "good European," who is the only lasting foundation for any workable League of Nations. Both sides need each other because each can contribute the psychological elements most lacking in the other.

German intellect has enriched our common civilization as much as has French intellect or English or American. Now Germany has temporarily seceded from us. But this international western civilization (no contradiction between international and western) must again be common to all when all work out some synthesis in way of life between the rational humanism of the clear, sunny Mediterranean sky and the elemental and dynamic thunder-forces of the formless nordic mists. If there can be any solution to the German problem, this is it, this finding of a *modus vivendi* between both sides of the Roman *limes*.

Metaphorically, every German must find his Mediter-

---

[8] Thomas Mann: *Betrachtungen eines Unpolitischen* (Berlin, 1918).

ranean. This concept is most beautifully expressed in the following ode to the beautiful "middle" sea:

Of thee the Northman by his beachèd galley
Dreamt . . . O sacred Mediterranean.
Unseen he loved thee; for the heart within him
Knew earth had gardens where he might be blessed,
Putting away long dreams and aimless barbarous
      Hunger for battle.
Thy langours thawed his bosom. . . . His racked spirit,
By thy breath tempered and the light that clothes thee,
      Forgot the monstrous gods. . . .[9]

*   *   *

1961 postcript:

Simultaneously an anti-Nazi and an anti-democratic underminer of the Weimar Republic, Stefan George reversed Napoleon's "J'aime le pouvoir comme artiste" to "J'aime l'art comme pouvoir." "Art as power" was a lure particularly sinister for the neo-romantic German audiences of the 1920's and early 1930's, as shown when several such Nietzsche-and-George disciples as Ernst Bertram tried to reconcile these two prophets of the superman with Führer Hitler. Yet Bertram soon became disgusted with the Nazis, and one of Germany's most active and daring anti-Nazi underground leaders was likewise a George disciple: Claus von Stauffenberg. He was the hero who set off the anti-Hitler bomb and *coup* of July 20, 1944; much of his stubborn nonconformity he owed to George and Nietzsche.[10] George had orginally willed his literary papers to Stauffenberg. They are now guarded in Switzerland by Robert Böhringer.

[9] G. Santayana: "Odes," V; quoted in *Comprehensive Anthology of American Poetry*, ed. Conrad Aiken (New York: Modern Library; 1929).

[10] For P. Viereck's later, fuller accounts of George and Nietzsche see his George chapter in *Dream and Responsibility* (University Press of Washington, D.C., 1953); his George article in *Antioch Review*, Spring, 1949; his indexed Nietzsche discussions in *The Unadjusted Man* (Beacon Press, Boston, 1956) and in *Conservatism: From John Adams to Churchill* (Anvil Paperback, Van Nostrand Co., Princeton, N.J., 1956). For Viereck translations of George, Hofmannsthal and Hölderlin, see *The Literary Review*, vol. 3, no. 2, 1959.

CHAPTER IX

REALPOLITIK: FICHTE, HEGEL, TREITSCHKE, HITLER

〜〜〜〜〜〜〜〜〜〜〜〜〜〜〜〜〜〜〜〜〜〜〜〜〜〜〜〜〜〜〜〜〜

> *War is the prime fact of Life, is Life itself. . . . The beast of prey is the highest form of mobile Life. . . . In the Faustian Kultur the proud blood of the beast of prey revolts against the tyranny of pure thought.*
>
> — OSWALD SPENGLER [1]

FROM FICHTE TO HITLER

Almost as hard to define as " Kultur " and " dæmonic " is *Realpolitik*. The word has seeped through all layers of the German population. In foreign-policy discussions it is a favourite equally of professors and of humble beer-table strategists. The word is pronounced with a long, throaty, truculent " r." Its pronunciation in *Realpolitik* connotes " r-r-ruthless " (*r-r-rücksichtslos,* Hitler's favourite adjective) and " r-r-realistic " (*r-r-realistisch*).

Realpolitik tends to mean ruthless power-politics. It

---

[1] O. Spengler: *Man and Technics* (New York: Alfred A. Knopf; 1932), pp. 22, 79–80; *Jahre der Entscheidung* (Munich, 1933), p. 14 (English translation, *The Hour of Decision,* New York, 1934).

means the most callous pragmatism (it "works"). It
means force (notably militarism and war) plus bluff of
force as the twin principles of foreign policy. As
Treitschke, the favourite nineteenth-century historian of
the Nazis, put it, war is the supreme court of history. We,
too, might cynically state the existence of war as an objective fact of life, a perhaps unavoidable though obviously
deplorable fact. But the Nazis state it as a fact to exult in,
sometimes even as the highest and all-absorbing national
goal.

Literally *Realpolitik* means "realist politics." It is about
as realistic as smashing the street-corner traffic lights or
substituting Stone Age clubs for due process of law. Fortunately reality is not at the beck and call of the self-styled
realists. Hitler and Rosenberg are following an unrealistic
and suicidal *Realpolitik* when they advocate that Germany
rule the globe not by peaceful consent but " by the victorious sword of the master race," for as a more truly realistic
Frenchman said, " One can do everything with bayonets
except sit on them."

Mein Kampf is a pæan to war. It has become almost a
parlour game to quote scary passages from *Mein Kampf*.
The right time for such quotations would have been before
the Munich Pact and the present war. Now they afford
every journalist a facile way of being wise after the event.
But now the time is too late for stopping Hitler with mere
words, with mere polite horror at purple passages from
the Nazi Bible.

On the other hand, such quotations are always justified
when they increase America's understanding of Hitler.
The self-analytical passages which follow best reveal his
emotional attitude toward war. They show the influence
upon his imagination of the 1813 War of Liberation. They
show him as an emotionally " unruly " youth who regrets

being born in an age of peace and as a man who vows to do something to bring about that great age of bloody wars which Nietzsche (probably more ironically than seriously) preached all too successfully to too many Germans.

> During the years of my unruly youth . . . the future appeared to belong to the " peaceful competition of nations." . . . I looked upon this period of " quiet and order " that awaited me as an unmerited mean trick of Fate. Even as a boy I was not a pacifist. Why could one not have been born a hundred years earlier? For instance, at the time of the *Wars of Liberation!* . . . The fight of the year 1914 was certainly not forced upon the masses, good God! but *desired* by the entire Volk itself. . . . To me personally those hours [1914] appeared like the *redemption from the annoying moods of my youth.* Overwhelmed by impassionate enthusiasm, I had fallen on my knees and thanked Heaven [for the outbreak of the World War] that it had granted me the good fortune of being allowed to live in these times. . . .
>
> Germany will either be a world power or not at all. . . . A highest race as the master nation, based upon the means of an entire globe, will be called upon. . . . Only the might of a triumphant sword will in the future assign us territory. . . . One makes alliances only for fighting. . . . The industrious labor of the German plow needs only to be given land by the sword." [2]

Perhaps the most far-sighted point of *Mein Kampf* is that Germany should model herself on the War of Liberation, reacting to the defeat of 1918 as she reacted to the defeat by Napoleon in 1806. Hitler sees the subsequent triumph over France of 1813–15 as the result of the nationalist regeneration propagandized by such Volk-nationalists as Stein, the poet Arndt, Father Jahn, Fichte, and the ro-

---

[2] Hitler: *Mein Kampf* (Reynal & Hitchcock ed.), pp. 204–5, 210, 946–7, 949–50, 959, 985, 977–9, 950, 953, 581. (Italics mine.)

mantics. Their role is to be imitated by the Nazis, according to Hitler, Rosenberg, and the rest. This plan of vengeance against France turned out in 1940 as predicted. In both 1806 and 1918 German humiliation released the angry energies needed for German triumph.

Mein Kampf said in 1925:

> A span of time equal to that which, between 1806 and 1813, sufficed to infuse a totally collapsed Prussia with new Life-force and fighting determination has not only lapsed unused, but on the contrary has led to an ever greater debilitation of our State [due to the fact that] the leadership of our destiny has, since the end of the War, been in the hands of Jews.

But let Jewry and its concomitant, democracy, be replaced by Hitler; then the miracle of the War of Liberation will be repeated. Here again Hitler turned out to be a prophet with honour in his own country.[3]

In the pre-Hitler past, *Realpolitik* was perhaps equally practised (tacitly) by all nations. But with frank perversity and perverse frankness, nineteenth-century Germany, like the Italy of Machiavelli, went furthest in rationalizing this deplorable practice into a glorious ideal of theory. Fichte's *Speeches to the German Nation*, during the War of Liberation, are the philosophic foundation of modern German *Realpolitik*. He preached a double moral standard: what is wicked for the individual to do becomes holy if done by the state. Unlike the individual, the state should use for victory, if needed, all possible frauds, violations of law, and violent crimes. The collective Volk-ego should be bound by no external laws or limits.

The historical background for Fichte's *Speeches* explains why so extreme a *Realpolitik* caught the German imagina-

---

3 Ibid., p. 970.

tion at that particular time. This historical context was the coming War of Liberation against Napoleon. So great were the hates of German romantics for what they called the French tyranny, and so great seemed the odds against its overthrow, that even the most bloody and scoundrel-like means seemed justified.

The historical situation led the romantics to the extrem-est statements of the Germanic racial myth that had yet appeared. German nationalism and Francophobia were widespread only among the middle class, to which most romantics belonged, and even there only among a noisy minority. Both the aristocrats and the peasant masses were apathetic to the crusade Jahn and Fichte preached. The German masses realized they were in many ways bet-ter off under Napoleon's semi-liberal Jacobin rule than under their German feudal masters. Therefore the roman-tic-school publicists of the War of Liberation turned to a tactic which Hitler has directly borrowed from them. They preached nordic self-worship and race hatred of every-thing French in order to stir to white heat the apathetic public feeling against Napoleon. Moreover, unlike mod-ern propagandists of the Goebbels school, the romantics sincerely believed the Germanic myth they preached.

Often their race hate included not only France but also the German Jews. That fact, too, appears less mysterious when viewed not in vacuo but in its historical context. Napoleon, as son of the French Revolution, made a point of freeing German Jews for the first time from their medi-æval ghetto restrictions. Consequently many Jews were more loyal to Napoleon than to their native Germany and have made poor nationalists ever since. From those days on, following the tradition of Fichte and Jahn, German psychology closely links racial myth and *Realpolitik*, the former justifying the use of the latter.

Fichte in his *Speeches* says: " Between states, there is
neither law nor right save the law of the strongest "; Germany, living more metaphysically than all other races, is
" the Volk, metaphysically destined, which has the moral
right to fulfil its destiny by *every* means of cunning and
force." Starting the myth of racial purity, Fichte calls the
Germans the most unmixed of all peoples and the closest
to the mystic powers of nature. Their unique purity and
their romantic idealism make the Germans not merely
" a Volk " but " *the* Volk."

This superiority justifies " *the* Volk " in seizing whatever *Lebensraum* it needs and expelling or enslaving other
Volk. In doing this, Germans must not be deterred by legality or by their own written promises, for *the* Volk is
above all such scraps of paper and above such sentimental
rubbish as international morality. *The* Volk must impose
a German peace on Europe. This peace must be based
not on treaties and written pledges but on brute force
alone, a self-justified force.

These axioms of Fichte's *Realpolitik* were developed
into a philosophic glorification of war by his fellow-roman-
ticist Hegel. Thence they were carried even further by
Treitschke and Houston Chamberlain and all the other
philosophers and historians who form the long but unbroken chain linking Fichte's nineteenth-century theories
with Hitler's twentieth-century practice.[4]

Ludendorff, the greatest German general of the first
World War, took up these theories of the German romantic school and carried them furthest of all. He
founded a new Wotan religion exalting "total war" as the
highest German mission, with which all civilian life must

---

[4] J. G. Fichte: *Speeches (Reden an die deutsche Nation)*. This and
the preceeding paragraph follow H. W. Steed's (debatable) summary of
Fichte in Kolnai, op. cit., pp. 8–9 — partly unjust to the partly cosmopolitan Fichte.

be co-ordinated. Ludendorff not only practised these theories in 1917 but preached them personally in Munich to his young disciples, Hitler and Alfred Rosenberg.

Like most major German thinkers, Fichte, Hegel, Treitschke, Chamberlain, and the rest suffered from the "two souls in one breast." This book deals chiefly with their anti-western soul for the simple reason that this is a book on the roots of nazism. Keeping this restriction in mind, the reader must guard against underestimating the importance of the other soul. It would be anti-German in the most unjustified and unchivalrous sense of the word to conclude from the evidence of this book that German thought has been one-sidedly anti-western and proto-Nazi. Both souls are of almost equal importance in Germany in the long run, and so far nazism has triumphed only in the short run.

Fichte is the first influential German who consciously and systematically combined nationalism with socialism and with a totalitarian system of education. That makes him a special Nazi hero today. But both Fichte and Hegel, like almost all the romantic school, originally started as Jacobin internationalists eager to exchange German for French citizenship. In fact, after the hurly-burly of the War of Liberation was done, Fichte returned in part from his fanatic national-socialist totalitarianism to cosmopolitan liberalism.[5] But this liberal soul of the greatest Germans is no more noticed by modern Nazi Germans than is Langbehn's conversion to Catholicism and to the Mediterranean.

In practice *Realpolitik* by its very brutality and clearcutness seems a pretty simple matter. Actually few psy-

---

[5] There is a summary of Fichte's alternating nationalist and cosmopolitan phases in R. Aris: *History of Political Thought in Germany from 1789 to 1815* (London, 1936).

chological motives of states and statesmen are more complex. *Realpolitik* is often and superficially explained as the " self-interest " of the state. But how meaningless! Exactly whose self-interest is meant, and exactly what or who is the " state "?

When Hitler sacrifices the lives and liberties of German individuals to his lawless power-politics, such *Realpolitik* is explained even by many of his foreign enemies as the " ruthless self-interest " of the " German Volk." That means the self-interest of a collective organic mystical entity which is greater than the sum of its individuals. Not only can we doubt the objective existence of such an entity, but in so far as it does exist (and doubtless it exists subjectively and psychologically) we should challenge as monstrous the notion that Hitler is acting in its interest.

So let us make much but not too much of *Realpolitik's* glib and apparently " obvious " explanation: self-interest. In addition, modern *Realpolitik* springs from the welding of the two chief anti-Christian heresies of the nineteenth century. These two are the " social Darwinism " (" dog eat dog," in plain English) of the west-European materialists, and the " subjective idealism " (egoism, in plain English) of the German romantic philosophers. Both these attitudes led Germany, and not only Germany, to a relativist view of ethical restraints. Both destroy the traditional Christian view, which treats morality not as relative and national but as absolute and universal.

A favourite attitude of romantic literature is to feel oneself so exalted that one acts on a plane " beyond good and evil." This notion is basic to *Realpolitik*. What sea-change did this romantic notion suffer during its evolution from Nietzsche and Stefan George to Hitler and Goebbels respectively?

Like Nietzsche's word " superman," his famous phrase

"beyond good and evil" was distorted into a favourite catchword of Nazi intellectuals. They forget he qualified that phrase by distinguishing "bad" from "evil" and by warning that he never meant "beyond good and bad." Like every civilized person, he believed in restricting national and personal conduct by standards of "good and bad." Repeatedly he called "nationalism the neurosis from which Europe suffers [by which] the Germans, with their Wars of Independence [1806–15] robbed Europe itself of its meaning and intelligence; they have led it into a blind alley." [6]

Nazism converts the twin Nietzschean concepts of superman and "beyond good and evil" into what Nietzsche most loathed: German nationalism. Hitler does this rather neatly in one of the most revealing passages of *Mein Kampf*.[7] Nietzsche's superman was an individual. Hitler collectivizes the superman into a whole organic "master nation" (Germany) and the ordinary man into the "slave nation." Hitler's justification for this "inequality of races" is "the innermost will of nature." For such German romantics, mother nature, in contrast with the ethics which man forces upon nature, is "justification" for almost every aggressive animal impulse.

Hitler demands, in so many words, that his superman "master nation" rule the "entire globe." For it is the sacred will of mother nature "to promote the victory of the better and stronger and the submission of the worse and weaker." Note his linking of "better" with "stronger" and of "worse" with "weaker." This linking not merely assumes that might is right but assumes it with that unquestioning matter-of-courseness which typifies and explains the brutality innate in all fascist thought and action.

---

6 Nietzsche: *Ecce Homo*, p. 127.
7 *Mein Kampf* (Reynal & Hitchcock ed.), pp. 579–82.

Again typically, Hitler concludes this passage by rightly insisting that his national religion of Volk " cannot grant the right of existence to an ethical idea if this idea represents danger for the racial life of the bearers of higher ethics [the Germanic race]." This is a direct collectivizing of Nietzsche's "beyond good and evil." Thereby Germany's posthumous nationalizing of Nietzsche and Stefan George is complete. In fact, an editorial footnote to this entire passage of Hitler's calls it " probably an allusion to Nietzsche " and links it with the misunderstood influence of Nietzsche and George.

Nietzsche described his superman as, above all, a " good European." The latest Nazi editions of their hero Nietzsche simply cut out the great part of his anti-nationalist passages. Especially they cut out his famous passages praising the Jews. He praised them as chief spreaders of rationalism in Germany. No slight problem for the Nazi censors are his warnings to Germans that Wagnerian anti-Semites would be the ruin of Germany and Europe.

Most German preachers of aggressive *Realpolitik* honestly deem it justified. Many sincerely consider it not a necessary evil but a necessary good, justified by Darwinian survival of the fittest. Many others justify it not merely pragmatically but in a mystical, metapolitical sense. This justification often arises from the German romantic concept of the dæmonic, which passes into the demonic as readily as Lucifer passed from archangel of light into prince of darkness. Just as the dæmonic individual can and should break all laws, so can and should a dæmonic German nation as a whole. That justifies its boundless ambition, which Hitler and Rosenberg jointly summed up as " Germany mistress of the globe by the victorious sword that takes over the world in the service of a higher Kultur."

The romantic view of the dæmonic is that the genius

and superman and Führer, whether individual or nation, whether in art or foreign politics, are justified in breaking all law — artistic, moral, political, or international. Goethe is claimed as the fountainhead of this view, with some justification in the case of the early *Faust*. But such elements were mostly repudiated in Part Two of Goethe's *Faust*. The wiser, more classical Goethe repudiated the irresponsible romanticism of his "Storm and Stress" period.

Goethe, defining the relation of genius to law, wrote: "Genius *above all* is willing to obey the law, for genius knows that art is not nature." This is the direct opposite of the dæmonic justification for *Realpolitik* and of the closely related romantic cult of nature and instinct. To romantic metapolitics, a nation practising the most ruthless and bloody *Realpolitik* could be justified as expressing the natural goodness of the collective Volk-instinct. But Goethe ended one of his greatest sonnets:

Whoever wants greatness must confine himself.
The master is revealed only by [ability to work within] limitation,
And only law can give us freedom.[8]

HEGEL AND DESTINY

War and unidealistic selfishness have always existed in all countries. How do the Nazi and fascist excuses for war differ from those of the past? The wars of the seventeenth and eighteenth centuries, of the Hapsburgs and of Louis XIV, had a dynastic motive. The nineteenth-century wars of capitalist imperialism had an economic motive. But these examples of aggression and their apologists had little inkling of that fantastic philosophy by which it is the

---

[8] Goethe's sonnet *Natur und Kunst*.

idealistic duty, the categorical imperative, of the national organism never to cease " becoming "— regardless of rational gain.

Today's romanticism applies the false contrast of becoming versus being to collective politics, instead of to æsthetic individuals like Faust. Becoming means ever growing and ever bursting all external disciplines and boundaries. The sole alternative, by this political philosophy, is the death resulting from the non-striving contentment of Faust's " tarry, you are so fair! "

Other states, such as the United States, England, and France, are not without fancy philosophic excuses for their less recent aggressions. America's version was Manifest Destiny. A fashionable British lecturer will describe India and the Crown Colonies, for certain audiences, in terms of the White Man's Burden and of that far-off, divine event of Dominion Status to which the whole creation moves. In contrast, his mind will rarely turn to reasons like *sacro egoismo* and the " need to expand or explode." Yet these are two reasons Mussolini gave for his economically unprofitable conquest of Ethiopia.

In other words, we are confronted by two almost opposite brands of culture and national psychology. There is nothing either mystic or indecent about an overcrowded nation's need to expand, even at the price of war. What drives the American and English sense of logic to desperation is that Hitler and Mussolini always couple, as a matter of course, the demand for expansion from overpopulated quarters with the·demand for even more children. The inconsistency strikes Americans and Englishmen as either imbecilic or subtly sinister. Yet romantic nationalists feel sincerely and almost instinctively that a national " organism " is doomed whose growth, both in population and in area, is static — not even declining, but merely static.

The "deepest" theologian of romantic *Realpolitik* is Hegel (1770–1831). His philosophy is a subtle, incomprehensibly subtle, refinement of the three romantic assumptions. His is a universe of pantheistic state-organisms, forever at glorious and bloody war with each other. Each, in turn, incarnates what Hegel calls an "Idea of God." Each, in turn, evolves ceaselessly through thesis and antithesis to ever grander organic syntheses.

Hegel tries to show that once Jews, then Hellenes, and now Germans have, in turn, ousted one another as the *Weltgeist*. This *Weltgeist* is the pantheistic Spirit of History. "The German Spirit is the Spirit of the new world" because it most follows what Hegel calls "Heart," has most avoided the corrupting "fusion of Roman and German blood," and has a unique feeling for organic "national totality." [9]

A dangerous expression of the romantic "repetition" is Hegel's identification of the good with the successful (what he calls "the Rational" with "the Real"). The state serving the *Weltgeist* is good no matter what it does and is. Why? *Because* it does and is (repetition). Or, more accurately, because it becomes.

Hegel is still very much alive today, among millions of men who never heard of him, in his two rival groups of disciples of Marxists and Nazis. Marx, through Feuerbach, turned Hegel's dialectic idealism into dialectic materialism. Applied to national lines, nazism and fascism substitute the German or Italian nation for Hegel's ideal of the Prussian state. Marxism substitutes the proletariat for it and transfers bodily to class lines the doctrine of ever changing thesis-antithesis. But, of course, with Marx-

---

[9] G. W. F. Hegel: *Philosophie des Rechts,* sec. 358; *The Philosophy of History,* tr. by J. Sibree (revised ed., New York, 1900), Part IV, especially pp. 341, 349–52, 420–1.

ism we are ever so much more " modern " and self-consciously hard-headed. We substitute a " common sense " economic interpretation of history for Hegel's mystic one and for Christianity's moral one. That proves we have grown too clever to be gulled by " superstitions." How " boldly " we emancipated ones thereby strike a " death-blow " at the " opiate of the people "!

Both nazism and Marxism justify the most immoral war and *Realpolitik* on national and class lines respectively. Their justification is their evolutionary relativism and Hegel's identification of Real with Rational. Having no external moral absolutes, such as the Christian and Jewish religions provide, both nazism and Marxism call a development good if it seems historically " inevitable," " destined," " determined " — " the Wave of the Future." Unfortunately for the rest of us, they won't sit back to let their so-called inevitable Destiny take care of itself.

The *Realpolitiker* defines Destiny and the " best " Kultur as military superiority. Such a definition is not merely mistaken but contemptibly, unforgivably, bestially mistaken. The climax of such Hegelian success-worship — from books into bullets — is Hitler's well-known motto that " the sole earthly criterion of whether an enterprise is right or wrong is its success." [10]

Old-fashioned socialists saw only two kinds of economics: production for profit (capitalism) and production for use (socialism). The need for subordinating economics to a foreign policy of expansive *Realpolitik* has caused a new kind of socialism. This new kind, Hitler's kind, nationalizes control of industry almost as much as would Marxist socialism, but for the purpose of war rather than

---

[10] Quoted in F. Czernin: *Europe* (New York, 1939), p. 291.

of prosperity. The best economic label we can coin for this is production for abuse.

Most Marxists deem the state completely determined by economics. Most Nazi romantics deem economics completely determined by the state. In both cases, what confronts us is a theory, *not* a condition.

TREITSCHKE, NIETZSCHE, AND BISMARCK

During the 1914 World War, Prussianism was accused of the same *Realpolitik* and "might makes right" as nazism today. Such premature crying of "Wolf, wolf!" leaves us few new epithets strong enough for the Nazis. As the contrast with Hitler shows, the alleged "might makes right" of Bismarckian and Hohenzollern Germany and of Prussian militarism was self-limited by a stern Protestant sense of duty and by that genuine *noblesse oblige* which so often atones for snobbery.

In 1914 many of our leading journalists and professors tried to prove Treitschke and Nietzsche the godfathers of the World War and the chief founders of German *Realpolitik*. Their names, frequently linked as twins, appeared throughout the pro-British propaganda of that day. The name Wagner almost never appeared.

How justified was the naming of Treitschke and Nietzsche — and how justified was their linkage? Over the naming of Treitschke, we cannot quarrel with the British publicists of yesteryear. Treitschke's influence on German mentality, especially through the German educational system, was enormous and baneful. A Saxon with Czech ancestors, he made desperate efforts to become more Prussian than the Prussians. He did indeed become the most eloquent historian of Prussia's rise. From Bismarckian statism

he soon evolved to racist nationalism, preaching it with the
fanaticism typical of Germans with Slavic surnames. He
tried to make aggressive war a popular national German
cult.

Treitschke and the Wagnerian Houston Chamberlain
were among the historians most enthusiastically discussed
by German college youth before June 1914. Their cult of
racism and war was increasing steadily even before the
World War. Therefore the Treaty of Versailles cannot be
blamed for their cult; it would probably have continued to
increase in any case.

To re-read Treitschke in 1940 is even more fruitful than
in 1914. The program for German foreign policy which he
preached in the nineteenth century is the program Hitler is
practising today. Treitschke preached and predicted the
replacement of the British Empire by a German Empire,
and, as means to this end, a coalition of "have-nots" by
which Spain would take Gibraltar, Italy Malta, and so on
for the British Empire's other key posts. Like the Englishman Houston Chamberlain and the Frenchman Gobineau,
the Slavic-named Treitschke preached and predicted the
enslavement of the Slavs in the Balkans and in *Mitteleuropa* by a Germanic super-race. Professor Treitschke's
advantage over the hundreds of more pedantic nationalist professors was his flair for quotable slogans. Such pithy
gems of his as: "The Teuton, a born conqueror, takes his
property where he finds it," circulated too freely among
Teutons and not freely enough among non-Teutons.[11]

As usual, Treitschke's pre-Nazi attacks on ideals of peace
and democracy were accompanied by pre-Nazi anti-
Semitism. In the 1880's he preached to Germans the "primeval contrast between Aryan and Semitic sensibilities."

---

[11] Heinrich von Treitschke: *History of Germany*, tr. by Eden and
Cedar Paul (New York, 1919), V, 529.

Like Wagner, he accused Jews of importing into German the "French ideas" of rationalism, legalism, and democracy. By such ideas the Jews were "undermining the foundations of state, church, and society." Like Hitler, Treitschke accused the Jews of importing such horrid concepts as emancipation of women and a free press. Freedom of the press he denounced alternately as a mask of Jewish radicals and of Jewish capitalists. Like Wagner's earlier Bayreuth manifestoes, Treitschke made Judaism synonymous with the sordid, materialistic symbol of "gold" in the minds of millions of Germans. In addition, "the Jews have in common with the French the gracefulness of vice," a dangerously "alluring" grace which is "utterly un-German." [12]

What of the linkage in America and England of Nietzsche with Treitschke and with Prussian militarism? Here is an example of the hysteria produced by this linkage in the America of 1917. Agents of the Department of Justice drew up an official procès-verbal to hunt down agents of "the German monster, Nietzsky," although this monster was both dead and mis-spelled as well as being the most anti-German of all philosophers. [13]

Actually Nietzsche gave us a brilliant accusation against Treitschke and against the whole school of historians who falsify history in order to indoctrinate nationalism. Labelling himself the "despiser of Germans *par excellence*," Nietzsche complained: "At the Prussian court I fear Herr von Treitschke is regarded as deep." Nietzsche warned against the popularity of "anti-Semitic history" and Prussian "court history, for which Treitschke is not ashamed of himself." Nietzsche rightly explained the triumph of the

---

[12] Ibid., pp. 530, 511, 517, 534, 541.
[13] Cited in H. L. Mencken's introduction to Nietzsche's *Antichrist* (Borzoi Pocket Book ed., New York, 1923), p. 15.

Treitschke school of history by the fact that " German historians " have " banned . . . that *broad* view of cultural values " and replaced it by the narrow view that " first and foremost a man must be ' German,' he must belong to ' *the* race '; only then can he decide upon all historical values. . . . ' I am a German,' constitutes an argument, ' Deutschland über Alles ' a principle." [14]

The hero of Treitschke's writings and lectures, the incarnation of his ideals of *Realpolitik* and Teutonic aggressiveness, was Bismarck. Today German unity seems a matter of course. But it seemed a miracle when, after centuries of disunity, Bismarck's genius plus the Prussian army united the Germanys in 1871. Naturally enough, Germans reasoned that whatever means were used to achieve such a superb miracle must be superb means indeed and must be a model for future foreign policy. What were these interesting means? Blood and iron! With results that speak for themselves, every German schoolboy was taught Bismarck's most parroted sentence: " Not by speeches and majority votes are the great questions of the day decided . . . but by blood and iron." [15]

Actually Bismarck's greatness as a European, as well as a German, lies not in his aggressive war policy of 1862–71 but in his self-restrained peace policy of 1871–90. The immorality of his *Realpolitik* was absurdly exaggerated by his bloodthirsty worshipper Treitschke — and by Bismarck himself in the malicious memoirs of his embittered old age. Bismarck's memoirs boast — incorrectly, as it happens — of deliberately causing the bloody Franco-Prussian War of 1870 by falsifying an official telegram to his King, the famous " Ems telegram."

---

[14] Nietzsche: *Ecce Homo* (Modern Library ed., New York), pp. 125, 129, 130.

[15] Quoted, for example, in C. D. Hazen: *Europe since 1815,* p. 255.

Consider the effect on a whole generation of German schoolboys of reading such boasts in their hero's memoirs. Such traditions, in themselves trifling, helped make modern Germans psychologically submissive to the political immoralities of the Nazis, against which Goethe's Germany would have instantly revolted. Not Bismarck but the Bismarck legend is Germany's curse today.

The revolutionary National Assembly of 1848 tried to unify Germany by relatively more peaceful and ideal means. It failed. In contrast, Bismarck did achieve German unity — by *Realpolitik*, by fraud and brutality and war. 1870 versus 1848: this inaccurate and oversimplified contrast became an object-lesson for the German people. A conclusive military defeat of Germany would have the wholesome psychological effect of reversing her object-lesson. Under Hitler such a defeat could not again be explained away as a 1918 " stab in the back " by a " Jewish-democratic " Reichstag! Such a defeat would discredit *Realpolitik* with Germans in the same way that Bismarck's *Realpolitik* discredited the alleged 1848 idealism.

But such a reversed object-lesson can only work on Germany if, not as in the first World War, her enemies themselves live up to the high international standards they preach. England's aggressive Boer War, with its bloody pre-Nazi concentration camps, remains a far from remote memory in many German minds. So does England's post-armistice blockade of 1918–19, which starved so many German children to death. Today England appeals rightly to the German people for a revolution against Hitler's inhumanity. Why do even anti-Nazi Germans tend to dismiss such appeals as hypocritical? It is important for us to realize that the German people are honestly convinced, partly correctly and partly by propangandist exaggerations, that British imperialism has long practised the same inhumanity as Hitler's against the people of Eire, India, Africa, China, and her own English slums.

To bring practical and lasting results, the united defence of the democracies against militaristic *Realpolitik*, and against nazism in general, must be always on two fronts: abroad, against the present German practitioners; at home, against any native brand of the same thing, no matter how bushy its democratic false whiskers, no matter how many American flags it waves, no matter how sincerely the domestic brand happens to conflict with German and foreign brands.

CHAPTER X

A DIFFERENT VIEW OF THE GERMAN REPUBLIC

Between the old romanticism we have been considering and its twentieth-century triumph in Hitler came a brief fifteen-year intermezzo, the Weimar Republic.

Both nazism and the Weimar Republic are fruits of the fertile German nineteenth century: nazism, from the Jahn and Wagner undercurrent of the War of Liberation and 1848; the Weimar Republic, from the liberal top-current of these same two revolutions. Just as westerners exaggerated the liberalism of 1813 and 1848, so they exaggerated the republicanism of the Weimar Republic, which never contained so many republicans as we then thought. The permanent bureaucracy and the courts and the army were never widely nor deeply republicanized.

The Republic's two Presidents, Ebert and Hindenburg, were both monarchists who in 1918 had not wanted the Republic. Ebert represented the moderate Left, the Social Democrats; Hindenburg represented the moderate Right, the Nationalist party and the Junkers. The extremists of Left and Right, the Communists and Nazis, were even less republican, wanting dictatorship instead of monarchy.

For twenty years, by unstable coalitions of minorities and by American financial loans, this quasi-Republic managed to persist. But let us remember its origin before fondly hoping that Germany could, with the fall of Hitler, become a democracy easily. It was decreed from above by a temporary and incompatible coalition of Social Democrats and the army. With what motives? According to Chancellor Scheidemann's frank confession, he proclaimed the Republic for the Social Democrats (against Ebert's wishes) merely as a means of sidetracking German workers from following Russia into communism. The motive of the generals was much cleverer. They could easily have crushed the tiny uprising against the Kaiser; that is now certain. They preferred to stand by passively or even, like Hindenburg, to advise the Kaiser's flight. Why?

The cleverer ones among them had a twofold motive. First, German democracy was partly a ruse to win from Wilson a peace with more lenient military clauses than would be granted to the Kaiser, that well-meaning and war-guiltless scapegoat of the war. When the devil is sick, the devil a monk would be. When the Brest-Litovsk and Pan-German annexationists were sick, Wilsonians they would be. In another generation Germany would again be strong enough for them to throw off their republican mask. Then they would continue the unfinished World War of 1918.

This ruse succeeded only partly. The ruse failed to gain Wilson's Fourteen Points as hoped. Had it done so, the decent peace-loving core of Germany might have returned to the fold of the west and booted out the war-makers. But the ruse did prevent the French from actually annexing the Rhineland, and later it hastened their evacuation of it. Had Germany not staged or, rather, stage-managed a democratic " revolution," Wilson could never have prevented the French from separating the Rhineland. And without a remilitarized German Rhineland, Hitler could not have resumed the World War.

Secondly, when the republican mask was no longer needed, the annexationists could get rid of it by accusing the Republic (which they had helped establish!) of treason and the stab in the back. The Social Democrats and Centrists signed the Treaty of Versailles unwillingly and *on army advice,* solely because the generals informed them that resistance was impossible.[1] Yet the same militarists could later get rid of the Social Democrats by blaming them for signing the treaty.

An aggressive, expansionist motive was behind many of the pious pleas for relaxing the Versailles Treaty as well as behind much of the sudden professed republicanism of 1919. These facts should have been shouted from the housetops in Germany, England, and France in 1933. Today they are merely historical curiosities. They illustrate the strategic superiority of the totalitarian mind over the futilitarian mind of the pre-1940 French and British governments. The latter is symbolized by Neville Chamberlain's gullible faith in the possibility of peace and compromise with the Pan-German–Brest-Litovsk–Ludendorff-Hitler tradition.

I am not insinuating that the aggressive motive behind the Weimar Republic and behind the anti-Versailles agitation was the motive of Germany as a whole. That would be a slander against the Germans. The largest party, the Social Democrats, genuinely wanted peace, and so did most Germans. But the Social Democrats were the dupes in their 1918 alliance with the army to set up the Republic. It would also be a slander to insinuate that the ma-

---

[1] Hitler: *Mein Kampf* (Reynal & Hitchcock ed.), pp. 269–76, 972, footnotes.

jority of army leaders were consciously using the Republic and its pious Wilsonian phrases merely as a breathing-spell for plotting new war. Yet that is all the Republic finally turned out to be; the plot did exist consciously in such generals as Ludendorff, and — the plot worked.

The war-wishing minority of bureaucratic and military officials held many key posts throughout the Republic. They helped push Hitler into power. When General Ludendorff in 1918 deemed defeat certain, and not till then, he suddenly urged the parliamentary responsibility which he had always opposed. The parliament, whose largest party was the Social Democrats, should now rule — and in consequence sign the peace treaty. Ludendorff's motive was certainly not love of democracy and of parliamentary rule. His was the dual motive: to get an easier peace and then to shift from himself to the "democratic backstabbers" the blame for losing the war in the first place. Thus considered, there is no inconsistency behind Ludendorff's privately urging Ebert into power with high praise and then publicly heading Hitler's 1923 putsch against the Ebert Republic.

None of these facts are cited to justify the dishonourable betrayal of the promised Fourteen Points at Versailles and the sadistic economic flagellation of Germany that followed. On the contrary, that was the surest way to drive the German people into the camp of the war-planning Ludendorff-Hitler minority. Our job then was, and will be after any future victory, to reconcile and synthesize the Germans with the west, to which they half belong. Whether the west treats them justly or unjustly has often determined which of their "two souls in one breast" they follow.

The Munich Pact principle was not in itself bad. What was scandalously bad was that the British and French governments applied it to Hitler, with whom peace was pragmatically improbable, instead of to the earlier Social Democrat and Centrist regime. Often the Social Democrats and Centrists were not sincerely democratic nor anti-monarchic, but they at least did sincerely represent Germany's western soul. With them peace was both pragmatically possible and morally desirable. According to Centrist Chancelor Brüning,[2] he and the murdered General v. Schleicher in 1932 hoped to lead Germany into a liberal-conservative monarchy. With this the more right-wing Social Democrats and liberals, the more left-wing conservatives and nationalists, and the Centrists would in the 1930's have replaced the insufficiently anchored Republic, which in part they had played at only to please Wilson.

Both they and Hitler sought to solve the manifest political and economic untenability of the Versailles republican set-up. Their liberal western solution for revising the Versailles Republic was racing neck and neck with Hitler's dictatorial anti-western solution. In 1933, by only a slim margin and perhaps not inevitably, Hitler won the race.

---

[2] Source: private Harvard conversations; also two 1938 letters, available in my files, from Dr. Brüning about his 1932 talks with Schleicher, Hindenburg, and the Crown Prince on stopping Hitler with monarchy. But what was really needed to crush the Nazi criminals was not such a subtle intrigue in high plates but broad-based anti-totalitarian solidarity, and this was sabotaged by Moscow in practical politics and by Germany's own romantic heritage in metapolitics.

CHAPTER XI

PROPHET LAUREATE
OF METAPOLITICS: PART I

~~~~~~

*A new peace shall make Germany mistress of the globe,
a peace not hanging on the palm fronds of pacifist
womenfolk but established by the victorious sword of a
master race that takes over the world in the service of a
higher Kultur.*

— *Joint prediction in the 1920's
by* ALFRED ROSENBERG *and
by* HITLER's Mein Kampf

*The war which began before all the world on May 10,
1940 [the date of Germany's invasion of Holland and
Belgium] is the greatest of revolutionary wars. An outworn era is crumbling to dust beneath the marching feet
of the German army.*

— *Prediction by* ROSENBERG *in 1940*

WHO IS ROSENBERG?

Alfred Rosenberg is Hitler's official highbrow, the prophet
laureate of metapolitics.

Most Americans follow Rauschning's *Revolution of*

Nihilism in underestimating Rosenberg's influence and in exaggerating both Nazi nihilism and Nazi cynicism about ideology. Nature abhors a vacuum even in ideology. No vacuum could give the daring Volk-armies now overrunning Europe their energetic will to power. The Nazis are nihilistic toward western and Christian civilization. But they are replacing with new values of their own this vacuum which their nihilist phase creates. Too narrow to see or to want to see these new and alien values is the doctrinaire type of anti-Nazi.

Today German youth is still being educated most uncynically and unnihilistically in that metapolitics of which Rosenberg is the most articulate example. He is editor in chief of the official Nazi newspaper, *Der Völkische Beobachter* (*The Folkic Observer*), and the official Nazi magazine, *Nationalsozialistische Monathefte* (*National Socialist Monthly*). I shall treat him less as a person than as the ablest and most revealing symbol of German metapolitics. Even if his person is ever liquidated in a new purge, thousands of younger Germans will still perpetuate the symbol. Using him as the most convenient jumping-off point, this chapter is actually a survey of current Nazi credos in general.

Many of Rosenberg's basic assumptions are sincere and brilliant nonsense. That is no reason for America to continue ignoring them. They are tremendously important *because* they are nonsense: nonsense plus mass will-power is the very stuff of which history is often made. The time has come for serious analysis of this man and his works.

From 1919 on, Rosenberg has been Germany's most ardent and consistent prophet of a " crusade " against Soviet Russia. In the 1920's he and his friends Hess and Professor Haushofer were responsible for Hitler's well-known *Mein Kampf* passages on the joys of annexing the Ukrainian wheatfields.

Rosenberg represents the moderate wing of nazism, while his enemy Goebbels represents the so-called " national bolshevist " wing. Both are anti-bourgeois, considering the bourgeois Weltanschauung synonymous with the liberalism they detest. Being literally national socialist, both have always violently opposed the so-called capitalist system of economics, which they deem synonymous with democracy ("plutodemocracy"). But Rosenberg's opposition tries hard to be in the lordly old Teutonic Knight tradition, with an agricultural viewpoint, while Goebbels's opposition tries to act more proletarian, with a big-city viewpoint.

The German *Who's Who* describes Alfred Rosenberg as follows: Born in 1893 in Reval. Of Protestant family. "Ancestors: Baltic merchants and manual labourers." Since 1921, chief editor of the official Nazi paper, *Der Völkische Beobachter*. "Commissioned by the Führer for the entire philosophic (*Weltanschaulich*) education of the movement." His chief youthful training: to be an engineer.[1]

Rosenberg was brought up in Reval (Tallinn), the capital of the small Baltic state of Estonia. While he lived there, Estonia was part of the Czarist Russian Empire. He walked among the Esths (members of the " Baltic race ") with mingled rage and fear. A slave race he deemed them, who should some day be put in their place again by the German minority which had ruled them in the ancient days of the Teutonic Knights. The World War gave Estonia for the first time in history national independence from both its Russian governors and its German agricultural landlords. For twenty years the Esths could taste

---

[1] H. Degener, ed.: *Wer Ist's?* (10th ed., Berlin, 1935), p. 1325.

some democratic liberties for the first time in all their tragic history. Then Stalin reconquered Estonia in 1940, and Hitler made it a battlefield in 1941.

Rosenberg's family was a pretty even mixture of proletarian and petty-bourgeois origins, never rich, never connected with the aristocratic German "Baltic barons" whom he so admired and who alone can claim descent from the Teutonic Knights. Unlike his rival Goebbels, Rosenberg is without scholarly training or Ph.D. Despite that, or because of it, he is the leading Nazi interpreter of German history.

A racial mixture of Balt and German, born and educated in Estonia and then spending the World War in Russia, Rosenberg is naturally a two-hundred-per-cent German patriot. The most fanatic German nationalists are generally produced outside Germany in some land where Germanism is not a matter of course, but something constantly threatened with submergence in alien culture. Too frequent to be coincidences are the following outstanding examples:

Wagner's German nationalism was created by his lonely years in Paris. Hitler in some ways is a typical Sudeten German, surrounded by Slavs in the Hapsburg Empire. Göring, though born in Germany, was brought up in the Hapsburg province of Styria. Until the mysterious airplane flight to Scotland in May 1941, the Führer's dearest friend and the next in succession after Göring was Rudolf Hess, whose youth was spent in Egypt. Hitler's Minister of Agriculture and chief proclaimer of "blood and soil" (*Blut und Boden*) is Darré, whose youth was spent in Argentina. Goebbels's nationalism reached its fever pitch under the Belgian and French armies of occupation in the Rhineland. The fanatically nationalist Ernst Bohle, director of all propaganda among Germans abroad, was born in

England and spent his first sixteen years in South Africa.[2]

Napoleon spoke French with an Italian accent. Stalin speaks Russian with a Georgian accent. Hitler speaks German with an Austrian accent. Rosenberg speaks German with a Baltic accent. He even reprinted, in a book of his speeches, an interview stressing his Baltic accent.[3]

Only the aristocratic Baltic barons could remain purely German in stock. The classes from which Rosenberg sprang, the proletarian and lower middle classes, were inextricably interbred with their Baltic neighbours. That is indisputable. German racists herd the Balts with the Slavs and Jews as the destined slaves of the nordic super-race.

Of all Nazi leaders, Rosenberg and Goebbels are the two to whom Jewish ancestry is most frequently attributed by popular German gossip. Lacking proof, such frequent gossip about them and about Hitler should be rejected as false. It is too smartly paradoxical, too obvious and cheap an anti-Nazi weapon to be trustworthy. It descends to the Nazi level of taking " race " and the Aryan nonsense seriously. But false or true, the mere existence of such gossip encourages Rosenberg and Goebbels in being Germany's two-hundred-per-cent anti-Semites, just as such gossip encouraged the too much protesting behind Wagner's anti-Semitism. Rosenberg's facial and physical features are not typically German (nor Jewish) but typically those found among Balts.

Rosenberg fled to Munich from Russia's Red revolution. In Munich, with Eckart, Röhm, Hess, and Hitler, he built the original nucleus of Hitler's present Nazi party. In Bayreuth he was a welcome guest at the house of Wagner's widow and children and son-in-law Chamberlain. Rosen-

---

[2] Sidney B. Fay: " Goering," in *Events*, New York, February 1940, p. 133.

[3] Rosenberg: *Blut und Ehre* (17th ed., Munich, 1938), p. 350.

berg impressed Munich's bohemians, especially Hitler and
Eckart, as a profound thinker because of the vagueness,
obscurity, and pretentiousness of his speech.

Rosenberg is a thoroughly German thinker (with important
exceptions which will be treated in the section on
" Russian Influences "). He should not, except technically,
be called a White Russian; and merely physically, not culturally,
is he a Balt. His foreign environment only fanned
the flames of his cultural Germanism. He incarnates the
typical traits of German romanticism. That is why Hitler
in 1934 created for Rosenberg the special office of " Director
of Party Education in Weltanschauung."

In 1936 I watched Rosenberg and Goebbels speak at the
Nürnberg party rally. Whereas the brief tirade by Goebbels
lashed the listeners into frenzy, Rosenberg's endless
schoolma'amish lecture made them fall asleep. The
prophet laureate's personality has the pedantry of a scholar
without the scholar's soundness and objective truth-seeking.
An ineffectual speaker he certainly is. But as a
journalist and pamphleteer he has spread nazism effectively
to millions.

Goebbels wins over the proletariat by his demagogics,
and many of the educated by his superior brains. Rosenberg
bores both the uneducated and the well educated, but
is the god of the semi-educated, whom earnest dullness
and obscure grandiloquence impress as scholarly and authoritative.

FOREIGN POLICY [4]

Unlike Ribbentrop and Goebbels, the Rosenberg group
refused to work with Communists internally and preferred

[4] Rosenberg best summarizes his foreign policy in *Mythus des 20.
Jahrhunderts* (142nd ed., Munich, 1938), pp. 637–77; and in his pamphlets
Wesensgefüge des Nationalsozialismus (6th ed., Munich, 1933)
and *Der Zukunftsweg einer deutschen Aussenpolitik* (Munich, n.d.).

an English to a Russian alliance externally. Stalin should have taken warning from the ominous fact that even during the Hitler-Stalin alliance Hitler retained Rosenberg as his chief philosopher and as editor of the chief Nazi daily. Hitler's invasion of the Soviet in June of 1941 is Rosenberg's hour of triumph.

All too sincerely Rosenberg pictures a " Jew-ruled Russia " plotting Marxist world-revolution as "mask" for " Jewish international bankers." He is convinced that the Red revolution was secretly financed by Wall Street, by firms like Kuhn Loeb, an " alien " German myth frequently repeated by that two-hundred-per-cent American, Father Coughlin. This slander is, of course, preposterous — but no more so than the counter-slander of American Marxists that Hitler is just a tool of the capitalists. A *national* socialist, Rosenberg has won millions of Germans to his "mask" theory of international (Jewish) socialism by his cheaply priced pamphlets. These bear such titles as *International High Finance; Plague in Russia: Bolshevism; The Mark of the Jew.*[5]

Rosenberg's and Hitler's passionate hate of Soviet Russia is mainly anti-Semitic and anti-Comintern rather than anti-Russian. During Stalin's purges in the 1930's the Nazi press stressed that most of those " liquidated " were Jews and Comintern internationalists and hinted — already then — that perhaps Stalin or some other *national* Communist would be good for a little pact. Long before the brief Russian pact of 1939, Rosenberg envisaged " friendship " with a " nationalist Russia " at the expense of Poland. Poland, " incapable " of maintaining a state of its

---

[5] Rosenberg: *Die Internationale Hochfinanz* (Munich, n.d.); *Pest in Russland, der Bolschewismus* (Munich, 1937), condensed version of 1922 issue; *Die Spur des Juden im Wandel der Zeiten* (Munich, 1920).

own, " should bear the chief burden of German expansion." [6]

More basic than Rosenberg's Russophobia was his dream of " Germany mistress of the globe . . . by the victorious sword of a master race." [7] " The globe " includes South America according to all existing planetary maps, but doubtless to point this out to Americans is just English-Jewish-capitalist propaganda by "hysterical war-mongers."

Rosenberg's consistent foreign policy was prophetically summed up in 1938 as " a sweeping extermination of honourless democracy . . . the spiritual undoing and historically overdue decomposition of the west, linked to an organic penetration and rearrangement of the east." Nor was Rosenberg such a bad prophet when he wrote, prior to Hitler's chancellorship, that " no considerations can be taken for Poles, Czechs, etc., who are as impotent as they are valueless and overbearing. They must be driven back to the east, so that the soil may become free to be tilled by the horny hands of Teutonic peasants." [8]

Himself a product of Germany's *Drang nach Osten,* Rosenberg voices the eternal mission of the mediæval Teutonic Knights: to conquer and colonize the Slavic east. Today Hitler is converting into appalling reality the Rosenberg theory about what to do with Slavs. Hitler has appointed Arthur Greiser to rule an important sector of conquered Poland. On August 26, 1940 Greiser gave a nationwide broadcast to all members of the Nazi youth movement. He called Slavic soil the " land of our destiny." To the whole new generation of German youth he cried:

---

6 Kolnai, op. cit., pp. 642–3.
7 Rauschning: *Revolution,* p. 184.
8 Kolnai, op. cit., pp. 642–3.

" The Pole is the servant of the German and will remain it forever." [9]

The famous passages on eastern expansion in Hitler's *Mein Kampf* were directly inspired by Rosenberg and Professor Haushofer. Both have been close collaborators since the party's early Munich days. One is a metapolitician, the other a geopolitician! Haushofer coined the interesting word " geopolitics " to describe national policies based on the geographical need for *Lebensraum* and to justify imperialism's age-old penchant for aggressive territorial expansion. Rosenberg provided the philosophic props for the pages in *Mein Kampf* on eastward expansion, while Haushofer " supplied the scientific basis for this foreign policy." [10] As a young student in Munich, Hess was Haushofer's favourite pupil.

At first Hitler founded two rival Foreign Offices side by side: the " Ribbentrop Bureau " and Rosenberg's " Foreign Politics Office." But the former soon triumphed completely in the 1930's, owing to Ribbentrop's greater diplomatic successes. Thereafter, Rosenberg has remained extremely important as Germany's philosopher and educator but is of no importance nor power as a diplomat.

Rosenberg believes in eventually setting up " world peace." What kind of world peace? " A ' world peace ' is to be installed not by disarmament of armies and fleets " — that would be too mild! — " but by the *sweeping extermination* of honourless democracy." Such sentences should be headlined in any nations fighting Germany who are in danger of losing their fighting morale. [11]

[9] Associated Press dispatch from Berlin, August 26, 1940, in *Boston Daily Globe,* Greater Boston ed., p. 1.

[10] Hitler: *Mein Kampf* (Reynal & Hitchcock ed.), pp. 937–40, 950–3. Cf. Haushofer's innumerable books and his magazine *Zeitschrift für Geopolitik.* Heiden: *Hitler,* pp. 177–8.

[11] Rosenberg: *Mythus,* p. 671.

Watching Rosenberg and Goebbels argue foreign policy in a public Nuremberg* rally in 1936, the author found Goebbels intelligent and lowbrow, a showman and demagogue of great genius, and found Rosenberg stupid and highbrow, a doctrinaire and *idéologue* of great Germanness. Their rivalry was a case of the quick brown fox jumping over the not lazy but theorizing dog. In person — fanatic about abstractions, didactic about systems, and far less corrupt financially than the gangsters around him — Rosenberg is the German Revolution's nearest equivalent of Robespierre. Except that Rosenberg spoils his stance of austerity by stinking daintily of perfume and wearing dirty expensive white gloves.

Superseded by the more activist, less theoretical careerists like Goebbels and Ribbentrop in propaganda policy and foreign policy respectively, Rosenberg's long-run strength lies in his practical weakness: in his being the turgid pseudo-philosopher most expressive of the turgid Nazi mind. Hitler recognized this when, during his imprisonment, he made Rosenberg his substitute head of the Party. Rosenberg best ideologizes the German "need" to invade Russia. Therefore, bringing invaded Russia his blueprinted "sweeping extermination" in 1941 would inevitably bring the superseded Rosenberg back into administrative prominence, would indeed climax his hitherto non-activist career by letting him talk himself not merely into best-selling books with uncut pages but into a noose.

Rosenberg has a charming plan for America to cede its Far Eastern possessions to Japan. His geopolitical col-

---

* 1961 postscript: Ten years later in the same town of Nuremberg, Rosenberg addressed a rather different audience, which hanged him for his genocide instead of cheering him for it. His death-chamber memoirs uphold Nazi dogma as much as before but now condemn Hitler, probably sincerely, for not practicing nazism's "pure theory." An ideologist to the end!

league Haushofer, in a book reprinted by the Nazis in 1938, has published plans for German dominance in part of South America: "Important sections of Latin America are significant for our future because of the sparse population of their vast expanses." It is a duty to call such unrepudiated writings by high Nazi officials to the attention of the American people, who will soon be hearing the usual Nazi non-aggression pledges.[12]

INFLUENCE OF WAGNER, CHAMBERLAIN, LAGARDE, JAHN

Whence Rosenberg's ideas? His most important source is Houston Stewart Chamberlain. This becomes indisputably apparent from reading Rosenberg's *Myth* side by side with Chamberlain's *Foundations*. Rosenberg is honest about this. He makes no attempt to conceal what he calls his "grateful homage" to Chamberlain, and the official Catholic refutation of both men calls Chamberlain "Rosenberg's direct teacher."[13]

Rosenberg's theories are drawn from Chamberlain's hard work in historical research. But Wagner is the ideal of "creative Aryanism" who inspires Rosenberg's emotional ecstasies about the German mission. That is why Rosenberg cites Wagner more frequently than any other to symbolize Aryan ideals.

For example, Rosenberg cites Wagner's *Tristan* to symbolize the nordic's sense of honour. He quotes *Die Meistersinger* and *Tristan* to symbolize the nordic's Faustian

---

[12] Ibid., p. 673. Karl Haushofer: *Geopolitik des Pazifischen Ozeans* (3d revised ed., Heidelberg and Berlin, 1938). Eugene Lyons: "Hitler's Blueprint," in *American Mercury*, New York, August 1940, pp. 398–400.

[13] Rosenberg: *An die Dunkelmänner unserer Zeit* (33d ed., Munich, 1938), pp. 65–6. "Studien zum Mythus des XX. Jahrhunderts," in *Kirchlicher Anzeiger für die Erzdiözese Köln*, Cologne, October 1934, pp. 72–3. Roberts: *House*, pp. 49–50.

striving for the infinite and the nordic's loneliness. He cites a Wagner letter to symbolize the self-justified selfish Life-force of the dæmonic nordic. Many more examples abound.[14]

To get a statistical idea of the influences behind Rosenberg, I have counted the number of references in the text of *Myth,* many of which are not contained in its index. Among political theorists, Wagner received the largest number of favourable references, Chamberlain the second largest, Lagarde the third. The book was begun before Hitler was famous, and he is referred to only about three times. In contrast, among unfavourable references, Judaism got the largest number, too overwhelming to count, more than the sum of all four above favourable references. The ancient Etruscans got the second largest number of unfavourable references (for reasons to be treated later). Not only are unfavourable references to these two vastly more frequent than the favourable references to Wagner, Chamberlain, and Lagarde, but the former are denounced vastly more passionately than the latter are praised. Hate prevails over love, war over peace, as Nazi motives.[15]

Romanticism and Nietzsche also receive favourable references — about as many as Lagarde. The result of counting the number of references is no coincidence, but is confirmed by an article Rosenberg wrote for his newspaper in 1933. There he named what he deems the four chief fountainheads of nazism, none other than " the apparent opponents Nietzsche and Wagner, the great seer Paul de Lagarde and as a prophet Houston Stewart Cham-

---

14 Rosenberg: *Mythus,* pp. 401–2, 388, 316.
15 Ibid., Wagner, pp. 275, 316, 388, 401, 402, 443, 444, 445, 427–34, etc.; Chamberlain, 81 ff., 112, 142, 430, 532, 553, 623, 683, etc.; Lagarde, 138, 237, 443, 454, 456, etc.; Judaism, *passim;* Etruscans, 54, 60 ff., 138, 383, 384, etc.

berlain." Despite popular American fallacies, Nietzsche
has by far the least connection with nazism of all these
fountainheads, and Wagner by far the most.[16]

The same newspaper article by Rosenberg attacked the
" reactionaries " and " aristocratic clubs " who would make
Moeller van den Bruck the fountainhead of nazism. Bruck
is the writer who did most to popularize the phrase " the
Third Reich." But where nazism is a *mass* movement
breaking class distinctions, Bruck corresponds more to the
popular American fallacy of seeing nazism as a new Prussianism, as a restoration of Junker aristocracy and exclu-
sion of the proletariat. That is why American writers have
often — and wrongly — made Bruck a chief Nazi source.
Though Bruck tried as hard as the Nazis to synthesize much socialism with his nationalism, he remained incurably an aristocratic gentleman of Prussian tradition,
whereas the Nazis' very essence is that they are neither
aristocrats nor gentlemen, and few of them Prussians.[17]

Rosenberg's additional reason for denying nazism to
Bruck was that Bruck, like so many Prussian Reichswehr
conservatives, was realistic enough to advocate military
alliance with unconservative Russia. But the more basic
reason for repudiating Bruck was his Prussian and aristocratic lack of organic folkdom. In 1939 a younger Nazi
published a book correctly attacking Bruck as " un-Nazi "
for three reasons: he was no racial determinist (too mild
an anti-Semite); he lacked folkdom; his Protestant Christianity was too deep to make him a complete totalitarian.[18]

To call Lagarde a proto-Nazi is more easily justified. He
had already called the Kaiser's Germany of 1870 a " Jew-

[16] Rosenberg: " Gegen Tarnung," article in *Völkischer Beobachter*,
Munich, December 8, 1933. Reprinted in Rosenberg: *Gestaltung der
Idee* (7th ed., Munich, 1938), p. 17.

[17] Arthur Moeller van den Bruck: *Das Dritte Reich* (Hamburg, 1922).

[18] Helmut Rödel: *Moeller van den Bruck* (Berlin, 1939).

ish-German Reich." Lagarde is a major precursor of nazism's new anti-Christian theology. That is why Rosenberg
calls him the " great German dreamer . . . who spoke out
the eternal German dream." His long-forgotten writings
were reprinted by the Nazis under the new title of *Writings for Germans*.[19] But the influence of Lagarde and the
rest on Hitler and his party is completely outshone by
Richard Wagner.

Wagner's vast influence Rosenberg explains by the fact
that "Wagner, beside Lagarde, fought alone against the
whole bourgeois-capitalist world of the Alberichs." Alberich is the dwarf in Wagner's *Ring des Nibelungen* who
symbolizes the lust for " gold " and the unheroic bourgeois pettiness of capitalists and Jews. Wagner's lone-wolf
stand against these Alberichs made "Bayreuth the true
foundation of Life amid a bestial age." Wagner's " mission " was to " serve his Volk " by " foreseeing the dawn "
of nazism. Writing prior to Hitler's seizure of power in
Germany, Rosenberg predicts: " The inner worth of Bayreuth towers, ever Life-giving, out into the coming German Reich." [20]

Rosenberg's *Myth* consists of three parts. Each part is
based on a typical quotation from a great German leader.
What three characters does Rosenberg choose? For Book
One he chooses Frederick the Great. Nazis make this most
tolerant, artistic, and cosmopolitan of German kings, who
was *plus français que les français*, whose wars were no
more nor less aggressive than his neighbours', into a symbol of Prussian militarism. With Frederick as with that
other Francophile German, Nietzsche, the Nazis twist the

[19] Paul de Lagarde (Bötticher); *Deutsche Schriften* (2 vols., Göttingen, 1878–81), reprinted by Nazis 1933 as *Schriften für Deutsche*.
Rosenberg: *Mythus,* pp. 457–8.
[20] Ibid. pp. 443–4.

Athenian into a Spartan despite himself. The Nazis invade
and loot the remote past as well as the present. They enslave the dead as well as the living and usurp ideas as well
as territories.

More appropriate are Rosenberg's choices for the other
two parts: Wagner for the second: symbolically nazism
thereby imposes on eighteenth-century Prussian militarism
the new force of romanticism; Father Jahn for Book Three,
the all-important book on current events. Rosenberg
chooses a long Jahn quotation on how the " holiest moment " in history is when the masses " awaken " into awareness of " the eternity of their own Volkhood." [21]

ROSENBERG'S BASIC LINGO AND BASIC ASSUMPTIONS [22]

The Old Testament of the Nazi religion is *Mein Kampf*.
Though far less directly influential, the New Testament is
The Myth of the Twentieth Century by Hitler's Saint Paul
and prophet laureate. Outlined in 1917, it was finished in
1925 and first published in 1930. By 1938 *Myth* had run
into 142 editions and had sold 713,000 copies. Since Hitler calls it today's greatest philosophical book, it merits our
detailed scrutiny as a key to the Nazi mind.

Rosenberg conceived and outlined the basic ideas of
Myth prior to Versailles. As a result, his book and philosophy would have been essentially what they are now
(except for a certain emotional bitterness) if Germany had
won the World War. As expressed by Rosenberg, the Nazi
credo is not a hypocritical propaganda-device improvised
by demagogues for the sake of grabbing power. Nor is the

---

[21] Ibid., pp. 274–451.
[22] This section is an interpretative condensation from Book I of Rosenberg's *Mythus, passim.*

credo an emotional reaction to the injustices of Versailles. It is a logical product, deliberate and consistent, of Germany's nineteenth-century political romantics. Throughout our scrutiny of *Myth*, this nineteenth-century background should be kept steadily in mind.

Precisely what myth does Rosenberg mean by his title? The best response to this frequent query is the blurb on the book's cover:

> "The myth of the twentieth century" is the myth of blood, which under the sign of the swastika unchains the racial world-revolution. It is the awakening of the race soul, which after long sleep victoriously ends the race chaos.

To understand these slogans we must contrast them with what they replace. "The racial world-revolution": in contrast with the French and Russian world-revolutions, in contrast with the liberalism of the former and the Marxism of the latter, in contrast with the capitalism of the former and the proletarianism of the latter. In contrast with their economic interpretations of history and in contrast with the church's Christian interpretation of history, the *Myth* is a racial interpretation of history. "History no longer means war of class against class nor of church dogma and dogma, but blood and blood, race and race." [23]

"Myth"! What a significant word! Rosenberg is a romantic writing in German; he is not an eighteenth-century rationalist writing in French. Therefore he uses "myth" not sarcastically but piously, not with curled lip but wide-eyed with wonder. His use of "myth" covers far more than a literal English translation could convey. His special use of the word covers something like this: necessary faith, or inspiration, or unifying mass yearning, or folktale truer than truth.

---

[23] Ibid., pp. 1–2.

Rosenberg's philosophy stands or falls on this basic assumption: God created man not as an individual nor mankind as a whole, but individual races of men. These are the building blocks of history, the only lasting units. The individual man has no soul, nor has humanity. Only a race has soul. The whole of a race is infinitely larger than the sum of all its parts — larger by a soul, an invisible soul that is more real than reality. When Rosenberg writes: " The Volk is more than the total of its members," he uses the very words of Novalis and Adam Müller of the 1800 romantic school.[24]

A nation is the political expression of the race. Here Rosenberg repeats the Wagnerian contrast of an organic society versus an atomistic society. The chief morality and justification of an organic (living) group body is its being organic (living). Life for Life's sake: salvation through subjective egoism instead of through obedience to objective universal standards. God is reached not by building on the rock of the Christian church but by each race lifting itself by its own boot-straps. In such metaphysics the individual can exist only for the nation instead of the nation for the individual.

Volk nationalism is sharply distinguished from Prussian statism. The mere state, for Hitler, Wagner, and Rosenberg, is soulless if inorganic (unfolkic). An unfolkic state deserves no loyalty, no " Prussian duty." When one nation conquers other nations, it must not interbreed with them into one common international state, but must erect a state in which the higher and purer race rules the lower. Hence the Nazi enslavement of Poles, Czechs, and Jews.

Rosenberg's second basic assumption is that no two races have the same soul. Therefore no two races can understand each other; no two speak the same moral, æsthetic,

---

[24] Ibid., p. 437.

or intellectual language. Like an iceberg, the race soul is mostly submerged. But it has two visible projections. The first is the physical differences between ethnic groups; let us admit that these are scientifically proved. The second is spiritual differences; this assumption, essential to all Nazi Weltanschauung, is scientifically unprovable.

Nazism is the revolt against conditioning by environment. Rosenberg denies that environment can give German morals or culture to, say, a Jew or a Slav. Such qualities are determined unalterably before birth. Partly they are determined by physical heredity and partly by metaphysical race soul. Nazi scientists prefer the former determinant for the sake of practical eugenics. But Nazi philosophers, like Rosenberg, prefer the latter determinant as less materialistic. Rosenberg defines " personality " as the combination, in ever varying proportions, of these two determinants: physical heredity and mystic non-physical race soul. Cross-breeding breaks up this divine — literally divine — combination of body and spirit. Both become a lifeless hulk, no longer being animated by race soul, and " personality " is annihilated.

Hegel's " state " embodied collectively and pantheistically an ever evolving, ever fluid " Idea of God." Rosenberg keeps this Hegelian framework, substituting nation for state, race soul for Idea. Marx, too, kept the Hegelian evolutionary dialectic, substituting not nation but class for state. Beyond external or universal laws of good and evil, the nation (or class) obeys only its sacred inner dynamics, ever expanding against its antithesis, ever becoming and never being — this all sounds Faustian and very Hegelian and equally Wagnerian, and very, very German.

This, then, is the lingo. How does Rosenberg's Bible apply it to history? As Frick, Nazi Minister of the Interior, pithily decreed: " Race determines thought." [25] No " personality," as defined above, obeys the same laws or has the same historical value as any other personality. All great achievements of history, specifically Hellenic, Roman, and European culture, are accompanied by the Germanic personality. Conversely, all periods of degeneration spring from its contamination by an alien personality, a mixture of alien soul and alien blood.

The last of these degenerate interludes, crows Rosenberg, ended in 1933. The job of nazism is to build a golden age by repurifying the race soul. Alien elements must be cut out as ruthlessly as a doctor cuts cancer. Should a sick body democratically tolerate its disease germs? Then why, argues Rosenberg's false analogy, should the German collective body tolerate democratically its non-Aryan germs?

RACIAL INTERPRETATION OF HISTORY

The first book of *Myth* is entitled " The Conflict of Values." It contains Rosenberg's famous racial interpretation of history. " Conflict of Values " refers to Aryan versus non-Aryan. " Aryan " is a more inclusive term than " Germanic," and " non-Aryan " is broader than " Jewish." But like Wagner's essay on race of 1881 and like Chamberlain, Rosenberg usually treats the Germanic race and the Jews as the only Aryans and non-Aryans worth bothering about in modern times.

Explaining all history's boons and banes as good and bad race respectively, Rosenberg gives us a brand-new history of the whole world. Certainly an unconventional history, based on the infallible intuitions of Rosenberg's some-

---

25 Vernon Bourke: " Philosophical Antecedents of German National Socialism," in *Thought*, Catholic Quarterly, New York, Vol. XIV, June 1939, p. 236.

what nordic blood instead of on mere facts and footnotes. The pages on the origins of man are the most interesting because there Rosenberg's imagination can soar most freely, in regions so remote that no known facts exist to clip its bold wings. Bold certainly is Rosenberg's explanation that the ancient lost continent of Atlantis was the origin of all good things.

To do Rosenberg justice, we must note that at one time he refers to Atlantis as an excellent " hypothesis " — oh, admirable self-restraint! — instead of as an entirely proved fact. A hundred per cent certain is merely that all good things derive from some single " nordic prehistoric Kultur-centre." Though such painful caution soon vanishes as the pages advance, Rosenberg does attain superhuman self-control when he describes the following vision as " not quite untenable "!

> Where today the waves of the Atlantic roar and giant ice-bergs roam, a flourishing continent once towered, where a creative race reared a great Kultur and sent its children as sea-rovers and warriors into the world . . . streams of Atlanteans on their swan-boats and dragon-boats.[26]

This vision is sheer poetry, possibly good poetry. The swan boats *à la* Wagner's *Lohengrin*, the roaming icebergs, the blond godlike children *à la Siegfried* conquering the globe on their dragon-boats — all this so intoxicates Rosenberg's imagination that he throws to the winds his lapse into bourgeois caution, which led him to refer timidly to these glories as perhaps a " hypothesis." Now he assumes the hypothesis is proved and derives from it the rest of his book.

The book traces how migrating Atlanteans gave the whole non-Aryan globe its Aryan ruling castes, spreading

[26] Rosenberg: *Mythus,* pp. 24–5.

everywhere their noble blessings — such as war. The book traces the process with the pictorial detail of an eye-witness. The details strangely resemble the stage-settings of Wagner's operas. To prove that these hypothetical inhabitants of a lost continent had blue eyes, blond hair, and godlike physiques is child's play for a Director of Weltanschauung. He " proves " it — being an archæological as well as philosophical genius — by discovering " pure nordic types " on ancient Egyptian, Libyan, and Indian relics.[27]

From Atlantis the blond master-race streamed in four great migrations: first, over North Africa; second, the Indo-Aryan wave over Persia and India, followed by the Doric Greeks and the Latins, who created the Hellenic and Roman civilizations; third, the Teutonic wave over Europe, after the Roman Empire decayed from mixing its blood; fourth and most recent, the colonizing of the whole globe by the roving Germanic element of western Europe. Great Britain led the fourth wave because Germany proper was not yet unified. In so far as the British Empire makes the coloured races subservient and pleases Rosenberg, it is Germanic. In so far as it displeases Rosenberg by rivalling Germany, it is the globe's capitalist exploiter, hence Jewish.[28]

All four migratory waves he calls " nordic," a broad, vague term. As earth's " master race " — Rosenberg's favourite term for flattering his audience — they enslaved the dark-haired inhabitants of the non-Atlantean continents. From this original racial enslavement came Hindu caste divisions, Rosenberg's favourite social institution. No democratic nonsense about equality! Unfortunately the rulers eventually interbred with their slaves. That

[27] Ibid., pp. 26–9.
[28] Ibid., p. 25. Rauschning: *Revolution,* p. 194.

caused the downfall of all history's empires, as Rosenberg at great length tries to prove. The Teuton wave has kept its purity best of the four, so that it has the best chance of building, by ruthless war, the world empire of the future.[29]

For propaganda purposes, the name of Jesus is too good to attack. The dilemma of all anti-Semites is how to provide Jesus with a family tree compatible with the Nazi Nürnberg laws. Already Houston Chamberlain, Eckart, and Hitler guessed and hoped that possibly Galileans were not Jews. No sooner said than proved. In Nazi thought, hypothesis and hope are synonymous with fact, and Nazi theology has made Christ's Galilean ancestry Aryan by decree. To bolster this up in the grand manner was Rosenberg's job: in addition to the four main migrations from lost Atlantis, stray little islands of blonds settled amid the non-Aryan world, and Galilee was such a " nordic stratum," untainted in the very core of Jewry.[30]

The book roams through all the history of all countries. Everything is dogmatically " explained " and every past historical mystery solved. Thereby the book becomes an unconscious parody of Spengler's work, which was equally ambitious and all-embracing but immensely wiser. Rosenberg chides Spengler for his environmental instead of " racial-organic " explanation of cultures.[31] But there is no need to go on summarizing Rosenberg's hundreds of pages of racial interpretation of history.

ART

The second book of *Mythus* does for art what the first does for history and politics: it is a racial interpretation of

---

29 Rosenberg: *Mythus*, pp. 28, 31, 34, 52, 54, 75 ff., 83 ff.
30 Ibid., pp. 27, 76.
31 Ibid., pp. 403–4.

art. Duly catalogued are the colour of the hair of all famous artists through the ages; and so the problem of art, too, is solved forever. Art is a Good Thing, we are told, and nazism intends to " spread " art right and left among those exquisite connoisseurs, " the masses." True art and true religion must spring not from the atomistic individual but collectively from the organic Volk. This romantic notion Rosenberg derived from Wagner's famous essay *The Art of the Future*. From Wagner's essay Rosenberg chose a quotation about Volk art as basis for the whole second book.

Nordic art is not form-bound, contemplative, classical, but striving and dynamic like Faust. Wagner is the greatest of artists because his art incarnates the " collective art-life " of the " nordic soul." This art-life is defined as the " nordic beauty-ideal " plus love of " nature " plus " hero-honour " plus " heroic will-power." The reader is thereupon overwhelmed with examples of these categories from Wagners operas *Tristan and Isolde, Lohengrin, Die Meistersinger,* and *Siegfried*. Throughout the book, Wagner exemplifies the racial earmarks of nordic art.[32]

The world's great art may seem separate achievements. Actually all are organically one. " A nordic hero-saga, a Prussian march, a Bach composition, an Eckehart sermon, a Faust monologue, are only diverse utterances of one and the same soul," the collective race soul of the blond godlike children of Atlantis. This " eternal force " was " first united under the name Wotan " and later " incarnated in Frederick the Great and Bismarck." But " nordic blood " will continue thus to " work and weave with nordic soul in mystic union " only so long as " men are ready to die " for belief in " the Myth." [33]

[32] Ibid., pp. 433–4, 443, 274.
[33] Ibid., p. 680.

Proud of his ability to see both sides of a debate, Rosenberg concedes that the unpatriotic might cite ancient Greece and the Italian Renaissance as examples of unnordic greatness in art. A great part of the book refutes this heresy by showing how every great Italian was really a blond nordic who strayed south by accident. Rosenberg does this by punning: he shows how each great name resembles some Germanic name, from which it is derived possibly, ergo hypothetically, ergo indubitably. For example, " it is today certain that Dante was of Germanic ancestry," because the name of Italy's greatest poet, Dante Alighieri, came from " Durante Aldiger, a pure Germanic name." [34] This was written before the Rome-Berlin axis.

Rosenberg attaches great importance to quotations from such apparent non-nordics as Euripides, Aristophanes, Dante, and others, showing that they were gentlemen who preferred blondes. Yet colour of hair not only has no connection with thought and morals but is not even a race characteristic. Statistically, a majority of Germans and even of the " purer nordic " Scandinavians are dark-haired, a minority blond. Not a small but an overwhelming majority of Nazi leaders are brunets. Blondness is a physical gene appearing according to the three-to-one ratio of the Mendelian law of heredity and not linked with mental qualities. Yet Rosenberg spends pages of probably " sound " scholarly research unearthing ancient poems whose heroines and heroes had blond hair. [35] With similar laboriousness, one could list many poems with brunet heroes and brunette heroines.

[34] Ibid., pp. 81, 70 footnote.
[35] Ibid., pp. 287, 295.

ROSENBERG'S LASTING INFLUENCES

Rosenberg unveils the secret of history in a single sentence: " Naught can change the one fact that the 'meaning of world-history,' shining out from the north, has passed over the whole earth, borne by a blue-eyed blond race." [36]

The racial quackery of nazism in general and Rosenberg in particular is not being unfairly oversimplified by me, but is as crude as here demonstrated. Yet *Myth* is taken seriously both by Nazis who swear by it and by anti-Nazis who swear at it. *Myth* has received many serious, long, and detailed refutations. Separate books of refutation are now at hand from Catholic, Lutheran, Anglican, scientific, democratic, militarist, and French viewpoints. [37] The justified motive for this is the book's great influence on German schooling and the need to combat that influence.

However, Nazis will inevitably expand beyond much of Rosenberg's rigid dogma in their new phase of becoming the globe's proconsuls. Meanwhile western scholars, embarrassed at seeming aloof and wanting to do their bit to " fight the Nazi Antichrist," will go right on refuting

---

[36] Ibid., p, 28.

[37] Refutations of *Myth*, or critiques of Rosenberg:

Catholic: *Kirchlicher Anzeiger für die Erzdiözese Köln,* Cologne, " Studien zum Mythus des XX. Jahrhunderts," October 1934; " Nachtrag zu den Studien," December 1934.

Lutheran: Walter Kuenneth: *Antwort auf den Mythus* (Berlin, 1935).

Anglican: Nathaniel Micklem: *National Socialism and the Roman Catholic Church* (London, 1939).

Scientific: University of Paris: *Racisme et Christianisme* (Paris, 1939), by a number of Catholic professors, including scientific refutation of racism by Albert de Lapparent.

French democratic: Pierre Grosclaude: *Alfred Rosenberg et le Mythe du XXme. Siècle* (Paris, 1938).

Attack by a German militarist: A. Haselmayer: *Der Fall Rosenbergs und fällt Hitler mit?* (Munich, 1931), in rebuttal of Rosenberg's *Der Fall Ludendorff.*

Also innumerable periodicals.

Rosenberg's inaccurate historical footnotes long after the Nazis have forgotten them.

When I say Germany's proconsul era outgrows the rigid dogma of *Myth,* I mean mainly the doctrinaire interpretations of history and race. These are what American and British scholars most associate with Rosenberg's name, but they are not his most important influences. For example, non-Germans know Rosenberg the influential philosopher but not Rosenberg the influential editor. Untranslated are his widely circulated pamphlets. All together he has had a fourfold permanent influence on history:

1. As prophet in drawing the main outlines of the Führer-state in the last book of *Myth.* They will last as long as Nazi Germany.

2. As journalist and pamphleteer.

3. As Nazi educator.

4. As the leading foe of the Christian churches.

These four influences will now be taken up. The fourth will be included in the separate chapter on " Nazi Religion versus Christian Religion."

CHAPTER XII

PROPHET LAUREATE
OF METAPOLITICS: PART II

~~~~~~

It takes more than machines of terror to make a Nazi Blitzkrieg. It takes soldiers with minds schooled to withstand the shock of their own frightfulness. That is where Rosenberg comes into the picture. In molding Germany's "psychology of frightfulness," Rosenberg wields an influence as powerful as that of the much-publicized Goebbels and the much-feared Himmler and his secret police. Rosenberg has directed Germany's psychological rearmament.

— H. C. WOLFE *and* H. HAUSER [1]

THE COMING REICH

The last book of *Myth* is entitled "The Coming Reich." By the Jahn quotation under its title, it proclaims its intention to carry on the lines laid down in Jahn's *Folkdom.* Rosenberg repeats spontaneously most of the points we examined in Jahn totalitarian Volk state. These will not be

---

[1] In the *New York Herald Tribune.* Cf. note 19 to this chapter.

repeated here. Instead let us consider where Rosenberg advances far beyond Jahn.

Rosenberg begins by announcing that the bourgeoisie is decadent and doomed, both economically and psychologically, both as ruling caste and as " liberal " way of life. This death announcement certainly proved true for Germany. Rosenberg would replace the bourgeois by a new Teutonic Order like that of the Middle Ages. This time it must not spring from any privileged class, he insists, but from the mass of the German Volk. To achieve its great missions and to wage war effectively, the new Teutonic Order must rule dictatorially and abolish such nonsense as political parties and free elections. Its sense of responsibility, the sense of honour inherent in its nordic blood, will be sufficient restraint. It needs no irresponsible parliament and free press to restrain its will-power. By implication this new Order will be the Nazi party.[2]

The new Order must be built on the right spirit. Rosenberg cites 1813 as the best example of the right spirit: the spirit of the War of Liberation, the days of Jahn and Fichte and Arndt. Those days and that spirit are the chief historical inspiration of those Nazis who know history, especially Hitler. Why? For two reasons. Then romantic nationalism first passed from books into bullets. And then, as after Versailles, war seemed the only realistic reply to a harsh and humiliating French peace.[3]

To awaken the new Order from the dozing German Volk, Rosenberg calls for " sermons which hypnotize and writers who knowingly inspire hearts." [4] " Knowingly " is the key-word here; it implies the whole Nazi propaganda technique. Note the juxtaposition of " knowingly," with its

[2] Rosenberg: *Mythus,* pp. 541–51. Elaborated in Rosenberg: *Der deutsche Ordensstaat* (Munich, 1934).

[3] Rosenberg: *Mythus,* p. 541.

[4] Ibid., pp. 521–2.

intellectual connotations, and "inspire hearts," with its dæmonic and emotional connotations. Typically German is the "knowingly" intellectual brand of anti-intellectualism, the very brainy worship of the "heart," the thorough and bureaucratic *organization* of "spontaneous inspiration." Only the Germans can triumphantly combine supreme hysteria with supreme efficiency.

Rosenberg reserves much of his most ferocious hate for the Jesuits and the Catholic hierarchy. Therefore his outline for the new Order consciously imitates Jesuit techniques and the Roman hierarchy. Through a succession of secular priests, bishops, and archbishops, the new Teutonic Order must rise like a pyramid from the German Volk, getting ever narrower, with the Führer at the pinnacle.[5]

Rosenberg should not be accused of wanting dictatorship as a principle. He minces no words against oppressive dictatorships like that of Soviet Russia and "stock-market Jews." His will be a *good* dictatorship, a Volk dictatorship. He follows the spirit of Wagner's complicated distinction between king and monarch. Rejecting alike government by parliament or by kaiser (monarch), Rosenberg demands the Volk-king, the hero-dictator risen from the ranks, whom Jahn and Wagner prophesied.

The qualities and justification of the Volk-king are outlined in the Führer section of the chapter on Wagner's metapolitics. This Wagnerian concept is basic to nazism. Rosenberg says: "We want to see in a German king a person like ourselves" (that is, not what Wagner called a "monarch," not an aristocratic kaiser, no class distinctions), "but yet the incarnation of a hero myth" (that is, not a prosaic democrat, but Wagner's mythical reborn Siegfried-Barbarossa). "The future will find the form of a

---

[5] Ibid., p. 546.

German national-socialist Volk-Führerdom." This will
" incarnate the yearning of the race of today for the coming Reich." [6]

The gist of the Führer myth is that the Führer *is* (incarnates) the Volk, instead of ruling it detachedly like monarch or economic class or representing it like a democrat.
The Führer is an organic part of the Volk instead of a
detached atom. This myth is absolutely basic to Hitler's
rule today. Of course, it is only a myth: after all, Hitler's
rule is also maintained by army, concentration camps, and
mendacious propaganda and not simply by incarnating
the romantic chimera of a subconscious Volk-will. But so
deeply has political romanticism steeped the German
masses in this myth that without it even army, concentration camps, and the lying press could not keep Hitler in
power. Hitler's rule rests on a combination of terror and
enthusiastic popular consent, of which neither by itself
would maintain him.

The new Nazi religion is for once right when it reacts
against the self-destructive economic materialism of our
democracy. The anti-economic reaction is typical of German thought in general rather than to the credit of the
Nazis. But as usual Germans react too far. Like most romantics, Rosenberg can spare few pages for anything so
uninspired as economics.

Even when at last he seems to tackle economics, he begins to " soar " the minute we turn our head, and we end
up in the clouds again, feeling more " noble " than ever.
In metapolitics even the price of potatoes must be heroic.
Grosshungern is a favourite German word, meaning to
starve oneself into greatness. For western democracies to
laugh at this sort of thing, as they have in the last decade,
is suicidal, for Germans have so often won their wars by

---

[6] Ibid. p. 559.

greater willingness for mass sacrifice than their foes. Realization of these facts of sacrifice sets a clear task for the peoples still retaining a free way of life, a task that is being realized only slowly by America's wrangling economic pressure-groups.

Already in the 1840's Wagner had established " gold " in German minds as the symbol of Frenchmen, capitalists, Jews. Consider the motif of sinister gold in his *Nibelungen Ring.* The Nazi poet Bangert wrote a book called *Gold or Blood.* Rosenberg uses that slogan as follows:

Blood is true socialism, based on a " racially-organically welded society." Gold is false socialism, Judaism, Marxism, democracy, " economic exploitation by finance," Freemasonry. " The great mission of the new German worker movement is to uproot from German life as *an alien Syrian-Judaic plant* the Marxist materialism and the finance-capitalist rear gard." Typically Nazi, Rosenberg judges an idea by its racial origins rather than by its objective merits or demerits. In other words, if Marxists and capitalists don't like Germany, they should go back to Syria, where they came from.[7]

Rosenberg would like America to join Germany in socialism of blood by revolting against Syrian-Judaic Wall Street. The United States is " the glorious land of the future " provided we breed a stock " consciously north-European, purged of blacks and yellows and Jews . . . that is to say, the destruction of the concept New York." Without being particularly enamoured of " the concept New York," we must yet suspect all such " white-Protestant-American " appeals. Such appeals will be the basis of a national American fascism, disguised behind " anti-fascist " (really anti-alien) slogans. Already it has

---

[7] Otto Bangert: *Gold oder Blut* (Munich, 1927). Rosenberg: *Mythus,* pp. 670–1, 15–17.

been remarked that Rosenberg's phrases about America would elect him straightway Imperial Wizard of the Ku Klux Klan — were it not for his Jewish-sounding name. Though wanting us " purged of yellows," Rosenberg urges us for our own good to hand our " Far East possessions to Japan." So already before Hitler's rise to power, the Japanese, because of their militarism and their Faustian striving, were unofficial Aryans.[8]

ROSENBERG AS JOURNALIST

Nazism's two most influential men of action were Göring and the purged Captain Röhm. But they were never influential as men of ideas; hence they are outside this book's scope. Since the 1920's Goebbels and Rosenberg have ranked as the two leading Nazi journalists and the two leading men of ideas. Hitler's mass appeal is unthinkable without their propaganda. Rosenberg the journalist has converted to nazism and war-fervour many a humble home that never heard of Rosenberg the philosopher.

His flood of anti-Semitic, anti-bolshevik, and anti-church pamphlets has already been mentioned. So has his role as editor of the official daily newspaper and of the official magazine for the party élite. His flood of effective articles and ineffective orations is reprinted at intervals in books with such titles as *Blood and Honour*.[9]

These reprinted books cover his activity from 1919 till the present. They will afford the historian an indispensable record of Nazi ideology from day to day. Their demands, prophecies, and programs have been pretty consistently carried out since then by Hitler — including the crusade

[8] Rosenberg: *Mythus,* pp. 671, 673. Kolnai, op. cit., p. 607.

[9] Rosenberg: *Blut und Ehre* (17th ed., Munich, 1938), speeches and articles of 1919–33; circulation of 130,000 in 1938. *Gestaltung der Idee* (7th ed., Munich, 1938), speeches and articles of 1933–5.

into the Russian Ukraine. From 1919 on, the leitmotiv of Rosenberg's articles and speeches is the mission to crush democracy both in and outside Germany and to dominate the world by force.

In his popular articles Rosenberg's racism is far cruder than in *Myth*. He does not give his simple hearers headaches with too much scholarly research into Atlantean swan-boats and Etruscan pottery. But all have heard of Shakespeare and are proud of it, and so Rosenberg proclaims in his newspaper *Der Völkische Beobachter:* " We regard Shakespeare, with his nordic delineation of the world, as a *German* classic." [10] In such popularized racism, Rosenberg has a knack of stating what everyone likes to hear — that is, what flatters most a nation with a (quite unjustified) cultural inferiority complex.

His most influential pamphlet by far is called *Nature, Fundamentals, and Goals of the National Socialist German Worker Party: the Program of the Movement.* It is all-important as the party's first official booklet. The first edition of 1922 was read and officially approved by Hitler. From then till now, despite all changes of policies, it has been disseminated by the party press — 150,000 copies by 1930, 350,000 copies by 1938. Following are familiar ideas which this pamphlet successfully put across.[11]

It begins in the Wagnerian tradition of contrasting German idealism with Jewish materialism. Nazi " idealism " declares war on " all materialistic, mammonistic thoughts." [12] Rosenberg's ceaseless attempt to saddle materialism on democracy must be emphatically repudiated. In so far as the democracies are indeed only " materialistic,

---

[10] *We Americans* (Boston: Atlantic Monthly Co.; 1939), p. 22.

[11] Rosenberg: *Wesen, Grundsätze, und Ziele der N.S.D.A.P.; das Programm der Bewegung* (Munich, 1933; 1st ed., 1922).

[12] All quotations in this and the seven following paragraphs are from Rosenberg: *Wesen,* pp. 6–8.

mammonistic," they will be conquered by fascism — for lack of self-sacrifice and hard work. But democracy consists of more than the Bank of France! The hard-working, independent-thinking citizenry who built the free countries of the west, and who in England and elsewhere die for freedom today, have more reservoirs of courage, sacrifice, and sense of duty than all the vaunted Nazi idealism.

In the days of the German Republic, Marxism was not yet so discredited as today. Its demoralizing materialist doctrines, though not really practised by the Republic, were so widely preached that Rosenberg's oversimple formula of Nazi idealism versus democratic materialism came as a welcome change to millions. His formula especially caught the fiery imagination of the youth movements. The way for the west to fight the formula's appeal is not to justify it by clamouring for ever higher business profits and by striking for ever lower hours in indispensable airplane factories (as during the regime of the French Popular Front). The way to fight it and win the imagination of the new generation is to show that the free peoples in their greatest crisis can be even more productive, unselfish, and co-operative than the most efficient slaves.

The correct beginning for every Nazi pamphlet is to list all it damns, always a list huger in space and fervour than that of what is praised. Not only is Rosenberg's pamphlet " against " democrats, Freemasons, and sin, but sweepingly " against *all* parties whether of Right or Left " (italics his) as " equally guilty of the German Volk's woe." Sensitive about belonging to nazism's less radical wing, Rosenberg leans backwards to declare himself especially " against " all who " look down on the Volk-comrade in working clothes as on a second-rank citizen." Rosenberg not merely piously deplores this snobbish attitude but cleverly observes that it " puts welcome weapons for agitation in the

hands of alien-folkic Volk-seducers." To translate these
compound nouns and adjectives of Rosenberg's into round-
about English phrases, instead of literally, might make
smoother reading but would miss the inimitable hippo-
potamoid grace of the original.

The pamphlet sets romanticism's usual false issue of
red-blooded vitalism versus abstract intellect. " Interest in
abstract, bloodless axioms sharpened the gap between
mental labourer and manual labourer." One of nazism's
most popular propaganda appeals, as found in Wagner,
Eckart, Rosenberg, Hitler, Goebbels, is the Sherlock
Holmes exposé of secret sinister masks. The pamphlet as-
serts, and millions of Germans believe that " Marxism pre-
tends to fight the exploiting world-capitalism, but has
worked ever since its origins hand in hand with international banks and stock markets." Like the Bolsheviks and
like Goebbels, Rosenberg finds the 1918 German Revolution a " betrayal " in which the " anti-capitalist, plundered
workers " were tricked into a " stock-market revolution "
with the masked " purpose " of delivering " Germany's national industry and agriculture into the hands of the super-
state of finance-capital."

Here in Rosenberg, approved by Hitler already in 1922,
occurs that sarcastic phrase: " plutocratic democracies,"
which Hitler was to use with such effect for home consump-
tion during the war of 1940. The most dramatic statement
of the pamphlet is this: " That was the greatest fraud of
the nineteenth century, as it finally triumphed in Moscow
in November 1917 and in Berlin in November 1918: the
anti-capitalist world-revolution led by the lackeys of world-
capitalism." Here we hit upon the modern world's basic
issue of social philosophy, as Rosenberg sees it: the " fraud
of the nineteenth century " (the " stock-market revolution ") versus " the Myth of the twentieth century " (the

revolution of German folkdom). The contrast must be
kept in mind throughout.

What made possible " this monstrous world-fraud " by
which " the lackeys of capitalism " sneak into leadership
of anti-capitalist revolutions? Rosenberg's pamphlet explains this neat stunt by alleging that " in the nineteenth
century the leadership of the Volk-exploiting capitalism
as well as of Marxism came into the hands of one and the
same Volk: the Jews. Hence Marxism was and is basically
a *race* war " (italics his).

What enabled the Jews to acquire this " leadership " in
the first place? The pamphlet blames the French Revolution, which Rosenberg urges Germany to reverse. The
blunder of the French Revolution, he charges, was this: it
was the first major movement to let the Jews out of the
mediæval ghettoes. Emancipation and legal equality of
oppressed races resulted from its " decadent " ideas of
liberté, égalité, fraternité, from which Hitler and Laval
would purge France in 1940.

What enables the Jews to retain their " stock-market
dictatorship " of the globe when they are so outnumbered
by their Aryan slaves? The secret Jewish world-masters
achieve this, screeches the pamphlet, by their technique of
" through division to rule." They it is who have set Protestant against Catholic. They it is who have set German
capitalist against German worker.

This allegation borders on persecution complex. Rosenberg's pamphlet borrows this allegation from his friend
Eckart's pamphlet of 1919, *Bolshevism from Moses to
Lenin.* Eckart's pamphlet, which consists of educational
dialogues between him and his pupil Hitler, traces every
division and disaster of history to Jewry's " divide and
rule." Eckart and Rosenberg and their pupil Hitler derived this hysterical *idée fixe* from the forged *Protocols of*

the Elders of Zion and, in less extreme form, from Wagner.[13]

Rosenberg insists the party system must be swept away because " the parties were no longer a helpful organ in the Volk organism. . . . National Socialism admits openly that it is a battle-party which may perhaps never compose a numerical majority, but it does so in the firm faith that it incarnates a Volk movement which will decide Germany's destiny. . . ." [14]

This is shrewd propaganda to justify the tyranny of a Nazi minority over Germany, but it is far more than that. It sincerely expresses Germany's widespread political romanticism. The only unit valued is the group organism; separate parties must go. The Nazis, though a mathematical minority, " incarnate " the whole Volk in Wagnerian fashion. Rosenberg unwittingly illustrates the influence of Rousseau, godfather of German romanticism. Rousseau preached that a minority might express the people's " general will " (the organic will, in romantic-Wagnerian terminology) more than some majority of individual interests, which merely expresses the " will of all " (the sum of atomistic wills, in romantic-Wagnerian terminology).

On economics Rosenberg's pamphlet has the same program as his friend Eckart and his foe Goebbels. " A German government will first of all advance to the state ownership of the stock markets and banks." It is typical of Nazi propaganda that after every such statement expressing the partly sane sentiments of Marxist socialism, an insane conclusion of anti-Semitism is immediately drawn. The purpose of this is subtly to ease the German masses from their peaceful trade-union socialism into in-

[13] Dietrich Eckart: *Der Bolschewismus von Moses bis Lenin, Zwiegespräch zwischen Hitler und Mir* (Munich; 1st ed. has 1923 on cover and 1924 inside; 2nd ed., 1925).

[14] Rosenberg: *Wesen,* pp. 10–11.

sane anti-Semitism, thence into aggressive nationalism, thence into war. That is why Rosenberg follows his relatively sane demand for nationalizing banks with this flow of rhetoric:

" All the ' reparation-questions ' would at one blow become immaterial if every Volk would jail its bankers, its parasitic usurious stock-market Jews, and use for the good of the nation the cash they swindled from every Volk." [15]

Also typical of fascist propaganda are the glowing promises of freedom and prosperity which the common people can achieve if only they'll take " direct action " to exterminate parliamentary government. Rosenberg says: " All parliaments depend on high finance, which enslaves the peoples. . . . The parliamentary representatives represent not the interests of the Volk but the interests of those economic spheres which paid for their elections." [16] Partly justified, and only partly, this most basic of all slanders against parliamentary democracy was first popularized by Karl Marx. Then in Wagner and Lagarde and Chamberlain this slander evolved into anti-Semitism and anti-Marxism, a posthumous irony for Marx.

The pamphlet elaborates Rosenberg's drastic views on foreign policy, already familiar, and sheds the familiar tears over unjust Versailles. The rest of the pages give the masses detailed explanation of Hitler's original Twenty-five-Point program, already summarized in the chapter on " Hitler and Wagner." Rosenberg subjects each of the Twenty-five Points to his metapolitical higher criticism and proves they will give everything to everybody.

Do any Germans fear the dictatorial means of the only party which can bring " freedom and bread "? More in sorrow than in anger Rosenberg raises his brows at such a

---

[15] Ibid., pp. 24–5.
[16] Ibid., p. 45.

fear and lulls it back to sleep by this solemn promise: the
Nazi dictatorship is but a needed interlude in the Volk's
march to greater freedom and will wither away when no
longer needed. As soon as the folkic Weltanschauung triumphs, " then the National Socialist Labour Party has fulfilled its mission and can leave the scene." With admirable
self-denial, National Socialism " scorns to establish itself
immortally as a political party." [17] Instead, it will merely
last — so Hitler informed Germany in a speech *after* getting the dictatorship — " for the next two thousand years."

ROSENBERG AS EDUCATOR

" Hitler's teacher was Alfred Rosenberg, the young Russo-
German who joined Hitler in 1920 and is to this day the
officially appointed trustee of National Socialist ideology." [18] Little time need be spent on Hitler's repetition of
Rosenberg's ideas because that is too obvious to anyone
who has glanced at *Mein Kampf*. We should have to re-
produce almost every other page of *Mein Kampf* because
almost every view I have quoted from Rosenberg is repeated there, often in exactly the same phrases and almost
the same sentences.

Never having finished high school, the Führer received
from Rosenberg his higher education, especially in history
and racism and his view of non-German lands. Rosenberg
in turn is echoing earlier romantics. It was he and Eckart
who in 1923 introduced Hitler to Frau Wagner and Chamberlain at Bayreuth. All three men combined to steep the
Führer in Wagnerian metapolitics, which is his inspiration
during today's war.

Rosenberg is the educator not only of Hitler; he has been

[17] Rosenberg: *Wesen*, p. 11.
[18] Olden, op. cit., p. 148.

labelled "the educational dictator of German youth."[19] His aim is to prepare youth psychologically for the merci- lessness needed in order efficiently to bomb civilians and build empires. Whether for future class war or present national war, Nazi education moulds the mind and body for merciless war. That makes Rosenberg and Goebbels as important as the military leaders in preparing and winning Hitler's war:

> In his talks with Hitler, Rosenberg advocated psycho- logical re-armament for Germany, a complete regimenta- tion of thought. *Hitler was fascinated.* . . . Once the Nazis came to power, the entire resources of the new state were thrown behind Rosenberg's philosophy. The press and the schools hammered home his views . . . of the "master race." What the Nazis are doing in the conquered Czech and Polish lands is a practical application of Rosen- berg's philosophy.[20]

Rosenberg says in his 1930 preface to *Myth:* "This is the mission of our century: out of a new Life-myth to create a new human type."[21] That best sums up the aim and successful achievement of Nazi education: a new hu- man type. "Education" is here used in the broad sense to include all didactic diffusion of ideas. Most of the earlier sections on Rosenberg's ideas should be classified under education, for most of these ideas are being taught to young Germans. But in addition some interesting con- crete examples must be cited of Rosenberg's influence; also of Nazi methods in general.

His racism influences the country on the two quite dif- ferent levels of highbrow and lowbrow. The latter over-

---

[19] H. C. Wolfe and Heinrich Hauser: "Doctor of Frightfulness," in *This Week,* magazine section of the *New York Herald Tribune,* June 30, 1940, p. 6.
[20] Ibid.
[21] Rosenberg: *Mythus,* p. 2.

shoots his own intentions and is futilely deplored by him as
an absurd vulgarization of his truths. For example, the
First Vice-Mayor of Königsdorf officially decreed that, in
order to further race purity, " cows and cattle which were
bought from Jews, directly or indirectly, may not be bred
with the community bull." [22] Rosenberg deserves full
credit for abhorring Hitler's old friend Julius Streicher and
his *Stürmer*. The *Stürmer* has the distinction of being the
vulgarest sheet on the face of the globe. It is dedicated to
slanderous sex scandals about Jews and the Christian
clergy.

Rosenberg's more highbrow racism is presented to university students as a logical " science " by Professor Hans
Günther. Günther is also an editor of *Race, a Monthly for
the Nordic Idea,* published in Berlin, Bremen, and Leipzig. It makes racism respectable among the educated
classes by having a dazzling array of Herr Doktors and professors among its editors and contributors. It is the organ
of Rosenberg's Nordic Society, outgrowth of the interesting Thule Society.

Thule is the legendary nordic island of the sagas. The
members of the Thule Society narrowly escaped execution
by the Munich Soviet dictatorship of 1919 when they distributed anti-Semitic pamphlets urging revolt. The members included the three most important early founders of
the Nazi party, who met each other in the Thule Society
before they made the acquaintance of a young Austrian
immigrant named Hitler. The three men were Rudolf
Hess, Eckart, Rosenberg.

To spread Kultur, Hitler in 1935 awarded prizes to his
choices as the leading German literary figure and the leading German scientist. Rosenberg had the honour of award-
ing the two prizes personally at the Party Congress. The

[22] *We Americans,* p. 6

two choices are naturally highly significant of the Reich's future Kultur. The winners were Hanns Johst and Günther. Günther has already been cited for his heroic efforts to make the Rosenbergian race-religion scientifically respectable. The poet Johst is best known to Americans for his often misquoted line: " When I hear the word ' culture,' I slip back the safety-catch of my revolver." [23]

This isolated line does him injustice because he is more the starry-eyed than the mad-dog brand of Nazi. In 1927 he wrote a play glorifying Tom Paine as the propagandist of the American Revolution. Johst's later plays, folkic, dashingly dæmonic, metapolitical, exalt a politics based on romanticism's organic and dynamic assumptions.

Johst, Rosenberg, and Goebbels unite to preach and practise that militarized up-to-date romanticism which they call " steel romanticism." That phrase is more significant than appears at first glance, for it sums up the synthesis of the two antitheses of tough Prussianism and dreamy Wagnerian romanticism. Johst, Rosenberg, and Goebbels reveal a really intelligent self-insight in summing themselves up with such brilliant aptness. This " steel romanticism " they constantly urge upon budding young authors as the Third Reich's official literary school.

Since great talent continues to be born under any regime, this generously subsidized literary school may produce, in a bad cause, some very good writers. The greatest modern German writer, Thomas Mann, courageously chose exile. But such distinctly major figures as Gerhart Hauptmann, Hans Fallada, Hermann Stehr, Hans Grimm, Rudolf Binding, Hans Carossa, Gottfried Benn, Ludwig Klages, and Erwin Guido Kolbenheyer chose to remain in Nazi Germany, where they are widely read today. Hitler's most

---

[23] Rosenberg: *Gestaltung*, p. 364. *We Americans*, p. 22. *Time*, New York, June 5, 1939, p. 83.

distinguished Norwegian admirer is the great novelist and
Nobel Prize winner Knut Hamsun, who has urged his
countrymen to fight democracy and to support none other
than Alfred Rosenberg's personal friend and disciple, the
Norwegian traitor Quisling. With his earthy, folkic peasants, Hamsun is in many ways a willing Nazi model for the
roots-in-the-soil phase of steel romanticism.

Today in Germany the great Rilke is posthumously the
favourite poet and, along with Stefan George, the most
imitated. Being harmlessly unpolitical, Rilke is tolerated
as the subject of some particularly intelligent writing inside Germany today. Such love of art for art's sake survives to a surprising extent the Nazi preaching of art for
the Volk's sake. Germany today is far from the literary or
cultural desert which American intellectuals think it to
be or would like it to be.

But the future? Too often the hand made to pluck the
violin or shape the clay is trained only to pull the machine-
gun trigger. The art of creating is canalized into the arti-
sanship of killing. The traditional German fervour and
technical virtuosity are retained all too invincibly in these
less æsthetic applications.

Rauschning points out that more sophisticated Nazis
mock Rosenberg's glorification of the nordic. Yet this
glorification is systematically disseminated among children
in schools and among adults in his network of Nordic Societies. This network reaches many for whom *Myth* is too
deep. Rosenberg and hundreds of fellow nordic enthusiasts tour the country addressing the Nordic Societies.
These earnest and humourless societies meet regularly at
Lübeck to hear a speech from their prophet Rosenberg
or to get a telegram from Sven Hedin pledging nordic
solidarity. Rosenberg also reaches the public with free
anti-Semitic exhibitions. In Frankfort am Main, he

founded an " Institute for Exploring the Jewish Question " and allows the public no lull in anti-Semitic agitation.[24]

Rosenberg's nordic philosophy is propagated by the state not out of love for philosophy for its own sake but for its practical effect in encouraging aggressive militarism. Hitler could drag Germany into war partly because millions of Germans have been steeped in Rosenberg's religion of nordic superiority, the supreme nordic virtue of bloody war, and the nordic mission to conquer the world. The official *Nazi Primer* for schoolchildren is filled with the Rosenberg and Günther teachings of race superiority: the nordics " are predisposed to *leadership* by nature, which distinguishes the nordic race from all others." [25]

The Hitler Youth movement, through which almost all young Germans must pass, is steeped in Rosenberg by his disciple Schirach. With what results? Typical is this verbatim dialogue in a German youth hostel. A young member of the Hitler Youth is explaining the gist of his history lessons to an American student:

"We learn about the superiority of the Indo-Germanic races, the blond, the blue-eyed peoples, in all branches of human activity. There was never a great general, statesman, or philosopher who was not Indo-Germanic."

"How about Hannibal and the Phœnicians who kept the Indo-Germanic Romans at bay for so long?"

"I am not quite sure about Hannibal, but if he was great, he was Indo-Germanic."

"How can you prove it? How does one know what was Indo-Germanic and what was not? "

"One looks in old church books."

"And before there were churches? "

24 *Münchner Neueste Nachrichten*, Munich daily, June 22, 1939, p. 2, and August 12, 1939, p. 1. A typical Rosenberg speech to a Nordic Society is reprinted in Rosenberg: *Gestaltung*, pp. 339–48.

25 H. L. Childs, ed.: *Nazi Primer* (New York, etc., 1938).

"One looks at the ancestor pass (*Ahnenpass*)."

"But there were no ancestor passes before 1933."

"But Hannibal was Indo-Germanic. He was a great general, so he must have been." [26]

Nordic superiority was only the positive side of Rosenberg's job of "psychological re-armament" for Hitler's long-planned war. The negative side was to detach youth from Christian influences. Christianity's crime is that it teaches peace and love instead of war and hate. Ley tries to detach the labouring classes from Christianity, and Schirach the youth. The courageous Protestant manifesto of August 1936 protested: "In the training camps the conception of the world contained in the Rosenberg *Mythus* frequently is taught. . . . The Christian population of Germany notes with great perturbation that it is being ridiculed and scorned in every way in the *press, theatres, lectures, and mass meetings* for its faith in the will of Jesus Christ." Schirach boasts: "Rosenberg's way is also the way of the German youth." [27]

Before 1933 the universities and churches took pleasure in refuting Rosenberg and laughing him down. Since 1933 he has taken pleasure in forcing his teachings on them. Their catalogues suddenly sprout forth courses with such titles as "Aryan Weltanschauung." Professor Bergmann, author of the pagan "Twenty-five Theses," teaches his pupils the Chamberlain-Rosenberg version of history: "That the human race is still alive in spite of having been Christianized, it owes only to the entry of the healthy German peoples into history." [28]

At the University of Munich, against the will of both

---

[26] Ernest Zaugg: "German Youths," in *Christian Science Monitor*, Boston, November 7, 1939.

[27] Lichtenberger: *The Third Reich* (New York, 1937), pp. 341, 334.

[28] *We Americans*, p. 16.

professors and students, young Nazi officials, anti-church
disciples of Rosenberg, gave "*compulsory* lectures" at
which students were forced "neatly to write down" and
learn the following "fighting song":

The old Jewish shame is at last swept away;
The black band of rascals [Catholic priests] rages on.
German men, German women, beat the black band to a
   jelly.
Hang them on the gallows. . . . Ravens have been wait-
   ing.

Plunge the knives into the parson's body.
We'll be ready for any massacre.
Hoist the Hohenzollerns high on the lamp-post!
Hurl the hand-grenades into the churches![29]

In 1938 a young Nazi broke into a church at Neuhausen
and smashed the baptismal font and the altar crucifix. The
church demanded punishment. The trial was held before
a Nazi court. His defense was that he intended to make a
habit of smashing baptismal fonts at every chance. Verdict: not guilty. Such is the fruit of a Rosenbergian education.[30]

The anti-Christian propaganda and the general inflammatory agitation of the Nazis, as well as the example set
by government-sponsored burning and looting of Jewish
shops, can have only one culmination. That is the bloody
"second revolution" for which the party's younger, national-bolshevist wing yearns. Compared with the models
of the French and Russian revolutions, nazism's first revolution seems too bloodless for its ardent supporters, despite
all the "heads rolling in sand" and the "night of the long

---

[29] Heiden: *Hitler*, pp. 351–2.
[30] *Mein Kampf* (Reynal & Hitchcock ed.), p. 691, footnote.

knives." Hitler promised: " There will be no peace in the land until a body is hanging from every lamp-post! " [31] Can he restrain his mobs from executing that promise?

The second revolution will apply to all German capitalists the bloody violence and the state confiscation which the first revolution applied to Jewish capitalists. Perhaps the accumulated anti-church incitement will at last bear its logical fruit in mobs literally " hurling the hand-grenades into the churches." There may be church burnings. Though Rosenberg would deplore them, he more than any other man would be to blame for them. Since he leads an anti-national-bolshevist wing of the party, younger Nazis may liquidate him in the very same purge as his hated Christian and Jewish foes.

All able-bodied Germans must serve six months in the labour camps. These were taken over from the Weimar Republic, but vastly expanded. The labour camps have become Nazi Germany's most admirable institution because of their spirit of genuine friendly co-operation between all social classes and regional groups. Hitler announced their purpose to be the overcoming of class distinctions in common constructive tasks such as planting new trees and helping out overworked farmers. Here is an aspect of Nazi life for which I, witnessing it in 1937, felt tremendous respect. K. Hierl, the head of the Labour Service, says sincerely and wisely: " The universal duty of equal labour service raises the category ' worker ' to a patent of nobility for every German." [32]

Unfortunately Hierl also says all too truly: " Above all, the Labour Service must be a vast school for educating the

---

[31] Heiden: *Hitler,* p. 52.
[32] Generalarbeitführer von Gönner, ed.: *Spaten und Aehre* (Heidelberg, 1937), p. 89.

Volk." [33] And German education no longer means teaching the mind to reason, but stultifying the reasoning power with one-sided official propaganda. This aspect naturally wrecked my enthusiasm for the labour camps. Thereby nazism tacitly rewrites the classical formula to *mens insana in sano corpore*.

The Nazi indoctrination is based on "the handbook of German youth in Reich labour service." [34] Since millions are taught from this book, it is of interest and importance to us. It reviews German history and German thought in simple terms comprehensible to all classes. The names it cites can be safely taken as the official brain-heroes of popular Nazi thought. They include all the chief names we have been treating, Rosenberg, Houston Chamberlain, Father Jahn, Fichte, Herder, Arndt, Stein and the other heroes of the War of Liberation, and some of the romantic school.

The book instils the concepts of society which Hitler learned from Wagner's metapolitics and from Rosenberg. Liberalism is branded as incurably capitalistic, democracy as being not freedom but "the dictatorship of Judaism." Marxism, capitalism, liberalism, democracy, and conservatism are all branded as atomistic in contrast with that welded organic whole, that subconscious general will, which alone frees the Volk by incarnating it in a Führer. Rosenberg's magazine, the Twenty-five Points, and *Mein Kampf* are officially urged upon all the camp workers for a simple understanding and "spiritual deepening" of the "new Weltanschauung."

The handbook accuses the Weimar Republic of driving the proletariat from nationalism to Marxism. It is very im-

---

[33] Ibid., p. 104.

[34] Gönner, op. cit. The citations from it that follow are from pp. 30–50.

portant that the book does not even partly blame the
proletariat for this but blames the bourgeoisie. The bourgeois tried to "monopolize nationalism" and make it upper-class instead of socialist, thereby driving the proletariat
into the hands of the "fake" Jewish socialism of Marxism.
But today the "real" Aryan socialism wins back the proletariat to nationalism. That this chain of thought is being
instilled into all the next generation will have tremendous
consequences.

This chain of thought is the one point where the book
goes beyond the more moderate social teachings of Rosenberg and Hitler. The labour-service leaders belong at least
partly to the national-bolshevist wing of Goebbels and Ley.
Rosenberg and Hitler would have blamed the middle class
and the proletariat equally instead of solely the former
in Goebbels's fashion. American leftists tend to dismiss
violent Nazi anti-capitalism as merely a lot of hypocritical
phrases to fool the workers. This accusation is partly true,
but misses the main point.

The main point is the future. You can't year after year
violently agitate the masses with radically anti-capitalist
phrases, no matter how little really intended, without having to obey the clamorous mass demands thus created.
Mob energy will do wonders for its exploiters. Before tapping it, they pep it up with ever more radical promises and
toss it ever more innocent victims, such as the Jews. But it
is easier to start an avalanche than to stop it when you no
longer need it or can no longer satisfy it. The stubborn
genie of the *Arabian Nights* simply would not return into
the bottle, and the Nazis won't escape the law that all
revolutions devour their own demagogues. Ever faster
progression toward national bolshevism can be clearly predicted and will continue quite apart from whether Germany is an ally or a foe of Soviet Russia.

Liberal socialists and even Marxists would be superficial to rejoice in this German development. Its inevitable economic bolshevism will be the opposite of the socialist utopia they picture. It will very likely be restricted jealously, at least for a long time, to Rosenberg's "Germanic master nation." It will grind down its millions of non-German slaves, as *Mein Kampf* and *Myth* confidently predict. It will make possible ever more efficient military aggression, from which no continent will necessarily be safe and "isolated." Led by the inhumanly ruthless young Führers produced by Nazi schooling, the Nazi tyranny will trample down all sparks of individuality and all those democratic liberties which Marx assumed were inherent in socialist economics.

On an analogy with the French Revolution, a post-Hitler world — in non-racist hands — may emerge economically happier owing to Hitler, thanks to his economic unification of Europe and his removal of stifling local tariff-systems and talent-wasting class lines. National bolshevism, whether the Hitlerite or Stalinist version, does emancipate the ordinary citizen from the economic insecurity of depending on the laissez-faire fluctuations of unemployment, stock markets, and "capitalist" wage-slavery. But . . . what price economic bliss in terms of moral degradation?

MALE-LEAGUES IN GERMANY

Many modern nationalists, including Rosenberg, make much of the term "male-league" (*Männerbund*). It refers to warriors linked unto death by loyalties supposedly "nobler" than the emotions men feel for women. Up through the hierarchy, each follower must love his respective Führer not as one loves a woman but as one loves a god. These emotional loyalties form Germany's cult of the divine Führer. Schirach instils them into the youth movement.

Sometimes frankly unsublimated and physical, these emotions are more often claimed to be strictly religious rather than sexual. Just as politics becomes metapolitics across the Rhine, so we might say that sex in the Führer-cult becomes a sort of meta-sex, shrouded in mists of vague idealism. Too rhetorical to deserve the name " religion," religiosity is a better word. Male-league religiosity makes everybody feel very noble and soar at least verbally beyond the base physical.

Rosenberg insists that his Teutonic Order to save Germany must be a male-league. Participation of women would cause decadence. A state is founded, he argues, not on family but on male-league. All history's creative groups were male-leagues, welded inseparably by honour, battle, and comradeship. To prove this, he cites the ancient Greeks, the Teutonic Knights, the Prussian Officer Corps, the Nazi party. Like many Nazi writers he is more enthusiastic about male comradeship than about love of females.[35]

Rosenberg carefully avoids the word " homosexual," nor have we any right to assume he implies it. It is surprising to American readers how many German nationalist writers of the 1920's were not afraid of the word. Their inspiration was the male-league and Führer-cult, often frankly homosexual, that gathered round the great poet Stefan George. Despite his own aristocratic contempt for the Nazis, many of his followers had great influence in converting German youth to Nazism. A Nazi " youth leader " (*Jugendführer*) has published *Stefan George and the Youth,* showing this metapolitical poet's vast influence on German youth. George's former follower, the well-known nationalist Hans Blüher, wrote books lyrically urging more

---

[35] Rosenberg: *Mythus,* pp. 546, 493.

homo-eroticism in the proto-Nazi youth movements. Hans Blunck, the Nazi "Führer of Literature," boasts: "The state of today has grown out of the youth movement and the exquisite virile cohesion of the male-leagues (*Bunds*)."[36]

(The republican youth movements and labour camps were an entirely different matter. Let no one disparage them. Under leaders like Eugen Rosenstock-Hüssy they made their section of German youth a free bulwark against the Nazi youth movements.)

The hardboiled desperado Röhm, founder and chief of the Storm Troopers, gathered round him a loyal homosexual male-league. The most powerful Nazi after Hitler, Röhm had Germany's youth entrusted to his tender mercies. Politically his group was more revolutionary-socialist than Hitler or Rosenberg. Röhm's alleged plan was to seize supreme power by replacing the small aristocratic army of the Reichswehr with a Volk-army of Storm Troops. This was somewhat akin to the old dream of Jahn and Wagner in days of the Free Corps of the War of Liberation and of the Revolution of 1848. Röhm and his male-league were sent before firing squads by Hitler, Göring, and the Reichswehr in the 1934 purge.[37]

Rosenberg bitterly attacks the undue influence of women today. He wants them to be state-subsidized breeding-machines. Raising the German birth-rate is so

---

[36] Stefan George, complete works published by Bondi, Berlin, 1927–34; note especially *Der siebente Ring, Der Stern des Bundes, Das neue Reich*. Note proto-Nazi works of his disciple Friedrich Wolters. The "youth leader" Theodor Dschenfzig: *Stefan George und die Jugend* (Munich, 1934). Hans Blüher: *Die Rolle der Erotik in der männlichen Gesellschaft* (Jena, 1921); *Führer und Volk in der Jugendbewegung* (Jena, 1924); *Philosophie auf Posten* (Heidelberg, 1928). Kolnai, op. cit., pp. 67–88, 105.

[37] Ernst Röhm: *Die Geschichte eines Hochverräters* (Munich, 1928). Roberts: *The House that Hitler Built*, pp. 106–19. Heiden: *Hitler*, pp. 344–90.

all-important to him that it might justify polygamous
breeding. The Nazi government today encourages its soldiers to beget as many legitimate or illegitimate children as
possible while home on leave. Jahn had long ago urged
subsidized breeding. Love becomes just another munitions
factory, to produce cannon fodder. Rosenberg cites
America as a horrible object-lesson of feminism. As comic
relief, he makes some really quite clever remarks on bul-
lied American husbands and their social-climber wives.
Worthy of a *New Yorker* cartoon is Rosenberg's description
of the American husband fleeing to his club to play golf
when his wife fills the home with Women's Book Club
meetings.[38]

RUSSIAN AND EASTERN INFLUENCES ON GERMANY

The anti-Semitic tradition of German romantics was a matter of cultural battles, not of criminal physical violence.
Rosenberg, intellectually dominating Hitler in the early
1920's, brought Russia's pogrom tradition of physical violence to Germany. No German romantic, not even Wagner
and Chamberlain, produced such crude and barbarous
anti-Semitic slanders as the Russian forgeries called *The
Protocols of the Learned Elders of Zion*. These Rosenberg
spread throughout Germany, though even Goebbels has
admitted they might be forgeries. Hitler in *Mein Kampf*
defends them, whether true or not, as pragmatically indispensable because " once this book has become the common
property of a people, the Jewish danger is broken." [39]

---

[38] Rosenberg: *Mythus,* pp. 493–513.
[39] Sergius Nilus: *The Great in the Little* (2nd ed., Tsarskoye-Selo,
Russia, 1905); in appendix, " Protocols of the Learned Elders of Zion."
Hitler: *Mein Kampf* (Reynal & Hitchcock ed.), pp. 423–4.

The Protocols claim to be first-hand documents of a Jewish plot to enslave the globe. The plot consists of the twin " Jewish " systems of international socialism and usurious finance-capitalism, respectively causing the twin evils of Red dictatorship and bourgeois democracy. Widely circulated in the Germany of the 1920's, Rosenberg's pamphlets spreading this brand of anti-Semitism include *The Congress of World Conspirators at Basel, Immorality in the Talmud, The State-Hostile Zionism, International High Finance*. Also influential was his translation of the nineteenth-century French anti-Semite Gougenot des Mousseaux.[40]

In 1905 Sergius Nilus, a Russian mystic, first published the Protocols. Very likely he is also their forger, deriving them in part from a nineteenth-century pamphlet against Napoleon III. But Nilus may have been secretly given them by the Grand Duchess Elizabeth.

Nilus claimed to trace his exposé back two thousand years, the greatest historical discovery of all times! His discovery was more hysterical than historical: " According to the records of secret Jewish Zionism, Solomon and other Jewish learned men already in 929 B.C. thought out a scheme in theory for a peaceful conquest of the whole universe by Zion." Nilus's job was to supply scholarly justification for the pogrom policy of the pro-Czarist, anti-democratic vigilantes known as the Black Hundreds. The Protocols were circulated among the Russian peasants by the Czarist police in order to canalize the " dangerous " anti-Czarism of the 1905 famine days into " safe " anti-Semitism.

[40] Rosenberg: *Der Weltverschwörerkongress zu Basel* (Munich, Eher, n.d.); *Unmoral im Talmud* (Munich, n.d.); *Der staatsfeindliche Zionismus* (Munich, n.d.); *Internationale Hochfinanz* (Munich, n.d.). H. R. Gougenot des Mousseaux: *Der Jude,* tr. from French by Rosenberg (5th ed., Munich, 1921).

Gruesome days of bloodshed followed. Throughout Russia great multitudes of peasants talked incessantly of the machinations of the Jews and demanded vengeance for their wrongs. They took up axes and guns to purge the cities of the "alien Jews" who were seeking world domination. There were six hundred and ninety such massacres simultaneously planned and executed immediately following the distribution of Nilus' Protocols.[41]

The book's subsequent editions of 1913 and early 1917 were signals for similar pogroms. The book included a forged document wherein the secret leaders of Jewry boastfully predict: "When the time is ripe, the Jews with their monopoly of gold will stage a vast economic crisis and throw the workers out of jobs. The latter will then resort to violence as in the French Revolution, which was the work of our hands." This curious prediction seemed justified to millions of Russians and Germans by the Red revolutions of 1917–20 and by the world-wide economic depression. The Protocols were distributed among the White armies, inciting them to slaughter 120,000 Jews during 1918–21. White Russian refugees — above all, Rosenberg — brought the Protocols and the pogrom spirit into Germany and into the Nazi party.

Successful in winning the German masses from the Marxist parties was the Hitler technique of lumping together as Jewish the two most hated isms in Germany, finance capitalism and bolshevism. Since the Nazis learned this technique chiefly from the Protocols, the latter is one of the most important books of our age, a forgery which cannot be refuted too often. Father Coughlin serialized the Protocols in his *Social Justice*, popularizing in the New World melting-pot that blood-soaked field-manual of Old

[41] Quotations are from *Liberty*, N. Y. weekly, New York, February 10 and 17, 1940; L. B. Davidson and F. L. Collins: "The Jews and the Freemasons," February 10, pp. 9–10.

World pogroms. "Noteworthy is the fact that Hitler's justification of the Protocols [as quoted from Hitler above] almost parallels the explanation given by the Reverend Charles Coughlin at the time they were reprinted in his periodical." [42]

Without the slightest question, anti-Semitic Germans of the romanticist tradition, Jahn, Treitschke, Lagarde, and Wagner, would have been horrified and nauseated by the physical violence of Black Hundreds and Nazis. This pogrom tradition and the Protocols are but an example of the general Russianizing of the German masses after the World War. This Russianizing derived equally in Germany from Comintern Communists and White Guard fascists. The psychological polarity of Germans was no longer with the west but with the east.

Books and crowd attitudes of the 1920's show Germans more and more turning against western civilization. Unfortunately they turned as much against its immortal qualities of rationalism, legalism, and individual freedom as against its all too mortal qualities of muddling smug capitalist democracy and sordid overemphasis of economics. More and more, Germans turned toward the cryptic east: toward its traditions of mass despotism and mass frenzy; of tribal indifference to staggering losses of individual lives; of Attila and Mahomet and Genghis Khan; of hungry hordes on the march.

Few of us then noticed the ancient and sinister undercurrents in German life. Few of us envisaged the logical consequence of nineteenth-century romanticism and Wagner: revolt against the west. Germany seemed so inseparable from western civilization, to which her great thinkers contributed perhaps more than any others. But Germans felt betrayed by their past faith in the western way of life

[42] *Mein Kampf* (Reynal & Hitchcock ed.), editorial footnote, p. 424.

when the west betrayed Germany: when the Wilsonian promises of a free, co-operative Europe were broken at Versailles, when the French brutally invaded the disarmed Ruhr in 1923, when the consequent currency-inflation wiped out the German middle class and all its comfortable peace-and-production aims of western capitalism.

This change in Germany was observed at work in the following little-known letter by the wise and foolish poet D. H. Lawrence. Naturally we reject his implication of mystic racism in his use of " the Germanic spirit." Yet the awakening national culture which Lawrence observed in the 1920's was really there. It was unnoticed by most of us, however, above all by German democracy's own leaders. The convulsive change through which Germany was passing is caught prophetically in his queer, overwritten letter. Note well how far back was the date of his letter: 1924.

> Immediately you are over the Rhine, the spirit of the place has changed. There is no more attempt at the bluff of geniality. It is as if all the life had retreated eastwards. As if the Germanic life were slowly ebbing away from contact with western Europe. Germany feels empty and somehow menacing. So must the Roman soldiers have watched the black massive hills: with a certain fear and with the knowledge that they were at their own limits. So it is with the French: this almost mystic fear. . . . Germany is very different from what it was two-and-a-half years ago, when I was here. Then it was still open to Europe. Then it *still looked to western Europe* for a reunion, for a sort of *reconciliation.* Now that is over. The barrier has fallen.
>
> The great leaning of the Germanic spirit is once more eastwards, towards Russia, towards Tartary. The strange vortex of Tartary has become the positive centre again, the positivity of western Europe is broken. So that all

Germany reads "*Beasts, Men and Gods*" with a kind of fascination. Returning again to the fascination of the destructive east that produced Attila.

These queer gangs of Young Socialists [embryonic *national* socialists], youths and girls, with their non-material professions, their half-mystic assertions, they strike one as strange. Something primitive, like loose roving gangs of broken, scattered tribes. . . . As if everything and everybody recoiled from the old unison [with the west], as barbarians lurking in a wood recoil out of sight. . . . The ancient spirit of pre-historic Germany coming back at the end of history . . . whirling to the Roman days, then to the days of the silent forest and the dangerous lurking barbarians.

Something has happened which has not yet eventuated. The old spell of the world has broken, and the old, bristling, savage spirit has set in. The war did not break the old peace-and-production hope of the world, though it gave it a severe wrench. The old peace-and-production hope still governs at least the consciousness. But it feels as if, virtually, it were gone. The last two years have done it. There is no work — consequently no money. The shopkeepers are in despair. . . . We have brought it about ourselves — by a Ruhr occupation, by an English nullity, and by a German false will. . . . *The hope in peace-and-production is broken.* The old flow, the old adherence is ruptured. And a still older flow has set in. Back, back to the savage polarity of Tartary, and away from the polarity of civilized *Christian* Europe. This, it seems to me, has already happened. And it is a happening of far more profound import than any actual event. It is the *father of the next phase of events.*[43]

Not even a Director of Weltanschauung, not even a nordic racial determinist, can escape entirely from the

[43] D. H. Lawrence: *Phœnix: Posthumous Papers* (London and New York, 1936), "A Letter from Germany," pp. 107–10. (Italics mine.)

influence of environment. Not till 1919, when he was
twenty-six, did Rosenberg leave the sinking ship of the
Russian Empire for Germany. For seven hundred years
the German branch of his ancestry had lived as a small
island among Balts and Slavs and fought to save from
assimilation its German ways. Saving kopeks and stealing time from his jobs to steep himself in the books of
German literature and philosophy, Rosenberg became
more romantic than native German romantics and more
Wagnerian than Bayreuth Wagnerians. Most fanatic of
German nationalists, number-one despiser of Russia and
eastern influences, Rosenberg — introducer of *The Protocols of Zion* — was the leading influence in the early Nazi
party of the Russianizing of Germany. This is the quite
unconscious irony behind his role in German history.

METAPOLITICS VERSUS ITS INTELLECTUAL
CRITICS

How a new national mentality works is illustrated by how
it answers its critics. Two kinds of answers are possible:
suppression and persuasion. Persuasion and appeals to
objective reason are not nazism's forte. Said the then Nazi-
style poet F. Jünger (later a brave anti-Nazi): "Why do we
need four walls? One wall is enough!"[44] To stand a critic
against a wall as a " traitor " may not be a very subtle way
of " refuting " him but has a certain pragmatic charm for
the Nazis: it " works." But it works only against the weak.
Against such strong organizations as the church, even the
Nazis must occasionally stoop to scholarly persuasion. Let
us see how.

Two great groups in the Third Reich are openly critical:
the universities, out of hate of intellectual fraud, and the

---

[44] Hitler: *Mein Kampf* (Reynal & Hitchcock ed.), p. 353, footnote.

churches, out of hate of paganism. The party's rough men of action delegate to the fine, un-Italian hand of Rosenberg the job of refuting both groups. From both groups emanate scholarly criticisms against educating German youth in the Chamberlain-Rosenberg distortions of history. I shall briefly summarize Rosenberg's most typical refutations of his church and campus critics.

The official Catholic refutation of *Myth* and of Houston Chamberlain is the most thorough and scholarly of all. Since Goebbels delayed censoring it, Rosenberg turned to persuasion as second best and published *To the Obscurants of Our Age*. Published in 1935, this government-encouraged pamphlet ran through thirty-three editions by 1938 and had a circulation of 660,000. Its arguments best reveal the level of intellectual honesty of the official thinker of what was once the "land of thinkers." Rosenberg defends himself against the charge that he gives few sources to substantiate his *Myth*. Defence is certainly called for; we should be fascinated to learn the sources for some of his astounding discoveries. His defence is twofold.

First, he omits sources not because he lacks them but because he is so extraordinarily learned that if he cited his sources for every statement, his book would consist " one third of footnotes! " [exclamation-mark his]. " One third " would equal all of 235 additional pages, a truly formidable threat.

Second, for readers not scared off by the first defence, Rosenberg draws up his heaviest artillery: the romantic argument of inspiration. Let dry Doctors of Philosophy putter around with such lifeless things as footnotes and objective evidence; genius soars above all that. " For the same reason, H. S. Chamberlain is also abused, to whom I pay grateful homage. He, too, is called ' dilettante '; he is ' unscientific.' " Rosenberg correctly recognizes that he and Chamberlain stand or fall together. Their scientific critics Rosenberg refutes by calling them "mental dwarfs." To sum up his twofold defence: first, he has the evidence but omits it for the humanitarian reason of keeping down the book's length; second — well, maybe he hasn't the evidence, but romantic geniuses can get along without such results of uninspired drudgery.[45]

The most stressed issue between the Catholic critics and Rosenberg's reply is over Christianity. The only novelty here is the great stress both sides put on Rosenberg's Etruscan theory. The theory is important because he justifies his anti-Catholic crusade by calling the papacy the non-Aryan, Etruscan half of Rome. Here at last he cited his sources in *Myth:* not only his imagination, but also a book by Albert Grünwedel.[46] Once a fine intellect, Grünwedel became somewhat of a raving lunatic, whose divine mission was to unmask the extinct Etruscans as almost Satans incarnate in their amours of some twenty-five hundred years ago. Grünwedel and Rosenberg foist on them every unprintable vice that a lonely bachelor's ingenuity can conceive. But however "lax" the extinct sex life of the Etruscans, historians know almost nothing of them, as Rosenberg's refuters convincingly point out.

In reply, Rosenberg does not deny Grünwedel's lunacy, but hits upon the charming euphemism that the poor fellow's "nerves were overstrained" by his "gigantic labours." If no one else values those gigantic labours, that is due to Catholic suppression of the evidence, and to the fact that these Catholic persecutors are "the Etruscans of our age." They plotted to have Grünwedel declared in-

[45] Rosenberg: *An die Dunkelmänner unserer Zeit* (33d ed., Munich, 1938), pp. 65–6.

[46] Albert Grünwedel: *Tusca* (Leipzig, 1922).

sane because he was about to expose their real identity as secret Etruscans.[47]

Rosenberg's conclusion is that the secret aim of the Catholic book against him is to suppress his truths by the same tactics they used against martyred Grünwedel: namely, to coop up the great Director of Weltanschauung in a padded cell. Rosenberg says that the " Etruscans of our age " are plotting to enable " the whole hostile press to represent me as a maniac, a *broken-down psychopath*." [48] If all these citations from Rosenberg strike the reader merely as comic relief, then this chapter has completely failed in its purpose. They would be comic if Rosenberg were a nobody, a harmless crackpot expounding them to gaping loafers. But the comic becomes tragic in view of Rosenberg's official position and of Germany's great intellectual past.

It is tragic that Rosenberg happens to be not the worst but the best philosopher that Nazi metapolitics can produce. Hitler was not intentionally ironic when he gave this man the title " Director of Weltanschauung " for the entire country. The world republic of letters is incalculably indebted to German scholarship and philosophy. Gratitude to Germany for this imposes, on intellectuals in particular, an urgent duty. The duty is to act, to act unitedly, on every spot of ground throughout the globe where the indivisible republic of intellect can still flourish, to act against a regime which turns the traditional German search for truth into an *opéra bouffe,* which sells the German soul for a mess of conquered territorial pottage.

By such a gesture of the intellectuals, the word " intellectual," so long a term of half-justified abuse, becomes

[47] Rosenberg: *Dunkelmänner*, p. 69.
[48] Ibid. p. 71.

a badge of honour. For this is the great issue of our age, not so much the battle of guns as the battle of ideas, a battle which, by the very universality of ideas, allows no neutrals, no spectators, no civilians. Like the inescapable voice of conscience, the din of this battle reverberates in even the most aloof ivory tower. From a million throats in a hundred different languages swells the conviction that this regime, no matter how omnipotent its material weapons, will be exterminated because such is the marvellous construction of the human mind that the idea of freedom *cannot* be exterminated.

If the church opposition to nazism demands freedom of Christian conscience, the university opposition demands academic freedom, the freedom of objective research for truth. How does Rosenberg defend nazism from the second of these two great sources of intellectual criticism? In 1934 Rosenberg delivered an important speech before the assembled professors and students of the University of Munich. The speech was called "Academic Liberty."[49] Its tone was purringly conciliatory because then the dictatorship felt not yet strong enough for its present gruff tone toward the universities. So Rosenberg magnanimously held out his arms to sceptics in his audience to persuade them that nazism stands for academic freedom.

To this glorious academic freedom, he adds only one slight qualification, a little gem of slippery Nazi wording: "the freedom of a truly Germanic, folkic knowledge and not of a liberal, irresponsible research." The word "truly" is particularly slippery. No well-propagandized despotism is ever "against" knowledge, freedom, justice, or Christianity; it is merely for "true" knowledge, "true" freedom, "true" justice, "true" Christianity.

---

[49] Reprinted in Rosenberg: *Gestaltung*, pp. 197–9.

Rosenberg and Hitler constantly justify political tyranny by accusing democracy of also being tyrannical. Analogously Rosenberg goes on to say that even if nazism does curtail the universities, they were never really free. This is the same sort of twofold argument by which he defended his lack of historical evidence. This time he is saying: first, we let you continue your glorious academic freedom; second — well, maybe we don't really, but you never had it before either.

So we are not surprised at his claim that the universities were never free in the Republic. What does surprise us is the specific reason he gives why they were not free. We expect his usual sort of reasoning: that they were enslaved by the plutocratic-Marxist Jews and Freemasons. But no, Rosenberg's reason for their former lack of freedom is that " hardly a university deemed it necessary to give an honorary Ph.D. degree " to those great thinkers who preached Nazi ideas before 1933. At last he has given himself away! He adds that these geniuses, panting vainly for the withheld " honorary Ph.D.," must therefore " die lonely."

To be sure, it is Houston Chamberlain and not himself whom Rosenberg cites as having " died lonely " without a Ph.D. But psychologically Rosenberg identifies himself completely with Chamberlain as a fellow victim of the persecuting " low dwarfs." The low dwarfs, as we saw earlier, are those utterly abandoned creatures who insist on proof and footnotes for any startling new rewriting of history.

How much better we understand the complex psychology of the leading Nazi thinker after he let this little outburst slip past his Freudian censor-mechanism! Behind all his loud heroic bluster against things bourgeois, whimpers a secret craving for that petty badge of respectability, the " honorary " Ph.D.

Prevalent in the late 1920's was the delusion that the Nazi demagogues were doomed because intellectually refuted. Their critics succeeded brilliantly in refuting them. Rosenberg's German critics generally won and made his intellectual arguments look ridiculous. But history makes these critics and intellectuals look ridiculous, far more so than the refuted Nazis. The ancient Greek historian Thucydides observed that in all revolutions " the blunter wits were the most successful. Apprehensive of the cleverness of their opponent, they feared to be worsted in debate and so at once had recourse to action." [50]

The intellectuals disproved the ideas of Wagner, Chamberlain, Rosenberg, Hitler; but meanwhile these ideas were building a new Germany and are now starting a new world war.

What nazism's critics and democratic opponents lacked, in and outside Germany, was its will-power, that power which turns words into deeds and which conquers unconquerable obstacles. The critics might refute nazism ever so brilliantly and argue ever so persuasively for freedom and justice. But these were no more than words unless willed into practice.

Too many American labour leaders, imitating the French Popular Front, would rather strike for shorter hours in defence industries than work to the limit in order to produce the maximum defence against military aggression. Too many capitalists, imitating the French " two hundred families," would rather make profits than increase their defence service to the limit, at a loss if necessary. They would rather avoid taxes than contribute the utmost to resist the Hitler menace and to end slums and soil erosion and share-

---

[50] Thucydides: *Works*, tr. by Crawley, (New York: Modern Library; 1934), p. 191.

cropping and all the other breeders of nazism and communism.

For ten years everyone has been talking about unemployment and analysing it brilliantly. But the unselfish will-power and united energy to solve it are still lacking in America. Few material problems can resist man's imagination and intellect, provided these are backed by courageous, unswerving volition. Hitler's triumph is in part the triumph of human volition over matter, of national political motive over economic motive, of faith over what logic called overwhelming odds. Consider Germany's material handicaps: in 1933 a country economically and psychologically in direst depression, dismembered by Versailles, with many unemployed, still crushed by the inflation and Reparations of the 1920's. Seven years later Hitler marches victoriously into Paris as head of an enormous central Europe of efficient economic planning, where unemployment is impossible and is replaced by labour shortage!

In 1924 Hitler and Rosenberg had been overwhelmingly refuted and laughed down by their intellectual critics and were consequently no longer deemed a menace. Hitler was preaching rearmament and victorious wars of conquest. His critics " brilliantly " refuted him by pointing out, quite correctly, that Germany was helpless, completely deprived by treaty of bombing planes, submarines, navy, heavy guns, and tanks, and with only a tiny army and a demilitarized Rhine frontier. They pointed out, quite correctly, that this helpless Germany was surrounded by rich, victorious neighbours, armed to the teeth, who had both the interest and power to keep Germany disarmed. In 1924, surrounded by scoffers, the brilliantly refuted Hitler replied:

To recover Germany's power you must not ask " How are we to make armaments? " but " How are we to breed the *spirit* that makes a people capable of bearing arms? " If that spirit rules a people, their *will* finds a thousand ways, any one of them leading to armament! Give a coward *ten pistols,* and when attacked he will fail to fire a single shot. He can do less with them than a man of spirit *with a mere blackthorn.*

On these words a wise English anti-Nazi comments:

This was not rodomontade, it was truth; as events showed when the time came. On Herr Hitler's accession to power in 1933, he at once began arming with feverish energy in flat defiance of the other Powers. Round him they lay, each with their ten pistols — that is, with armaments that could have stopped his action by the motion of a finger while he was still powerless to resist. And not one of them had the nerve to act. The man of spirit with a mere blackthorn has re-armed Germany. . . . Rarely has a man prevailed more conspicuously by his belief that spirit dominates matter, that where there is a will there is a way.[51]

---

[51] Hitler: *Mein Kampf* (Munich ed.), pp. 365–6. R. C. K. Ensor: " *Mein Kampf,*" no. 3 of *Pamphlets on World Affairs* (New York, 1939), pp. 28–9.

CHAPTER XIII

NAZI RELIGION VERSUS CHRISTIAN RELIGION

∞∞∞∞∞∞∞∞∞∞∞∞∞∞∞∞∞∞∞∞∞∞∞∞∞∞∞∞

*Should the subduing talisman, the Cross, break, then
. . . the old stone gods will rise from the long-forgotten
ruin and rub the dust of a thousand years from their
eyes; and Thor, leaping to life with his giant hammer,
will crush the Gothic cathedrals!*

— HEINRICH HEINE, *1834* [1]

The subject of this chapter is urgently pertinent in a day
when anti-Christian forces are increasing steadily all over
the world. Is Christianity doomed, like so many religions
before it, to be replaced by some more modern or adapt-
able creed? The Nazis and communists believe so, and so
do even many democrats. Let us survey contemporary Germany as the perfect object-lesson of this process whereby
a fanatic new religion seeks to replace the west's traditional faith.

In addition to his pupil Hitler, Alfred Rosenberg is cited
frequently because in words and deeds he is the frankest,
most consistent, and most important of the new religion's

---

[1] Heine: *Works,* tr. by C. G. Leland (New York, 1906), V, 207–8.

theologians. Now that Stalin has purged the old-Bolshevik
intellectuals and Soviet Russia has stopped philosophizing,
Rosenberg remains the leading anti-Christian philosopher
in the world today.

Much evidence suggests that the new religion has been
lastingly established among German youth by means of an
exclusively Nazi education. On the other hand, much evidence suggests that this new paganism, by scorning the
Christian " other cheek " tactics, by its very persecution,
has made Christ's modern martyrs a stronger popular force
in Germany than ever before. We urgently need to examine the collision between the new streamlined tidings
and the ancient " good tidings " of Easter morn.

CHRIST ARYANIZED

To do the Nazis justice, let us not ignore that they generally sincerely admire — or profess to admire — Christ
Himself. But for what reasons! For example, Rosenberg
— and here even Goebbels agrees with him — regards
Christ as one of a long line of Aryan heroes, ranging from
Wotan and Siegfried to Wagner and Hitler. Rosenberg
" proves " Christ an anti-Semitic descendant of Atlantis.

The Rosenberg-Goebbels-Hitler distinction between
nordic Christ and nasty Christianity leads us back, as usual,
to nineteenth-century romanticism. Rosenberg's endless
reams of meta-theology about this distinction are but a
franker and more radical restatement of Lagarde and
Houston Chamberlain. Lagarde, Chamberlain, and Rosenberg are all anti-Old-Testament and anti-church and dub
Saint Paul the villain of the drama.

Saint Paul, according to these three writers, betrayed
Jesus by founding His church on that obnoxious Judaism
which He died to destroy. Thereby the Christian churches

became just one more mask of the Jews, allied with Freemasons, Marxists, Tibetan lamas, and international bankers. The most villainous church of all is the Catholic because it is the most international.

All three writers worship Martin Luther — not Luther the great Christian, but Luther the German nationalist rebelling against the Mediterranean world and against Renaissance humanism. That is why Hitler links Luther with Wagner and Frederick the Great as his three chief heroes — the Luther who in 1542 wrote *The Jews and Their Lies*. Chamberlain says: " Luther is above all a *political* hero " rather than a religious hero; he founded " the future of German nationalism " by " emancipating " the nordic from international Rome. Rosenberg: " Luther shattered the alien crust over our life." Luther is sharply distinguished from the Lutheran church; the latter must be exterminated in so far as it uses " the Jewish Bible " (the Old Testament) and rejects racism.[2]

In 1937 Germany's Protestant leaders wished to attend the international Christian conference at Oxford, expressing the indivisibility of world Christianity. The German government forbade its Protestant pastors to attend. It fiercely attacked them in *The Black Corps,* official magazine of Hitler's S. S. bodyguards and tolerant to the pre-Christian pagan cults. Rosenberg rushed into print again with a pamphlet announcing that Luther would be a Nazi today and attacking the Lutheran churches as racial traitors. This pamphlet, *Protestant Pilgrims to Rome,* had a circulation of 620,000.[3]

---

[2] Heiden: *Hitler,* p. 318. H. S. Chamberlain: *Der Seher des Dritten Reiches* (3d ed., selections by G. Schott, Munich, 1939). Rosenberg: *Mythus,* pp. 129, 185, 250, 516, etc.

[3] *Das Schwarze Korps,* Berlin, organ of S. S. Guards and Himmler, September 2, 1937, etc. Rosenberg: *Protestantische Rompilger* (Munich, Eher, n.d.).

The clergyman Künneth had written *Reply to the Myth,* the Protestant refutation of Rosenberg's book. Künneth now again penned a vigorous defence of Protestant Christianity against Rosenberg's pamphlet. This time Künneth's rebuttal was suppressed by the German government, which thus officially backed Rosenberg's stand. But earlier, in 1934–5, the rebuttals of Rosenberg's *Myth* by Künneth and by the Catholic church had been openly distributed in Germany — while the Goebbels censorship bureau, by an "oversight," looked the other way. This burst of Nazi tolerance mystified many. It is explainable by Dr. Goebbels's love of democratic free speech — about Rosenberg. The impish little doctor welcomes every chance to embarrass the prophet laureate of metapolitics.[4]

Why are the Nazis so afraid of Christ's doctrines that they must either distort or persecute them? Nazis believe that His doctrine of brotherhood would cause the fall of any strong military state and did cause the fall of the Roman Empire, as Nietzsche argued so dazzlingly in his influential *Antichrist.* But Nietzsche rejected any racist explanation of history and abhorred the barbaric Teuton tribes who overran Rome. So Rosenberg's Nazis teach an explanation more suitable than Nietzsche's for educating Nazi youth, though equally anti-Christian. Except about the Etruscans, Rosenberg's explanation is largely based on Houston Chamberlain's *Foundations of the Nineteenth Century.* The following is a very brief summary of how Rosenberg explains why Rome fell and why the civilization-destroying invasions by the Teutons in bearskins were a blessing.

Christianity's crime is to spread the belief in salvation of the individual soul instead of the collective race-soul. This

---

[4] Micklem: *National Socialism,* pp. 180–1.

belief killed the Roman Empire by leading to internationalism and race mixture. Non-Aryan stocks can never rule the
world long, only disintegrate it. Rome was doomed, justly
doomed, because its original Aryan rulers were too tolerant
toward Etruscan and Semitic strains. Suddenly in the nick
of time, like Hitler in 1933, came the Teuton invaders.
They rescued from chaos what few Roman values the
Etruscans and Semites had left.[5]

Just who the Etruscans were and what their heritage,
no historian knows except the omniscient Rosenberg.
Nothing bad in Germany can be conceded to be German.
Whatever poisons among the Teutons can't be traced to
Jews are traced to those extinct Etruscan neighbours of
Rome.

The Etruscan heritage is blamed for all things diabolical,
from unprintable refinements of sexual perversion to
papacy and black magic. Rosenberg's lack of proof for
these accusations is pointed out in the scholarly Catholic
refutation. Rosenberg makes a long list of the most monstrous, incredible, and bloodthirsty sexual aberrations.
First he describes these for five pages, hardly concealing
how they fascinate him. Then he denounces the unknown
Etruscans for them with a hysterical fury hard to motivate
against a race extinct for two thousand years.[6]

Rosenberg's religious views stem directly from the following aphorisms by his " great German dreamer," Lagarde: " For every nation, a national religion is necessary."
" Paul brought the Old Testament into the church. By its
influence the Gospel was as far as possible destroyed."
" World religion in the singular and national religions in
the plural are the platforms of the two opponents." " Nations are thoughts of God." The last aphorism transfers to

[5] Rosenberg, *Mythus,* pp. 79–85; 60 ff.
[6] Ibid., pp. 61–5.

the nation Hegel's concept of states as incarnate Ideas of God.[7]

A book by Friedrich Delitzsch in 1920 also influenced Rosenberg against Paul and the Old Testament. The famous Catholic refutation of Rosenberg proves convincingly that Christianity is inseparable from the Old Testament, that the connection is umbilical and introduced not merely by Paul but by Jesus Himself. Hitler has called the Old Testament " the Bible of Satan "! Rosenberg calls it " tales of pimps "! He blames it in part for today's " frightful Jewish overlordship " in Germany. All this horrifies both Protestants and Catholics of Germany, especially his demand that " the so-called Old Testament must be *abolished*" officially. Ever more Nazi educators of the young follow his advice to replace instruction in the Old Testament by " nordic sagas from Wotan on." [8]

Mein Kampf and the Twenty-five Points of the official party platform demand "positive Christianity." Rosenberg defines positive Christianity as Germanic, negative Christianity as Etruscan-Syrian-Jewish-African. The latter is non-Aryan, the former carries on the spirit of nordic paganism. Rosenberg accuses the established churches, Protestant and Catholic, of always selling out Germany to the negative heritage, because of Paul's linking Christianity to Rome. Established Christianity was permanently corrupted by Rome's Etruscan-Syrian-Jewish-African elements.[9]

How much Christianity remains in Rosenberg, the " true Christian," after he throws out its love, its universal-

---

[7] Lagarde: *Deutsche Schriften*. Rosenberg: *Mythus*, pp. 457–8.

[8] Delitzsch: *Die grosse Täuschung* (Stuttgart and Berlin, 1920). Kirchlicher: *Studien*, pp. 72–7; and all the *Nachtrag* is on Paul. The Hitler quotation is from an officially endorsed pamphlet of Dietrich Eckart: *Der Bolschewismus von Moses bis Lenin* (2nd ed., Munich, 1925), p. 33. Rosenberg: *Mythus*, pp. 603, 614–15.

[9] Rosenberg: *Mythus*, pp. 78–9.

ism, the whole Old Testament, and all of the New Testament connected with Paul, and links Jesus with Wotan as just one more example of nordic blood? Rosenberg says: "Among the greatest missions of our century is to give the yearning of the nordic race-soul its form as a German church under the sign of the Volk-myth." [10] Our conclusion is that Hitler's and Rosenberg's positive Christianity means nordic paganism plus lip-service to a falsified Jesus.

MESSIAH HITLER AND THE NEW "CHOSEN PEOPLE"

Even lip-service to Jesus is scorned by those Nazis who worship the pre-Christian gods like Wotan, popularized by Wagner's Siegfried dramas. Nazi bookshops often teem with heathen books and newspapers. Christian Easter coincides with an old heathen spring festival, and Nazi heathen have been granted facilities for public Easter celebrations of their own. These celebrations have substituted for Christian songs the *Song of the Goths:* " Up the Viking banner, up the blue sun-flag! "

A leading Nazi heathen is none other than the supreme Reich Youth Leader, Baldur von Schirach. His irreverence for Christianity can go even further than Rosenberg's. None the less, he is Rosenberg's disciple, proclaiming in 1935: "Rosenberg's way is also the way of German youth." [11] Schirach appropriated his first name, Baldur, from the heathen god of love. His beloved German youth he indoctrinates with Rosenberg, with worship of the old heathen warriors, and with religious faith in Hitler as the New Messiah.

[10] Ibid., pp. 614–15.
[11] Schirach's magazine, *Wille und Macht,* " Führer-organ of National Socialist Youth," fortnightly, Munich. H. Lichtenberger: *The Third Reich,* p. 334. Roberts, op. cit., pp. 276–7.

Hegel had three concepts that in oversimplified fashion have captured the Nazi imagination: the embodiment of God's Idea in a specific state, exalting it above all ordinary states; the possibility of a new Chosen People to replace the Jews, whose mission is *passé;* the prediction that the Germanic peoples would now be the teleological agents of the God of History (*Weltgeist*). Against Jewish thesis, Germanic antithesis could be neatly set.

Two examples will suffice to show how the three Hegelian concepts are translated into Nazi paganism. A founder of the "German Christian Church" told a Berlin mass meeting that " the Nazi state " supersedes the churches because it "*embodies* the totality of God." And Pastor Leffler's book, *Christ in the Third Reich,* asks the world to " choose between Israel and Germany " as to which is the " chosen people " to embody the " God of History." Hitler is the new " Saviour whom God sent." Unlike Christ, this new Saviour is not sent to humanity as a whole but — an important Nazi distinction! — to Germany alone. "This is our faith: after two thousand years the Eternal has summoned the Germans to fulfil the mission that He laid in the cradle of the race." [12]

Once German universities were world-famous for their spirit of scientific inquiry. Today a tablet in Munich University quotes the creed of Ley, the Labour-Front Führer. Ley's creed: Hitler is his religion and nazism his faith; students should not seek to understand Hitler with their mere intellects but " with their hearts," in religious faith. In speeches to his labour unions Ley even more frankly makes Hitler god. Ley has learned from delightful experience that such flattery seldom goes unrewarded from above by this particular god!

---

[12] E. Lyons: " Dictators into Gods," in *American Mercury,* March 1939, pp. 266–8.

Ley's Labour Front is the world's largest labour union, inasmuch as every single German worker is forced to join. And all are required to listen to him. Ley has taken part in heathen nature-rites and made public speeches against the Gospels to the " proletariat." Ley said to fifteen thousand Hitler-Youths in 1937: " We believe on this earth *solely* in Adolf Hitler. We believe that National Socialism is the *sole* faith and salvation of our people. We believe that God has sent us Adolf Hitler." [13]

Dr. Engelke, a " German Christian," has said: " God has manifested himself not in Jesus Christ but in Adolf Hitler." An important pagan magazine, *Der Brunnen:* " How high Horst Wessel [the Nazi martyr] towers over that Jesus of Nazareth! " Hanns Kerrl is Minister for Church Affairs. In 1935 Hitler gave him dictatorial powers and the right to issue binding church edicts, including the power to dismiss or arrest clergymen at will. Kerrl in 1937: ' A new authority has arisen as to what Christ and Christianity really are — Adolf Hitler." [14] That is still a relatively modest claim, but Kerrl had proceeded to actual deification: " As Christ in his twelve disciples raised a stock fortified unto martyrdom, so in Germany today we are experiencing the same thing . . . Adolf Hitler is the true Holy Ghost! " [15]

The totalitarian state, whether Soviet or Nazi version, ceases to be total if it allows room for independent Christianity. As labour-Leader Ley puts it, " The party claims the *totality* of the soul of the German people." This totalitarian attitude was best summed up in Baldur von Schirach's boast to his German youth movement: " I am neither a Catholic nor a Protestant: I am a National Socialist." Hitler himself said: " We wish for no other God than

---

[13] *New York Times,* February 11, 1937. Roberts, op. cit., p. 275. Lichtenberger, op. cit., p. 341.

[14] *We Americans,* pp. 12, 17.

[15] *American Mercury,* loc. cit. in note 12.

Germany." [16] An old-fashioned German death-notice reads: "died in belief in God." Today newspapers sometimes carry as death-notice: "died in belief in Adolf Hitler."

The warrior heaven of pre-Christian Teutons was Valhalla. The climax of Hitler's funeral oration over President Hindenburg was: "Departed General, enter now into Valhalla!" Against pious Hindenburg's express will, Hitler had him buried amid heathen torches. Heathen fire-worship is gaining in Germany. Yet "the attraction of an old cross erected by sincere piety in the Black Forest will no doubt survive the fascination of the nightly dances around the sacred fire, staged on those same hills by neo-pagan youths in bathing suits." [17] We must guard against overestimating the importance of such pagan rites. Sometimes hysterically serious, generally they are mere boyish pranks.

In Hitler's concentration camps languish not only liberals and Jews but non-political and "Aryan" Catholic and Protestant ministers. "The arrest of the courageous pastor Niemöller is to be traced directly back to the tendencies unleashed by Rosenberg's book." Niemöller is the most famous victim but only one of many thousands martyred for the crime of being sincere Christians. For example, seven hundred pastors were arrested in Prussia at one fell swoop in 1935 for denouncing modern paganism from the pulpit. Open paganism, such as Wotan-worship, has very little mass influence; such revivals are too artificial. More dangerous and very successful is the Hitler-Rosenberg-Goebbels ruse of disguising nordic paganism

---

[16] Lichtenberger, op. cit., p. 335. Roberts, op. cit., p. 270.
[17] M. Demiashkevich: *The National Mind* (New York, 1938), pp. 401–3.

for the time being as positive Christianity. "Thus it was said in a students' training camp: When the party program mentions ' positive Christianity,' it really does not mean Christianity, but just a positive religious feeling in general. It was not wished to say this openly right at once." [18]

In 1936 the Evangelical Church Council, including Niemöller, sent directly to Hitler one of the most daring protests ever issued inside Germany. It stresses Rosenberg's vast influence, naming him more often than any other anti-Christian propagandist. It quotes his demand that " the general ideas of the Roman and Protestant churches " must be trampled down as " negative Christianity " by " the nations following nordic-racial principles." It expresses directly " to the Führer our uneasiness that he is often *revered in a form that is due to God alone*." It proclaims " strenuous resistance " as a Christian duty against the " active " Nazi war on church membership. The manifesto ends by posing " the clear question to the Führer whether the attempt to de-Christianize the German people is to become the official government policy." [19]

All the world is still asking that " clear question " today. Hitler's reply to this protest was — still more persecution.

Hitler's Reich-Bishop Müller has rewritten the Sermon on the Mount, substituting the military virtues for those of love, and German patriotism for humanity. The Psalms were similarly rewritten, substituting Germans for Jews as Chosen People. Hitler himself has always refused to take part in Wotan-worship, though tolerating it. Discarding both Wotan and Christ, some more sophisticated Nazis have invented a brand-new religion, the " German Faith

---

[18] Dutch, op. cit. p. 99. Lichtenberger, op. cit., pp. 333, 342.

[19] Lichtenberger, op. cit., pp. 338, 330; reprinted in full in appendix, pp. 329–39.

Movement." Most influential of these are Professors Hauer and Bergmann and Count Reventlow.[20]

Hauer had once been an able Protestant pastor and theologian. He based his new religion of the " race spirit " on the romantic and Hegelian concept of becoming as opposed to being. " National history is a becoming; it is the Spirit of the Race always in suspense, always in movement." Hauer's slogan: " Our Holy Land is Germany! " Only fifty-three thousand members registered officially in his German Faith Movement. He lost control of it owing to the jealousy of Rosenberg, whose thunder was being stolen.[21]

Even more than Hegel, Goethe's *Faust* led German writers to turn ceaseless lawless becoming into a religion of salvation. Rosenberg calls the god Wotan " eternally dissatisfied, the symbol of the nordic soul, eternally striving and becoming." Can Christianity ever kill the spirit of Wotan in Germany? Rosenberg says: " Wotan, as the eternal mirror of the primeval soul-forces of the nordic man, is living today as five thousand years ago." [22]

In his famous Twenty-five Theses, Professor Bergmann tried — vainly — to set up a new Nazi religion for German schools. It was based on pantheism, subjectivity, nature-worship, and Volk instincts, all via the romantic school and Rousseau. He called his theses " a catechism of the German religion." Religion must be mystic and Germans the most mystic of races; so the learned professor determined to out-mystic all other mystics with such theses as his 13th:

> The living world is the womb-mother of the high human mind. Knowing, Being, and Mind are a birth of the

[20] Micklem, op. cit., p. 47. Wilhelm Hauer: *Deutsche Gottschau* (Stuttgart, 1934). Count Ernst zu Reventlow: *Wo ist Gott?* (Berlin, 1934).

[21] Roberts, op. cit., p. 276. Lichtenberger, op. cit. pp. 193–4.

[22] Rosenberg: *Mythus,* p. 679.

All-Mother. The mother-child thought is hence the right indication of the God-world secret. We speak in a modern nature religion of the Mind-child God, who rests in the womb of the All-Mother.

More comprehensible and far more typical of Nazi thought today are Bergmann's other theses. They are contrasts between the Germanic and Christian-Semitic religious instincts. The Germanic craves a pantheistic God identified with romantic "force of nature"; the Semitic and Christian craves the "other-worldly God." The Germanic craves the salvation of the Volk as an organic whole; the Semitic and Christian craves "salvation of the *individual*." The Germanic craves a hair-on-the-chest "heroic ethics"; the Semitic and Christian craves an ethics of peace. Therefore "we of the German religion demand" that this new religion be taught in the schools instead of "Christian instruction," which should be regarded as "no longer a religion." [23]

Racism is itself less a science or philosophy than a religion, an anti-Christian brand of mysticism. It worships blood as sacred, but only the blood of its own tribe, making it a narcissistic self-worship. Hauer's mystic new religion is in the last analysis racism. And Professor Hans Günther's scientific racism is in the last analysis a religion, although he is the official Nazi "scientific" authority on race. Rosenberg frankly calls faith in race "mystic" in the religious sense of the word.

Like everything Nazi, the race-religion antedates Versailles, deriving its scientific pretensions to a great extent from Otto Hauser (not to be confused with Hauer). No compromiser, Hauser warns nordics to avoid mating not

---

[23] Ernst Bergmann: *Die 25 Thesen der Deutschreligion* (Breslau, 1934). Translated in Friends of Europe *Publications,* no. 39 (London, 1936).

only with Jews but with fellow Germans of the short, round-headed, Alpine stock, to which Hitler belongs. Here is a perfect metapolitical gem from Hauser's race-religion of 1915:

> The Alpine is pre-eminently a man of business . . . diligent but unfair . . . no interest in anything save himself and his money. . . . He will marry for money instead of for inclination and will seek in the brothel the sexual excitement he cannot find at home. Not until he has predominant admixture of nordic blood does he get the better of his inward baseness; not until his skin has the rosy pallor of the nordic.[24]

Already Fichte, more than a century ago, combined "true" Christianity with a religion of the German Volk's divinity: "The German nature, being *deep,* has instinctively seized upon the true essence of Christianity and *discarded* with abhorrence the corruption that obscured it. The spirit of the German is the living source of all the suns and rushes to create new things forever. The German mind is the selfconsciousness of God."[25]

WAR IS HEAVEN!

American schoolboys learn General Sherman's famous phrase: "War is hell!" German schoolboys today learn that the heaven of nordic religion is Valhalla, a warrior paradise of bloody war daily, where even the beautiful ladies — the Valkyrie of Wagner's operas — swing no

---

[24] Hans Günther: *Der nordische Gedanke unter den Deutschen* (Munich, 1925); *Herkunft und Rassengeschichte der Germanen* (Munich, 1925); *Rassenkunde des deutschen Volkes* (13th ed., Munich, 1928). O. Hauser: *Rasse und Rassenfragen in Deutschland* (Weimar, 1915). Quotation reprinted in Magnus Hirschfeld: *Racism* (London, 1938).

[25] Fichte as summarized by G. Santayana: *Egotism in German Philosophy* (New York, 1940), pp. 62–3.

mean battleaxe. If racism reaches the state of frenzy where it becomes literally a religion for many Nazis, so does war — or, more broadly, so do the military and heroic virtues.

Rosenberg sums up the perennial German religious conflict as "honour" versus "love." Honour he uses in a distortedly militaristic sense of the word. He damns "international Christianity" as based on the "enfeebling idea of love and humanity" and as open to all. Instead he demands a "German Volk-Church" based on "national honour" and open only to "nordics." He traces through history how Christian doctrines insidiously filled Teuton warriors with love, peace, turning the other cheek, universal instead of tribal standards, and good will to all men, even to non-Germans.[26]

These doctrines Rosenberg derived from three great Germans: Wagner (before his pious *Parsifal* days), *The Antichrist* of Nietzsche's last mad days, and Spengler. This prostration of the tame Herr Professor before the wild virile beast of prey is but a form of the romantic school's "corybantic prostration before Life" (dynamism). Wagner wrote: "Our clergy-ridden civilization reduced the health-exuding warriors of the north into weak-nerved cripples." Nietzsche: "Christianity aims at mastering beasts of prey; its *modus operandi* is to make them ill — to make feeble is the Christian recipe for taming, for 'civilizing.'"[27]

Spengler is the perfect example of how the unmoral romantic worship of life for Life's sake evolves naturally, under the pressure of German military needs, into worship of war and hatred of the Christian virtues. Spengler starts harmlessly enough with the old romantic postulate that "Life exists simply for its own sake" and that the "irra-

---

[26] Rosenberg: *Mythus,* pp. 621, 599–636.
[27] Wagner: *Prose,* I, 259, 249–66. Nietzsche: *The Antichrist,* ed. cit., pp. 74, 42–3.

tional blood " and not " reason " is what " controls Life."
These cloudy banalities of " German idealism " reveal their
sinister potentialities when Spengler goes on to assume
that " war is the prime fact of Life, is Life itself." If war
and Life are synonymous, then does not war, too, " exist
simply for its own sake "?

No wonder Spengler's logical next assumption is that
" man is a beast of prey " and that " believers in social
ethics are only beasts of prey whose teeth have been pulled
out." Contrasting Kultur with civilization, he defines his
" Faustian Kultur " as the heroic revolt against reason by
the " proud blood of the beast of prey." Spengler's final
conclusion is that " The great beasts of prey are noble creatures of the most perfect type and without the lies of
human morality due to weakness." This sentiment is the
perfect primer for rearing young Nazis, even though
Spengler and the Nazis clashed violently over other important issues.[28]

It is over-obvious to stress merely that such sentiments
in pre-Hitler Germany paved Hitler's way. To understand
nazism we must go even further back. We must stress
again the books-into-bullets process by which the assumptions of the innocent ivory-tower romantic school of 1800
evolved into Nazi Kultur's bloody military crusade against
civilization today. War, which " is Life itself," is worshipped as a religious ritual in the same sense in which romantics worshipped " Life."

After the World War, General Ludendorff formed a
nordic group to combat everything Christian. His motto:
" War is the highest expression of the racial life." Ludendorff recognized that a religion of war was more likely to
win the new " total war " for which he prayed than a re-

---

[28] Spengler: *Jahre der Entscheidung* (Munich, 1933), p. 14. *Man
and Technics* (New York, 1932), pp. 22, 79–80.

ligion of love. He was converted by his bluestocking wife
Mathilde, who wrote *Redemption from Jesus Christ*. Most
Nazis consider themselves sufficiently subtle when they
" discover" that all foes are tools of Judaism. Mathilde
goes them one better in subtlety: even the Jews are tools!
At a Nazi party congress she unmasked the subtlest plot in
history, shrieking that Jews, capitalists, Reds, democrats,
and Freemasons were all puppets of the insidious Dalai
Lama, who pulled their strings from his fiendish laboratory
in Tibet, where he plotted to persecute Germany.[29]

On Rosenberg and Hitler, Ludendorff's personal influence was enormous. He had barely missed achieving his
dream of Pan-German world-conquest, and now they felt
they must carry on the old man's torch. When Ludendorff
threw in his lot with them in 1923, he was performing a
symbolic, almost ritualistic act: he was providing the historical continuity between Germany's first World War and
that second war which Hitler planned with conscious and
consistent monomania from November 1918 on.

Ludendorff was the World War's greatest military genius. In 1918 his nerves cracked and he began writing
crank pamphlets with such titles as *Annihilation of Freemasonry by Unmasking Its Secrets*.[30] Yet he still had
enough prophetic power to pick Hitler and marched at his
side in the 1923 beer-hall putsch. At that time, with historic prescience, Germany's hero-dictator of 1917, the 1917
preacher of annexing the Ukraine, told the courtroom he
" loved Hitler like a son." In 1941 the son fulfils the father,
and again the grey-coated Reichswehr is on the march.

---

[29] Neo-pagan articles in Erich Ludendorff's biweekly *Volkswacht*.
New York Times, Sunday, June 16, 1940, p. 8E. Erich Ludendorff: *Der
Totale Krieg* (Munich, 1935). Mathilde Ludendorff: *Erlösung von Jesu
Christo* (Munich, 1931).

[30] E. Ludendorff: *Vernichtung der Freimaurerei durch Enthüllung
ihrer Geheimnisse* (Munich, 1927).

Hitler broke with Ludendorff for losing pious Bavarian votes with such public proclamations as " Your most important duty is to protect your children from Christian influences. They have destroyed our people, and only priests and Jews have profited thereby." Ludendorff angrily called Hitler's party " entirely Judaized "! [31] Hitler, the shrewder politician, always paid lip-service in public to " positive Christianity." But privately he, too, shared Ludendorff's anti-Christian ideas and " discerned, in the form which Rosenberg gave them, the philosophic foundation of the National Socialist movement." That is why Hitler " gave Rosenberg a free hand in connection with his anti-Christian propaganda and placed the party apparatus at his disposal for this purpose." [32]

TWO CURRENT EVENTS

A reliable foreign correspondent vouches for two thought-provoking events of the 1940 war-front. Both show how deep-rooted in German youth this racist and Führer religion has already become. Both events are the concrete fruit of the teaching of Rosenberg, Schirach, Ley, and the rest. A wounded German prisoner in France desperately needed a blood transfusion. But when approached by the doctor and blood donor, the prisoner insisted: " I will not have my German blood polluted with French blood! I would much rather die." So the French racial inferiors could only shrug their un-nordic shoulders with very Gallic shrugs and — soon after — bury the prisoner, a martyr to the new religion of racism.

The second event: One of those very young German aviators was shot down in France and dying. A priest crept

[31] Lichtenberger, op. cit., p. 192. R. Olden: *Hitler*, p. 183.
[32] Heiden: *Hitler*, p. 170.

to him under a bombardment to offer the last Christian comforts. The dying boy replied: " The Führer is my faith. I don't want anything from your church. But if you want to be good to me, get my Führer's picture out of my breast pocket." The priest got it. The boy kissed the picture, with the usual beatific expression attributed to Christian saints and martyrs, and murmured: " My Führer, I am happy to die for you." [33]

THE DARK GODS AWAKEN

Through romantic incantation and mass ecstasy Nazi religion would reawaken the elemental powers of pre-civilization days. Awake again after centuries are the days and powers of totem and tabu, as expressed in tribal cult, blood cult, and war cult. The purpose of these primitive powers, according to the metapolitical mystique, is to launch and win a bloody war of Kultur against civilization. This barbaric war-cult was dismissed by unimaginative English " appeasers " as harmless childish rhetoric. Yet under Rosenberg and Goebbels it was fanatically indoctrinated into the youth from the day the Nazis took power.

For example, already in 1933, when peace and rationalism still seemed attainable goals to the west, the following from a Nazi oration was delivered in Munich. Like much of the better poetry of German romanticism, such speeches are fascinating in their pathology, and genuinely impressive and awe-inspiring in their frank revolt against two thousand years of civilization. With the heroic insanity of such an oration of 1933, seven years of training in fanatic Nazi paganism set out to smash those two thou-

[33] Sonia Tamara dispatch in *New York Herald Tribune*, July 15, 1940, p. 8.

sand years of Christian and western striving for a creed
of peace and reason:

> Here we will not speak the warm words of peace, the
> words Home and Fatherland. Our words are spoken in
> the face of the awful summons of war. Youths, young
> hands are raised in an oath before this monument which
> is erected to the sublimity of bloodshed — and Michael
> is the Angel of Death — and you are swearing that your
> lives belong to the Reich and your blood to the Führer.[34]

What Hitler deems the " new " religious force of nazism
is the oldest of all forces. It is not so much anti-Christian
as pre-Christian, as old as Cain, as old as the terrible stark-
ness of nature before Christianity came to tame and restrain nature. In the year 1940 this new — this old — force
seems to triumph militarily and psychologically over the
Christian civilization of the west. So appalling a triumph
makes us almost superstitious ourselves, almost feel like
saying: the sorcerous ritual of metapolitical witch-doctors
has conjured up the old tribal thunder-gods to aid their
non-non-Aryan " Chosen People," has conjured up from
the German subconscious the most terrible and elemental
of pre-Christian atavisms.

The discussion of this new-old Nazi religion is best
closed with an old warning to the better half of Germany
and to the west. This old warning was voiced prophetically by the poet Heine more than a century ago. Germany's nationalistic and anti-monarchic radicals had just
failed in another of their periodic revolts against Metternich's conservative and Christian internationale of monarchs. Heine consoled the rebels by proving, with bitter
irony, that the thwarted German revolution would triumph
in the future and that its violence and nihilism would make

---

[34] Reprinted from Munich in *New York Times,* October 31, 1933.

other western revolutions milk-and-water affairs. With astounding foresight, he showed how a brand-new religion, revolting against Christianity, would grow from the romantics; that is, from the subjective idealism, nationalism, and " fanaticism of the Will " of the Fichte school and from " the Nature philosophers."

" These doctrines," wrote Heine in 1834, " have developed revolutionary forces which only *await the day to break forth and fill the world with terror and astonishment.*" The German " Nature " cult would have " terrible " results because its atavistic return to the " primitive powers of Nature " would " evoke the demoniac energies of old Germanic pantheism." The eventual result would be a reawakening of " that battle-madness which we find among the ancient Teutonic races, who fought for the very love of fighting." The Christian Cross has for centuries kept tame " that brutal German joy in battle," but Heine concluded:

> Should the subduing talisman, the Cross, break, then will come roaring forth the wild madness of the old champions, the insane Berserker rage, of which the northern poets sing. That talisman is brittle, and the day will come when it will pitifully break. The old stone gods will rise from the long-forgotten ruin and rub the dust of a thousand years from their eyes; and Thor, leaping to life with his giant hammer, will crush the Gothic cathedrals! [35]

ON THE OTHER HAND

On the other hand, let us not decide too hastily whether Christianity can survive Nazi rule. Thor has not yet won the majority of Germans; they are too deeply civilized a people. Rosenberg's religious views are rejected as evil by most of the older, pre-Nazi generation and as madly ex-

---

[35] Heinrich Heine: *Works,* tr. by C. G. Leland, V, 207–8.

tremist by many Nazis themselves. The contemptuous attitude to Christianity of Hitler, Rosenberg, Ley, Schirach, Goebbels, and Himmler is silently deplored and sabotaged by many moderate Nazis. It is openly abhorred and sabotaged by such powerful ruling circles as the Prussian army officers of tough and devout Protestant tradition.

It would be intolerant to Germany to ignore these powerful elements within the ruling framework. Their wholesome moderating influence has again and again succeeded in halting some Nazi persecution of Christian beliefs and in protecting from the Gestapo many a village Hampden, many an unknown Niemöller. Nazism as a new secular system of politics and economics has probably converted a majority of Germans. But only a large minority have been converted by nazism as a new religion. Only a minority — this point must, out of fairness to Germany, be underlined.

Therefore we must not exaggerate the danger to Christianity under Hitler today, even though, if he had his own way, he would probably throw out Saint Paul and the Old Testament as the " Bible of Satan." Hitler's effort merely to set up a German-Christian church under Reich-Bishop Müller was met by such a spontaneous mass resistance that even Hitler had to compromise. Not even Hitler is omnipotent. Germany is still a Christian country today.

But perhaps only today. The fatal danger is tomorrow, if the present Nazi educational tendencies continue. These show every sign not only of continuing but of ever intensifying as the Nazis feel themselves ever securer from foreign or internal reprisals. Tomorrow the present members of the Hitler-Youth and of the Führer-training schools will be the ruling generation. And we have just seen from specific evidence what their new-old religion will be.

CHAPTER XIV

METAPOLITICS IN ACTION: THE THEOLOGY OF TERROR

〰〰〰〰〰〰〰〰〰〰〰〰〰〰〰〰〰〰〰〰〰〰〰〰〰

In the most important matter — and that is civilization — the Germans are no longer of any account. It is not only manifest that German civilization declines, there is also sufficient reason for it. We expend our means on power. . . . It costs dear to attain to power; power stupefies. . . . Civilization and the state— let us not delude ourselves with regard to the matter — are antagonists. One flourishes at the expense of the other.

There is no longer a single German philosopher that counts in Europe. . . . The Germans — they were once called the nation of thinkers; do they really at present think at all? "Deutschland, Deutschland über alles" ("Germany above all"), I fear that has been the end of German philosophy.

—NIETZSCHE, 1889 [1]

"WORLD-POLITICAL THOUGHT-GROOVES"

Whoever would see twentieth-century metapolitics in action, let him read a little Nazi magazine called *Der Welt-*

[1] Nietzsche: *Works* (New York: Macmillan edition; 1908), XI, "Twilight of the Idols," pp. 155–6, 152.

kampf ("*The World-Battle* "). It is boosted in Rosenberg's Nazi handbook officially beamed upon by the Führer. *World-Battle* advertises that an honest-to-goodness Herr Doktor edits it as "a monthly for world-politics, Volk-Kultur, and the Jewish question of all lands! " (the exclamation mark is the Herr Doktor's). Founded by Rosenberg in 1924, *World-Battle* is still going strong today. It enjoys glowing official approval by Otto Dietrich, the Reich Press Chief. Let us examine this magazine as a concrete object-lesson in metapolitics.[2]

Deliberately, *World-Battle* aims neither at the merely uneducated nor at the merely educated, but at the cream of the Nazi crop: the semi-educated. It is an ideal example of all those crank sheets of beer-drenched philosophy with which Germany has teemed since 1870.

Upon whose hard-earned pfennigs do such sheets thrive? Upon those semi-educated folk, pathetically sincere, whose pride is the glib Kultur-lingo which they toss around at Sunday picnics of the Patriotic Thinkers Club. In America we are not exactly unfamiliar with such things. In modern Germany, once you get the hang of it, such lingo practically writes itself. It is a verbal witch-brew by metapolitical medicine-men. By the following verbal tricks ye shall know them, the proto-fascist intellectuals who paved the way in nineteenth-century Germany and may pave it elsewhere today.

Their lingo includes all that sounds Wagnerian, highfalutin, half-digested, irresponsible, super-heroic, and, above all, vague. It includes romantic scorn of legality and reason, romantic worship of unhumanized nature and of the alleged natural goodness of mob instinct, mass action,

---

[2] *Weltkampf*, monthly, Munich, 1924–40 (obtainable at the New York Public Library). Dietrich, January 1939. The advertisements of *Weltkampf* which I shall quote throughout are from the end of Alfred Rosenberg: *Wesen* (Munich, 1933 and 1938).

lynch law. It includes the mystic lispings of what Jahn and Wagner and Rosenberg call "the subconscious, collective Folk-soul." All that was needed to transform these folk-oracles into political and military deeds — books into bullets! — was the advent of an inspired oracle-interpreter, a folk-priest, a Führer.

Put the diction of *World-Battle* under the microscope, and you find a rhetorical earmark by which its metapolitics may be detected. It is the amusing fetish of big Germanic compounds based on the prefix "world" (*Welt*). Such ponderous words conjure up spurious connotations of solemnity and depth. These connotations give readers a tremendous spiritual "kick," which we dare not contemptuously ignore in estimating nazism's mass appeal. The prefix "world" can sometimes make Germans feel blissfully tragic. In contrast, the mere adjective "international" (*internationale*), in German an importation from the French, sounds nasty, alien, and unwashed. The title *World-Battle* sounds ever so much more Aryan and sublime to its subscribers than would *International Battle*.

"World" can also sound thrillingly sinister. The fifty-pfennig *World-Battle* world-battles "against the vampire of all workers, the international parasitic world-finance-capitalism (*Weltleihkapital*)." The prefix "world" is quite unnecessary here, because the parasitic vampire is in the same breath called "international." But apparently no truly nordic shopkeeper is getting his money's worth of world-philosophical lore unless the prefix *Welt* is generously squandered. How glorious to feel that even though you are a sturdy folkic shopkeeper and not a dirty intellectual, you can still flaunt a great big *Weltanschauung* (world-philosophy) with the best and fight in a *Weltkampf* (world-battle), and even experience *Weltschmerz* (world-woe), a *Kitsch* for which we prefer to coin the word "*Weltschmalz*."

Equally glorious is it to be able to expose across your beer table the conspiracies behind every innocent mask. That is why *World-Battle* also advertises itself as a sure cure "against Marxism, [which secretly is] the advance guard of high finance; against the international secret societies, the deadly foes of German folkdom." As special tidbits for fans, a monthly feature section prints the very latest scandals of international " world-Judaization (*Weltverjudung*) " from " all earth lands," the prefix " world " being superfluous as usual.

The constant stringing together of " world " with " international " by Nazis is far more than a mere redundancy. It is used for persuasive dramatic connotations. It is linked to diabolical plots against Germany. In propagandizing the semi-educated, a deliberate *sloppiness* of thought, by exploitation of connotation, lends authenticity and solemnity to some outrageous new program. In short, the typical formula is " international " plus the tautological prefix *Welt* plus a " conspiracy."

The arch-conspirator of this formula is always Jewish capitalism (and/or Marxism), stamped on the reader's imagination by vivid metaphors of monsters, real or supernatural, such as spiders, octopuses, boa constrictors, and vampires. An effective example is a Nazi poster of 1921:

" MANUAL AND WHITE-COLLAR WORKERS OF MUNICH! Like a giant spider, the Jewish international world stock-exchange capital creeps over the peoples of this earth, sucking their blood and marrow. . . . By an enormous MASS DEMONSTRATION of all . . . who condemn the present parliamentarianism . . . we want the resurrection of the German Volk." Hitler, Rosenberg, and Eckart had begun streamlining the new party they had just captured. Six thousand Germans responded to this " international world " poster in a packed, frenzied mass meeting.[3]

The words " mass " and " MASS DEMONSTRATION " are the key. Germany has one of the world's highest literacy-rates; Nazi appeals could never work in an uneducated country. They are effective only where the masses are educated but not well enough, and not educated into individuals but into that lowest common denominator, the mass man. Nazi propaganda among the lower middle class — for example, *World-Battle* — presupposes not ignorance of history and philosophy but half-knowledge. This half-knowledge is at least as high as that of George Babbitt in our western democracies. Mass man is he who is laudably well educated in ideas of sweeping social change but deplorably uneducated in critical discrimination between them, laudably well educated in the mass organization of vast material power but deplorably uneducated in the needed moral restraints of power.[4]

Germany was historically ahead of us in being ripe for collectivism. Americans may get a less fascist version from similar causes. These causes are more basic and world-wide than Versailles: — An over-mechanized and over-specialized industrial society is spawning mass men, instead of responsible, self-disciplined *individuals* rooted in the universal moral values. Of course, " mass man " and " lower middle class " should be used as terms of social psychology and never of social snobbery; the rich are as susceptible to mass-man mentality as the poor.

During the Hitler-Stalin pact of 1939–41, *World-Battle* denounced, as Judaism incarnate, no longer Russian communism but " English high finance." The magazine's special War Issue of 1939 explained England's aggression against peaceful Germany as the direct result of the Jewish

---

[3] Hitler: *Mein Kampf* (Reynal & Hitchcock ed.), pp. 534–6.
[4] José Ortega y Gasset: *The Revolt of the Masses* (New York, 1932).

world-vampire bribing Churchill and Eden with huge
piles of gold.

Right under its title, *World-Battle* advertises its mission
as " schooling " readers in " world-political questions " and
teaching them " to think in terms of grand world-political
thought grooves (*weltpolitische Gedankengänge*)." How
reassuring to read that it world-battles not merely
" against " vampires but also " against " world-chaos and
" for liberty, Kultur, and moral cleanliness! "

In her aristocratic and individualistic days, Germany
was magnificently the west's greatest " land of thinkers and
poets." What of the modern Germany of the mass man?
Hitler appoints an Alfred Rosenberg as official thinker for
the " land of thinkers "! Even at the time of the Hitler-
Stalin pact, *World-Battle* continued to boost " Rosenberg's
work " as " one of the most important fundamentals of National Socialist world-philosophy." [5]

Linking all opponents in one compound gives the Nazi
metapoliticians their denunciatory gusto. It gives their
German audience the delicious, shuddery thrill of feeling like a wolf at bay against all world-conspiracies. For
example, a typical epithet by Rosenberg — the editor of
World-Battle must have remarked: " I wish I'd said that! "
— is " democratic-Marxistic-plutocratic." All is written
as one single, quivering, venom-bloated adjective, from
which nothing is missing except the Freemasons and the
Dalai Lama of Tibet! [6] In short, an Alfred Rosenberg —
and every shabby-genteel café from Munich to Berlin
teems with his like — is but a more literate version of
World-Battle. His compound nouns are but slightly more
interminable, slightly more unpronounceable, slightly
more foggily " impressive." If only the Teutons of heroic

Hermann the Cheruscan had lost to the Romans the battle of Teutoburg Forest, if only they had become part of the great Mediterranean *civitas* . . . if only Germany had passed through a real eighteenth century, that mental discipline of the Latin-French tradition, that unpretentious clarity, that fastidiously classical humanism, that well-balanced scepticism, that laughing rationalism!

Objective inspection of Germany's metapolitics shows something terribly wrong somewhere but something hard to lay a finger on. Surely the defect of her " world-political thought-grooves " is not only economic but psychological. Germans need that bread and security which anti-aristocratic Marxism would offer. They may even need that *Lebensraum* for which the anti-aristocratic Nazis are now warring. But equally Germans need that training which is the best spirit of aristocracy — that is to say, the training in sane sense of proportion, in unbreakable universal standards, in emotional self-control, in the necessity of imposing classical form upon even the most inspired and dæmonic content. Universal standards — that is what romantic anti-legalists consciously reject when they exalt Kultur against civilization.

Painfully, over æons, civilization stamps its traditional and conservative values upon men. Only within these values, or traffic lights, are freedom and objective justice possible. One by one Hitler efficiently smashes the traffic lights of the " common basis of humanity." With them, freedom and objective justice inevitably vanish in Germany. Nazism scorns personal freedom and objectivity and all universal, unnational values as being the " superficial " civilization of the sunny Mediterranean, in contrast with that "deeper" Kultur of northern fogs, that misty metapolitics, that "queer mixture of mysticism and brutality."

Kultur versus civilization — say the self-styled "typical" Germans, say many romantics, says Spengler, say Wagner and Chamberlain and Rosenberg. Kultur plus civilization, Kultur within the inviolable framework of a common humanity — says the immortal "other Germany," say Lessing, Kant, Hölderlin, the classical half of Goethe and Nietzsche, Max Weber, Hofmannsthal, Rilke, Thomas Mann.

CAPTAIN HITLER OF KÖPENICK

The town of Köpenick in Brandenburg was an old centre of traditional Prussianism. " In 1906," recounts the *Encyclopædia Britannica,* " the place derived ephemeral fame from the daring feat of a cobbler, one William Voigt, who, attired as a captain in the army, accompanied by soldiers, whom his apparent rank deceived, took the Mayor prisoner, on a fictitious charge of having falsified accounts, and absconded with a considerable sum of municipal money." [7]

Is it not clear what makes Germans, of all people, the most susceptible to authoritarianism? Not a captain in the army but " *attired* as a captain in the army." Hilariously the imposter ruled all Köpenick, adored by its patriotic inhabitants. Being Germans, they were instinctively obeying an impressive uniform regardless of what was inside it — even if a criminal swaggered inside it. Yet they were all " decent " people, as are most Germans still today, and would have been horrified at the thought of adoring a criminal.

" Accompanied by soldiers, whom his apparent rank deceived, took the Mayor prisoner." Who in 1906 guessed

---

[7] *Encyclopædia Britannica* (13th ed., London and New York, 1926), XV, 897.

that what took place comically in Köpenick would take place tragically in all Germany? In no freely debated election did Hitler poll more than a large minority of votes. In 1933, by a brilliant blend of palace intrigue and terror, the Austrian artist and Bavarian corporal dons Prussia's highest metaphorical uniform of authority. And Germany has obeyed him slavishly ever since.

But the Prussian aura only accounts for half his prestige. In addition there are uniforms of Weltanschauung. Wagnerian romanticism has moral and intellectual prestige as enormous as the physical prestige of Prussianism. What if a captain of Köpenick appeared in Germany with the magic uniform of romanticism in addition to that somewhat outworn uniform of militarist state authority? Would not such an imposter win many times more success and adoration than the simple cobbler of 1906?

Prussianism by itself, for example the Nationalist party, failed completely to attract the masses under the German Republic. Prussianism, meaning efficient state bureaucracy and aristocratic militarism, is prosaic and uninspiring to the masses. It lacks the emotional glamour of German romanticism. Nazism, unaristocratic and national-bolshevist to the root, the culmination of a hundred years of romantic Volk movements, is not Prussianism except in spurious externals. Nazism, as Hans Kohn once brilliantly put it, is the strange new child of a marriage between romanticism and Prussianism.[8]

An illegitimate child, let us add, a child later legitimatized by a coercive shotgun marriage. How incongruous and yet how irrefutably real, that combination of Potsdam with Munich: of the disciplined goose-stepping martinets with wild-eyed desperado bohemians of Germany's Green-

---

[8] Hans Kohn: *Revolutions and Dictatorships* (Cambridge, Mass., 1939), pp. 200 ff.

wich Village. Not accidental but psychologically essential
are that bohemian private life and those artistic, philosophic, or literary ambitions of so many leading Nazis and
proto-Nazis — Hitler, Goebbels, Eckart, Houston Chamberlain, Rosenberg, Baldur von Schirach. Not to mention
Wagner and the literary warriors of Jahn's Free Corps.

To Americans, seeing only the marching soldiers and not
the exotic new glow in the hearts of those soldiers, Prussianism seems the dominant parent. But actually the inspirational fire-centre of this expansive dynamism is
romantic. Not the noble cosmopolitan romanticism of
Herder's day, but the industrialized political romanticism
prophesied by Wagner. The Nazi revolt against western
civilization is romanticism transferred from the middle
classes to the masses, welded to a sort of national bolshevism, saturated through and through in that mass-man
revolt which is sweeping all mechanized industrial society, in mutually hostile forms, from Moscow and Tokyo
to Paris and New York.

NEANDERTHALERS IN AIRPLANES

Self-styled invincible Prussian efficiency and militarism
are merely the means of what is happening in Germany,
the means used by romantic dynamism for romantic ends.
Ultimately even the Volk romanticism as well as the Prussianism is transitional. By far the most obvious and most
publicized earmark of nazism is fanatic nationalism. But
is it not, by this very fanaticism, a sort of *Indian summer* of
nationalism? Is it not the last violent *rigor mortis* of the
senile concept of autonomous national sovereignty — a
nationalism to end all nationalism?

Despite Hitler himself, both the Prussianism and the
nationalism are masquerade. They are unconscious mas-

querade, temporary masquerade of the totalitarian world-revolution of the mass man. For good or for ill? Utopia or the Terror? The imagination reels at such ultimate vistas and dares not presume to make snap judgments on them any more than on earthquakes, on cosmic collisions.

But no! Let us presume a little, after all. Let us dare to judge the unjudgeable. To know establishes the duty to act. To be aware of the universals of reason and of Christian ethics establishes the iron necessity to judge and to resist any " corybantic prostration before Life," before even the most invincible and dynamic life-forces if they burst the moral law and the civilized disciplines of God and man. The inevitable is not the same as the good, the powerful is not the true, nor is death on the battlefield for these truths so futile and naïve as blasé liberals led us to think in days of the pacifist Oxford Oath.

The Roman world-civilization fell before barbarians from the outside. Our Christian, western civilization is falling, citadel after citadel, to a stealthier invasion, the barbarian invasion from below. The invader is the mass man, and we are to blame for him. We produce him through unjust plutocracy and economic bungling. We have failed to train the thwarted masses in civilization's universal traffic lights. The result is apes in evening dress, Neanderthalers in bomb-laden airplanes, very efficient and intelligent barbarians speeding debonairly in civilization's latest-model motor-cars: applying to uncivilized ends the highest technical achievements of civilization.[9]

Barbarism does not mean lack of brains or lack of material efficiency; the Nazis have all that, and so do our own native mass men. Whoever believes that the end justifies the means is a barbarian invader of western and Christian civilization. Barbarism is psychological, ethical, religious

---

[9] Cf. Ortega y Gasset, op. cit., *passim.*

in category. Barbarism means blindness, blindness to the standards of conduct which civilization has over æons imposed upon human nature. This process is artificial — in the best sense of the word. The mass man's barbarism is natural. So is lynch law.

Goebbels has said: "Important is not what is right but what wins." No! Hitler: "Success is the sole earthly criterion of whether an enterprise is right or wrong." No! Lüng (a chief Nazi brain-hero): "'Humanity' is an abstraction which cannot be translated into practical life." [10] No, it is a passionate precious reality. Is heroism a monopoly of Nazi Kultur? Again, no. Heroism is not always a spurious rhetorical spree but the inextinguishable firecore of freedom in an age when freedom must live either dangerously or not at all.

Even if the barbarian invasion is inevitable, even in that case let us set the clear-headed courage of intellectual honesty against "nordic heroism," let us here quote Spengler against what Spengler stands for:

> We are born into this time. There is no other way. Our duty is to hold on to the lost position, without hope, without rescue, like that Roman soldier whose bones were found in front of a door in Pompeii, who during the eruption of Vesuvius died at his post because they forgot to relieve him. That is greatness. The honourable end is the one thing that can *not* be taken from a man.[11]

After the victories of 1870, militarism and mass politics canalized many of those same great German talents and energies which had been canalized into philosophy and music in Goethe's era. If nazism exploited *merely* the

---

[10] Goebbels in *The Atlantic Monthly*, Boston, June 1940, p. 792. Hitler in F. Czernin: *Europe* (New York, 1939), p. 219. Pidder Lüng in Hitler: *Mein Kampf* (Reynal & Hitchcock ed.), p. 352.

[11] Oswald Spengler: *Man and Technics*, pp. 103–4.

worst qualities of Germans! But it also exploits their very noblest qualities: for example, their traditional readiness to sacrifice material self-interest for an ideal. Their readiness for voluntary collective self-sacrifice is exceeded only by that of the Japanese.

During Germany's western and individualist phase, these anti-materialist qualities helped her produce the heights of truth and beauty, of philosophy and music. Without these qualities today's Germany would never tolerate the vast sacrifices it makes to Hitler's ambitions. Thence the tragic irony of a Nazi Germany and thence its extraordinary success. Enlisted in a worthier cause than nazism, what contributions to humanity these German abilities of character and technics could accomplish! — and shall yet accomplish, atoning for nazism and for the bloodshed of today.

I have tried to show that Wagnerian romanticism is the most important single fountainhead of Nazi ideas and ideals. How appropriate, then, how peculiarly fitting, that nazism's nineteenth-century prophet, in his best and sanest moments, damned the Nazis in advance. In those inspired moments Wagner warned that Germany would some day sacrifice all her best qualities of wisdom, art, science, and peace for the sake of ruling the world by military power. Fitting conclusion for this book, in which Wagner has played so central a role, is Wagner's truest prophecy:

> Is the German already tottering to his fall? . . . The unity and European power which the Germans lost in their fights for the Reformation had to be given up that they might keep the idiosyncrasies which mark them not for *rulers* of the world but for *betterers* of the world. . . . The beautiful and the noble came not into the world for profit, nay, not for the sake of even fame and recognition, and everything done in the sense of this teaching is " Ger-

man "; and therefore is the German great, and only what is done in that sense can lead Germany to greatness. . . . *Woe to us and to the world* if the nation itself were this time saved [and] the German Volk remained but the German spirit had taken flight [for sake of power]! The hardly thinkable is closer to us than we fancy.[12]

[12] Wagner, in 1865 and 1879: *Prose*, VI, 124; IV, 163–4.

THE ROOTED GERMAN
(restored 1940 ending)

(This alternative conclusion of the 1940 typescript, deleted by a consultant as "unrealistic exaggerations which the pig-headed young author would regret 20 years from now," is now pig-headedly restored, 20 years later, as an ending more relevant now than then.)

The German enigma is not Hitler. Nor is it the behavior of either frauds or police-sadists (these are latent in all countries in about the same proportion, though hardly in the same high posts). The real enigma is the honest, un-sadistic German majority that unleashes them rather than throwing them in jail. Hitler's shoddy day-dreams are not interesting. What is interesting is that an outstanding edu-cated nation crusades for them.

Mein Kampf was a best-seller long before the German people, voting uncoerced in the free Reichstag election of September 1930, increased the Nazi seats from 12 to 107 and made them the biggest party in Germany. By then, Hitler had said in *Mein Kampf* (to pick a typical threat at random): "If at the start [of World War I] we had *held under poison gas* twelve or fifteen thousand of these He-brew subverters of our people . . . then the sacrifice of a million Germans at the front would not have been in vain. . . . The timely elimination of 12,000 bums . . ."[1]

Note the revealing phraseology, the sadistic physical

---

[1] *Mein Kampf*, official German edition, p. 772, italics and translation mine. Hitler's actual words for *"held under poison gas"* are "unter Giftgas gehalten."

force implied in saying not plain "gassed" but "*held* under." So explosive an aggressiveness as this diction hints at can never become the tool of the various German industrialists and generals and foreign Munich-men who all hope to control the uncontrollable. The German enigma is: just what kind of behavior could those millions of pro-Hitler voters, from 1930 on, expect of the monster-mentality that composes such "held under" threats? We have no inside facts about what goes on in his "rehabilitation" camps; we make no charges, no predictions. We merely record that such threats are typical of Hitler's book, that his book is no classified secret document, that millions of Germans own it, and that at least a few must have browsed in it. These few must have included some of the cheering public and also some influential dignitaries with access to press, radio, and other means of warning the public, — that public to whom Hitler appeared (to cite the famous prize-winning painting of him in the Munich House of German Art) with starry eyes and stainless armor. Why did no one paint our knight more appropriately: with a gas chamber?

We are not spreading "war-mongering rumors" against what our own Stainless Knight of isolationism would call "the wave of the future." It is not a question of rumors only or of speculating about Hitler's words rather than actual deeds. Well-publicized among Germans, already before Hitler came to power and during a period when he still depended on their consent rather than coercion, were the many actual deeds of butchery. For example, his headlined support of the open and bloody Potempa murder of 1932. Some day the same Germans, now cheering Hitler's strut into Paris, will say to their American friends and to their brave German anti-Nazi friends: "We did not know what went on, we did not know"; and when that day of know-nothing comes, there will be laughter in hell.

Admittedly they cannot know what goes on in that intimate confrontation when an SS guard stands face to face with a helpless prisoner. Admittedly. Suppose, further, that one grants each average German the right to disbelieve all concentration-camp reports unless personally witnessed by him. Even so there has been so much[2] he did witness while cheering: — the peculiar disappearances all around him, the brotherly hands stretched out to him for help and stretched in vain, and the urns of ashes in the mail all over Germany after what very openly happened in June 1934 and again in November 1938.

Not to know and yet to know: perhaps this will be the heaviest moral burden ever borne by any culture. No one is speaking of inherited "racial" determinisms but of freely-accepted cultural roots; only the uniquely German roots (the metapolitics) explain the enigma of those cheers, that burden. Will the historic curse of the Wandering Jew be replaced by the curse of the Rooted German? — doomed to re-enact again and again his pendulum-swings between free western civilization and an explosive, overcompensating Kultur of romantic white armor, which turns out to be a white poison-gas chamber where people get *"held under."* Or else, will the Rooted German finally exorcize the nightmare? — by the agonizing honesty of knowing what he "doesn't know." Or in a breezy alternative, shall brisk new generations, with jobs to do, simply forget and go about their business? Meanwhile a war is on; Paris has fallen; Lord, forgive them — first defeat them, then forgive them — for they well know what they do.

---

2 1961 postscript to above 1940 text: Hitler's extermination-expert, R. Hoess, wrote in *Commandant of Auschwitz* (New York, 1960): "When a strong wind was blowing, the stench of burning flesh was carried for many miles and caused the whole neighborhood to talk about the burning of the Jews." He notes, of still another camp, that whenever a bus with victims drove past, even the German children chortled in the street: "There comes the murder box again!"

BIBLIOGRAPHY
(revised 1961)

≈≈≈≈≈≈≈≈≈≈≈≈≈≈≈≈≈≈≈≈≈≈≈≈≈≈≈≈≈≈≈≈

The written sources on which this book is partly based are listed with full detail throughout the text in the footnotes. A broadly inclusive bibliography is often less convenient for the reader than are smaller bibliographies on more specialized topics. Moreover, five broad and unspecialized bibliographies on nazism have already been compiled; to them the reader is referred, as follows:

BOUTILER, PHILIPP, editor. *Nationalsozialistische Bibliographie: Monathefte der Parteiamtlichen Prüfungskommission zum Schutze des Nationalsozialistischen Schrifttums*. A monthly, from January 1936 on.

FEDER, GOTTFRIED, editor. *Nationalsozialistische Bibliothek*. Munich, 1928–35, Heft 1–54.

PINSON, KOPPEL S. *A Bibliographical Introduction to National Socialism*. New York, 1935.

UNGER, ERICH. *Das Schrifttum des Nat.soz., 1919–1934*. Berlin, 1934.

In Re: Germany. Edited by JAMES LOEB, JR., published by The Writers and Educators Committee of the "American Friends of German Freedom," New York. A monthly critical bibliography, listing the current books and magazine articles about Germany as they appear.

Leaving a general bibliography of Nazi Germany to the above five sources, and to the footnotes the listing of this book's sources, the following bibliography limits its scope to four figures, chosen because they are among the most important antecedents of Nazi ideas and because their role as metapoliticians is relatively unknown in America. Three of them are the three men treated at greatest length in this book, Jahn, Wagner, and Rosenberg. The fourth specialized bibliography is of Wagner's son-in-law, Houston Stewart Chamberlain, the important personal link between Hitler and the proto-Nazi intellectuals of the nineteenth century.

The Jahn and Wagner bibliographies aim not at completeness but at inclusion of the works most directly used for the Jahn and Wagner chapters. That is because, unlike the case of Rosenberg, there is no dearth of Jahn and Wagner material in American and British libraries. Such is not the case with Chamberlain and Rosenberg, especially the latter. Therefore my bibliographies on these two men do attempt to be as complete as possible on their own writings. These two bibliographies are larger than those on Chamberlain and Rosenberg in any American library, because some of the books (such as Rosenberg's interesting jingoistic pamphlets) appeared not to be exported by the Nazi government outside of German territory.

A brief bibliography on the problem of " romanticism " is to be found in footnote two of the " romanticism " chapter and also *seriatim* throughout that chapter.

1961 POSTSCRIPT ON GENERAL BIBLIOGRAPHY OF NAZISM: After 1945 the captured Nazi documents would fill a book merely to itemize. Suffice it to mention the 42 volumes of Nuremberg testimony entitled *Trial of the Major War Criminals* (Nuremberg, International Military Tribunal, 1947–49); the Rehse Collection in the Library of Congress; the Hoover Library in California (good on press of 1920's); and the captured Nazi records microfilmed at Alexandria, Va. and deposited in the World War II Records Division, National Archives. *In re* the latter: since the 1950's, the U.S. National Archives and Records Service, Washington 25, D.C., has been sending out free, to historians who request it, a series of *Guides to German Records,* conveniently listing microfilmed material. Among excellent German libraries, scholars will want to consult the Reichsjugend Archiv; the Institut für Zeitgeschichte in Munich; the Institut für europäische Geschichte in Mainz; the Institut für politische Wissenschaft in West Berlin; the Weltkriegs-Bibliothek of the Landes-Bibliothek in Stuttgart; and the Federal Archives of the Bonn Republic at Coblenz. A useful short one-volume collection of documents is W. Hofer, ed., *Der Nationalsozialismus, Dokumente 1933–1945*, Frankfurt a. M., Fischer-Bücherei, 1957.

HOUSTON STEWART CHAMBERLAIN

BOOKS BY CHAMBERLAIN

Arische Weltanschauung. 3d enlarged ed., Munich, 1916.

Auswahl aus seinen Werken. Breslau, 1934.

Briefe, 1882–1924, und Briefwechsel mit Kaiser Wilhelm II. 2 vols., Munich (*c.* 1928).

Includes important letter from Chamberlain to Hitler.

Bühnendichtungen. Munich, published by Bruckmann (n.d.).

A book of three original plays by Chamberlain.

Cosima Wagner und Houston Stewart Chamberlain im Briefwechsel, 1888–1908 (by Chamberlain and Cosima Wagner). 2 vols., 2nd ed., Leipzig, 1934.

Deutsches Wesen. 2nd ed., Munich, 1916.

Essays including the important " Richard Wagners Bayreuth."

Deutschlands Kriegsziele. Oldenburg i. Gr., 1916. Pamphlet of 16 pages.

Drei Vorworte. Munich, Bruckmann (n.d.). 35 pages.

Contains his prefaces to 3d ed. of *Goethe,* to 14th ed. of *Grundlagen,* and to his collected works (*Gesammelte Hauptwerke*).

England and Germany. (n.p.) 1914. 62 pages.

Foundations of the 19th Century. 2 vols., tr. from German by John Lees, intro. by Lord Redesdale, New York, 1914.

Its first impression is dated Nov., 1910; i.e., before the World War. A translation of *Grundlagen,* q.v.

Gesammelte Hauptwerke. 9 vols., Munich, Bruckmann.

Contains six of his most influential German works: " Richard Wagner "; " Grundlagen "; " Immanuel Kant "; " Lebenswege "; " Goethe "; " Mensch und Gott "; — q.v.

Goethe. Munich, 1912. 851 pages.

The book wanders from its subject to indulge in anti-Semitic passages made significant because of their uncanny resemblance to today's Nazi writings.

Die Grundlagen des 19. Jahrhunderts. 2 vols., 10th ed., popular ed. (*Volksausgabe*), Munich, 1912.

Under Nazis, this has been revived in a 20th ed. *Volksausgabe,* 2 vols., Munich, Bruckmann, *c.* 1938. 1264 pages. His best-known and most thorough work. Originally published 1899. The guiding influence behind Rosenberg's *Mythus.*

Hammer oder Amboss. Munich, 1916.

Series of pro-German war essays.

Heinrich von Stein (by Chamberlain in collaboration with Poske). Munich, Bruckmann (n.d.). 126 pages.

Herrn Hinkebeins Schädel. Munich, Bruckmann (n.d.). 71 pages.
  Little sketches described — by the author — as " humorous."

Immanuel Kant. 2 v., authorized tr. by Lord Redesdale, London and New York, 1914.
  Series of lecture-essays not only on Kant but also on Goethe, Leonardo, Descartes, Bruno, Plato.

Kriegsaufsätze. Munich, 1914. 95 pages.
  Essays with such titles as " German Love of Peace," " German Freedom " (as opposed to un-German freedom), and " Germany as leading World-State." This war propaganda, which has resemblances to Hitler's today, is mostly reprinted from periodicals of the autumn of 1914.

Lebenswege Meines Denkens. Munich, 1919.
  Includes such significant chapters as " My Education," " My Way to Bayreuth."

Mein Weg nach Bayreuth. Munich [1937]. 92 pages. Reprinted from *Lebenswege*, q.v.

Mensch und Gott. Munich, 1921.
  Influenced Rosenberg and Nazi program of " Positive Christianity." Distinguished between established churches and " true " Christianity. Against " corruption " of Christ's teachings by Jewish St. Paul, in the fashion of Lagarde & later Rosenberg.

Natur und Leben, ed. by J. v. UEXKÜLL. Munich, Bruckmann [*c.* 1928?]. 187 pages.

Neue Kriegsaufsätze. Munich, 1915. 102 pages.

Parsifal-Märchen. Munich, Bruckmann, 1900.
  Three legends of Parsifal.

Politische Ideale. Munich, 1915. 117 pages.

Rasse und Nation. Munich, 1918. 14 pages.

Rasse und Persönlichkeit. 3d ed., Munich [1937].
  Essays reprinted by the Nazis on Germans and Jews from standpoint of Aryan myth. Includes such separate essays of his as " Richard Wagners Regenerationslehre," " Deutsche Weltanschauung," " Kultur und Politik," " Die Rassenfrage."

The Ravings of a Renegade; being the war essays of H. St. Chamberlain, tr. by C. H. Clarke. London, Jarrold [1915?].
  Translation of *Kriegsaufsätze*, q.v., plus an anti-Chamberlain introduction by Lewis Melville, pseudonym.

Richard Wagner. London, 1900.
  Revived in new editions by Hitler. Cf. my Wagner bibliography.

Der Seher des Dritten Reiches, H. St. Chamberlain. 3d ed., ed. by Georg Schott, Munich, 1939.

Nazi selections from Chamberlain's various works. This book is very important because of the significance of what particular passages of his Nazis seek to revive among German youth today. Very important because taken by the *Reichsjugendführung* into the official Nazi *Jugendschriftenverzeichnis,* thus helping to mould the philosophy of the youth now growing up in Germany. Includes letter from Chamberlain to Hitler of October 7, 1923 and Chamberlain's birthday dedication to Hitler of April 20, 1924.

Wagner der Deutsche als Künstler, Denker, und Politiker. Leipzig Reclams Universal Bibliothek (n.d.).
Convenient anthology of Chamberlain's essays on Wagner, compiled from many books.

The Wagnerian Drama. London and New York, 1915.
Glorifies Wagner not merely as musician but as great dramatic poet.

Who is to Blame for the War? [2nd ed., New York, 1914], published by Vital Issue Co. 38 pages.
Same published [New York, 1915] by German-American Literary Defense Committee. 24 pages.

Der Wille zum Sieg. [2nd ed.] Munich, 1918. 59 pages.
Collection of pro-German war essays.

Worte Christi. Munich [1903]; 1st ed., 1903.
Selections from New Testament by Chamberlain.

Die Zuversicht. 2nd ed., Munich, 1915. 26 pages.

BOOKS ABOUT CHAMBERLAIN

BANSELOW, ALBERT. *Das Werk H. St. Chamberlains.* Munich, Bruckmann (n.d.).
Includes important bibliography of Chamberlainiana.

CHAMBERLAIN, ANNA. *Meine Erinnerungen an H. St. Chamberlain.* Munich [1923].
By his wife.

CURTINER, E. B. *Chamberlain gegen Schopenhauer.* Düsseldorf, 1910.
A study of the criticisms Chamberlain levelled at Schopenhauer in his *Immanuel Kant.*

GEPRAEGS, ADOLF. *Germanentum und Christentum bei H. S. Chamberlain.* Nürtingen, 1938.
A Tübingen Ph.D. thesis.

MEYER, HUGO. *H. St. Chamberlain als Völkischer Denker.* Munich, Bruckmann [1938].
Traces Chamberlain's intellectual development up through appearance of *Grundlagen.*

MCGOVERN, W. *From Luther to Hitler.* Boston, 1941.
Helpful Chamberlain summary, pp. 504–12, 620.

NIELSEN, WILLI. *Der Lebens- und Gestaltbegriff bei H. St. Cham-
    berlain.* Kiel, 1928.
    As a Kiel Ph.D. Stresses psychological background of Chamber-
    lain's philosophy.

ROSENBERG, ALFRED. *H. St. Chamberlain.* Munich, 1927.
    Rosenberg's homage to his personal friend and philosophic
    teacher.

ROSENFELD, PAUL. *Discoveries of a Music Critic.* New York, 1936;
    pp. 89, 116–22.
    One of the shrewdest brief summaries of Chamberlain.

SCHROEDER, LEOPOLD VON. *H. St. Chamberlain.* Munich, 1918.
    114 pages.
    First-hand information on Chamberlain's life.

SEILLIÈRE, ERNEST. *H. St. Chamberlain.* Paris, 1917.
    French war book on Chamberlain as the "latest philosopher of
    pan-German mysticism."

SPITZER, LEO. *Anti-Chamberlain.* Leipzig, 1918.
    Attacks Chamberlain's *Kriegsaufsätze* from philosophic view-
    point.

STUTZINGER, GERHARD. *Die Politischen Anschauungen H. St.
    Chamberlains.* Bottrop i. W., 1938.
    A Berlin Ph.D. thesis.

PERIODICAL ARTICLES ABOUT CHAMBERLAIN

Innumerable. Many listed in Banselow's book, q.v.

The two best periodical sources for Chamberlain material through
the years are *Bayreuther Blätter* (cf. the Wagner bibliography) and
Nationalsozialistische Monatshefte (cf. the Rosenberg bibliography). For example, in the latter magazine, see Heft 49, April 1934,
for article by Fritz Peuckert: "Chamberlain und Nietzsche," pp.
299–305, discussing the Chamberlain-Nietzsche dispute over Wagner and what all three of these thinkers had in common with nazism.

FRIEDRICH LUDWIG JAHN

BOOKS BY JAHN

Friedrich Ludwig Jahns Werke, edited with an introduction **by**
CARL EULER. 2 volumes, Hof. 1884–7.
Contains all Jahn's important works conveniently together.

BOOKS ABOUT JAHN

(FLJ = Friedrich Ludwig Jahn)

ANTONOWYTSCH, M. *FLJ, Ein Beitrag der Anfänge des deutschen
Nationalismus.* No. 230 in *Historische Studien.* Berlin, 1933.
Jahn's role in the development of modern nationalism.

ARIS, R. *Political Thought in Modern Germany.* London, 1936.
German political ferment caused by French Revolution and Napoleon. Good as background for Jahn.

BARTS, W. *Fremdwort und Sprachvereinigung bei FLJ.* Greifswald, 1936.
Jahn as language-purifier.

BRUNNER, KARL. *FLJ.* Leipzig, 1912.
Apotheosizes Jahn. Includes interesting pictures of the old man.

BUNGARDT, KARL M. *FLJ als Begründer einer völkisch-politischen
Erziehung (Idee und Gestalt).* Würzburg, 1938.
Appreciative rediscovery of Jahn as source of modern German
nationalism.

EULER, CARL. *FLJ.* Stuttgart, 1881.
Standard biography. Pro-Jahn, thorough, and dull.

FRIEDRICH, J. *Jahn als Erzieher.* Munich, 1895.
Short account of Jahn as educator. Cannot equal Piechowski.

HAYES, C. J. *Historical Evolution of Modern Nationalism.* New
York, 1931.
Standard pioneer study. Good as background for Jahn.

HITLER, ADOLF. *Mein Kampf.* New York, 1940 (Reynal & Hitchcock ed.).
Shows influence of Jahn's educational views.

MEINECKE, FRIEDRICH. *Das Zeitalter der deutschen Erhebung.*
Leipzig, 1906.
Recaptures mood of War of Liberation.

METTERNICH, PRINCE CLEMENS. *Memoirs of Prince Metternich.* 5 vols., London, 1880.

MONYPENNY, W., and BUCKLE, G. *Life of Benjamin Disraeli.* New ed., 2 vols., New York, 1929.

PERTHES, CLEMENT T. *Memoirs of Friedrich Perthes.* 2 vols., Edinburgh and New York, 1856.

Thoughtful comments on the problems of the age of Jahn and Metternich.

PIECHOWSKI, P. *FLJ — Vom Turnvater zum Volkserzieher.* Gotha, 1928.

Best summary of Jahn's " Volkstum " and his intellectual background.

PRÖHLE, HEINRICH. *FLJ's Leben.* Berlin, 1855.

Incomplete biography. Contains full text of valuable Hoffmann report on Jahn's trial as a " demagogue."

PRUTZ, HANS. *Preussische Geschichte.* Stuttgart, 1906.

SCHADE, F. *Die ästhetischen und ethischen Anschauungen FLJs.* Leipzig, 1928.

Contains a summary of Jahn's educational background.

SCHNABEL, FRANZ. *Deutsche Geschichte im 19. J.h.* 4 vols., Freiburg, 1929.

Best general background.

SCHULTHEISS, F. G. *FLJ.* Berlin, 1894.

Shorter, more popular presentation of material than in Euler.

SRBIK, H. VON. *Metternich, der Staatsmann und der Mensch.* 2 vols., Munich, 1925.

STEFFENS, HEINRICH. *Was ich erlebte.* 8 vols., Breslau, 1843. Memoirs of one of the leading anti-Jahn intellectuals.

THEUNE, B. *Volk und Nation bei Jahn, Rotteck, Welcker und Dahlmann.* No. 319 in *Historische Studien.* Berlin, 1937.

A Nazi in search of spiritual ancestors.

TREITSCHKE, HEINRICH. *History of Germany.* 6 vols., New York, 1915–19.

Jahn pictured as boorish but patriotic.

VALENTIN, V. *Geschichte der deutschen Revolution von 1848.* 2 vols., Berlin, 1931.

WENTZKE, PAUL. *Geschichte der deutschen Burschenschaft.* Heidelberg, 1919.

The nationalist student movement, in which Jahn played an important role. Part of a series published over a period of many years, *Quellen und Darstellungen zur Geschichte der Burschenschaften und der Einheitsbewegung.*

WILDT, K. *FLJ und das deutsche Turnen.* Rostock, 1931.

Good on political implications of gymnastics.

ZIEGLER, THEOBALD. *Die Geistigen u. sozialen Strömungen des 19. J.h.* Berlin, 1899.
Intellectual background.

PERIODICALS

Forschungen zur Brandenburgischen und Preussischen Geschichte
RUDOLF KÖRNER: " FLJ und sein Turnwesen," in XLI (1928), pp. 38–82.
Monatshefte der Comenius-Gesellschaft für Volkserziehung
TESCH: " Jahn als Volkserzieher," in Vol. XIX, no. 3 (Jena, 1903). Typical apotheosis.
Nationalsozialistische Monatshefte
ALFRED BÄUMLER: " FLJs Stellung in der deutschen Geistesgeschichte," in Vol. VII (1936), pp. 523–37.
Bäumler is a leading Nazi intellectual.
Preussische Jahrbücher
O. HERRMAN: " Der Turnvater Jahn," in Vol. CXVIII, Berlin, 1904, pp. 18–37.
W. MEYER: " Der Prozess FLJ," in VOL. CXXXVIII (Berlin, 1909), pp. 245–80.

1961 POSTSCRIPT: If any crucial new primary sources have been found on Jahn, they have eluded our vigilance. Of sizeable secondary sources in English, there are none before *Metapolitics* but many after; the latter include a good short discussion in Rohan Butler, *Roots of National Socialism*, N.Y., 1942 and a good long one in Hans Kohn, *The Mind of Germany*, N.Y., 1960. In Germany of the 1960's, a negative re-assessment of Jahn is in progress, including a de-politicizing of the gymnast societies. On August 9, 1958 the popular West German photo-weekly, *Quick*, featured a gymnast parade with Jahn's picture but also with this (perhaps pseudo-naive) headline: "GYMNASTS ARE NO NATIONALISTS – GYMNASTS ARE MODERN."

RICHARD WAGNER

[*sources for the two chapters on Wagner*]

WAGNER'S OWN WRITINGS

Autobiographische Skizze. Eine Mitteilung an meine Freunde, ed.
G. R. Kruse. Leipzig (n.d.).
> Reprint, with ed. notes, of Wagner's extremely important auto-
> biographical fragments of 1843 and 1852.

Mein Leben. 2 vols., Munich, 1911.
> His official autobiography, factually unreliable, psychologically
> revealing.

Richard Wagner's Prose Works, trans. and ed. by W. A. Ellis. 8
vols., London, 1895–9.
> My most valuable source. His complete works through life.

Art, Life, and Theories of Richard Wagner, trans. E. L. Burlingame.
New York, 1875.
> Sample selections from his essays, but not enough politics.

Wagner-Lexikon, ed. Carl Glasenapp and Heinrich v. Stein. Stuttgart, 1883.
> Wagner's ideas on everything alphabetically classified and quoted.
> Indispensable as brief general index to his works.

Wagner's Letters

> Often of political interest, especially letters to Uhlig, etc., to
> Roeckel, and to Praeger. (*RW* = *Richard Wagner*.)
>
> > *RW an Theodor Apel.* Leipzig, 1910.
> > *Briefe an Hans v. Bülow.* Jena, 1916.
> > *Briefwechsel zwischen Wagner und Liszt.* 2 vols., Leipzig,
> > 1887.
> > *König Ludwig zu RW.* 4 vols., Karlsruhe. (1936).
> > *RW an Mathilde Maier*, 1862–78, 2nd ed., Leipzig (1930).
> > *The Letters of RW to Anton Pusinelli.* New York, 1932.
> > *Echte Briefe an Ferdinand Praeger*, ed. H. S. Chamberlain
> > with a "Kritik der Praegerschen Veröffentlichungen." Bay-
> > reuth, 1894.
> > *RWs Briefe an Frau Julie Ritter.* Munich, 1920.
> > *RWs Letters to August Roeckel*, with essay by H. S. Chamber-
> > lain. Bristol and London (n.d.). (His fellow revolutionary).
> > *Ws Briefe an Theodor Uhlig, Wilhelm Fischer, Ferdinand
> > Heine.* Leipzig, 1888. (His Dresden friends).

Richard to Minna Wagner; letters to his first wife, ed. and trans. by Ellis. 2 vols., New York, 1909.

RW to Mathilde Wesendonck. New York, 1905.

RW an Mathilde Wesendon(c)k. Leipzig, 1918. New material.

BOOKS ABOUT WAGNER

BORGESE, G. A. *Goliath.* Revised ed., New York, 1938.
Influence of Wagner and Nietzsche on Mussolini and d'Annunzio, pp. 197, 200, 220, 290, 185.

CHAMBERLAIN, HOUSTON STEWART.
Cf. the Chamberlain bibliography, but note especially:
Cosima Wagner und H. St. Chamberlain im Briefwechsel, 1888–1908. 2 vols., 2nd ed., Leipzig, 1934.
Richard Wagner. London, 1900. More enthusiastic than scholarly.

CHANNON, HENRY. *The Ludwigs of Bavaria.* Tauchnitz edition, Leipzig, Hamburg, Paris, 1935.
Influence of Wagner on King Ludwig of Bavaria.

CYSARZ, HERBERT. "Wagner, Nietzsche, George," in *Jahrbuch des Freien Deutschen Hochstifts.* Frankfurt am Main, 1931.

CZERNIN, FERDINAND, COUNT. *Europe — Going, Going, Gone!* New York, 1939.
Includes some stimulating wise-cracks and *aperçus* on Hitler's Wagner cult.

DAVIS, ELMER. *Not to Mention the War.* New York, 1940.
Includes an essay on Wagner, summarizing Wagner's political heritage, pp. 186–90.

DINGER, HUGO. *Richard Wagners geistige Entwicklung.* Leipzig, 1892.
Best account of Wagner's transition from Feuerbach to Schopenhauer. Proof of his participation in the revolution.

DREW, ARTHUR. *Der Ideengehalt von Richard Wagners dramatischen Dichtungen.* Leipzig, 1931.
Excellent review of Wagner's chief ideas. Appendix on Nietzsche and Wagner.

ELLIS, W. A. *1849: A Vindication.* London, 1892.
Ellis, ed. of Wagner's *Prose Works,* soft-pedals Wagner's role as an active revolutionist. Disproved by Newman etc.

GANZER, K. R. *Richard Wagner, der Revolutionär gegen das 19. Jahrhundert.* Munich, 1934.
Best book from Nazi viewpoint.

German Dissertations Relating to Wagner, a collection of Ph.D.

theses about Wagner compiled by Widener Library, Harvard University, Cambridge, Mass.

GLASENAPP, CARL. *Das Leben Richard Wagners.* 6 vols., Leipzig, 1894–1911. Esp. Vol. II for 1848.

Best Wagner biography except Newman's. Longest, most thorough, but unreliable on controversial issues owing to dogmatic pro-Wagner bias.

GOBINEAU, COUNT ARTHUR (d. 1882). *Essai sur l'inégalité des races humaines.* 2 vols., 2nd ed., Paris, 1884.

Converted Wagner from cultural to racial nationalism.

GRUNDSKY, K. *Lessing und Herder als Wegbereiter Richard Wagners.* Stuttgart, 1933.

HEIDEN, KONRAD. *Hitler: A Biography.* Amer. ed., New York, Alfred A. Knopf, 1936.

Good for Wagner and Houston Chamberlain influence.

HILDEBRANDT, KURT. *Wagner und Nietzsche, ihr Kampf gegen das 19. Jahrhundert.* Breslau, 1924.

Published in Stefan George's series *Blätter für die Kunst.*

HITLER, ADOLF. Practical version of Wagnerian metapolitics.
     Mein Kampf. 13th complete German ed., Munich, 1932.
     Mein Kampf. Annotated ed., New York, Reynal & Hitchcock, 1939. Complete English trans.
     My Battle, ed. E. T. S. Dugdale. Boston, Houghton Mifflin, 1933. Abridged English trans.

KIESSLING, ARTHUR. *Der Geist des Romantischen im Denken und Schaffen Richard Wagners.* Leipzig (1925?).

KNOPF, KURT. *Die Romantische Struktur des Denkens Richard Wagners.* Jena, 1932.

MALHERBE, HENRI. *Richard Wagner, Révolutionnaire.* Paris, Albin Michel, 1938.

Includes important evidence on the question of whether Geyer was Wagner's real father.

MANN, THOMAS. *Leiden und Grösse der Meister.* Berlin, 1935. Wagner essay, p. 89. Best psychological study of Wagner.
     Freud, Goethe, Wagner. New York, Alfred A. Knopf, 1937. Condensed Eng. trans. of above essay, pp. 101–211.

MÜLLER, GEORG. *Das Recht bei Richard Wagner.* Berlin, 1914. Good for 1849.

MUELLER, G. H. *Richard Wagner in der Mai-Revolution, 1849.* Dresden, 1919.

Muenchner Neueste Nachrichten, newspaper. *Der Hitler-Prozess.* 2 vols., Munich, 1924.

Account of Hitler trial; quotes Hitler on Wagner.

NEWMAN, ERNEST. *Wagner as Man and Artist*. London, 1914.
  Superseded by following.
  The Life of Richard Wagner. 3 vols., New York, Alfred A. Knopf,
  1933, 1937, 1941. Though unfinished, by far the best biography;
  indispensable.

NIETZSCHE, FRIEDRICH. *The Case against Wagner*. 2nd ed., trans.
  by Ludovici, Edinburgh and London, 1911.
  Conveniently contains together his *Case of Wagner* and *Nietzsche
  contra Wagner*. Most brilliant psychological attack on Wagner.
  "Richard Wagner in Bayreuth," fourth part of *Unzeitgemässe
  Betrachtungen*. Leipzig, 189?. Most brilliant panegyric of
  Wagner. Contrast Nietzsche above!

NORDAU, MAX. *Degeneration*, trans. from 2nd German ed., New
  York, 1895, pp. 171–213: "The Richard Wagner Cult."
  Most ferocious and least brilliant attack on Wagner.

PLACZEK, SIEGFRIED. *Erotik und Schaffen*. Berlin and Cologne,
  Marcus & Weber, 1934.
  Wagner as transvestite and perfume fetishist, pp. 157–69.

RAUSCHNING, HERMANN. *The Voice of Destruction*. New York,
  1940.
  Includes eyewitness evidence of how steeped Hitler is in Wagner.

ROSENBERG, ALFRED. *Der Mythus des 20. Jahrhunderts*. 91–94th
  ed., Munich, 1936.
  Hails Wagner as Nazi prophet.

ROSENFELD, PAUL. *Discoveries of a Music Critic*. New York, 1936.
  Includes good brief summary of H. Chamberlain's nazification of
  Wagner's doctrines, pp. 80–90, 116–22.

ROSENSTOCK-HUESSY, EUGEN. *Die Europäischen Revolutionen*.
  Jena, 1931.
  Sums up Wagner's influence on Hohenzollern Germany, pp. 236,
  427–32.

RUPPRECHT, ERICH. *Der Mythos bei Wagner und Nietzsche*. Berlin, 1938; from *Neue Deutsche Forschungen*, Abteilung Philosophie, Band 28.

SHANKS, L. P. *Baudelaire*. Boston, 1930.
  Brilliant analysis, pp. 194–8, of how Baudelaire and Wagner psychologically stood for the same mood in different fields.

SHAW, BERNARD. *The Perfect Wagnerite*. Chicago and New York,
  1899. "Wagner as a Revolutionist," pp. 32–41.
  Stresses Wagner's socialism.

TINDALL, W. Y. *D. H. Lawrence and Susan His Cow*. New York,
  1939.
  Includes Wagner's metapolitical influence on Lawrence.

VISCHER, FRIEDRICH. *Kritische Gänge*. 2 vols. in one, Tübingen, 1844.
Essay " Vorschlag zu einer Oper," Vol. II, best sums up Wagner's later doctrine of Volk-opera based on Nordic heroes.

WELLER, ELISABETH. *Richard Wagner und der Völkische Gedanke*. Tübingen, 1927.
Useful compilation of Wagner's political remarks.

WESTPHAL, OTTO. *Feinde Bismarcks*. Munich, 1930. Chapter on Wagner.

WIEGLER, PAUL. *Geschichte der deutschen Literatur*. 2 vols., Berlin, 1930. Vol. II, pp. 504–6, Wagner as revolutionist.

ZINNIUS, K. W. *Schriften Richard Wagners in ihrem Verhältnis zur zeitgeschichtlichen Lage*. Heidelberg, 1936.
Typical pro-Nazi dissertation on Wagner.

PERIODICALS

Bayreuther Blaetter. Ed. and founded by Wagner.
Passim for ceaseless political editorials, letters, etc. Extremely important; overlaps the collected *Prose Works*. Note Nazi slant after 1933.

Common Sense. New York, monthly.
PETER VIERECK: " Hitler and Wagner," November and December 1939.
THOMAS MANN in reply article, January 1940.

Corona. Munich, Berlin, Zurich.
K. A. v. MÜLLER: " Richard Wagner und das 19. Jahrhundert," pp. 411–27; Jg. 1933, v. 3 (2); (April 1933). Wagner versus over-industrialization.

Life. New York, weekly.
B. LANSING: " Adolf Hitler," September 25, 1939. Evidence of Wagner influence.

Mass und Wert. Zurich.
THOMAS MANN: " Richard Wagner und der Ring der Nibelungen," Band 1 (1937–8), p. 377.

Die Musik. German periodical.
BASER: " Richard Wagner als Künder der Arischen Welt," Band 26 (1933), p. 85.
PAUL BECKER: " Wagner," Band 25 (1932), p. 321.

The Nation. New York, weekly.
B. H. HAGGIN: " Records," September 23, 1939, p. 330; and October 28, 1939, p. 476. Argues that even " the sound " of Wagner's music is filled with " menace " to democracy!

Nationalsozialistische Monatshefte. Official Nazi monthly, ed. by Alfred Rosenberg.
   Passim. For example, H. Schilling: " Richard Wagners ethischer Nationalsozialismus," Nr. 40, July 1933.
The New Republic. New York, weekly.
   REINHOLD HANISCH: " I Was Hitler's Buddy," April 5, 1939, pp. 239–42, and April 12, pp. 270–2. Wagner allusions.
Sueddeutsche Monatshefte. Munich, monthly.
   Sonderheft "Gegen Psychoanalyse," Jahrgang 28, Heft 11, August 1931: SEBASTIAN RÖCKL: "Erinnerungen eines Tapezierers an Richard Wagner." Evidence for Wagner's transvestitism as analysed in Placzek's book, q.v. [1]
Time. New York, weekly.
   Evidence for Wagner's influence on nazism in issue of February 26, 1940, pp. 24, 90.
Völkische Kultur. Dresden, Nazi periodical founded in 1933.
   J. M. VERWEYEN: " Richard Wagner der Deutsche," September 1933, pp. 184–9.
Zeitschrift für Musik.
   OTTO STROBEL: "Richard Wagner: Mitteilung an meine Freunde," Jg. 98, Heft 7, pp. 563–6 (July 1931). Important discovery of pages omitted from the 1851 autobiography by timid publisher because of their communistic and revolutionary enthusiasms.
   BOSSHART: " Richard Wagners Regenerationslehre," Jg. 100 (1933), p. 688.
Zeitwende. Munich, Nazi periodical.
   HANS JOACHIM MOSER: "Wagner und unsre Zeit," Band 9 (1933), p. 17.

1961 POSTSCRIPT: Here is no space or need — anyone can copy off a card catalogue — to list the immense post-*Metapolitics* material on political Wagnerism; none of it requires any major revising of the book's Wagner chapters. Indeed the thesis of those chapters has been further substantiated by the first-hand quotations from Hitler about Wagner in such new books — among others — as Kubizek, *The Young Hitler I Knew* and Ritter, ed., *Hitler's Table-Talk.* Ernest Newman's monumental *Life of Richard Wagner* was completed with vol. IV, N.Y., 1946 and remains the best of many biographies. Among new primary sources: unpublished letters of the Burrell collection appeared in J. Burk, ed., *Letters of Richard Wagner,* N.Y., 1950. Among new secondary sources: political Wagner allusions of particular interest to present readers may be found in

[1] Wagner's secret compulsions to dress in feminine robes and perfumes help explain his — and perhaps Hitler's — compensatory, pseudomasculine cult of Teuton warriors.

the following, to name only a few among others equally valuable:

JACQUES BARZUN, *Darwin, Marx, Wagner*, Boston, 1941.

W. BLISSET, "Thomas Mann: The Last Wagnerite," in *Germanic Review*, N.Y., Feb. 1960 (also Wagner articles in *Toronto Quarterly*, etc.).

W. DAIM, *Der Mann der Hitler die Ideen Gab*, Munich, Isar-Verlag, 1958.

JOSEF GREINER, *Das Ende des Hitler-Mythos*, Zurich-Leipzig-Vienna, Amalthea-Verlag, 1947.

E. HANFSTAENGL, *Unheard Witness*, Philadelphia, 1957.

J. KERMAN, "Wagner" in *Hudson Review*, Fall 1960.

HANS KOHN, *The Mind of Germany*, N.Y., 1960.

A. KOLB, *Ludwig II. und Richard Wagner*, Amsterdam, 1947.

A. KUBIZEK, *The Young Hitler I Knew*, Boston, 1955.

THOMAS MANN, *Adel des Geistes*, Stockholm, 1945; *Dr. Faustus*, N.Y., 1948; *Last Essays*, N.Y., 1959.

R. RIE, Wagner-Nietzsche article in *Journal of the History of Ideas*, N.Y., June 1952.

G. RITTER, ed., *Hitlers Tischgespräche*, Bonn, 1951.

R. DE ROUSSY DE SALES, *The Making of Tomorrow*, N.Y., 1942 (cf. his analysis of *Metapolitics*, pp. 254–268).

FRIEDRICH SELL, *Die Tragödie des Deutschen Liberalismus*, Stuttgart, 1953.

L. SNYDER, *Basic History of Modern Germany*, Princeton, 1957 (pp. 169–71 list parallel quotations from Wagner and Hitler).

L. SNYDER, *German Nationalism*, Harrisburg, 1952.

LEON STEIN, *The Racial Thinking of Richard Wagner*, N.Y., 1950.

See final pages of 1961 preface for quotations from some of this new Wagner-Hitler material.

ALFRED ROSENBERG

THE COMPLETE WORKS OF
ALFRED ROSENBERG

(including many works not found in any American library)

An die Dunkelmänner unserer Zeit. 33d ed., Munich, 1938; 1st ed., 1935. 112 pages. Circulation 641,000–660,000 by 1938.

An attack on the Catholic critics of his *Mythus.*

Blut und Ehre. 17th ed., Munich, 1938. Circulation 130,000 by 1938.

His speeches and articles of 1919–33.

Der Deutsche Ordensstaat. Munich, 1934.

Links nazism with the knightly old Teutonic Orders.

Der Fall Ludendorff. Munich (Eher? n.d.). Pamphlet.

Freimaurerische Weltpolitik. (Munich, Eher? n.d.).

Gestaltung der Idee. 7th ed., Munich, 1938. Circulation 75,000 by 1938.

His speeches and articles of 1933–5.

Houston Stewart Chamberlain als Verkünder und Begründer einer deutschen Zukunft. Munich, 1927.

Acknowledges his and nazism's intellectual debt to Chamberlain.

Die Internationale Hochfinanz. Munich, Eher (n.d.). Cited in his *Mythus,* p. 466, footnote. Pamphlet.

Kampf um die Macht. Munich, Eher (n.d.). Circulation 70,000 Essays of 1921–32.

Der Mythus des 20. Jahrhunderts. 137th–142nd ed., Munich, 1938; 1st ed., 1930. 713,000 copies printed 1938.

Hitler considers this book by his official " Director of Weltanschauung " the profoundest book by a living German.

Pest in Russland. Munich, Eher (1937?). 48 pages, condensed version of an original 1922 version. Circulation 28,000.

Bolshevism denounced (not so long before the Hitler-Stalin pact) as the new bubonic plague.

Protestantische Rompilger. Munich, Eher (n.d.). 64 pages. Circulation 620,000.

Attacks Protestant critics of *Mythus* as betraying Luther to the Catholic Church.

Die Spur des Juden im Wandel der Zeiten. Munich, 1920. 160 pages. Circulation 23,000.

Der Staatsfeindliche Zionismus. (Munich, Eher? n.d.).

Der Sumpf. Munich, Eher (n.d.).

The Weimar Republic compared to a " swamp " of corruption.

Unmoral im Talmud. Munich (Eher? n.d.). Pamphlet.

Quotes anti-Christian passages from Jewish Talmud.

Verbrechen der Freimaurerei. (Munich, Eher? n.d.).

Der Weltverschwörerkongress zu Basel. Munich, Eher (n.d.).

The horrendous Elders of Zion conspiring to enslave the gentile world.

Wesen, Grundsätze und Ziele der Nat.soz. Dt. Arbeiterpartei; das Programm der Bewegung. Munich, 1933. 47 pages. Circulation 170,000 by 1933, 350,000 by 1938 edition.

Endorsed by Hitler as official Nazi program; includes a complete list and discussion of the famous " 25 Points."

Das Wesensgefüge des Nationalsozialismus. 6th ed., Munich, 1933. 80 pages. Circulation 24,000–28,000.

Propaganda for a " German rebirth " through nazism.

Der Zukunftsweg einer deutschen Aussenpolitik. Munich, Eher (n.d.).

Destiny and *Lebensraum* demand an aggressive expansion.

BOOKS EDITED BY ROSENBERG

[*written by others*]

ECKART, DIETRICH. *Dietrich Eckart, ein Vermächtnis.* Selected works with intro. and notes by Rosenberg. 4th ed., Munich, 1937; copyrighted 1st ed., 1928; approved officially by Nazi party in 1935.

Eckart had tremendous influence on both Rosenberg and Hitler.

GOUGENOT DES MOUSSEAUX, HENRI ROGER (1805–76). *Der Jude, das Judentum, und die Verjudung der christlichen Völker.* Tr. from French by Rosenberg. 5th ed., Munich, 1921.

In addition to the more famous Count Gobineau, here is another nineteenth-century French source for modern Nazi racism.

Die Protokollen der Weisen von Zion. (Munich, Eher? n.d.). The notorious forgeries.

PERIODICALS EDITED BY ROSENBERG

[*fertile sources for his articles and editorials*]

Nationalsozialistische Monatshefte, monthly, Munich.

Official " Weltanschauung " magazine for Nazi party members.

Der Völkische Beobachter, daily, Munich.

Official state-subsidized newspaper of the Nazi regime. Bought

by Nazi party in 1920, edited by Dietrich Eckart and Rosenberg,
then by Eckart alone until his death early in 1925, then by Rosenberg until through today. Owned privately by Hitler.

Der Weltkampf, monthly, founded by Rosenberg in 1924, then edited by Dr. Ernst Boepple, Munich, Deutsche Volksverlag, 1924 through today.

Devoted to anti-Semitism and Wagnerian-Rosenbergian metapolitics.

BOOKS ABOUT ROSENBERG

DUTCH, OSWALD (pseudonym). *Hitler's Twelve Disciples.* New York, 1940.

Includes chapter on Rosenberg.

GROSCLAUDE, PIERRE. *Alfred Rosenberg et le Mythe du XXme. Siècle.* Paris, 1938.

GROSS, OTTO. *Erläuterungen zum Mythus des XX. Jahrhunderts.* Munich, Eher (n.d.).

Gross is a German Professor who worships the very air that the metapolitical Rosenberg walks on.

GRUENAGEL, FRIEDRICH. *Rosenberg und Luther.* Bonn, 1934.

A Heidelberg Ph.D. thesis.

HART, F. T. *Alfred Rosenberg: Der Mann und sein Werk.* Munich, 1939.

An apotheosis.

HASELMAYER, A. *Der Fall Rosenbergs und Fällt Hitler Mit?* Munich, 1931.

A pamphlet of 51 pages rebutting Rosenberg's *Der Fall Ludendorff.*

Kirchlicher Anzeiger für die Erzdiözese Köln. " Studien zum Mythus des XX. Jahrhunderts," Cologne, October 1934. " Nachtrag zu den Studien zum Mythus des XX. Jahrhunderts," Cologne, December 1934.

Anonymous, the official Catholic answer, distributed despite Nazi censorship.

KOLNAI, AUREL. *The War against the West.* New York, 1938.

Includes many pages on Rosenberg vs. the West.

KUENNETH, WALTER. *Antwort auf den Mythus.* Berlin, 1935.

A Protestant rebuttal to *Mythus,* more cautious and compromising than the above Catholic answer.

LICHTENBERGER, HENRI. *The Third Reich.* New York, 1937.

Includes a good summary of some of Rosenberg's philosophy.

MICKLEM, NATHANIEL. *National Socialism and the Roman Catholic Church*. London, 1939.
Chapter on "Herr Rosenberg and His Myth," pp. 15–23.
UNIVERSITY OF PARIS (by a number of Catholic professors dividing the chapters among them). *Racisme et Christianisme*. Paris, Flammarion, 1939.
Includes much discussion of Rosenberg by Ernest Seillière and others.

1961 POSTSCRIPT: Aside from the many memos about him by fellow Nazis (for example, Hans Fritzsche, *The Sword in the Scales*, London, 1953), the chief *post*-war primary sources about Rosenberg include his testimony at the Nuremberg trial (*Nazi Conspiracy and Aggression*, eleven volumes, Washington, 1947–49 and *Trial of the Major War Criminals*, 42 volumes, Nuremberg, International Military Tribunal, 1947–49) and also his *Letzte Aufzeichnungen* (Goettingen, 1955), written half-disillusioned in prison before being hanged. Among countless new secondary sources on Rosenberg, two categories of books and articles predominate: (1) those about the Nuremberg trials (for example, G. M. Gilbert, *Nuremberg Diary*, New York, 1947 and *The Psychology of Dictatorship*, New York, 1950; D. Kelley, *Twenty-two Cells at Nuremberg*, New York, 1947; W. Benton and G. Grimm, ed., *Nuremberg: German Views*, Dallas, 1955; W. Harris, *Tyranny on Trial*, Dallas, 1954; R. H. Jackson, U.S. Chief of Counsel, *The Nürnberg Case*, New York, 1947); (2) those about Nazi atrocities in occupied Russia (for example, A. Dallin, *German Rule in Russia, 1941–1945*, London, 1957 and G. Reitlinger, *The House Built on Sand*, New York, 1960).

SYNOPSIS OF ROSENBERG'S POSTS AND INFLUENCE

The reader may find useful a synopsis of Rosenberg's official posts, to bring up-to-date our two Rosenberg chapters of 1941. During Hitler's imprisonment, 1923–24, Rosenberg was appointed acting head of the Nazi party by Hitler. Ever since the Nazi press reorganization of 1921–23, Rosenberg was chief editor of the official party newspaper, *Der Völkische Beobachter* (along with his Wagner-cult friend, the increasingly alcoholic Dietrich Eckart). Rosenberg's three main posts: 1933–45, *"Reichsleiter"* of the party's Foreign

Policy Office (the APA); 1933–45, director of "the spiritual and ideological supervision of the party"; 1941–45, "*Reichsminister*" for the German-occupied Eastern Territories. In practice he was edged out of the first post by Ribbentrop; out of the second by Himmler, Ley, Goebbels; out of the third by Erich Koch, the Gestapo, etc. He was also founder of the 1939 Institute for Exploring the Jewish Question at Frankfurt am Main and President of the International Conference on the Jewish Question at Frankfurt, 1941. Through his Nordic Societies he was the negotiator arranging for the treasonable Fifth Column of Norway with his ex-Communist friend, Vidkun Quisling, thereby coining a new noun.

Because Rosenberg eventually lost his Führer's favor and because his turgid book *Mythus* appears unreadable to any one with a sense of humor, some excellent historians now minimize his importance for the Third Reich. But millions did read, believe, and "act on" his pamphlets and his *Völkischer Beobachter* articles, where he expressed (more simply) the selfsame racist-romantic credo as in *Mythus*. The records of the Nuremberg trial and of Dr. Gilbert, its attendant psychiatrist, show fairly convincingly that such death-camp organizers as Colonel Hoess of Auschwitz and Governor Frank of Poland were steeped in Rosenberg's writings and definitely influenced by them (though whether as real motive for genocide or mere rationalization we can never know, perhaps both). Dr. Gilbert interviewed Hoess rather shrewdly in an attempt to find out what convinced Hoess personally of the need to exterminate two million Jews in Auschwitz — and got as answer Hoess's reading of Rosenberg's *Mythus* (in addition to the more expected answer of *Mein Kampf* and Goebbels). Hoess added priggishly — a macabre priggishness in the given context — that at his death-camp it was "subordinates of narrow outlook" who read Streicher's *Stürmer* but that what Hoess called the less "superficial" executioners of Jews preferred to read Goebbels and Rosenberg.

Here are the off-the-record private comments on Hoess and Rosenberg by the other Nazi defendants (as secretly recorded by Dr. Gilbert).* Hans Frank (the self-flagellating mass-murderer): "Hoess testified how he exterminated two million Jews. . . . The things I said and the things Rosenberg said made those things possible." Von Papen (the self-exculpating collaborator): ". . . Hoess, the Commandant of Auschwitz, had read his [Rosenberg's] works. That was, of course, the crux of the whole thing." Admiral Doenitz (whom Hitler had appointed his successor): "That Rosenberg . . . these propagandists were really responsible for these terrible anti-semitic acts." Hans Fritzsche (of Hitler's propaganda ministry): "Rosenberg became the high priest of the Nazi ideology . . . the

* G. Gilbert, *Nuremberg Diary* (N.Y., 1947), pp. 267–80 and *The Psychology of Dictatorship* (N.Y., 1950), p. 256.

father of Nazi ideology." Of course, an author need not be held responsible for the crimes of his disciples and readers (these Nazi attempts to shift their guilt to Rosenberg are a transparent dodge), but the above does at least suggest that the author in question was really important and really read; and this importance, now often denied, is what we are trying to establish.

ROSENBERG VERSUS HITLER IN RUSSIA

In Russia Hitler became disgusted not only with Rosenberg's pompous inefficiency but with his basic occupation policy. Backed by Mussolini and motivated not by compassion but by brutal military needs and by his own 1917 stand with the White Russian armies, Rosenberg wanted a more cooperative treatment of millions of anti-communist Ukrainians, a potential new fascist army of Ukrainians marching against Stalin. Treat "those Nigger peoples" like slaves, make them "Germany's colonial Africa," retorted Hitler, echoed by Erich Koch, Rosenberg's main rival in Nazi-occupied Russia and originally from the national-bolshevik Strasser wing of the party.

Backed by Hitler against the Rosenberg-Mussolini dream of a non-colonial, multi-national, pan-fascist alliance, Koch boasted he would bring the Ukraine, even if anti-communist and pro-German, not national liberation but "the whip." In 1934 the same Koch had published a book urging Soviet-Nazi cooperation against western democracy; such cooperation he had discussed in a secret national-bolshevik meeting with Soviet Russia's Karl Radek and the once pro-Nazi and once pro-Soviet Theodor Oberländer, later a Bonn cabinet minister. Not till 1958 did Koch's Communist jailers allow his long-postponed trial as a leading war-criminal. Both Soviet Russia and Soviet Poland today hate public mention of the Ukrainian independence movement as much as Koch did in 1942, and his delayed trial in Poland significantly indicted him for his small-scale murder of non-Ukrainian Slavs rather than for his obvious large-scale crime, namely his mass-murder — against Rosenberg's will but with Hitler's and perhaps Stalin's — of Ukrainians. According to Reitlinger, Koch's death sentence (in contrast with Rosenberg's) has still, mysteriously enough, "not been carried out."[1]

---

[1] Reitlinger, *The House Built on Sand,* pp. 175, 438: "[Koch] had chosen the same victims as Stalin himself. For Koch's bitterest hate had been reserved for the Ukrainian nationalists, the favorites of Alfred Rosenberg and the pioneers of his anti-Soviet State. Behind all Koch's speeches on a 'nigger people' lurked the contempt of a man who had been almost a communist in his day for the flotsam and jetsam of the White Armies."

Many of Russia's Ukrainians, having been enslaved by Stalin-aides like Khrushchev in the 1930s, at first welcomed the Hitlerite invaders with pathetic flowers. By rebuffing his *Untermensch* welcomers into a still bloodier slavery, Hitler was subordinating political propaganda gains, military self-interest, and international or non-German fascism to the myth of race. This race dogma of metapolitics was reinforced by the Lebensraum dogma of geopolitics but perhaps equally by two of Hitler's sourest non-theoretical memories: his sullen Hapsburg boyhood among Slavs and General Ludendorff's Ukrainian fiasco of 1918. No wonder Stalin, having even more cause to resent Rosenberg's Ukrainian nationalists, once praised Koch and Hitler ironically for terrorizing them.

In the end Hitler seems to have deliberately humiliated Rosenberg, his once-revered teacher and quack-philosopher, and derided him in public as "a half-Russian." The final split between Hitler's kind of criminality and Rosenberg's kind is that of gun-man versus con-man — or, as they would have preferred to phrase it, man of will versus mind-gymnast, the latter a phrase from gymnast Jahn.

When the thousand-year Reich collapsed in 1945, Rosenberg went into brief hiding. He was captured when he appeared, quite needlessly, for hospitalization of a minor injury, sustained while drunk. The shadowy episode suggests half-tentative questions about how much Rosenberg, perhaps guilt-ridden about the Hitler practice of the genocide Rosenberg himself had theorized, was impelled by an unconscious need for punishment. In contrast with almost all other self-exculpations by ex-Hitlerites, Rosenberg at his Nuremberg trial seemed somewhat honest[2] in regretting the atrocities his own teachings had prepared and for which he was hanged. It was as if Lenin, himself a ruthless terrorist, had lived to witness with horror terrorism's logical extreme in Stalin. In his *Letzte Aufzeichnungen,* written while awaiting death at Nuremberg after the war, Rosenberg retaliated by ascribing to Hitler the responsibility for Germany's fate:

"The name National Socialism derives from the Sudetenland. . . . Never was the German soul more at one with itself than in 1933. Never did the Great-German Dream seem nearer fulfilment than in 1938. Yet the Reich never collapsed into greater ruins than in 1945. All this is included under a single name, but this one name must bear responsibility for all this before the Court of the German Nation."

[2] See Rosenberg's *Letzte Aufzeichnungen* and Fritzsche's *The Sword in the Scales.*

APPENDIX A

PRO AND CON:
Two Reviews of Original Edition:
JOSEPH C. HARSCH AND JACQUES BARZUN

Publisher's Note

As an interesting example of the opposite reactions evoked by such a controversial book about Germany prior to Pearl Harbor, the publishers here reprint two 1941 discussions of it, one favorable, one completely unfavorable. The former is by the foreign correspondent to Germany, Joseph C. Harsch; it appeared in the *Christian Science Monitor* (Boston, 7/12/41). The latter is by Professor Jacques Barzun, written in mid-1941 and published in January, 1942 in the scholarly quarterly, *Journal of the History of Ideas*. The Barzun discussion was presented in *Journal of the History of Ideas* in the form of a debate with Dr. Viereck; therefore, it is also necessary here to reprint Dr. Viereck's brief rejoinder. The issues which this interesting debate between these two scholars raises about Germany, and about the peculiar development which romanticism underwent in Germany, are issues that remain equally important for the reader of today.

Reprint from CHRISTIAN SCIENCE MONITOR,
Boston, 7/12/41
THE BOOKSHELF
Reviewed by Joseph Harsch, former Am. foreign corr.
in Germany.
The Origins of Naziism

If anyone still labors under the delusion that the current war in Europe is just another one of Europe's old imperialistic or economic rivalries, he would be well advised to read Peter Viereck's scholarly dissection of the origins and nature of

Naziism, METAPOLITICS (New York: Knopf. $3). The tragedy of the world is that only now, when Hitler's armies are running berserk over a continent and threatening the whole world, is it possible for a man like Mr. Viereck to diagnose the nature of the threat with any chance of the public bothering to notice. If such a book could have been read by millions 10 years ago, or even five years ago, history might have been different.

"Metapolitics" might well have appeared under the title of the first great book about the menace of Hitler Germany, Edgar Mowrer's "Germany Turns the Clock Back." It would have been a less forbidding title than a word such as Metapolitics, which was coined by German nationalists because no existing word in their language or any other European language was capable of expressing the unscientific, unethical, vague, to-be-sensed-by-German-alone-but-not-to-be-understood-rationally-by-anyone type of politics which lie behind Naziism.

Mr. Viereck has given us the explanation of why Germany today is turning the clock back. And it is an absorbing study. He takes the roots of Naziism back to the Napoleonic period, when the first nationalists of Germany found they had to coin something new to arouse popular support for their "war of liberation." The fact was that the armies of Napoleon had brought so many benefits in their wake that most Germans, particularly of the lower classes, found themselves better off under French rule, tyrannous and violent as it was, than under the former order.

To recruit the middle class to the cause of German nationalism the political leaders of the country subsidized Friedrich Ludwig Jahn, a Prussian schoolteacher with a mystic creed about the German folk being the true entity and the individual nothing. "Father Jahn" organized students in gymnastic societies, forerunner of the Hitler Jugend, taught a passionate hatred of everything foreign and a mystic reverence for all anti-social crudities which could be excused as primitively German, and left behind him a seed which germinated in the universities down through the next century.

"Father Jahn's" pupils were leaders in the 1848 revolutions, and they numbered among their group on the barricades Richard Wagner, pictured by Mr. Viereck as a major link between racial doctrines of "Father Jahn" and the culminating, atavistic, reversion of Germany under the banners of Hitler to the primitive, marauding hordes of Naziism to day.

During the first World War the tendency was to blame Germany's rampant militarism on Nietzsche. Mr. Viereck finds some justification for this in part of the great philosopher's career. But Nietzsche, like most of the others whom Naziism regards as spiritual ancestors of Hitler, including Langbehn, George, and Spengler, outlived a period of orgiastic revel in the cult of Germanic tribal mysticism and "returned to the west." Actually Wagner himself in his final period said many things which the Nazis keep very quiet about today. But Wagner founded the Bayreuth circle which included the French renegade Count Gobineau and the English Houston Stewart Chamberlain, two men who directly influenced Hitler; and he celebrated the German pagan cult in his operas.

The hope Mr. Viereck holds out for the survival of civilization is that just as Nietzsche and Spengler and even Wagner outgrew their worship at the shrine of racism and returned spiritually to the fold of western civilization, so too may the German people, provided, he says, their faith in the Germanic myth is shaken by military defeat.

One fact worthy of notice which Mr. Viereck produces is that Alfred Rosenberg's "Myth of the Twentieth Century," the philosophic textbook of Naziism, was conceived and outlined prior to the Treaty of Versailles. In other words, it was not Versailles which created Naziism, as all Nazis would have it.

This is an extremely important book, notable because it makes it possible for a normal western mind to understand at least partially the disease which has warped the thinking of the German people. This is no easy task because no German has ever been able to explain it intelligently. In fact the very inexplicableness of it is considered an essential of German racialism. But Mr. Viereck does let us get a glimpse of how and why the German nation has turned for a time from western civilization for an orgy in primitive emotionalism and international lawlessness. J. C. H.

A DEBATE ABOUT "METAPOLITICS" WITH JACQUES BARZUN[1]

Indictment by Professor Barzun

Mr. Viereck's book *Metapolitics* is an ardent attempt to psycho-analyze the religion of the Nazis. At least this is the purpose which the author declares in his Preface, having set to one side as fairly well established the economic and political antecedents of the new German imperialism. The term "metapolitics" is a piece of jargon borrowed as a convenient label from the usage of the Wagner circle, but the content of the term is what Mr. Viereck offers as the result of his investigations. As he sees it, metapolitics is made up of four things; romanticism, racism, a vague economic socialism, and faith in the *Volk*. It follows, still according to the author, that in adopting these principles, Germany is turning her back on all of western civilization, and that an understanding of the four streams of doctrine will help preserve us from the "new paganism" by refuting its constituent elements.

Mr. Viereck has done much reading in the literature of modern Germany and in those portions of the European tradition which seem relevant to the topic of our contemporary "chaos"; Nietzsche, Gobineau, Chamberlain, Hegel, Paul de Lagarde, Fichte, Carlyle — the list is by now almost standard. He writes, moreover, with a great deal of verve, and his re-exposition of these and other men's ideas is quick and simplified enough not to tax the casual reader's attention. Hence it is quite likely that the book will please and convince many people. Or rather, it will confirm by its evidence of sincerity and erudition many

[1] This debate appeared in *Journal of the History of Ideas*, City College, N.Y., January, 1942, Vol. III, No. 1, pp. 107–112.

latent prejudices, among them some possibly useful to the practical ends of pugnacity and group cohesion.

But if the history of ideas is viewed as an exacting discipline, this book must be judged an ill-advised publication on a narrowly conceived thesis. Like a number of similar attempts, it exemplifies the error of seeing the past only through the eyes of the present, or rather, of seeing the past only in the light of what is most striking and seems most important in the present. For if the author had examined the contemporary scene with a more fastidious enthusiasm for our national cause, he would not make the mistake of seeing Germany both as warring against western tradition and as a product of that periodic force in western tradition which is called romanticism. This contradiction is only one of many vitiating Mr. Viereck's passionate account. It is clear that he has been too busy finding evidence to ask himself what rules govern its admission and interpretation. To give an instance, he quotes Nietzsche with approval against nineteenth-century German imperialism and racism; but he includes Gobineau among the ogres as a convinced racialist. Now it is a fact that Nietzsche can also be quoted on Gobineau's side as a racialist, and Gobineau on Nietzsche's as an individualist. The problem of the historian becomes, therefore, that of deciding whether the thinkers whom he has chosen as representative are only unreliable weather vanes, or whether there is some reason for these real and apparent contradictions. When the historian has made his decision or discovered such a reason, he can be said to understand in something like its own terms the time or temper which he is discussing.

If Mr. Viereck so understood romanticism — and indeed the whole nineteenth century — he might still dislike its prototypes or disapprove of its works, but he would not be guilty of the caricature without resemblance which he produces under these names. He produces it, of course, with the aid of clichés and misleading short-cuts which are far from original — hence the ready persuasiveness of his demonstration. To speak of "Rousseauistic lispings about the noble savage" takes the place of analysis, as usual. But where did Rousseau idealize the savage, and why? To complain that Romanticism is not definable, because it has too many connotations, acts as a *prima facie* condemnation; but one misses the awareness that there are also a myriad inconsistent definitions of Classicism, Realism, Rationalism, Renaissance — all unsatisfactory to the degree that the concrete is not exhausted by abstract formulas. Again, to assert that romanticism is essentially German may make a complex state of affairs more simple, but it begs the ultimate question at the cost of suppressing eighteenth-century manifestations of romanticism in England, France, and Italy. Finally, in order to make romanticism and its sequel a certified plague, a writer must steadily confuse particular with general propositions, speaking of romanticists (or of "the nineteenth-century") in such a way that all romanticists, romanticists like all of us, or romanticists as opposed to the rest of mankind, may equally be meant. All these are no single instances but types of historical and logical malfeasance which Mr. Viereck repeatedly commits — often by mere epithet or implication — both in the main body of his work and in his *obiter dicta*.

This general criticism, I repeat, does not in the least depend on whether the author prefers classicism and I romanticism (as he seems to imply in a footnote referring to an article of mine). Its scope goes beyond the subject matter of any given movement and embraces instead the methods of all intellectual history. When Mr. Viereck discredits romanticism by accusing it of worshipping life, and quotes as proof a love scene from a pulp magazine; when he indicts in one bill of particulars Bergson, Jahn, and Chamberlain, together with the historical ideas of Herder, the poetry of Shelley, and the apologetics of tyranny; when he says with apparent unawareness of the concession, that romanticism has been refuted again and again but still survives . . . so that the task of civilization is to harness it, I submit that he is not only not fulfilling his function as an historian, but is as a writer fostering public bewilderment on matters high and dangerous.

Even as an historian of practical affairs his conclusions seem singularly naïve. He either ignores or forgets the double life — internal and external — which every European nation has led since the Roman Empire, and consequently treats national histories with reference to an impossible single standard, now internal, now external. To read him one would think that an imperialistic France led by Louis XIV and Napoleon had never sought after hegemony in Europe,[1] nor justified its acts in the name of glory, culture, and the right of might. One would never know that liberal revolutions succumbed to nationalistic passions elsewhere than in Germany, neither would one suspect that whatever metapolitics may be, politics keeps constant ways in defiance of ethics and civilization, as can be seen in its record from Thucydides to Winston Churchill, by way of Catherine de'Medici and Cecil Rhodes. Since, then, it might be argued that Germany's present actions are in line with the European tradition of Empire (ever accompanied by persecution), it follows that we must distinguish between the course of politics and the history of ideas. I say distinguish between, not dissociate from; for belief and action are related and it is precisely the art of the historian to make clear in what ways thought turns to good and evil in human hands. This distinction in no sense weakens the indictment against those who misuse ideas or deny the validity of civilized life, reason, and justice; any more than it levels present and past offenses to one and the same degree of evil. On the contrary, it permits value judgments by establishing a scale of comparison, and by showing how peculiar modern conditions (e.g., mass persuasion and mass action) give a new embodiment to an old curse.

As soon as we speak of scale and values, however, it becomes obvious that we must not mingle foul with fair and drag the aesthetics of Keats and Shelley (p. 31), the metaphysics of Bergson and Nietzsche, the psychology and religion of the non-rationalists (which should include Christians like Pascal and William James) into the morass of irresponsible or venal journalism, old and new. In a recent review of a book on

---

[1] In two periods of cultural classicism, as it happens.

351

Modern Dictatorship, Professor Koppel Pinson had to rebuke its author for making Hitler's educational theories derive straight from Goethe's lines, "Gray is all theory; only the golden tree of life is green." Mr. Viereck makes fundamentally the same allegation, even though he speaks, somewhat inaccurately, of Goethe's "conversion to Classicism." It is because of this allegation that his book begins with the romanticists, a few, at any rate, and that the four subheads of metapolitics merge into one condemnation of the so-called romantic spirit which is conveniently stretched to cover every kind of folly and knavery. To all these bills of attainder against our forefathers, it seems to me that the historian is bound to say, in effect: "If Goethe is right and Hitler does intelligently follow out his implied educational theory, then Hitler's educational theory is right." We must of course question — as does Professor Pinson — whether the link truly exists. We must further question — as does Mr. Viereck — whether Goethe is right, but it is surely the anti-historical method par excellence to argue that Goethe is wrong (and by extension, romanticism, the nineteenth-century, what you will) because Hitler is an alleged result.

JACQUES BARZUN

Columbia University, 1941

Reply by the Author of METAPOLITICS

Through the courtesy of the Editors I am permitted to reply in the same issue to Mr. Barzun's interesting and (if I may borrow one of his terms) somewhat "passionate" review. The first thing which it seems needful to say about it (for readers unacquainted with the book) is that the review has to do almost entirely with the two introductory chapters of *Metapolitics*, which deal in part with Romanticism. The second chapter draws up a precise definition of what the word "romantic," when used by me, is to be understood to mean. In his review Mr. Barzun neglects to define his own use of the word; but his previous brilliant exaltation of what he designates by "Romanticism" — in his *Darwin, Marx, Wagner* and in his *American Scholar* article, "To the Rescue of Romanticism" (1940) — makes evident that, in the main, he signifies by the term something quite different from what it means in the book he is reviewing. For the most part he is referring to one set of ideas, I to another. Since he overlooks this fact, and fails to notice my definition, it is not surprising that he accuses me of an unjust "caricature" of "romanticism," and of "suppressing eighteenth-century manifestations of romanticism in England and France." Mr. Barzun, in short, has provided an interesting parallel to the proverbial controversy over the color of the two sides of the shield.

Mr. Barzun pronounces my "passionate account vitiated" by the "contradiction" of "seeing Germany both as warring against western tradition and as a product of that periodic force in western tradition which is called romanticism." Here he finds a "contradiction" solely by failing to inform the reader of two facts. First, my book explicitly defines the "western tradition" and "romanticism" as the real "warring" opposites. Second, his linkage of "romanticism" with western tradition is according to his usage of the word, but not according to mine. His usage, if it were defined precisely, may be preferable to mine. But his unintentional failure to state that our usage is different, a failure convenient for converting any unalert reader, ultimately handicaps his cause by producing only "bewilderment on matters high and dangerous" in readers who check back from his criticisms to the actual pages that he is criticizing.

Through most of his critique of my introductory romanticism chapters (the actual book itself he understandably cannot waste his busy time on), the issue is never joined. He is talking, very brilliantly indeed, of something quite different from the book he is supposedly reviewing. And I cannot but register protest against the reviewer's giving readers the impression that the issue is joined.

His impressions of the personality behind the book are of less interest to the reader than the broader issue. So I shall not use my limited space to reply to them (nor to thank him for attributing to me "verve"). But I cannot permit to pass unchallenged his grave charge that I "unfastidiously" distort the "rules of evidence," apparently in order to bolster my support of anti-Nazi interventionism. Suffice it to remark that he cites not a single substantiated example of such alleged distortion. Actual events have made the interventionist cause so sound on its own merits that it hardly needs the additional bolstering of distortion by me or by anyone else. When he lists "Winston Churchill" as a subtopic under "defiance of civilization" and observes that "Germany's present actions are in line with the European tradition of Empire," he accuses me of naïvely implying that the British Empire is on a qualitatively higher moral plane than Hitler's empire. Here I agree; that is exactly what (on this point) my book intended to imply. Yet the superiority of England's empire to Hitler's does *not*, as Mr. Barzun believes, make me suppress the former's faults; pp. 207–8 are sharply critical of England's past aggressions and present economic abuses.

In his second and fourth paragraphs, he dismisses the book as a rehash of an "almost standard list" and implies that it contains little or no unfamiliar historical material. He lists these "almost standard" names in a way that gives the impression that his list summarizes the principal contents of my book. This raises two separate points. Does his list really describe the book? Is the book really without original scholarly contributions?

For the very reason that the figures which he names are already well known, my books treats them relatively very briefly: one of them, Carlyle, is mentioned only in a single sentence. The amazing and unexplainable fact is that Mr. Barzun's list of the contents completely omits the three authors chiefly dealt with in the book, Jahn, Wagner, Rosenberg; the chapters on these take up some two-thirds of the volume! Far from being "almost standard," the rôle of these men in producing the Nazi metapolitics has received little serious analysis outside Germany. As my book's bibliography indicates, many of their works, often unavailable in America, have never before been treated in any form; yet their crucial influence on German history, and on Hitler himself, is demonstrated in my text, with documentary proof in the notes. Rosenberg, the subject of the longest two chapters of all, is not only omitted from Mr. Barzun's "list" but is not once mentioned in the whole review.

Since he condemns the book's scholarship with such dogmatic finality, it is not improper to cite from two foremost authorities in the field a verdict directly contradicting his implication that the scholar can learn little new from the book. America's foremost historian of modern Germany, Professor Sidney Fay of Harvard, wrote of *Metapolitics*: "I have learned a lot from it and agree with almost all of it. . . . I like the book very much." Thomas Mann calls it a work of "profound historical insight" and calls its Wagner-Hitler discoveries "extraordinarily meritorious" because "for the *first* time in America" Wagner's Nazi metapolitics "here undergo a sharp and inexorable analysis."

In those few cases in which Mr. Barzun's vague criticisms are accompanied by specific examples, he is factually in demonstrable error. Here are some of these examples.

In *Metapolitics* he "misses the awareness that there are also a myriad inconsistent definitions of classicism." No one will "miss" this "awareness" who reads, for example, p. 21, where I stress the inconsistent definitions of classicism. Mr. Barzun dubs "somewhat inaccurate" my reference to Goethe's "conversion to classicism." Since Goethe himself referred constantly to his crucial conversion (as his *Wiedergeburt* in classic Italy) and later said, "The classical I call the healthy, and the romantic the diseased" (pp. 20, 28–9, 199), my reference is not "inaccurate," not even "somewhat." In his closing paragraph, Mr. Barzun charges that my book rests largely on the illusion that Hitler's educational theory is based on Goethe. Far from thus slandering Goethe, on p. 79 I cite Goethe's remark that "patriotism corrupts history" as the best rebuttal to Hitler's educational theories and, instead, trace them to Jahn.

In his most revealing sentence (its italics mine), Mr. Barzun flings forth as a trump card, "*To read him*, one would think that an imperialistic France, led by Louis XIV and Napoleon, had never sought after hegemony in Europe." On pp. 12–13 and 57, I stress that an imperialistic France under Louis XIV and Napoleon (both of whom I name) did seek after hegemony in Europe. Consequently, here Mr. Barzun's phrase "to read him" is an unfortunate slip because it will — together with his dearth of references to any of the book after the introductory chapters, and the factual errors above noted — give the (doubtless erroneous) impression that Mr Barzun simply failed "to read him." At all events, I am obliged to place on record the fact that Mr. Barzun's review shows almost no sign of even superficial familiarity with that seven-eighths of the book's contents which follows the introductory chapters, and that the review conveys to the reader not merely an incomplete but an amazingly misleading statement of the authors with whose doctrines and influence the volume is principally concerned, of the method which it employs, and of the nature of that "Romanticism" whose crucial historical relations to Nazism the book seeks (among other things) to demonstrate.

PETER VIERECK

Harvard University, 1941

APPENDIX B
Publisher's Note

Here in book form for the first time (never before available except as a letter of 1940 to a no-longer-existent magazine) is Thomas Mann's essay on the thesis expounded by Peter Viereck in his romanticism and Wagner chapters (when they appeared in magazine form in *Common Sense*, 1939). To this essay of Mann's (which was written as a letter to the editor* of *Common Sense*), the publisher has added Thomas Mann's subsequent statement of 1941 (never before printed) on the book version of *Metapolitics*.

_____
* Selden Rodman. Reprinted by his permission.

1. LETTER FROM THOMAS MANN[1]

To the Editor of *Common Sense*

Sir:

I am very grateful to you for your kindness in sending me the November issue of your magazine, containing the article on "*Hitler and Richard Wagner*," by Peter Viereck. Since I am an avowed admirer of the art of Richard Wagner, you assume that I must have many objections to this essay and might even be minded to protest against it. I must disappoint you. Such is not the case. I read Mr. Viereck's piece with very nearly complete approval and regard it as extraordinarily meritorious. For the first time in America, as far as I know, the intricate and painful interrelationships which undeniably exist between the Wagnerian sphere and the National Socialist evil here undergo a sharp and inexorable analysis which will put an end to much sentimental innocence. The dismay, confusion and disillusion this is likely to strike in many well-meaning heads and hearts are no different from the effects that spring from the first impact of knowledge generally. They must be accepted for the sake of the service thereby rendered truth.

I can well understand the bitter laughter that overcame your contributor on the occasion of that fashionable Wagner concert, when he heard the speaker solemnly distinguish between the Germany of Hitler and the Germany of Wagner — the latter a Germany of creative freedom, racial tolerance, and democracy. Creative freedom — I can still let that stand. They were indeed exceedingly free, those sensuously intellectual masterpieces by a musician-dramatist, a genius in the art of the theatre. Braving scorn and opposition, they embarked upon their triumphant course in a world still dominated by the classic ideals of humanism. It is certain that, had the word existed in Wagner's time, he should have been called a *Kultur-*Bolshevist.

---

[1] This study by Thomas Mann appeared in the January issue of *Common Sense* magazine, New York, 1940.

But racial tolerance? Democracy? There the outlook is gloomy. Nietzsche had not yet openly broken with Wagner — indeed, he may still have believed himself a disciple of Wagner — when he noted down: "*Meistersinger* — a lance against civilization. The German against the French." That is a mere statement of fact, not yet a taking of issue. But it is a sort of transition from purely critical appreciation to repudiation of Wagner's Germany. It lends significance to the fact that the *Meistersinger* was destined to become the favorite opera of our wretched Herr Hitler.

If two people like the same thing and one of them is inferior, is the object of their affection inferior too? One ought to read the incomparable piece of prose which Nietzsche dedicated to the prelude to the *Meistersinger*. One ought to reread his famous page on *Tristan* in *Ecce Homo*. Baudelaire was one of the earliest Wagnerians. Another favorite of his, aside from the creator of *Lohengrin,* was Edgar Allan Poe. The juxtaposition is bewildering, almost incomprehensible to German ears (if "German" is taken to be synonymous with a complete lack of psychological insight). Yet it shows who and what Wagner really was — disregarding the fact that he was a "German master craftsman" and "against civilization." He was a European creative artist who knew every last trick of his trade. He had soaked up all the romantic wiles of seduction to console, delight and enchant long-suffering worldly-wise souls. It was no accident that his works had a world-wide effect, such as was never before the lot of any German of stature. The creator of the most overwhelming dramatic spectacles offered by the West in modern times was a shrewd and soul-stirring stage director of ancient legends. His boundless urge and enthusiasm swept into their orbit all the emotional elements of his century — the democratic-revolutionary as well as the nationalist. Later and on a smaller scale, d'Annunzio became an imitator of this system.

Nietzsche spoke of the "twin optics" that dominated Wagner's enormous talents — his ambition to win the finest as well as the coarsest. He succeeded, and the result is a certain sense of discomfort felt by the one section of his admirers in the presence of the other. A further consequence of the ambitious ambiguity inherent in this artistry is a corresponding ambiguity inherent in all higher criticism of which it becomes the object. Such criticism will always have an element of discord and passionate irony. It will be a curious blend of abandon and distrust, calling to mind the philosopher's love of "life" which Nietzsche called the love for a woman who "fills us with doubt."

Wagner is one of the most complex phenomena in the history of art and intellect — and one of the most fascinating, because he offers the most profound challenge to one's conscience. I am somewhat taken aback by the fact that Mr. Viereck, in his excellent article, gives the impression that I had proved rather unresponsive in the face of the gravity of this phenomenon, as though I had contributed to the over-simplified notion that Wagner is an unmistakable representative of the "good" Germany, in contrast to the "evil" of Herr Hitler. He quotes a lecture of mine on Wagner's essays on the philosophy of art — quotes it inaccurately, or at least incompletely. I described Wagner's essays as astonishingly acute writings by an artist, though having the character of propaganda on his own behalf and being far removed from truly great essay-writing. Consideration kept me from commenting on the style of these "essays" — a style which, regarded purely as prose and apart from all content, doubtless has a strong National Socialist element. This was, after all, a Memorial Address requested of me by foreign societies in Amsterdam and Paris, on the occasion of the 50th anniversary of Wagner's death.

What Mr. Viereck does not know or has forgotten is that it was this very speech in 1933 which determined my emigration, or, more correctly, my failure to return to Germany. Its enthusiasm was so faint that it put the Nazis into a transport of rage. This vermin is affected by shades of difference as is a bull by a red rag. Yet it is these very nuances of difference that are the most indispensable element in any discussion of Wagner.

May I say that I miss ever so slightly a sense of nuance in

Mr. Viereck's revealing characterization of Wagner? I mean
the nuances of love, of passionate personal familiarity with this
artistry, which is, after all, admirable and gifted beyond measure. Wagner was full of such naïve wonder at his own works
that he spoke of them as "miracles" ("Wunderwerke"). And in
the end — this is the proper word. No term better fits these
unexampled manifestations; nothing in the history of creative
art does it fit better — even though we, on our part, may not
necessarily use that term as the absolute superlative. We were
never similarly tempted to describe as "miracles" other precious
and indispensable cultural properties, such as *Hamlet* or
Iphigenia or even the Ninth Symphony. But the score of
Tristan is a miracle — especially in its irksome affinity with the
Meistersinger, which almost defies mental grasp. It is still more
of a miracle when both of these are taken for what they really
are, mere relief from the minute, gigantic thought structure of
the *Ring.* Wagner's work is a veritable eruption of talent and
genius, the profoundly serious yet enchanting work of a sen-
suous sorcerer, drunk with his own wisdom.

It is a unique case, one subject to severe intellectual criticism (this must be admitted over and over) — this combination
of poet and musician in which both qualities necessarily lose
their pure character, becoming something different from what
they usually are, on a big scale or small. As a poet Wagner
was a musician; as a musician he was a poet. His relationship
to dramatic poetry was that of the composer; his music forced
his language back into a primitive state so that without their
music his dramas are only half poetry; nor was his relationship
to music purely musical; it was literary or poetic to the extent
that the spiritual and symbolic content of his music, its significant charm and interpretative magic, decisively influenced
this relationship.

It was from this dubious mixture of talents, developed to absolute greatness, that the *Ring der Nibelungen* grew. It is a
work that stands by itself. It seems utterly beyond modernity,
yet in the refinement, awareness and deliberate recency of its
technique it is extremely modern. Again, in its pathos and its

romantic, revolutionary urge, it is primitive — a world-poem interlaced with music and prophetic Nature. In it the original substance of life interacts; day and night hold colloquy; the mythical prototypes of man — the fair, blithe, golden-haired and those that brood in hate, grief and rebellion — engage each other in profound fairy-tale plot.

The tremendous thing about all this is a certain epic radicalism for which I shall never lose my enthusiasm. It is the radicalism of *beginning*, of going back to the first and original source of all things, the primeval cell, the first E-flat of the prelude to the overture. It is the obsession to rear a musical cosmogony, indeed, a musical cosmos, to be endowed with a meaningful life of its own — the ringing pageant of the world's beginning and end.

This blend of drama and music is often called impure, the work of a charlatan. I admit the charge. There are cases in which admissions of all kinds may be made — and still, something overwhelming remains. The parallelism between music and the creative world of things places the epic birth of the world in coincidence with the birth of music. The mythology of music is interwoven with that of the world. A mythical philosophy, a musical poem of Creation, grow up before our senses and proceed to unfold into a richly joined world of symbols rising from the E-flat major triad of the deep-flowing Rhine.

We are dealing with a work that is intensely German, to an exemplary degree. This conclusion is disquieting when we remember the relationships uncovered by Mr. Viereck. It leads to identifications which we are today profoundly interested in repudiating. But the truth is that such a work could only spring from the German spirit. Perhaps — though this is not certain — Jewish blood did its share. Certain qualities of this art — its sensuousness and intellectualism — speak in favor of the assumption. But first and foremost it is German. It is the German contribution to 19th-century creative art in the monumental tradition — the type of contribution which in other nations preeminently took the form of the great social novel.

Dickens, Thackeray, Tolstoy, Dostoyevsky, Balzac, Zola — their works, heaped up with the same urge for moralizing grandeur, constitute Europe's 19th century, constitute the world of literary and social criticism. The German contribution, the form which this greatness took in Germany, has no social element nor desires to have anything to do with it. Society is not musical; indeed, not even capable of creative art. The roots of creativeness go down into the pure humanity of the mythical age, into the timeless, non-historical proto-poetry of Nature and of the heart. That is what the German spirit desires. That was its instinct, long in advance of any conscious decision. So far as time and mind are concerned, the *Ring der Nibelungen* has a great deal in common with the Rougon-Macquart series. The essential and characteristic national distinction is that between the social instinct of the French work and the mythical, primitive, poetic spirit of the German. With the appreciation of this difference, the intricate old question: "What is German?" perhaps finds its tersest answer. Essentially the German spirit lacks social and political interest. Deep down, that sphere is foreign to it. But its accomplishments do not permit a purely negative evaluation of such a fact. Still, one is fully entitled to speak here of a vacuum, a failure, a deficiency. And in so decidedly social and political a time as ours, this often so productive deficiency may truly take on a fateful, indeed, a disastrous character. In the face of the problems of the times it may lead to efforts at solution which are poor evasions and which are by way of being mythical substitutes for truly social solutions. But that brings us to National Socialism.

National Socialism means: "I do not care for the social issue at all. What I want is the folk-tale". This formulation, to be sure, is the mildest, the most intellectual. The fact that in reality National Socialism is also filthy barbarism springs from that other fact, that in the realm of politics fairy-tales become *lies*.

National Socialism, in all its ineffable empirical vileness, is the tragic consequence of the mythical political innocence of the German spirit. You see, I go a little farther than Mr. Viereck. I find an element of Nazism not only in Wagner's questionable literature; I find it also in his "music," in his work, similarly questionable, though in a loftier sense — albeit I have so loved that work that even today I am deeply stirred whenever a few bars of music from this world impinge on my ear. The enthusiasm it engenders, the sense of grandeur that so often seizes us in its presence, can be compared only to the feelings excited in us by Nature at her noblest, by evening sunshine on mountain peaks, by the turmoil of the sea. Yet this must not make us forget that this work, created and directed "against civilization," against the entire culture and society dominant since the Renaissance, emerges from the bourgeois-humanist epoch in the same manner as does Hitlerism. With its *Wagalaweia* and its alliteration, its mixture of roots-in-the-soil and eyes-toward-the-future, its appeal for a classless society, its mythical-reactionary revolutionism — with all these, it is the exact spiritual forerunner of the "metapolitical" movement today terrorizing the world. This is the movement that must be beaten if a really new order is to arise in Europe.

Let us not deceive ourselves. National Socialism must be beaten. In practice this means, unfortunately: Germany must be beaten. It is meant, however, in a very definite sense — a spiritual sense too. For there is but *one* Germany, not two, not a good and an evil. And Hitler, in all his wretchedness, is no accident. He could never have become possible but for certain psychological prerequisites that must be sought deeper down than in inflation, unemployment, capitalist speculation and political intrigue. Yet it is true that nations do not always show the same face, that it depends on time and circumstances how their constant qualities appear. Germany today makes a frightful appearance. It torments the world — not because it is "evil," but because it is at the same time "good" — a fact with which Anglo-Saxon humor is fully familiar, as evidenced by the words of the estimable Harold Nicolson: "The German character is one of the finest but most inconvenient developments of human nature."

Germany must be beaten. That means it must be compelled
to re-activate all the constructive social elements in its fund
of tradition from earlier centuries. It must do so in order to fit
into the European Confederation, the comity of nations for
which Europe is ripe. Such federalism will require sacrifices
in national sovereignty and selfishness from *every* nation. This
war is waged in Germany's interest. It would be asking too
much, of course, for Germany to see this at the moment. But
the war is waged to bring about a state of affairs which will
free Germany from the curse of power politics, more depraving
for her than for any nation. It is waged for a pacified, de-
politicalized Europe which alone can provide an atmosphere
conducive to Germany's greatness and happiness. Such an atmosphere will restore political innocence to the works of Germany, and a clear conscience to those who admire them. They
will no longer have to sigh: It is great, it is splendid, but it is
"against civilization."

Yours very sincerely,

THOMAS MANN

2. LETTER FROM THOMAS MANN

September 7th, 1941

Dear Mr. de la Torre Bueno:

I have received the bound galleys of METAPOLITICS, and have
occupied myself thoroughly with it. I would be tempted to
write a review about it, but I fear that it would lead me too
far and I must avoid such excursions at the present time, because I am concentrating on my own work which will be inter-
rupted soon by a lecture tour. I will however, make the following statement which you may use at your discretion.

In general it must be said: if the World would really suc-
cumb to the Hitler-assault, and fall into slavery which would
happen ultimately because of moral weakness, of sympathy,
but of a very stupid, unknowing and mistaken sympathy — in
any event it will not be possible to accuse the American intel-

ligentsia of having contributed to this World debacle by their failures. What has been accomplished in the last few years in the great American Press, in the American Weeklies, in pamphlets and books as to enlightening work, is simply admirable, and has not been equalled in any other country. Whoever wanted to be informed in this country (but that is of course not everybody) had and has the opportunity, and among the best of those opportunities one may count the book of Peter Viereck.

I have long esteemed this young author as an intellect with profound historical knowledge and keen psychological observation, and after a few samples of the book which I read in magazines, I expected much of it. To one of those samples, an essay about Wagner and National Socialism, I have given my detailed comment in COMMON SENSE. The book as a whole, however, has still surpassed my expectations. I have read it with great interest, and consider it an excellent contribution to the critique of the German Nationalism and Racism, and with it to the clarification of the spiritual backgrounds of this war.

Of course, such a book may also have its dangers inasmuch as it lends a spiritual excuse to the actual crimes of the German Nationalism, and a sort of historic legitimacy to the political outrages of Hitler, and could thus weaken the physical defense against him. On the other hand, nothing is more important than understanding and recognition, and I consider it most meritorious how Viereck goes back to the sources of the German Nationalism which is the most dangerous in existence, because it is mechanized mysticism.

I believe it desirable that his book would find at least as wide a circulation as Rauschning's REVOLUTION OF NIHILISM, a work which METAPOLITICS surpasses and rectifies in many respects.

Sincerely yours,
THOMAS MANN

APPENDIX C

For the 1965 edition:

ACKNOWLEDGMENTS, WAGNER'S TRANSVESTISM, AND "HARSHNESS"

"Only Wotan, foaming with rage, can fight Jehovah! Back to harshness!"—F. Haiser

I. ACKNOWLEDGMENTS AND AGAIN WAGNER

The author is grateful to Harvard University library for use in this book of his "Romanticism" chapter, which, as 1939 winner of Harvard's Bowdoin Prize contest for a philosophical essay, belongs to the university library. For indispensable help during 1936–39 on the Jahn chapter, thanks remain due to the author's brother, G. S. Viereck, Jr., of Harvard Law School and the U. S. Army (killed in action against the Nazis in 1944). Inside the academic world: during his student days of 1933–40, the author received the discipline of much-needed criticisms and suggestions, about his romanticism and Wagner hypotheses, from the following scholars—Crane Brinton, Dana Durand, Sidney Fay, Hans Kohn, William Langer, Arthur O. Lovejoy, Reginald Phelps, Karl Viëtor. Outside the academic world: gratitude is owed to Alfred Knopf, Edmund Epstein, and Steven Frimmer, for the publishers of the 1941, 1961, and 1965 editions respectively, for their patience with tedious and time-consuming additions. Here, too, is the opportunity to thank Sir Ernest MacMillan, in 1940 conductor of the Toronto Symphony Orchestra, for his unpublished Wagner material, and to thank the psychiatrist Dr. Siegfried Placzek (who had examined Nietzsche during the latter's insanity) for acquainting us in 1940 with still-unpublished, psychologically illuminating material about Wagner and Nietzsche.

Dr. Placzek's evidence, for what he calls "Wagner's transvestite dependence"[1] on privately wearing feminine-style robes and perfumes imported from Paris, seems of legitimate concern to the historian; not because Wagner's private foibles are anyone else's business but because, in the given context, this private foible had a public, political consequence which his Nazi disciples made everybody's business: namely, his overcompensatory, pseudo-virile glorification of uncivilized Teuton warriors, and his violent self-projecting attack on the French and Jews as allegedly overcivilized, effeminate, and addicted to perfume. Related to our suggestion that Wagner's anti-Semitism is projective self-hatred, is Nietzsche's cryptic allusion (taken very seriously in the Ernest Newman biography) to Wagner's later suppressing an earlier admission that his real father was not the elder Wagner but the possibly Jewish actor Geyer. As a psychological parallel (more hypothesis, however, than certainty), there is now, of course, the new Hitler-family documentation in Jetzinger's book, *Hitlers Jugend*.

Not the harsh Jack the Ripper but the would-be-harsh Casper Milquetoast becomes the most dangerous, most uncompromising apostle of "back to harshness." And the masks of the harshness hysteria are endless: gymnastic militarism, muscle-flexing foreign policies, a doubly ruthless tyranny toward those whose softness—or whose minority status—one partly shares: a self-exorcism.

To return for just one sentence more to acknowledgings (in what is quite candidly a grab-bag postscript of omitted but necessary points for the 1965 edition): in the appendix the criticisms from *Journal of the History of Ideas, Christian Science Monitor,* and *Common Sense* are reprinted with the written permissions of the publishers of these three periodicals; in the main text the quotations from Yeats, D. H. Lawrence, and the American edition of *Mein Kampf* are reprinted with the written permission of the Macmillan Company, Viking Press,

[1]See also the Paris perfume letters, as well as the pictures of Wagner in transvestite costume, in *Sueddeutsche Monathefte,* Munich, August, 1931.

and Houghton Mifflin Company. But in quoting the American *Mein Kampf,* we have taken a liberty. Wherever necessary, we have seen fit to restore the German original of Hitler's words "Reich," "Kultur," and "Volk." For you lose the metapolitical emotional undertones of these words by using their merely political English equivalents. What other language or culture possesses or can even translate precisely the adjective "völkisch"? Is it not ever so much more than the common translations "folkic," "populist," or "narodnik"?

Hence, this is not really a book about German nationalism. (There are so many of those, often mere war propaganda, trying to make one's flesh creep with nationalist quotations that often are merely political and hence no worse than their British or French equivalents.) Rather, it attempts just what the title says it attempts: to understand *metapolitics.* The unique metapolitics of Volk has little to do with the universal politics of nationalism. Of nationalist politics, flag-waving, and imperialism Germany is no more guilty than her neighbors (Kipling in England, Barrès in France). In contrast, German metapolitics is an evil (not a Versailles-induced "sickness," to be cured with jargonizing Pollyanna therapies, but a narcissistic self-deifying evil) without equivalent in the annals of human destructiveness. Auschwitz simply has no equivalents. And already a half century before Hitler, the Wagnerian Konstantin Frantz—from whose letter[2] of 1878 we derived our term "metapolitics"—was proclaiming one key aspect of that term: "The Jewish people ... excluded itself from history, for instead the Germans became God's Chosen People."

Even after World War II, Wagner's Bayreuth festival continues to be the center of narcissistic wallowings for the German industrial bourgeoisie (technology plus ideology still make what Goebbels and Rosenberg called "steel romanticism"). For example, Berthold Beitz, the 1960 director of the Krupp armaments empire, gave money to the society for Wagner festivals on these non-musical, non-aesthetic grounds: "If you

---

[2] See pp. 3-5 of main text for definition and derivation of the title word.

want contacts to West Germany's industrialists you find them in Bayreuth. For that reason one has to go to Bayreuth; there you find the whole bunch together."

Nor is Jahn, the other outstanding Volk romanticist of these pages, forgotten in the 1960s. The German veterans' newspaper, *Deutsche Soldaten-Zeitung,* in August 1960 ran this headline: JAHN'S IDEALS ARE ETERNAL, above a glowing description of 15,000 gymnasts worshipping a Jahn memorial in Austria. From an opposite viewpoint, representative of the more thoughtful West Germans of the sixties, the superb anti-Nazi scholarly journal, *Deutsche Rundschau,* declared: "The so-called gymnast-father Jahn, in reality a rabble-rousing ruffian worthy of the SS, coined the infamous slogan: 'The Jews are Germany's disaster' (*'Die Juden sind Deutschlands Unglück'*)." And as for Nietzsche, the first voice to prophesy against the cult of Volk and Wagnerian anti-Semitism, to call Nietzsche (as do most of these books on German "nationalism") the precursor of Hitler, only makes us all the more bitterly recall still another Nietzschean prophecy: "I am terrified by the thought of the sort of people who may some day invoke my authority."

II. THE "BACK TO HARSHNESS" CRESCENDO

The all-embracing internationalism of Christianity embarrasses equally the ethnic separatism of Volk romanticism (Jahn, Fichte, Wagner, Langbehn, Lagarde) and the less ethnic separatism of Prussian or Austrian statism (Haller, Radowitz, Hegel, Goerres, Adam Mueller, Vogelsang). There are two ways out from the embarrassment. You can praise but distort Christianity, as did most of these nineteenth-century statists or Volk-ists. Or you can become openly anti-Christian, like General Ludendorff, Count Reventlow, Alfred Rosenberg, and (less openly) Hitler. The seething emotions behind the second approach are suggested by our favorite quotation from that racist of the 1920s, Franz Haiser (used as chapter epigraph for this new Appendix to our 1965 edition): "Only Wotan, foaming with rage, can fight Jehovah! Back to harshness!" (exclamation marks his, foam and all). Wotan was meant as shorthand symbol for aggressive Volk pride; he was not being put forward by these Nordic pagans as a god to be literally believed in. Similarly Jehovah was shorthand for the Christian as well as Judaic ethics of unharshness and "un-Volk."

Instead of thus attacking Jehovah and Christ on behalf of open militarist immoralism, the earlier approach turns the tables by calling militarism a new, a higher kind of morality, somehow integrated with Christianity by those deeper profundities of German philosophy. This approach was more the fashion among those respectable bourgeois militarists of World War I (whom the unrespectable gutter-gangs of Hitler ridiculed, then allied with, and then superseded). On a very brilliant level an example of this approach is the un-Prussian Prussianism, the somehow Wagnerian Prussianism expressed by the young Thomas Mann of World War I (in contrast with his later, truer role as the leading anti-Nazi humanist): "German militarism is the manifestation of German morality ...[and] refuses to recognize the civilian spirit as a final ideal of mankind."

Despite the deeply moving heroism of occasional individual Christian martyrs under Hitler, there was no mass resistance on Christian grounds. (Indeed, there was no mass resistance period.) The majority of German Christians, whether Protestant or Catholic, failed to see that the spiritual link of Christianity to Judaism is closer than to Nazi racist paganism and that their professed Christian values were despised by their Fuehrer. During World War II, Hitler remarked to his officers at his Table Talk: "The heaviest blow that ever struck humanity was the coming of Christianity. Bolshevism is Christianity's illegitimate child. Both are inventions of the Jew...Christ was an Aryan, and St. Paul used his doctrine to mobilize the criminal underworld and thus organize a proto-bolshevism." Though in no way out of character, this remark was never available quite so bluntly before the war (we had looked in vain for so frank a Hitler statement at the time of our first edition); therefore, at the time the majority of the German people were able to pretend to themselves that they were crusading (among other things) for Christianity against "atheistic Asiatic communism."

What they were really crusading for (to return to our foam-drenched Haiser) was "back to harshness." The harshness developed into a crescendo: from harmless rugged Spartanism (cf. Wagner's self-hating attacks on "French and Jewish" perfumes and effeminacy) to old-fashioned Prussian military killings and finally to new-fashioned romantic-daemonic genocide. You can plot a graph or extrapolate a curve of this development, simply by listing the titles and dates of (for example) Haiser's three main books. All three precede the Third Reich. The first book is merely a detached, a so-to-speak "Platonic" romance with tyranny. The second is a rather unspecific apology for the joys of enslaving the weak. The third is a very specific designation of the victim. But let the book titles and chronology speak for themselves: (1) *The Persuasiveness of Evidence: Style Versus Liberty*, 1916; (2) *Slavery: Its Biological Foundation and Moral Vindication*, 1923; (3) *The Jewish Question from the Viewpoint of Master-Morality*, 1926. Carry the curve one step further and what else is ahead but Auschwitz?

The same graph would show a corresponding crescendo from political thinking to metapolitical "emoting." Have we here chosen a merely isolated or accidental example? Not quite. For you can plot a similar curve for so many different authors of the period. For example, among others, the widely sold Hans Guenther. His titles, too many to list here, commence with such mild brew as *The Nordic Idea Among the Germans*, 1925; they progress to such middling frenzies as *Racial Knowledge of the Jewish People*, also from the late '20s; then after 1933 they attain such a metapolitical climax as *Fuehrer-Elite Through Racial Pruning*, 1936.

Though most Germans claim – often truthfully – to have known nothing of Auschwitz, yet how can that Final Solution be entirely separated from the above almost inevitable crescendo of increasingly murderous hysteria among representative writers? Privately most of these influential shamans and dervishes were self-hating unharsh intellectuals, trying to be super-harsh; publicly they thereby helped provide the catalyst of "moral vindication" (to quote one of their titles) for the unintellectual thugs and sadists. A normal society keeps the thugs and sadists (of whom Germany had no monopoly) in check; the checks break down when there is such a *carte blanche* vindication from above.

An age of conveyor-belt technology tends to produce mechanized conformity, regardless of whether its ideological "superstructure" is right, left, or center. These pressures of mass over person, of public life over private life, threaten individual liberty in America at least as much as in Germany. Then what talisman has so far saved American and British politics from likewise becoming totalitarian? In addition to such obvious factors as our empirical pluralist outlook, our relative lack of economic crisis, and our lack of Volk romanticism, the talisman involves the following attitudes. First, freedom not as an imported abstract novelty but as rooted concrete tradition (1688, 1787, the Constitution and the *Federalist* papers, as well as all those unwritten, inarticulate patterns that the Burkeans rightly talk of conserving). Second, too little grand opera and too much sense of humor for such quaint ecstasies as any "Wotan, foaming with rage." Third, a central consensus, a liberal-conservative balance, which distinguishes authority simultaneously on two fronts: from authoritarianism and from anarchy (an un-German as well as un-Russian distinction). This liberal-conservative consensus saved America from the pseudo-liberal left of the Henry Wallace extremists in 1948 and from the pseudo-conservative right of the Goldwater extremists in 1964.

INDEX

Alberich: 227

Amerikanische Rede by H. Grimm: 173 *n*

An die Dunkelmänner unserer Zeit by Rosenberg: 224 *n*, 273–4 and *n*

Annunzio, d': 128–9

Antichrist by Nietzsche: 284

anti-intellectualism: *see* rationalism

anti-legalism: *see* legalism

anti-rationalism: *see* rationalism

anti-Semitism: *see* racism, Jews

anti-vivisectionism: Wagner, 107–9; Hitler, 135

Aris, R.: 195 *n*

Arische Weltanschauung by Chamberlain: 115 *n*

Aristophanes: 237

Arndt: 48, 68, 85, 191, 241, 261

Arnim: 39–40

Art and Revolution by Wagner: 120 *n*

Art of the Future by Wagner: 236

Athenäum: 17 *n*, 28 *n*, 31 *n*

Atlantis myth: 233–5, 246, 282

Attila: 269

Augustus, Roman Emperor: 11–12

Austria: 71, 86, 157, 174

Autobiographical Sketch by Wagner: 97

Axis: 164, 237

Babbitt, Irving: 17, 18 *n*, 37 *n*

Bakunin: 99, 110, 120, 130

Balkans: and *Mitteleuropa*, 169; and *Lebensraum*, 174

Balts: 76, 272; and Rosenberg, 216–18

Bangert, Otto: 244

Barbarossa: 111, 126–7, 134, 142, 148, 242

Barrès, Maurice: 128–9

Battles: Teutoburg Forest, 11, 186, 309; Leipzig, 53; Waterloo, 53, 56, 69; Jena, 57, 58, 70, 71, 82

Baudelaire: defence of discipline, 20; on boredom, 100 *n;* and Wagner, 116; and neoromantics, 145

Bäumler, Alfred: 63 *n*, 90 *n*

Bavaria: 71, 109, 135, 311

Bayreuth circle: 91–3, 108, 115, 127–33, 135–7, 147–8, 157, 160, 218, 227, 252, 272

Bayreuther Blätter: 92 *n*, 108, 114 *n*, 115 *n*, 117

---

* Not included in this Index is the material in the new 1961 Preface and Appendix A and B and bibliography section.

Beauté, La, by Baudelaire: 20 and *n*

" becoming vs. being ": 45, 175, 200, 292

beer-hall putsch: 135, 148, 212, 297

Benn, Gottfried: 157, 255

Berchtesgaden: 160–2; Barbarossa and Hitler, 111 and *n*

Berenson, Bernard: 3

Bergmann, Ernst: 258, 292–3

Bergson, Henri: 18 *n*, 46

Betrachtungen eines Unpolitischen by Mann: 187

"beyond good and evil": 196–9, 231

Bertram, Ernst: 188

Beyond Good and Evil by Nietzsche: 48, 183 *n*

Bill of Rights: 179

Binding, Rudolf: 255

Birth of Tragedy by Nietzsche: 152

Bismarck: 37, 61, 147; unifies Germany, 55, 84; " blood and iron," 73; Wagner vs., 92–3, 107; tolerates Potsdam-Bayreuth alliance, 126–8; H. Chamberlain compares Hitler to, 149; vs. Pan-Germanism, 174; Nietzsche vs., 182–3; contrasted with Hitler, 203; misinterpreted, 206–7; Russian Pact, 213 *n*, Rosenberg on, 236

Black Hundreds: 267–9

Blätter für die Kunst: 47 *n*

Blücher, General: 69

" blue flower," the: 147, 165

Blüher, Hans: 157, 264–5; works, 265 *n*

Blunck, Hans: 145, 154–6, 159, 164–5, 177, 265

Blut und Ehre by Rosenberg: 218 *n,* 245 *n*

Boer War: 207

Bohle, Ernst: 217

Bolschewismus von Moses bis

Lenin by D. Eckart: 250 *n,*

book burning: in 1817, 85; by Nazis, 162–3

Borgese, G. A.: 17 *n,* 129 *n*

Börne: 94

bovarism: 22, 24, 123, 146

Brandes, Georg: 17

Brentano: 39–40, 42 *n*

Brest-Litovsk Treaty: 210–11

Brüning, Heinrich: 213

Brunnen, Der, periodical: 289

Bryce, James: 111

Buddhism: 118

Bungardt, K. M.: 63

Burke, Edmund: 13

Burschenschaften: *see* youth movements

Byron: 150

capitalism: 142, 147, 200; Chamberlain vs., 9, 251; Lagarde vs., 227, 251; Nazis vs., 134, 137, 140, 157–8, 202, 216, 220, 229, 244, 247–51, 261, 268–9, 305–6, 308; puppet of Dalai Lama, 297; romantics vs., 4; secret masters of communism, 248–9; Siegfried vs., 121, 139, 227, 243; Treitschke vs., 205; Wagner vs., 101–2, 105, 107, 118, 120–1, 122, 129, 131, 134, 142, 147–8, 243

Captain of Köpenick: 310–12

Carlyle: 17

Carossa, Hans: 255

Case against Wagner by Nietzsche: 100 *n,* 116 *n*

Catholicism: Centre party, 14, 211, 214; Nazis vs., 242, 259, 289–90; Nietzsche appeals to Pope, 181–3; refutation of *Mythus,* 224, 238 *n,* 273–5,

284–5; romantic converts, 46, 181, 185, 195; Spengler appeals to Pope, 181, 185; tragic split, 75–6, 185, 249; universalism of, 58, 181, 185, 283; *see also* Christianity

Central Europe by Naumann: 170 n

Centre party (Catholic): 14, 211, 213

Chamberlain, Houston: first discovers Hitler, 9; pictures Teutons as saving Rome, 10; on Luther, 13, 283; corrupts romanticism, 53; considers self "national liberal," 59; to Hitler through Eckart, 91–2, 111, 113, 115, 252; as link between Hitler and Wagner, 91–2, 111, 115, 137, 142, 147–50, 168, 252; on Wagner's part in 1849 Revolution, 99; considers Wagner a revolutionist, 109; vs. democracy, 113; popularized by Bayreuth circle, 115; "enraptured with Hitler," 115; lives on in Rosenberg, 115, 142, 183, 218, 224–6, 232, 251–2, 273–4, 277, 282–3, 310; endorses Nazi program, 137; Hitler names Berlin street for, 138; as example of armed bohemia, 157, 312; calls Hitler "heaven-sent," 149; on Christianity, 168, 282–3; links art and war, 171; develops *Realpolitik*, 194; "two souls" in, 195; predicts enslavement of Slavs, 204; entertains Rosenberg at Bayreuth, 218–19; sees Jesus as Aryan, 235; glorified in Labour Service book, 261; Catholics refute, 273; vs. Old Testament and St. Paul, 282; bibliography on, 319–22

Chamberlain, Neville: 211

Charlemagne: 14, 181, 185; disliked by Nazis, 12–13

Childs, H. L.: 257 n

Christ as Aryan: 235, 282–7

Christianity: Chamberlain vs., 258; Darwinism vs., 196; denounced as Jewish, 169–70; Hegel on, 202; Lagarde vs., 227; Ludendorff vs., 298; mass man vs., 313; Marxism vs., 146; nazism vs., 176–7, 229, 258–260, Chap. xiii — 281–302; nationalism vs., 4–5, 13, 75–6; "positive" or "German," 75–6, 151, 168, 286–92, 294, 295, 298, 302; pantheism vs., 26; Rosenberg vs., 239, 245, 258, 274; *Stürmer* vs., 254; Wagner vs., 110, 118–19; Western heritage, 5, 10, 179–81; *see also* Catholicism, Protestantism

Churchill, Winston: 308

classicism: misconceptions of, 20–1; romantics vs., 5, 20, 36–7, 42, 43–4, 46, 52, 132, 152; Wagner vs., 101, 108; Western heritage, 5, 7, 13, 309

Code Napoléon: 60

Coleridge: 17

Communication to My Friends by Wagner: 97 n

communism: *see* socialism, Stalin, Russia

Congress of Vienna: 68, 85

Coughlin, Father: 220, 268–9

Czechs: 61, 80, 141, 174, 203, 221, 230, 253

dæmonic: 6, 153, 166, 172–3, 189, 225, 242, 255, 309; defined, 150–1, 198–9

Dalai Lama: 297, 308

Dante Alighieri: 237

Darré: 217

Darwinism: 44, 116, 196

Davis, Elmer: 139 and *n*

" decadents," the: 14, 145–7

Decline of the West by Spengler: 10

Défense de l'Occident by Massis: 10

Degeneration by Nordau: 93 *n*, 97 *n*

Delitzsch, Friedrich: 286

Demiaskevich, M.: 290

democracy and parliamentarianism: 174; as critic of nazism, 278–80, 238 *n;* Dalai Lama's puppet, 297; German Republic, 14, 55, 122, 139, 154–5, 157–8, 159, 161, 163–4, 174, 209–13, 247, 260, 261, 277, 311; Hitler vs., 32, 134, 139, 192, 277; Jahn on, 72–3, 86; materialism, 243–4, 246–7; Nazis vs., 207, 248, 251, 261, 263, 308; neo-romantics vs., 145–6, 156; Rosenberg vs., 216, 222, 234, 247, 248, 251, 277; Wagner on, 60, 93, 101, 102–3, 104, 110, 112–14, 115, 121–2, 131, 148

Denmark: 61, 72, 122

Deutsche Gottschau by Hauer: 292 *n*

Deutsche Schriften by Lagarde: 169 *n*, 227 *n*, 285–6 and *n*

Deutscher Geist und Westeuropa by Troeltsch: 7

Deutscher Ordensstaat by Rosenberg: 241 *n*

Dietrich, Otto: 304

Dinger, Hugo: 99, 100 *n*

Dowson, Ernest: 145

Drang nach Osten: 76, 221

Dritte Reich, Das, by Moeller van den Bruck: 226

Dryden: 31

dynamism, 35, 36, 106–10, 134, 152, 166, 181, 236, 255, 312, 317; defined, 21–6; false analogy of, 43–7; and militarism, 295–6

Ebert: 209, 210, 212

Ecce Homo by Nietzsche: 128, 130, 183 *n*

Eckart, Dietrich: link between Wagner and Hitler, 91–2, 110–11, 115, 142; and H. Chamberlain, 110, 148, 252; predicts Hitler's success, 149; dedicates verse to Hitler, 156; as literary figure, 157, 176, 312; blames Jews for literary failure, 161–2; and origin of Nazi party, 218, 254, 306; impressed by Rosenberg, 219; sees Christ as Aryan, 235, 286 *n;* economic program of, 250 and *n*

Eckehart, Master: 8, 286

Eden, Anthony: 308

education for nationalism: Jahn's plan, 77–80, 88; Treitschke's part in, 205–7; under Hitler, 43, 215, 253, 257–9, 282, 286, 299, 302

Egoism in German Philosophy by Santayana: 47, 173

Eichendorff: 17, 42 *n*

élan vital: 46

Elizabeth, Grand Duchess: 267

Ellis, W. A.: 99, 100 *n*

Engelke: 289

England: nationalists of, 13,

52; romantic movements in, 18–19, 27, 145–6; fooled by *Ossian,* 40; Hitler charges plot by, 71; Reformation in, 76; misconception of Jahn in, 86; Wagner on, 112; and fascism, 114, 128, 137; as Wagnerian dragon, 140; impressed by Göring, 159; Rome civilizes, 179; White Man's Burden in, 200; conceptions of Nietzsche and Treitschke in, 203, 205; Treitschke on Empire, 204; distrusted by Germans, 207–8; policy toward Germany, 211–13, 307–8, 299; Rosenberg favors alliance with, 220; Anglican refutation of *Mythus,* 238 n; spirit of sacrifice in, 247; high finance, 307

Erlösung von Jesu Christo by M. Ludendorff: 297 n

Essai sur l'inégalité des races humaines by Gobineau: 116 n

Essay on Man by Pope: 31

Estonia: 216–17

Ethiopia: 200

Eton: 159

Etruscans: 225, 246, 274–5, 285

Euripides: 237

Evangelical Church Council: 291

evolution concept: 28; in Goethe, 44–5; in Hegel, 202

Failure of a Mission by Henderson: 160 n

Fallada, Hans: 255

Famous Fantastic Mysteries: 25

Faust, Faustian; 3 n, 22–4, 27, 36, 38, 45–6, 66–7, 83, 165–7, 186, 199, 200, 292; Hitler as, 175; in Spengler, 181, 189, 296; in Rosenberg, 236, 245; and Japan, 245

Fay, Sidney B.: 218 n

Feder, Gottfried: 176

Feuerbach: influence on Wagner, 94, 102–3

Fichte: on Volk, 6–7, 51, 294; to Hitler, 7, 18, 33, 189–99, 261, 294; preaches *Realpolitik,* 11, 192–4; theory of science of, 30–1; socialism of, 33, 38, 125, 157, 195; Nietzsche vs., 48; Rosenberg on, 48, 241; compared with Jahn, 68–9, 89; on religion, 294

Fleurs du mal by Baudelaire: 100 n

Follen: 85

Foundations of the Nineteenth Century by Chamberlain: 115 n, 284; Rosenberg's debt to, 224

Fourteen Points: 210, 212

France: 167, 187, 227, 244; and War of Liberation, 54–8, 65, 80–4; vs. Prussia in 1870, 7, 152, 206; other conflicts with Germany, 12–13, 47, 49, 67, 75, 200, 210–11, 217, 241, 270, 279; and German Republic, 210–13; Nazi vengeance, 154, 192; Popular Front, 247; " 200 families," 278; French proto-Nazis, 114, 128, 267; romantic movements in, 18–19 30, 145–6

Franconia: 158

Franken, poem by George: 184 n

Frankfurt Diet: 87, 162, 207
Frederick the Great: 65, 77, 82; misinterpreted by Nazis, 227–8, 236; as Hitler's hero, 283
Free Corps: in War of Liberation, 80–4, 88, 89, 265, 312; modern, 149
Free Masons: 283, 297, 308; Rosenberg on, 247, 277
" French ideas ": 56, 174; benefit Germany, 13–14; origin of reaction against, 49–50, 54–8; Jahn vs., 65–6, 68, 77–8, 84; romantics vs., 27, 29, 31–2, 41, 193, 195; Wagner and, 93–9, 102, 104, 109, 113, 118, 125, 131, 133, 244; and 1848 Revolution, 61; Rosenberg vs., 249
French Revolution: 12, 20, 29, 31–2, 41, 65–6, 71, 193, 249; smashes German social order, 54–8; universal military service, 82; compared with Nazi revolution, 259, 263
French Revolution of 1830: 93–4
Freud: 24, 40, 277
Freud, Goethe, Wagner by Mann: 93 n, 97 n, 98, 100 n, 115, 128 n, 131 n
Führer concept: in Jahn, 72–3; in Wagner, 106, 110–14, 122, 125, 131, 134, 142; in Chamberlain, 137; in Rosenberg, 242–3; in male leagues, 263–4; and the dæmonic, 198–9
Fünfundzwanzig Thesen der Deutschreligion by Bergmann, 258, 292–3
Funk, Walther: 157–8, 176

Gautier: 145
Gegen Tarnung by Rosenberg: 226 n
Genealogy of Morals by Nietzsche: 90
general will vs. will of all: 32, 250
Genghis Kahn: 269
Geopolitics: 170, 222–3
Geopolitik des Pazifischen Ozeans by Haushofer: 223 n
George, Stefan: vs. life-worship, 47 and n; Schirach imitates verse of, 162; Nazi roots in, 157, 168, 171, 176, 196, 198, 264; and " secret potentates," 172–3; pro-Western phase, 178, 182, 185; repudiates Nazis, 183–4; popular in Reich today, 256
German Diet: 68
German Empire of 1871: *see* Second Reich
German Faith Movement: 291–2
German Opera by Wagner: 94
German Republic: *see* democracy
Germany Speaks: 154
Geschichte eines Hochverräters by Röhm: 265 n
Gespräche mit Eckermann: 29
Gestalt psychology: 34
Gestaltung der Idee by Rosenberg: 183 n, 226 n, 245 n, 276 n
Gestapo: 302
Geyer, Ludwig: 95–6 and n
Gibraltar: 204
Glasenapp, Carl: 99, 100 n
Gobineau, Arthur: 91, 115–17, 128, 169, 204
Goebbels: disciple of Wagner, 91, 124, 131, 132, 148; en-

joys *Meistersinger*, 138; as littérateur, 157, 161–3, 165, 171, 176, 312; imitates Jahn's book-burning, 162; as success-worshipper, 196, 314; Rosenberg's rivalry with, 216–17, 284; stirred by Rhineland occupation, 217; as orator, 219; war-cult in, 240, 299; as Nazi journalist, 245; economics of, 250; on Christianity, 282, 290, 302

Goethe: 17, 207; " two souls " in, 3, 6, 187; reflects the West, 9, 186, 314; as classicist, 20, 199, 310; and Life-worship, 22–3, 36; warns against romanticism, 28–9, 186; pantheism in, 30; hailed by *Athenäum*, 31; evolution theory of, 44–5; at Weimar, 55; satirizes Teutonicism, 66–7; on patriotic corruption of history, 79; and " dæmonic," 150, 167, 199; and lawless " becoming," 292

Gold oder Blut by Bangert: 244

" gold vs. blood ": 5, 97, 99, 117, 157–8, 165, 244

Gönner, Generalarbeitsführer von: 260 n, 261 n

Göring: 149, 217, 245, 265; impresses the English, 158–9

Götterdämmerung by Wagner: 136

Great in the Little, The, by Nilus: 266 n

Greece: *see* Hellenic tradition

Greiser, Arthur: 220–1

Grenzboten, periodical: quoted, 7–8

Grillparzer, Franz: 50 and n

Grimm, Hans, 157, 159, 173–4, 177, 255

Grimm brothers: 39

Grosse Täuschung by Delitzsch: 286 n

Grünwedel, Albert: 274 and n

Guérard, Albert: 16

Gundolf, Friedrich: 17 n, 183

Günther, Hans: 254, 255, 294

gymnasts: *see* youth movements

Hamlet: 45

Hamsun, Knut: 256

Hanisch, Rudolf: 133 n

Hannibal: 257–8

Hapsburgs: 61, 70, 76, 140, 170, 199, 217

Hauer, Wilhelm: 292

Hauptmann, Gerhart: 255

Hauser, H.: 240, 253 n

Hauser, Otto: 293–4

Haushofer: converts Hitler, 170; on Russia, 216, 222; on South America, 223

Hazen, Charles: 61 and n

Hedin, Sven: 256

Hegel: 18, 33, 195, 286; state-worship, 38, 89 n; combined with *Realpolitik*, 47, 191; influence on Wagner, 94; as precursor of Nazism, 199–203; and Rosenberg, 231; and Nazi paganism, 288, 291

Heine, Heinrich: on romanticism: 17 and n; and " Young Germany," 94; influences Wagner, 94–5; prophecy, 281, 300–1

Heinrich von Ofterdingen by Novalis: 165 and n

Helenic tradition: 118, 201; and the West, 179; confused conceptions, 20–1; Jahn's version, 69; Rosenberg on, 234, 237, 265

Henderson, Nevile: 159, 160 n

Henry VIII: 76

Herder: 55; as tolerant nationalist, 37, 61, 77, 78, 88; folksong theory, 39; evolutionist, 43; to Hitler, 50–4, 156, 261; and neo-romantics, 168

heredity vs. environment: 231–2

Herkunft u. Rassengeschichte d. Germanen by Günther: 294 n

Hermann the Cheruscan (Arminius): as a symbol, 11–13, 15, 180–1, 186, 309

Hermannschlacht, Die, by Kleist: 11–12

Herodom by Wagner: 114

Herzensergiessungen eines kunstliebenden Klosterbruders: 42 n

Hess, Rudolf: 136, 149; as poet, 158; and Russia, 215–16; born in Egypt, 217; as Haushofer's pupil, 222; and Thule Society, 254

Hess, Hermann: 255

Hierl, K.: 260

Himmler: 240

Hindenberg: 209, 290

History of Germany in Nineteenth Century by Treitschke: 52 n

Hitler, Adolf: metapolitics of, 3, 134–5; Fichte to Hitler, 7, 18, 33, 189–99, 261; reads Spengler, 10; and Houston Chamberlain, 9, 110–11, 115, 137–8, 142, 147–50, 282–3; like Kleist, 11–12; on Luther, 13, 283; vs. " other Germany," 14–15, 28; romanticism to Hitler, 16, 18, 31–3, 38, 50–4, 62, 165, 186, 243; deified, 34, 151, 287–91, 298–9; avenges German defeats, 49; vs. provincialism, 55–6, 71; vs. " French ideas," 56; unlike Napoleon, 60; like Jahn, 65–6, 69–72, 74–6, 79–80, 88, 182, 209, 269; and *Lebensraum,* 72, 174–5; and " positive " Christianity, 75–6, 168, 286; and Wagner, 91–2, 96, 98, 108, 110–11, 114–15, 117–18, 120, 122–3, Chap. vi — 127–43, 227, 283; as orator and showman, 124, 135, 150; as friend of Wagner family, 132–3, 148; admires Wagnerian music, 133, 138, 160; early years of, 133–4, 160–1, 190–1; and the arts, 79, 133, 136, 148, 154, 155–68, 312; in beer-hall putsch, 135–6, 212; and Hess, 136, 149; as Wagnerian hero, 136–7, 139–40; Twenty-five Points of, 137, 251; names street for H. Chamberlain, 138; exalts Volk, 140–2; vs. Hapsburgs, 141; vs. Prussianism, 141; in early days of party, 143, 218–19, 254, 309; neo-romantics triumph in, 145; as dæmonic, 151, 172; vs. capitalism, 154, 157–8, 262; Röhm dedicates verse to, 156; and Nationalist party, 163–4; and Lagarde, 168–9; on *Mitteleuropa,* 169–70; and Langbehn, 171, 185; as Faustian, 175; intellectual supporters of, 176; denounced by Jünger, 177; repudiates Mediterranean heritage, 179; 1934 blood purge of, 181, 265; horrifies Spengler, 181, 185; Stefan George vs., 185; distorts Nietzsche, 185, 197–9; contrasted with Mann, 187; and *Realpolitik*, 189–91, 195–6, 198, 200, 202–3; and War of Liberation, 191–3, 241; disciple of Ludendorff, 195, 297–8; population policy of, 200; socialism in, 202–3; like Treitschke, 205; and Bismarck legend, 207; fools Neville Chamberlain, 211; bureaucratic support of, 212; not inevitable, 213; war prediction of 1920, 214; and Russia, 215–16, 220, 262, 307–8; ancestry, 217; Austrian accent, 218; fulfils Rosenberg's prophecies, 219–22, 245–6, 248, 252–3; as " capitalist tool " myth, 220; sees Jesus as Aryan, 235; on democracy, 248, 277; Hamsun admires, 255–6; promises bloodshed, 260, 317; accomplishments, 263, 287–98; defends *Protocols*, 266, 269; Coughlin parallels, 268–9; anti-Christianism under, 281–302; on Frederick the Great, 283; calls Old Testament " Bible of Satan," 286, 302; exploits Prussianism and romanticism, 310–13; exploits German idealism, 315; *see also* Nazis, racism, Chamberlain, H., Wagner

Hitler Prozess: 143 *n*

Hoffmann, E. T. A.: 152

Hofmannsthal, Hugo von: 47, 310

Hohenzollerns: 14, 141, 203, 210, 259

Hölderlin: 21, 310

Holy Roman Empire: 14, 54, 55, 75, 126, 131, 185

Holy Roman Empire by Bryce: 111

homosexuality: 264–5

Hour of Decision by Spengler: 189 *n*, 296 *n*

House of German Art: 79, 136

Hugenberg: 163

Hugo, Victor: 17

Humboldt: 55

Hutten, Ulrich von: 13

Hymnen an die Nacht by Novalis: 41

I was Hitler's Buddy by Hanisch: 133

Immermann: 174

In the Path of the Führer by Ribbentrop: 158

Institute for Exploring Jewish Question: 257

Internationale Hochfinanz, Der, by Rosenberg: 220 *n*, 267 *n*

Ireland: 175, 179, 208

Italy: 52, 94, 192; fascism, 128–9, 164, 201; Renaissance, 13, 237, 283; Treitschke's plans for, 204

Jackson, Andrew: 174

Jacobinism: 193; " German Jacobinism," 65–6, 71–2, 82

Jahn, Friedrich Ludwig: 14, 56–7, 62, 162, 172, 181, 191, 193, 261, 305, 312; Herder to, 50–3; life summarized, 63–4; as German Jacobin, 65–6; cult of primitivism, 66–8; from provincialism to nationalism, 71–2; favours mass participation, 72–3; " republicanism " in, 72–3;

Führer concept, 73–4; racialism, 74, 87; on Christianity, 75–7; schemes for nationalist indoctrination, 77–9; on art, 79; Free Corps, gymnasts, and student leagues, 64, 68, 75, 80–7, 93; significance today, 88–9; compared with Hitler, 66, 70, 71, 72, 74, 79–80, 88, 209, 269; and Wagner, 123; and Rosenberg, 228, 240–2, 265; and Röhm, 265; bibliography on, 323–5

Jahre d. Entscheidung by Spengler: 189 *n*, 296 *n*

Japan: 156, 164–5, 315; Rosenberg's plans for, 223, 245

Jefferson, Thomas: 174

Jesuits: Jahn vs., 76; Rosenberg vs., 242

Jews: and Americanism linked, 9; Chamberlain on, 9, 115, *passim;* Judaism vs. pantheism, 26; "Chosen People" concept borrowed from, 38, 69, 288; Grillparzer on, 50 and *n;* Jahn on, 70, 87; liberated by Napoleon, 87, 193; Wagner and, 94–5, 99, 104–5, 108–9, 113, 117–20, 122, 129, 131, 148, *passim;* Wagner's parentage attributed to, 95–6 and *n*, 218; "Jewish gold," 99, 157–8; Hitler on, 142, 192, 205, 268, 290, 317, *passim;* Nazi artists' resentment of, 154, 156, 161–2; contributions to Western civilization of, 179; praised by Nietzsche, 198; incarnate "world-spirit," 201; Hegel on, 201; Treitschke on, 205; enslavement of, 218, 230;

Goebbels on, 218; Rosenberg vs., 218, 220, 225, 231, 235, 246, *passim;* and French Revolution, 249, 268; barred as cattle-dealers, 254; looted, 259; and *Protocol* forgery, 249–50, 266–9, 272; treatment in Russia, 267–9; Coughlin on, 268–9; *see also* racism, Jews blamed for

Jews and Their Lies by Luther: 283

Jews blamed for: industrialism, 9; Russian revolution, 29–30; Marxism, 66, 118, 142, 220, 244, 262, 268, 306, 307; democracy, 104, 113, 157, 192, 267; intellectualism, 108; '48 Revolution, 109; free press, 118; anti-vegetarianism, 119; German emigration, 122; capitalism, 142, 157, 205, 220, 244, 267, 268, 306–7; Nazi literary failures, 156; hurting animals, 167; Christianity, 168–9, 282–3, 286–7, 292; "French ideas," 205; Kaiser's Germany, 226–7; materialism, 246; Catholic-Protestant split, 249; obeying Dalai Lama, 297; dominating Nazi party, 298; English high finance, 307; *see also* racism, Jews

Johst, Hanns: 159, 255

Judaism in Music by Wagner: 104–5

Jude by des Mousseaux: 267 *n*

Jüdin von Toledo by Grillparzer: 50 *n*

Jung, Edgar: 177

Jünger, F. G.: 177, 272

Junkers: 122, 72, 126, 141, 163, 209, 226

Kant: 9, 310
Keats: 31, 41
Kerrl, Hanns: 289
Kipling: 52
Klages, Ludwig: 157, 177, 255
Kleist, Heinrich von: 11–12
Knaben Wunderhorn, Des: 39–40
Know Thyself by Wagner: 117 n
Kohn, Hans: 8 n, 17 n, 311
Kolbenheyer, Erwin: 159, 255
Krieck, Ernst: 165, 176, 177
Kroeck: 165
Ku Klux Klan: 245
Kultur: *see* Western civilization
Kultur Senate: 154
Kulturbolshevik: 130, 162, 166

Labour Front: 140, 288–9
Labour Service: 260–2
Lagarde, Paul de, (pseud. for Bötticher): 174; bovarism in, 24; on Christianity, 168–9, 227, 282; racism in, 168–9, 251, 269; coins "master Volk," 169; *Mitteleuropa* concept in, 169–70, 173; war-cult in, 171; exalts Saxon peasant, 174; hailed by Rosenberg, 225–7; would be horrified today, 269
Langbehn, Julius: as proto-Nazi, 169–73, 174, 176; repudiates past ideas, 178, 180–2, 184–5
language purification: 77–8
Lassalle: 157
Lawrence, D. H.: phallism in, 25; as Wagnerian, 128; on Germany, 270–1
Lebensraum concept: 309; foreshadowed by Jahn, 72; by Fichte, 194; in Grimm,

173–5; in Haushofer, 222–4
Leffler, Pastor: 288
legalism and anti-legalism: 5, 28, 43–4, 59, 60, 269, 309; Mediterranean heritage, 179–80; "natural man," 20, 52, 304; "beyond good and evil," 196–9; in Herder, 52; in A. Müller, 37; in Wagner, 108, 109, 110, 124, 134; in Treitschke, 205; in Troeltsch, 7
Leiden u. Grösse d. Meister by Mann: *see* Freud, Goethe, Wagner
Lenin: 120, 131, 250 n
Lerner, Max: 175 n
Lessing: 14, 310
Ley, Robert: 140, 298, 302; deifies Hitler, 288–9
liberal label: misapplied to certain nationalists, 58–60, 72–3, 86; Wagner's early, 94–5, 99–106
Liebestod by Wagner: 167
Life of Richard Wagner by Newman: 93 n, 94 n, 96 n, 97 n, 100 n, 102 n, 110 n
life-worship: *see* dynamism
Little Herr Friedemann by Mann: 22
Lohengrin by Wagner: 133, 136
Lorenz, A.: 96 n
Louis XIV: 12, 199
Louis Philippe: 112
Lovejoy, Arthur: 18 and n
Lucinde by Schlegel: 22 n
Ludendorff, Erich von: romantic origin of total war, 194–5; Republic as a ruse of, 210–12; influence and ideas, 296–8
Ludendorff, Mathilde: 297

Ludwig of Bavaria: 109, 114

Lüng, Pidder: 314

Luther: 13, 58, 76; as nationalist, 283

Lyons, Eugene: 233 *n*, 288 *n*, 289 *n*

Machiavelli: 192

MacMillan, Ernest: 136

Macpherson: 40

Madame Bovary by Flaubert: 22 and *n*

Madariaga: 79

Mahomet: 269

male leagues: 263–6

Malherbe, Henri: 95

Mallarmé: 145

Malta: 204

Man and Technics by Spengler: 189 *n*, 296 *n*, 314

Mann, Heinrich: 162

Mann, Thomas: 131 *n*, 183 *n*, 310; on bovarism, 22 and *n;* on Wagner, 92, 93, 97 *n*, 98, 100, 115, 127–8, 130, 135; books burnt, 162; nationalist phase, 186–7; chooses exile, 255

Marie Antoinette: 53

Marxism: *see* socialism

mass man: 307, 312–14

Massis, Henri: 10

master race: 172, 218; in Hitler, 191, 197–8; in Lagarde, 169; in Rosenberg, 221, 234, 263; in Treitschke, 204; super-man into super-race, 196–9

materialism and anti-materialism: 4, 315; in Wagner, 94 97, 103, 118, 120, 246; in second romantic movement, 145–8; and Nazi " idealism," 243–4, 246–7

Mazzini: 52, 62

Mediterranean spirit: *see* Western civilization

Mein Kampf: 9, 53, 138 *n*, 139 *n*, 143 *n*, 211 *n*, 214, 262, 280 *n*, 286, 307 *n*, 314 *n;* low-brow romanticism of, 33; foreshadowed by Jahn, 69–70, 79–80, 87 *n;* on education, 79–80; influenced by Wagner, 108, 111, 115 *n*, 117, 135, 141; Hitler's youth described in, 113–14; dictated to Hess, 136; borrows from Chamberlain, 137; in U. S., 190; on militarism, 190–2; distorts Nietzsche, 197–8; influenced by Haushofer, 210, 222, 224; influenced by Rosenberg, 210, 222, 224, 252; as " Old Testament " of nazism, 228; required Nazi reading, 261; paralleled by Coughlin, 269; predicts gassing of Jews, 317–19

Mein Leben by Wagner: 94 *n*, 99, 100 *n*, 118 *n*

Meinecke: 33 and *n*

Meistersinger, Die, by Wagner: 98, 103, 127, 131; favoured Nazi music, 91, 138; often seen by Hitler, 132; " a lance against civilization," 182; quoted by Rosenberg, 224–5

Mellish, W. H.: 98 and *n*

Mendelian law: 237

Mephistopheles: 23–4

metapolitics: defined, 3–5, 134; of Wagner, 92, 97–9, 103–25; as new mass force, 124; Wagner to Hitler, 132, 134, 252, 261; Chamberlain to Hitler, 48–9; of Rosenberg, 214–15, 220–59; and its critics, 272–80; appeals to youth, 147,

215; and neo-romantics, 168; and *Realpolitik*, 199; heroizes hunger, 243; and meta-sex, 264; jargon in *Weltkampf*, 304–8

Metternich: conservative internationalism of, 58–60, 64, 70–2, 85–6, 300; Rosenberg vs., 59; vs. Jahn, 64–5, 71–2, 85; Wagner vs., 109

Meyerbeer: 94 *n*, 95, 105

Michael by Goebbels: 165 *n*, 183

Middle Ages: 126, 241; confused conception, 20–1, 46

militarism: *see* war-cult

Mitteleuropa, book and concept: 72, 169–70, 204

Moeller van den Bruck: 226

Monroe Doctrine: 223

Mousseaux, Gougenot des: 267 and *n*

Müller, Adam: 37; political oracle of first romantics, 32–3; and Rosenberg, 230

Müller, Georg: 99, 100 *n*

Müller, Reichsbischof: 76; rewrites Bible, 291; resisted, 302

Munich Pact: 190, 212–13

Münster, town of: 49

Mussolini: 52, 93; and Wagner, 128–9; *sacro egoismo*, 200

My Part in Germany's Fight by Goebbels: 138

Mythus d. 20. Jahrhunderts by Rosenberg: 8 *n*, 48, 88 *n*, 129, 224, 227 *n*, 245 *n*, 256, 262, 264 *n*, 266 *n*, 283 *n*, 285 *n*, 286 *n*, 292 *n*; on democracy, 222; most frequent favourable references, Wagner, Chamberlain, Lagarde, 225; unfavourable references,

Jews, Etruscans, 225; basic lingo and assumptions of, 228–31; great influence of, 228, 238–9; racial interpretation of history in, 232–5; on art, 235–7; refutations of, 238 *n*, 258, 273–6, 284–5

Nanking, sack of: 165

Napoleon: invades Germany, 12; Jahn vs., 54, 64, 70, 83, 191; and modernization of Germany, 55–8, 65; contrasted with Hitler, 60; hatred of, 72; liberates Jews, 87, 193; as dæmonic, 150; Italian accent of, 218; on power, 188

national socialism: *see* Nazis, socialism, Hitler

nationalism: *see* universalism

Nationalist party: 163, 209, 213

Nationalsozialistische Monatshefte: 215

Natur und Kunst, sonnet by Goethe: 20, 199

Naumann, Friedrich: 170

Nazi Primer: 257

Nazis, nazism; romanticism into Nazism, *see* romanticism; vs. Western civilization, 5, 180, 215; proto-Nazis and, 7, 150–1, 169–73, 177, 182, 185–6; vs. Charlemagne, 12; vs. " other Germany," 14–15, 23, 28, 62, 195, 209, 212–15, 302, 309–10; storm troops foreshadowed, 38, 67; and education, 43, 78, 88, 258–9, 273, 276–8; and Wars of Liberation, 54, 57–8, 192, 241, 261, 265; Herder and, 52; vs. Metternich, 59; as disciples of Jahn, 73–4, 77, 85, 88; Volkstum as favoured word of, 64;

plebiscites of, 79; Wagner as fountainhead of, 91–2, 126, 130, 132, 135, *see also* Wagner; and *Meistersinger,* 91, 98, 138; and the fascintern, 128–9; in 1932 election, 136; Twenty-five Points of, 137; first meeting of, 139; artistic leaders, 153–6, 312; book-burning, 162–3; intellectuals and, 175; Langbehn repudiates, 180–1; 1934 purge of, 181; Spengler horrified by, 181–2; and Nietzsche, 183, 197–8, 227, 285; George repudiates, 183–4; and Goethe, 186; aggression and Hegel, 199–203; compared with Prussianism, 203–7, 226, 311–12; and the Republic, 207; left-wing vs. right-wing, 216, 219–20, 247, 259–60, 262; original nucleus of, 218; and the New World, 221–3; and Lagarde, 226–7; distort Frederick the Great, 227–8; basic testaments of, 228, 238, 245; enslavement of Slavs, 230; favour heredity vs. environment, 231–2; contrast idealism and materialism, 246–7; secret plots in propaganda of, 248–51; and Rousseau's general will, 250; Rosenberg on mission of, 251–2; and Thule Society, 254; literature under, 255–6; vs. Hohenzollerns, 259; vs. Christianity, 258–9, 273–6 281–302; labour camps, 260–2; Russian influences on, 268–9; mass appeal of, 305, 307, 311–12; combine romanticism and Prussianism, 311–12; exploit noblest and worst qualities, 214–15; bibliographies on, 317; *see also* Hitler, socialism, etc.

Near East: 224

neo-classicism: 31, 36, 41, 46; *see also* classicism

Netherlands: 72, 122, 170, 174

Neue Reich, Das, by George: 265 *n*

Newman, Ernest: 92 *n,* 93 *n,*

Nibelungen, The, essay by Wagner: 111 *n,* 136

Nibelungen Saga: Jahn boosts, 80; and Wagner, 110, 134; and Hitler, 134; significance to-day, 138–40; Goethe vs., 186

Niemöller, Pastor: 75, 290, 291, 302

Nietzsche: bovarism in, 24; on racism, 48, 90, 183, 198, 284; on Wagner, 48, 90, 95, 99, 116, 128, 130, 152, 183; on Bismarck, 48, 183; defines nationalism, 77; on German gullibility, 144; vs. philistinism, 153; and metapolitics, 168; visited in asylum by Langbehn, 172; insanity, 172, 182; converted to West, 178, 182–8, 310; appeals to Pope, 182; war-cult in, 182, 191; inspires Mann, 186; on superman, beyond good and evil, 196–9; and *Realpolitik,* 203, 205–6; on Treitschke, 205–6; hailed by Rosenberg, 225–8; Nazis distort, 188 *n;* cf. 1961 Preface

Nietzsche's Zusammenbruch by Podach: 48 and *n,* 172 *n,* 183 *n*

Nilus, Sergius: 266 *n,* 267–8

Nordau, Max: 93, 96, 97 *n*

Nordic Society: 254–5, 257 *n*

Nordischer Gedanke unter d. Deutschen by Günther: 294 *n*

Norway: 256

Not to Mention the War by Davis: 139 *n*

Novalıs (pseud. for von Hardenberg): and definition of romanticism, 17, 47; political ideas of, 33; Storm Troops foreshadowed in, 37–8; emotionalism in, 41, 42 *n;* "blue flower" and, 165; and Rosenberg, 230

Nuns Fret Not, sonnet by Wordsworth: 27

Nuremberg Party Congress: 98, 124; Goebbels at, 223; Rosenberg at, 223, 254–5; M. Ludendorff at, 297

On Meyerbeer's Huguenots by Wagner: 94

organic vs. atomistic: 7, 59, 196, 235, 261; mathematical fallacy of, 29–34; state and Volk, 5, 37–40, 51, 52, 55, 64, 73–4, 88–9, 250; in Wagner, 97, 103, 107–8

Ortega y Gasset, José: 307 *n*

Ossian: 40

Otto the Great: 185

Paine, Thomas: 255

Pan-Germanism: from Herder to, 51; Hitler on, 53; in Wagner, 134; in Grimm, 173; Bismarck vs., 174; Nietzsche vs., 183; and German Republic, 210–11; in Ludendorff, 297

Pan-Slavism: 51

Panthea, poem by Wilde: 41 *n*

pantheism: romantic's, 26, 31, 46–7; Goethe's, 30; Schopenhauer and Wagner, 104; Nazi, 292–3; Heine warns vs., 301

Parsifal by Wagner: 118, 185, 295

particularism: Jahn vs., 63–4, 70–2, 83–4; Hitler vs. 54–6, 71

Paul, Jean: 42, 55

Paul, Saint: 282, 283, 285–7, 302

Pauli, Gustav: quoted, 19 and *n*

Perfect Wagnerite by Shaw: 121 *n*

Pest in Russland by Rosenberg: 220 *n*

philistinism: 129, 153

Philosophie des Rechts by Hegel: 201 *n*

Philosophy of History by Hegel: 201 *n*

Phœnicians: 257–8

Placzek, Siegfried: 96 *n*

Poland: 57, 61, 141; inspires Wagner, 194; enslavement of, 222, 230; Rosenberg on, 220–1, 252

Pope, Alexander: 31

Pope, the: 181, 182, 185

Potsdam-Wagner alliance: 127, 255, 311

Prose by Wagner: 93 *n,* 94 *n,* 97 *n,* 100 *n,* 101 *n,* 104, 106, 108 *n,* 110 *n,* 116 *n,* 118 *n,* 119 *n,* 120 *n,* 121 *n,* 315–16

Protestantische Rompilger by Rosenberg: 283

Protestantism: 46, 75–6, 181, 185, 203, 216, 249; vs. Nazis, 226, 258, 283, 289–91, 302; refutations of *Mythus,* 283 *n,* 284, 258

Protocols of the Elders of Zion: 249–50, 266–9, 272

Proudhon: 120

provincialism: *see* particularism

Prussia: 142; yoked to France,
57; and Jahn, 63–5, 67, 70–2,
73–4, 81–3, 86–7; suppresses
Saxon revolution, 99; Wagner
favours splitting of, 102; governed by Göring, 158;
Treitschke on, 203–6; officer
corps, 265; 700 pastors arrested in, 290

Prussianism: un-German qualities of, 26–7; and Wagner,
126–8, 140–1; Hitler vs., 141;
and Hegel, 201; compared
with nazism, 203–7, 226, 302,
311–12; distinguished from
volk-worship, 230; combined
with romanticism, 255, 311–
12; exploited by Hitler, 311

Quisling: 256

*Race, a Monthly for the Nordic
Idea:* 254

racism: 4, 5, 38–40, 53, 59, 193,
298; in Houston Chamber-
lain, 9, 137, 115–16, 232; in
Fichte, 6–7, 194; in Gobineau, 115–17; in H. Grimm,
173–4; in Günther, 254–5,
293; in Hauser, 293–5; in
Hegel, 201; in Hitler, 87,
133–4, 137, 141–2, 158–8,
192, 205, 268, 290; in Jahn,
69–70, 74, 87; in Lagarde,
168–9; in Langbehn, 170–3;
in Rosenberg, 8, 220–1, 229–
32, 232–5, 245–55, 256–9,
293; in Russia, 266–72; in
Treitschke, 204–6; in Wagner, 95, 97, 99, 104–6,
114–20, 122, 130–1, 232;

Nietzsche on, 48, 90, 182–3,
198, 284; Christ aryanized,
287–9; vs. Christianity, 291–
4; vs. the West, 187–8; *see
also* Jews

*Rasse u. Rassenfragen in
Deutschland* by Hauser:
294 n

*Rassenkunde d. deutschen
Volkes* by Günther: 294 n

rationalism and anti-rationalism: 41, 46, 59, 60, 94, 155,
205, 242; first romantics, 7,
19–20, 28–9, 32, 151; neo-
romantics, 145–6, 152, 168;
in Wagner, 97, 103–4, 105,
108–9, 124, 134; and the
West, 5, 9, 269, 309

Rauschning, Hermann: 136 n,
182, 221 n; on dynamism,
43; underestimates Rosen-
berg, 214–15, 256

Realpolitik: 11, 47, 160; in
Fichte, Hegel, Treitschke,
Hitler, Chap. ix — 189–208;
Nietzsche vs., 182

Reich Chamber of Literature:
145, 154

Reichsbank: 158

Reichstag: 73; denounced by
Wagner, 194; war on, 213 n,
222, 230; Rosenberg on, 220–
1, 252

Reichswehr: 102, 141; and the
Republic, 209–10; and Ver-
sailles Treaty, 211; and Social
Democrats, 211–12; favours
Russian alliance, 213 n, 226;
Röhm vs., 265

Rembrandt als Erzieher by
Langbehn: 170

Renaissance: 13, 58

Reventlow, Ernst zu: 176, 177,
292

Revolt of the Masses by Ortega: 307 *n*, 313 *n*

Revolution by Wagner: 102, 108

Revolution of Nihilism by Rauschning: 43 and *n*, 214 *n*, 221 *n*, 234 *n*

Revolutions of 1848–9: 14; reinterpreted, 58–62; Jahn and, 84, 87; Wagner and, 98–104, 109, 265; bibliography on Wagner's role in, 100 *n*

Rheinfront: 34

Ribbentrop: as dramatist, 158; rivalry with Rosenberg, 222

Richard Wagner, Revolutionär gegen 19. Jahrhundert by Ganzer: 106

Richard Wagner, Revolutionaire by Malherbe: 95 *n*

Richter, Jean Paul: 42, 55

Rienzi, by Wagner: 98, 103

Rights of Man: 179

Rilke: 256, 310

Rimbaud: 145

Ring of the Nibelung by Wagner: 119, 121, 139, 243; anticapitalism in, 229

Robespierre: 32, 223

Röckel: 99–100

Rödel, Helmut: 226 *n*

Röhm, Ernst: 103, 149, 218, 245; as poet, 156; on Volk-army, 265

Roman civilization: 10, 18, 171; contributions to the West, 179–80, 184, 309; Roman wall as symbol, 5, 6, 146, 187; Nietzsche on, 284; Rosenberg on, 234, 284–6; Spengler on, 313; Wagner vs., 98

Romantic Structure of Wagner's Cogitation: 93

romanticism: as element of metapolitics, 4; classicism vs., 5, 20–1, 28, 36, 41–2, 43–4, 45, 52, 132, 152; first romantic movement, 11, 14, 21, 28, 42 *n*, 44–7, 51–3, 54, 62, 78, 88–9, 123, 125, 138, 145, 152, 155, 160, 165, 191–5, 266, 269; neo-romantic movement, 14, 145–8, 160, 167–8, 168–73, 176–7, 200, 282–3; into nazism, 16, 23, 26, 28, 29, 30–1, 33, 34, 37–8, 43, 50–3, 55–6, 88–9, 123–5, 135, 138, 140–2, 145, 147, 150, 155–6, 159, 164, 168, 174–6, 193–203, 228, 261, 283, 299–300, 315; defined and analysed, 16–47; difficulties of definition, 17–21; outside of Germany, 18–20, 22–3, 27; as typically German, 19–20; life-worship in, 21–6, 36; made easy, 25; "the weight of too much liberty," 26–8; three basic assumptions of, 28–9; the mathematical fallacy, 29–34; Hitler's lowbrow version of, 33; repetition, 34–42; in art, 36–7; and the state, 37–8, 140; and Volk, 38–40, 140, 236; ego and emotion glorified, 40–2; influential romantic novels, 42 *n;* false analogy of dynamism, 42–7; in Wagner, 43, 53, 56, 93, 106–8, 123–5, 135, 138–9, 140, 160; and *Realpolitik*, 47, 198–9; stands self-condemned, 47; corruption of romantic nationalism, 50–4; in Jahn, 50, 52–3, 56, 63–4, 66, 69, 78, 88–9, 123; in Chamberlain, 53, 160; and

the Wars of Liberation, 54–
60, 241; and the Second
Reich, 127; and militarism,
140, 166, 171, 176, 228, 255,
311; exploited by Hitler,
140–2, 243, 310–12; in Hess,
158; in Goebbels, 161, 163,
165; and " the German soul,"
164–7; in Hitler's speeches,
165; in Rosenberg, 165, 219,
225, 229–30, 248, 250; Nietzsche warns against, 183;
Goethe warns against, 186; in
Ludendorff, 194; and Hegel,
201; " steel romanticism,"
255–6; synthesized with the
West, 309–10; and Prussianism, 310–13; *see also* becoming vs. being, dyna-
mism, legalism, rationalism,
Volk, Kultur vs. civilization *under* Western civilization

Rosenberg, Alfred: romantics
pave way for, 6; admires
Master Eckehart, 8, 236; prefers Saxons to Charlemagne,
12; on Luther, 13, 283; denounces Metternich, 59; admires Jahn, 88, 228, 240–1;
and Wagner, 91, 115, 131,
142, 183, 224–7, 232, 234,
236, 242–3, 246, 251, 292,
295, 304–5; and Chamber-
lain, 115, 142, 183, 218, 224–
6, 232, 251–2, 273–4, 277,
282–3, 310; as example of
armed bohemia, 148, 157,
312; hate dominates writings
of, 161, 225; as disciple of Lagarde, 169–70, 225, 285; converts Hitler to *Mitteleuropa*
idea, 170; as disciple of Langbehn, 172, 181–3; sees Shakespeare as German, 172; underestimated in U. S., 176,
214–15; names nazism's four
fountainheads, 183, 225; compares Nazis to 1813 nationalists, 191–2; as disciple of Ludendorff, 195, 297; back-
ground and origin of, 214–19;
vs. Jews, 218, 220, 225, 231,
235, 246, 249; preaches crusade vs. Soviet, 215–16, 219–
22; influences *Mein Kampf*,
216, 222, 252; helps found
Nazis, 218, 252; made Weltanschauung Director, 219,
252, 275; as typical romantic,
219; calls Marxists tools of
capitalism, 220; wants Germany to rule world, 221;
preaches conquest of Slavs,
221, 253; vs. democracy, 222,
246–8, 281; rivals Ribbentrop, 222; refutations of, 224,
238 and *n*, 258, 273–6, 278–
9, 284–5; attacks van den
Bruck, 226; distorts Frederick the Great, 227–8, 230;
basic lingo and assumptions
of, 228–32; lasting influence
of, 228, 238–9, 252–4; romantic roots of, 229–30, 248,
250, 255, 273; distinguishes
Volk and state, 230; on the
race-soul, 230–1; racial interpretation of history in, 232–5;
glorifies Atlantis, 233–4; sees
Jesus descended from Atlanteans, 235, 282; racial interpretation of art, 235–8; calls
Dante German, 237; pro-
nounces doom of bourgeoisie,
241; calls for new Teutonic
Order, 241, 264; hates Catholicism, 242; Führer-cult

in, 242–3; denounces capitalism and Marxism, 244, 246–51; as journalist, 245–52; vs. materialism, 246–8; as "educator," 252–63; influences German youth, 252–3, 256–8, 261, 273, 289; awards cultural prizes, 254–5; preaches "steel romanticism," 255; vs. Christianity, 258–60, 273–6, 281–7, 291–2, 298, 302–3; gives compulsory lectures at Munich, 259; makes much of male-leagues, 263–4; attacks American feminization, 265–6; spreads *Protocols,* 266, 272; "Russianizes" Germany, 272; damns Etruscans, 225, 274–5, 284–5; on academic liberty, 276–7; vs. Old Testament, 282–3, 285–7; and *Weltkampf,* 304–6, 308; bibliography on, 326–9

Rosenstock-Hüssy, Eugen: 127, 265

Rousseau: 51; Life-worship in, 22; "general will vs. will of all," 32; and Wagner, 101; to Rosenberg, 250; and Nazi pantheism, 292

Ruhr, French occupation of: 12, 270

Russia: 99, 120, 210; Russian revolution, 29, 65–6, 218, 248, 254, 268, 269; Rosenberg's crusade vs., 215–18, 220–3, 245–6, 308; alliance with Germany, 220, 262, 307–8; 1941 invasion of, 220; Nazi explanation of purges, 220–1; and Reichswehr, 226; influences Germany, 266–72; purge in, 282

Sachs, Hans: 98, 136
sacro egoismo: 200
Sade, Marquis de: 164
Sand: 68, 86
Santayana, George: 47 n, 173, 188 n
Saxons: 12–13, 14, 113, 170, 172, 174, 181
Saxony: 71, 99, 102, 111, 114, 120
Schacht, Hjalmar: 157
Scheidemann: 210
Schelling: 30
Schiller: 9, 55
Schirach: 156–7, 175, 298; vs. Christianity, 287, 289–90, 302; as poet, 162, 312
Schlegel brothers: 17, 21–2 and n, 28, 30, 32, 39, 41, 47
Schleicher, General Kurt von: 213 n
Schleiermacher: 36, 89 n
Schleswig-Holstein: 61
Schmitt, Carl: 157 and preface
Schnabel, Franz: 62
Schopenhauer: 103, 104, 106, 125
Schriften für Deutsche: see *Deutsche Schriften*
Schwarzer Korps: 283
Scott-James, R. A.: 180 n
Second Reich: 92, 107; and Wagner, 126–8, 140–1, 147; denounced as Jewish, 226–7
secret plots "unmasked": 248–51, 297, 306
Seher des dritten Reiches by H. S. Chamberlain: 9 n, 149 n, 283 n
Shakespeare: as a "true German": 171, 172, 246
Shaw, G. B.: 121
Shelley: 31
Siebenter Ring by George: 265 n
Siegfried as symbol: 110–11, 127, 129, 134, 136, 138–42, 148, 153, 242, 282

Siegfried by Wagner: 110, 123
Siegfried Line: 139
Slavs: 76, 217, 272; Pan-Slavism, 51; enslavement preached, 204, 218, 221
Social Democrats: long period of strength, 14; psychological weaknesses, 163–4; and the Republic, 209–13; as scapegoats of annexationists, 211
Social Justice: 268
socialism, Marxist: 128, 131, 176, 268, 307; Dalai Lama's puppet, 297; denounced as Jewish, 66, 118, 143, 244, 267, 268, 277, 306, 307; "Jewish-capitalist" puppet, 157–8, 220, 248–52; Hegelian roots, 94, 201–3, 231; in Germany, 122, 140, 142, 209, 210, 219; psychological handicaps, 126, 146–7, 309
socialism, Nazi: 4, 157–8, 163, 202–3, 216, 220, 226, 243–4, 247–52, 261–3; "national" or "Brown bolshevism"; 65–6, 210, 259–60, 262, 263, 311–12; collectivism in Jahn, 73–4, 240; in Fichte, 33, 195; Wagnerian, 53, 94, 99, 100, 101, 105, 107, 120–1, 122, 125, 128, 130, 134
Sokol: 80
Song of the Goths: 287
South America: Wagner's emigration scheme, 119; Nazi threat to, 221, 223
Spain: 164, 204
Spaten und Aehre by von Gönner: 260–2
Speeches to the German Nation by Fichte: 7 *n*, 11, 68, 192–4
Spengler, Oswald: 10, 168, 189;

pro-Western conversion, 178; 181–2, 184, 185; chided by Rosenberg, 235; romanticism in, 295–6, 310; vs. Spengler, 314
Spur d. Juden im Wandel d. Zeit by Rosenberg: 220 *n*
Stalin: 131, 216; Georgian accent, 218; pact with Hitler, 213 *n*, 220, 262, 307, 308; and the purge, 282; moral price, 263
Stauffenberg, Claus von: 188
Stefan George u. d. Jugend by Dschenfzig: 264, 265 *n*
Steffens, Heinrich: 75
Stehr, Hermann: 255
Stein, Freiherr vom und zum: 39, 48, 65, 74, 82, 191, 261
Stendahl: 17
Stern d. Bundes by George: 265 *n*
"Storm and Stress": 14, 54, 199
Storm Troops: 38, 53, 66, 68, 75, 82, 85, 103, 105, 113, 156, 165, 167, 265
Strasser, Otto: 177
Streicher, Julius: as watercolour artist, 158; Rosenberg vs., 254
student leagues: *see* youth movements
Stürmer: 158, 254
Sturzo, Luigi: 179
subjective idealism (egoism): 196
Sudeten Germans: 217
superman: 42, 151, 172; qualities of, 150; super-man into super-race, 197–9
Swabia: 71
Sweden: 122
Swinburne: 145
Switzerland: 72, 103, 122, 184

Tat, periodical: 159

Teutonia: 71

Teutonic Knights: 216, 217, 241–2, 264

Theune, B.: 63, 70 *n*, 76, 87 *n*

Thirty Years' War: 13, 75, 131; contemporary significance, 49–50, 57

Thompson, Dorothy: 27–8 and *n*

Thucydides: 278

Thule Society: 254

Thyssen: 66

Tieck, Ludwig: 37 *n*, 39, 42 *n*, 152

Totaler Krieg by Ludendorff: 297 *n*

Treitschke, Heinrich von: 52 *n*, 59, 66–8, 77, 84, 89 *n*, 194–5, 203–6, 269

Trespasser by Lawrence: 128

Tristan by Wagner: 106, 123; quoted by Rosenberg, 224–5

Troeltsch, Ernst: 7

Tusca by Grünwedel: 274

" Twenty-five Points ": 137, 251, 261, 286

Twilight of the Idols by Nietzsche: 303

" two souls in one breast ": 3, 6, 10, 14, 20, 177, 184, 187, 195, 212

Über die Religion by Schleiermacher: 37 and *n*

Ukraine: 216, 246, 297

United States: 79, 85–6, 158, 162, 207, 256, 304, 307; H. Chamberlain on, 9; romantic movements in, 18, 145; Hollywood romanticism, 23; emigration to, denounced by Jahn, 87; and Wagner, 123; misconceptions of Germany in, 141, 220, 262, 312; Lang-behn on, 172; and democracy, 174; Mediterranean heritage in, 179; quoting Hitler in, 190; Manifest Destiny, 200; and Treitschke, 203, 205; and Nietzsche, 203, 205, 226; loans to German Republic, 210; underestimates Rosenberg, 214–15, 239; and Nazi Germany, 221, 223; aid to Britain, 223; materialism in, 243–4; Rosenberg appeals to, 244–5; Johst glorifies Revolution of, 255; Rosenberg mocks feminism in, 266; defence effort in, 278–9

universalism vs. nationalism: 10, 14, 50–3, 58–60, 133–4, 162, 179–83, 185–7, 283, 295, 309, *passim*

University: Halle, 64, 169; Jena, 64; Greifswald, 64; Leipzig, 64, 94; Harvard, 85; Göttingen, 169; Berlin, 169; Paris, 169; London, 169; Munich, 258–9

Unmoral im Talmud by Rosenberg: 267 *n*

Unschuld des Werdens: Der Nachlass, Die, by Nietzsche: 90, 183 *n*

Vandals: 67

vegetarianism: in Wagner, 107–8, 119; in Hitler, 135

Verlaine: 145, 167

Vernichtung der Freimaurerei by Ludendorff: 297 *n*

Versailles Treaty: 8, 9, 11, 49, 57, 105, 139, 142, 158, 168, 169–70, 186, 204, 211, 212, 213, 238, 239, 241, 251, 263, 270, 279

Vienna Art Academy: 160

Viereck, Peter 92, 188 *n*, 213

Voigt, William: 310

Volk concept: xi, 4, 5, 8, 36, 58–9, 134, 261, 287, 293, 305, 312; Germans as *Ur-Volk*, 6–7; in Fichte, 6–7, 192–4; in romantics, 38–40; from Herder to Hitler, 50–4, 311; in Jahn, 66–70, 72–4, 87–8; indoctrination of, 77–80; and Volk-army, 83–4, 89, 102, 265; in Wagner, 93, 97–8, 103, 105–7, 110–13, 118, 120, 123–5, 131; vs. static state, 140; in Hitler, 141–2, 198; vs. legalism, 152; artists as carriers of, 154; and Social Democrats, 164; vs. Western civilization, 167–8; as a religion, 168–9; in Lagarde, 168–70; in Langbehn, 170–3; "Volk without room," 173–5; and *Realpolitik*, 199; in Rosenberg, 230, 235, 240, 250; vs. Prussianism, 230; *see also* master race

Volk im Werden, periodical: 165

Volk ohne Raum by H. Grimm: 173–5

Völkischer Beobachter: 215, 216, 227 *n*, 246

Volkswacht, periodical: 297 *n*

Voltaire: 54

Vom Kaiserhof zur Reichskanzlei by Goebbels: 133 *n*

Von d. Welt-Seele by Schelling: 30 and *n*

Wackenroder, H. W.: 42 *n*, 151

Wagner, Cosima: 91–2, 127, 148, 252

Wagner, Frederick: 95–6

Wagner, Richard: metapolitics coined by admirer of, 4; and Chamberlain, 9, 91–2, 99, 109–10, 111, 113, 137, 142; romantic roots of, 6, 93, 107, 108, 132; denounces Christianizing of Northmen, 11; and dynamism, 43, 106–10, 135; Nietzsche on, 48, 90, 100, 116, 128, 130, 152, 183, 198; to Hitler, 53, 62, 91–1, 98, 108, 111, 112, 117, 129–43, 147–8, 158, 168, 182, 209, 248, 261, 283, 294; liberal phrases used by, 60; favours amateur political army, 82, 102, 265; and nationalization of the masses, 88, 91, 122, 139–40, 312; and Gobineau, 91, 115–17, 128; and Rosenberg, 91, 115, 131, 142, 183, 224–7, 232, 234, 236, 242–3, 246, 251, 292, 295, 304–5; and Eckart, 91–2, 110–11, 115, 142, 162; Thomas Mann on, 92–3, 98, 100, 115, 127, 135; petulance toward Bismarck, 92–3, 127; multitude of books on, 93; variable attitude toward "French ideas," 93–9, 133; damns "Jewish music," 96, 104–5; as student at Leipzig, 94; influenced by Hegel and Feuerbach, 94; internationalist phase, 93–4; influenced by Heine and Meyerbeer, 94–5; story of Jewish ancestry of, 95–6; inclinations to luxury of, 96–7, 101; returns from Paris to Germany, 97, 217; identifies self with Hans Sachs, 98; participates in 1848–9 Revolution, 99–103;

socialistic ideas of, 101–2, 120–2, 132, 227; takes refuge in Switzerland, 103; repudiates Feuerbach for Schopenhauer, 103–4, 107; repudiates revolutionary past, 104; defines Volk, revolution, freedom, 105–6; Führer-cult of, 106, 110–14; as antivivisectionist, 107–9; as vegetarian, 107–8, 119; denounces Jews as destructive intellectuals, 108; revolt against classical rules in, 108; repudiates '49 Revolution as Jewish, 109; links Siegfried and Jesus, 110; sees Christ as Aryan, 110, 282–3; glorifies Siegfried and Barbarossa, 110, 114, 134, 139, 142; conception of republicanism in, 112–13; urges King Ludwig to head united Germany, 114; racism of, 114–20, 134; religious ideas of, 118–19; favours emigration to South America, 119; denounces industrialism, 120–1; final synthesis of Volk and communism in, 122–5; attitude toward Second Reich, 126–8; influences Barrès, 128; D. H. Lawrence admires, 128–9; inspires d'Annunzio, 128–9; contrasted with Hitler, 129–32, 269; dislike of the state in, 131; art most important to, 131; and Goebbels, 138–9; as link between two romantic movements, 152; accuses Lagarde of monopolizing anti-Semitism, 169; fascinated by " secret potentates," 172; " collapse before the Cross " of, 185; Treitschke like, 205; and steel romanticism, 255; prophecy of German doom by, 315–16; bibliography on, 330–5

Wagner, Siegfried: 91, 127, 132, 148

Wagner, Verena: 132

Wagner, Winifred: 132, 148

Wagner as Man and Artist by Newman: 92 n, 96 n, 97 n

Wagner by Chamberlain: 109–10, 117

War of Liberation: 162, 195; popularizes Hermann symbol, 11; revolt vs. West during, 14; Nietzsche on, 48, 182, 190; Rosenberg on, 48, 241; importance today, 53–8, 154, 156, 209, 241, 261, 265; reinterpreted, 58–62; fanatic students in, 84; links folksong and folk-army, 89; Wagner on, 93; romantic nationalism in, 123; Goethe vs., 186; Hitler on, 190–3, 241; breeds *Realpolitik,* 192–4

war-cult: 314, 227, 238 n; in first romantics, 5, 11–12, 38; in Jahn, 52, 84; in Treitschke, 29, 204–5; " nation in arms," 82; in Chamberlain, 137; Greenwich Village, 178; in Nietzsche, 152, 181, 185; in Spengler, 181–2, 185, 295–6; and *Realpolitik,* 190–1; in Hegel, 201; in Rosenberg, 231, 257, 292, 294–7; in Wagner, 294; in Ludendorff, 296; discounted by English, 299; militarism and romanticism mingled, 138, 166, 171, 176, 228, 255, 311

Wartburg celebration: 85

" Wartburg circle ": 159
Was Ich Erlebte by Steffens: 75
Weber, Max: 310
Weimar, Duchy of: 55
Weimar Republic: *see* democracy
Weltbürgertum u. Nationalstaat by Meinecke: 34 *n*
Weltkampf, periodical, 303–8
Weltverschwörerkongress zu Basel by Rosenberg: 267 *n*
Wesen, Grundsätze u. Ziel d. N. S. D. A. P. by Rosenberg: 137 *n*, 246–7, 304 *n*, 308 *n*
Wesendonk, Mathilde: 95, 96 *n*
Wessel, Horst: 165, 167; " towers over Jesus," 289
Western civilization: 140; defined, 4–5; Christian element, 179–81, 281; Mediterranean contributes, 3, 13, 19, 117, Chap. viii — 178–88, 283, 309; Russian influences on Germany, 219, 266–72; Kultur vs., 3–15, 19, 60, 78, 98, 167–8, 181, 184–7, 296, 299–301, 309–10; harnessing romanticism to, 56, 309–10; mass man vs., 312–13; Germany's case vs. the West, 12–13, 269–70; in Germany, 62, 163, 195, 302, 315
Westphalia, Treaty of: 49
Wieland: 55

Wilde, Oscar: 41, 145
Wilhelm Meister by Goethe: 31
Wille u. Macht, periodical: 287 *n*
Wilson, Woodrow: 61, 270; and the German Republic, 210–13
Winckelmann: worship of Greece, 21
Witukind: 181
Wo ist Gott by Reventlow: 292 *n*
Wolfe, H. C.: 240, 253 *n*
Wolters: 157, 265 *n*
Woolf, Virginia: 175 *n*
Wordsworth: 27, 52
Wotan: 5, 12, 26, 236, 282, 286, 287, 290, 291, 292

Yeats, quoted: 5, 175
" Young Germany ": 94
Young Hegelians: 94, 103
youth movements: 265; Burschenschaften, 80, 84–7, 94; gymnasts, 53, 64, 68, 80–2, 87, 94; Nazi, 3, 135, 157, 221, 253, 264–5, 267–8, 282, 287, 289, 300, 302

Zarathustra by Nietzsche: 183
Zaugg, Ernest: 257–8 and *n*
Zeitschrift für Geopolitik: 222 *n*
Zionism, 267